WITH

Looking at Race and Gender

OTHER

in Visual Culture

EYES

LISA BLOOM, EDITOR

University of Minnesota Press

Minneapolis — London

An earlier version of "Ghosts of Ethnicity: Rethinking Art Discourses of the 1940s and 1980s," by Lisa Bloom, was published in *Socialist Review* 94, no. 1/2 (Winter/Spring 1995): 129–64; reprinted by permission of the author. "Constructing National Subjects: The British Museum and Its Guidebooks," by Inderpal Grewal, was originally published as "The Guidebook and the Museum," in *Home and Harem: Nation, Gender, Empire, and the Cultures of Travel,* by Inderpal Grewal (Durham, N.C.: Duke University Press, 1996), 85–130; copyright 1996 Duke University Press, reprinted with permission. "Dark Continent," by Francette Pacteau, was originally published in *The Symptom of Beauty,* by Francette Pacteau (Cambridge: Harvard University Press, 1994, and London: Reaktion Books, 1994); copyright 1994 by Francette Pacteau, reprinted by permission of the publisher. "'A World without Boundaries': The Body Shop's Trans/National Geographics," by Caren Kaplan, was originally published in *Social Text* 43 (Fall 1995): 45–66; copyright 1995 Duke University Press, reprinted with permission. "You Make Me Feel (Mighty Real): Sandra Bernhard's Whiteface," by Ann Pellegrini, was originally published in *Performance Anxieties: Staging Psychoanalysis, Staging Race,* by Ann Pellegrini (New York: Routledge, 1996), 49–64; copyright 1996, reproduced by permission of Routledge, Inc. Lines from "No License to Die," by Esther Fuchs, in "Daughters of Sunshine: Diasporic Impulses and Gendered Identities," by Irit Rogoff, were originally published in *No License to Die,* by Esther Fuchs (Tel Aviv: Ecked Publishing House, 1983). Poetry by Sutapa Biswas in "Tracing Figures of Presence, Naming Ciphers of Absence: Feminism, Imperialism, and Postmodernity in the Work of Sutapa Biswas," by Griselda Pollock, was used by permission.

Published by the University of Minnesota Press
111 Third Avenue South, Suite 290
Minneapolis, MN 55401-2520
http://www.upress.umn.edu

Library of Congress Cataloging-in-Publication Data

With other eyes : looking at race and gender in visual culture / Lisa Bloom, editor.
  p. cm.
  Includes index.
  ISBN 0-8166-3222-7 (hardcover). — ISBN 0-8166-3223-5 (pbk.)
  1. Feminist art criticism. 2. Feminism and art. 3. Art and race. I. Bloom, Lisa.
  N72.F45W57 1999
  704—dc21   99-29675

Printed in the United States of America on acid-free paper

The University of Minnesota is an equal-opportunity educator and employer.

11 10 09 08 07 06 05 04 03 02 01 00 99   10 9 8 7 6 5 4 3 2 1

CONTENTS

ACKNOWLEDGMENTS

Feminist visual cultural studies has yet to enjoy regular funding and support in the U.S. academy within women's studies, art, or art history departments if only because of its very interdisciplinary nature and its commitment to an engaged feminist and antiracist scholarship in the arts. The publication of this anthology along with others perhaps testifies to a change. There is much that transpires in the halls and classrooms of academe and in art schools that remains as tacit or anecdotal knowledge that never reaches print and thus does not enjoy the kind of public scrutiny a publication affords. At best, the present volume can hint at the fraught and often difficult circumstances that oversaw its conceptualization.

This anthology has been in the making for some time. As a result, the perseverance of my colleagues in this anthology as well as of those readers and students who went over various drafts of these essays has been critical to its completion. I would especially like to thank the anthology's contributors for bearing with me and the press through long delays. I would also like to thank Caren Kaplan, Eric Smoodin, and Ella Shohat for encouraging me to begin this work, since the idea for this anthology came out of a dinner conversation I had with them after a conference on colonial discourse at the University of California, Santa Cruz in 1993.

Over the past four years I have been able to work with some wonderful students whose sympathies and solidarities have sustained me. My special thanks to Christina Hanhardt for her practical and extremely helpful assistance when she was my research assistant and for her excellent work on the anthology's index. I also thank Heidi Brant and Wendy Norris for the exquisite poster they designed for the conference Gender and Race Politics in Visual Culture, based on this anthology and held at San Francisco State University on April 10, 1997. Louis Juska and Mary Mizelle were a wonderful conference committee, and I thank them for their help.

Colleagues and friends have inspired and assisted this work at various points. I especially want to thank Amelia Jones for her extremely attentive and helpful comments on the whole manuscript. I also wish to thank my colleagues at San Francisco State who offered encouragement and moral support during the difficult times when this anthology was being completed: Judith Bettelheim, Whitney Chadwick, Inderpal Grewal, Mark Johnson, Margo Kasdan, George LeGrady, Akira Lippit, Ann Robertson, and Tim Sampson. Louisa Castner was an excellent copy editor, and I want to thank her for her wonderful work on this manuscript. Finally, Roddey Reid has played an especially important role, emotionally and intellectually, through and beyond the writing of this text.

Material support is also of course important, although not always in itself decisive. A Mellon Postdoctoral Fellowship from Stanford University supported my research at the beginning of the project. As the project neared completion, certain individuals and organizations enabled the scholarship in this anthology to reach a wider audience in the Bay Area. I thank the following supporters of the conference Gender and Race Politics in Visual Culture: Bill Berksen at the San Francisco Art Institute, David Hannah at Stanford University's Art Department, Paul Dorn at the College of Creative Arts, San Francisco State University, and the following organizations at San Francisco State: Student Activity Fee Funds, Office of Research and Sponsored Programs, Vice President's Mini Grant Program, and Department of Women's Studies.

INTRODUCING *WITH OTHER EYES: LOOKING AT RACE AND GENDER IN VISUAL CULTURE*

Lisa Bloom

How does a feminist movement for social change "de-Westernize" itself?
—Caren Kaplan, "Postmodern Geographies," in *Questions of Travel*

It is, in fact, art history's continuing adherence to a theory of immanent aesthetic value that has prevented historians from fully examining the ways in which the work is related to all the other institutions and practices that constitute social life.
—Norman Bryson, Michael Ann Holly, and Keith Moxey, "Introduction," in
Visual Culture: Images and Interpretations

This book's cover shows a tightly cropped black-and-white close-up photographic portrait of Franz Roh, an art historian, taken in 1926 with his eyes closed. I chose to begin with this image that draws attention to the art historian's shut eyes both to give an example of how images are being read differently now in the context of a burgeoning new scholarship, as well as to reexamine the preeminence given to the "eye" and the notion of emotionally detached, objectively accurate vision in the discipline of art history. This image works suggestively to present a subversive and furtive glance that challenges the gaze of the art historian, who ordinarily attempts to control the look, in the sense that he takes the study of the object and the artist as his chief professional aim and leaves himself out of the picture. Sexual, racial, and social meanings tend to be imposed on objects and artists that are extensively defined, not on the art historian. Lucia Moholy, the photographer, attempts slyly to turn the tables when she makes Roh the object of her gaze. However, Roh seemingly in trying to evade her surveillance makes himself difficult to capture. He shuts his eyes and in so doing exempts himself from her scrutiny.[1]

This anthology seeks to address how contemporary cultural critics and historians have thrown open the field to new questions that undermine older ways of art historical seeing. Therefore, it is meant not just simply as a response to traditional art historians, nor does it have much to do with the figure of Franz Roh in particular (who indeed was a rather complex figure in his own right).[2] Rather, it continues a discussion that is occurring both inside and outside of the field of art history regarding a feminist visual culture and how it can develop new paradigms of social criticism that do not rely on either the traditional underpinnings of the discipline nor on unitary notions of "woman." In the discipline of art history, it is only fairly recently that feminist art historians, cultural critics, and artists have begun to reexamine mainstream ways of looking as well as the issue of spectatorship in this regard.[3] This has been a difficult task since, unlike within the field of film studies, an idea of innocent vision as simple perception continues to haunt the discipline. No matter how anachronistic, a "trained eye" and a good visual memory are skills still revered today in art history, in which learning about art involves primarily "developing an eye" in order to unlock the purported secrets of art.

One of the tacit assumptions that still guides the normal activity of the art historian, according to books that describe the discipline to undergraduates such as Mark Roskill's *What Is Art History?*, is that "the artist is long since dead, like the corpse in a mystery (or unwilling to talk about what he did), and much is lost or missing, both in the way of works and in the way of evidence."[4] Within this scenario, art history is constructed through narratives of absence and loss. Yet this emphasis is not to simply mourn the loss of irretrievable objects but, rather, to regard it as a highly productive opportunity to put to test the powers of the discerning eye and reestablish the rightful value and the true artistic merit of objects. According to Roskill, this is a long, laborious process in which success is equated with a prolonged, contemplative gaze: "A work of art is affected in the way in which it is seen. . . . And if it is to give up its secrets, assuming it has some, it most often has to be worked at. Particularly if it is a great work of art, it does not spontaneously lay itself open to us."[5]

What is striking about this passage is that both the duration of the look and the viewing process itself are construed as incontrovertibly masculinist, as evidenced by the way in which sexual difference is inscribed in the very language and formulation of the act of looking. Moreover, there is a disturbing voyeurism evoked in likening the work of art to a female body that will ultimately yield its secrets and "lay itself open to us." Spectatorship within the discipline is constructed here as an ordinary part of the development of a craft or skill in which an opposition between woman as image and man as bearer of the look is naturalized as part of an apprenticeship that leads to art historical mastery. This naturalized process of looking was challenged by both early feminist film theory, in particular Laura Mulvey's highly influential 1975 essay "Visual Pleasure and Narrative Cinema," as well as John Berger's well-known 1972 book and film series *Ways of Seeing,* which acted as a catalyst for considerations of sexual difference and spectatorship specifically in the field of art history.[6] However, both Mulvey's and Berger's arguments of a strict separation between active and passive roles in looking according to sexual difference have a certain currency in traditional art history in the sense that the viewing practices defined the gendered process of investigation in the profession.

The process of looking in the field doesn't always focus exclusively on filling in missing or lost evidence, especially when it comes to contemporary art, nor does the way that art reveals its so-called secrets follow the normative heterosexual script suggested by Roskill, Berger, or even Mulvey. Such a monolithic conception of seeing could not account for the appeal of this profession to a broader group of practitioners, particularly gay men and lesbian women or/and critics of color or Jewish women who partially fill its ranks.

WITH

OTHER

EYES

This doesn't mean that all art historians do engage in a masculinist way of looking, and it doesn't mean that lesbian women, straight women, or women of color cannot adopt a position of sexual or racial voyeurism. Rather, since all kinds of men and women can and do derive pleasure from looking at works of art, this fact suggests that the process of looking might transpire in a more multiform "bisexual" fashion.[7] Consider, for example, the genre of the nude and the homoerotic dimension involved within the most basic and supposedly neutral of scholarly practices: male art historians viewing male nude figures by male artists. Or the more clichéd and predictable heterosexual voyeurism at work in the analysis of white female nudes, or the opportunities for interracial looking available in viewing, for example, the Polynesian nudes of Paul Gauguin[8] or the black male nudes in Robert Mapplethorpe's *Black Book*.[9]

Regarding the issue of spectatorship, there are other possible viewing practices. Consider the following two alternatives. The first turns on what bell hooks refers to as "oppositional looks," a process in which the gaze functions as a site of resistance.[10] Rather than viewing works of art or film through a disembodied process of visual detachment, a spectator can place herself in a position of agency through a more embodied subjective viewing process that takes into account questions of difference, sexuality, and power. For hooks, however, the experience of this more critical viewing process will be neither uniform nor universal for all women. What she advocates is a different kind of looking, which neither rests on the ideology that art is a universally understood experience nor relies on the professional look of objectification or connoisseurship. In her book *Black Looks*, hooks directly acknowledges how race and colonialism structure feminist ways of seeing, and it is in this sense that her concept of the oppositional gaze departs from earlier feminist notions of looking. She emphasizes in particular how empowering confrontational viewing practices are for black women who construct their own ways of seeing to "speak" their experience:

> Like that photographic portrait of Billy [Billie] Holiday by Moneta Sleet I love so much, the one where instead of a glamorized image of stardom, we are invited to see her in a posture of thoughtful reflection, her arms bruised by tracks, delicate scars on her face, and that sad far-away look in her eyes. When I face this image, this black look, something in me is shattered. I have to pick up the bits and pieces of myself and start all over again—transformed by the image. (7)

Hooks's reading of the photograph of Billie Holiday situates the image not in relation to the kind of inquiry that Roskill's analysis does (her concern is obviously not with uncovering secrets in the archive, or with questions of attribution, dating, authenticity, and rarity) but in terms of a discourse of feminist African American experience—a perspective rarely addressed in conventional art history. In doing so, hooks demonstrates her presence and point of view in the way she chooses to look. Thus, hooks's perspective is significant in how it constructs a way of seeing in which the process of investigation is part of the object of knowledge.

The second viewing practice turns on imitation and parody and suggests a process of looking in which the meaning of race and ethnicity or the experience of racialization is by no means uniform or univocal across racial and white ethnic groups. For Ann Pellegrini's theory of spectatorship, it is important that what race, sexuality, and ethnicity mean differs among Jews, Asians, Latinas, and blacks as well as within these social groupings. There is also not the same expectation that hooks has that viewing practices, whether they are confrontational or not, will be affirming, or the assumption according to Mulvey that they will be readable through a male gaze. In this sense Pellegrini's theorizing challenges both the terms through which Laura Mulvey advanced her interpretation of the male gaze and visual pleasure, as well as hooks's notion of an oppositional gaze. For her article in this collection, Pellegrini chooses as an example for her theory the film *Without* You *I'm Nothing* about a Jewish lesbian performer, Sandra Bernhard, whose performance about her desire to be black, by impersonating Nina Simone, Diana Ross, Cardilla DeMarlo, Prince, and Sylvester functions as a parody of her inability to translate herself across racial boundaries:

> What prevents Bernhard's impersonation from being a "simple" act of appropriation is its open failure to forge an identification between her black audience of address and herself. The audience withholds its belief, refusing to authorize Bernhard's vision of herself. Moreover, Bernhard sets herself up as an object of ridicule for that audience, conspicuously dramatizing the distance between her audience's and her own self-understandings. Bernhard's performance is self-ironizing. The audience does not "get" Bernhard; Bernhard does not "get" her audience. But the very misrecognition is to some degree what compels the performance.
>
> . . . Yet so obnoxious is much of Bernhard's performance, so arcane many of her jokes, that the film ultimately frustrates any lasting identification between even its (phantasmatically) white audience and Bernhard, thereby leaving no place to "fix" identity within or through the film.[11]

Pellegrini seizes on this example of Bernhard's perverse repetition of racial and sexual stereotypes in order to undo them, and in this respect her article offers a theory of spectatorship that shifts theoretical discourse of looking relations to yet a third position that is neither the neutral and universalizing gaze of art history nor the oppositional gaze of bell hooks in her reading of the Billie Holiday photograph.

Though crucial new work by feminist theorists such as bell hooks and Ann Pellegrini challenges existing methodologies and looking relations by questioning how art history continues to determine the truth of its objects within its own discourse while erasing the positions—national, racial, sexual, class-based, and gendered—from which these discourses are spoken,[12] it has not been enough to destabilize the virtually unmarked position of universality from which it claims to see or pass judgment.[13] The discipline of art history is still primarily in the business of determining what may be considered legitimate and reliable knowledge and what must be marginalized, as well as gauging the merits of works of art with a certain aloofness and disengagement from social relations altogether. Despite the concerted efforts and groundbreaking work of a number of art historians, artists, and critics over the past twenty-five years, including the writing coming out of important traditions of feminist scholarship, Marxist-based social art history, and more recently scholarship influenced by the writings of Jacques Lacan and Michel Foucault,[14] the authority of this art historical gaze that claims to "transcend" time and place persists in the new work as well as the old, particularly in terms of the way that the implicitly ethnocentric agenda of art history gets reproduced. This persistence makes it still an urgent issue for younger scholars, such as the contributors to this volume (including me), to address. In certain ways our project is even more complex than those of our more established colleagues, since we are now questioning so many underlying assumptions of the discipline at once, at a moment when there is an even greater resistance to change. Moreover, we are trying to define a different kind of looking, which takes into account sometimes incompatible theories of representation, performance theory, feminist theory, and colonial discourse that are each contested on their own, and even more controversial when put together.

My idea of putting together this anthology came about initially as an attempt not only to critique a continuing cultural investment in traditional art historical narratives that insist on the disengaged look of the universal man, but to imagine what the field could look like if it did not place at the center of its discourse the "discerning" eye but were more self-reflexive about how the discipline transmits and reproduces its racial and gendered premises. As an image of scholarship, detachment is a gendered privilege of knowing no bodies, of being, in Donna Haraway's words, "a conquering gaze from nowhere," a gaze that claims "the power to see and not be seen, to represent while escaping representation."[15] What I am proposing, then, is a greater attention to the complex discursive and rhetorical dimensions of visual culture and the ways in which scholarly attention makes gender, ethnicity, sexuality, class, nation, and race peripheral.

Following the recommendation of feminists such as Haraway and others who claim that feminists should work from their embodied perspectives in order to produce what she calls "situated knowledges," I find that much of the impetus behind putting together an anthology such as this one comes out of my own personal investedness in intervening in the discipline of art history, and what I have come to see as its ideological assumptions. As a feminist scholar who teaches visual culture in an interdisciplinary women's studies program at Josai International University in Japan and has a multidisciplinary Ph.D. from the History of Consciousness program at the University of California, Santa Cruz, I have been deeply influenced by the changes brought about in the humanities and social sciences by feminist cultural studies, particularly the way it has reformulated what counts as both pedagogical practices and scholarship. Since I have found cultural studies and feminist theory so genuinely responsive to both my intellectual and pedagogical concerns, specifically how they shift awareness away from the consumption of knowledge to the production of knowledge, I wondered how it would be possible for the field of art history to change to become compatible with feminist cultural studies but with an emphasis on the visual arts.

One of the ways that this anthology responds to this question is through presenting scholarship that treats art not as something that can be taught in a disinterested way as information to memorize, or as a conduit to high culture, but as a vital and living tradition that is constantly being negotiated in everyday life. Many of the authors in this anthology start from the notion of what it means to be a cultural subject, and this point of departure takes the form of a renewed emphasis on the autobiographical. However, this turn to the autobiographical is meant to be quite distinct from earlier autobiographical tendencies that privileged the author. An author-based presumption of speaking from the heart, or confessing one's essence, has been replaced by the autobiographical expression of a writer or artist as an embodied individual within the process of cultural interpretation. Since Roland Barthes's well-known proclamation of the "death of the author," there has been a shift away from the author or the artist to a privileging of the reader or spectator.[16] The abandonment of author-based interpretations and the elevation of women as readers and spectators have had many beneficial effects on feminist scholars. For some of the authors in this anthology, including me, these changes have opened up a whole history of masculinist discourses and artistic traditions to feminist appropriations and recontextualizations. For it enables any art historical text or work of art, however masculinist, to be read from a feminist point of view. This elevation of spectators to the position of textual and visual creators is an empowering development that underscores the erotic source of looking and complicates the question of spectatorship and consumption. This new framework in which women are no longer put into place by the power of the white male gaze has informed a rethinking of what we do, not only in the field of women's studies but also in art history and the arts in general.

From such an autobiographical turn, then, this anthology addresses the impact of gender, race, and sexual politics of imperialisms and nationalisms on contemporary visual culture and its practices. Though this set of issues has been influential in cultural studies and American studies, there has been little attention paid to them in the traditional disciplines that study visual representations, in particular art history. Thus the multidisciplinary focus of visual culture suggests not only the need to point to some significant blind spots in the traditional disciplines of the visual arts, but the need to remap the field in a way that is more responsive to important scholarship that is already under way in other disciplines such as anthropology, American studies, women's studies, ethnic studies, film, and even literature where cinema studies, popular culture, and cultural studies are taught.

Though the purpose of the anthology is to intervene in the way the discipline of art history is taught, the contributors to this volume refuse to do this simply by wrangling over the canon and traditional aesthetics. Rather than refighting battles that have been taking place for the past twenty-five years in the visual arts, we propose to make apparent the breakdown of the divisions between disciplines, which has resulted in an ever-widening gap between student multidisciplinary interests and what is taught in academic departments of art history. It is into this gap that this anthology will insert itself. This is why I use the term *visual culture* rather than *art, film,* or *media* to signal a shift in emphasis in the visual arts toward work that broadens conventional notions of traditional "high cultural" agendas to include so-called impure visual practices (television, video, popular culture, photography, advertising, computer technologies, junk, altars, and so on). Such work by its very nature dispenses with hierarchical cultural distinctions such as high versus low, elite versus mass, modern versus folk, Western versus non-Western, as well as with academic departmental divisions like film versus television, theater versus performance studies, art and art history versus communications.

Yet the study of visual culture is not just about expanding the dominion of objects to encompass a broader range of cultural forms within the discipline. The admission of popular culture, advertising, video, and so forth into the curricula of art history departments alone will not bring about change, as we have seen during the moment when feminists and postmodernist artists such as Cindy Sherman and Barbara Kruger were accommodated into the canon, or more recently when artists of color such as Jean-Michel Basquiat, Martin Puryear, Betty Saar, Fred Wilson, James Luna, among others, began to appear in art history coffee-table books and surveys.[17] For as long as these "new" artists and their work get included as merely the new subjects that make up a fixed culture, their disciplinary descriptions will do no more than create storehouses of knowledge having almost nothing to do with lived culture, much less its transformation. Unfortunately, accommodation of new artists and new kinds of art has shown that their inclusion does not necessarily lead to a different framing of the whole, which would ideally affect those critics and artists who never do feminist theory, multiculturalism, or postcolonial discourse at all.

Another purpose of the anthology is to rethink already ongoing debates that are focused on multiculturalism. Though current high-profile cultural events organized around multiculturalist themes have widened the field, what is absent from these events is an understanding of the way, for example, that the notions of race and ethnicity are tied to questions of gender and sexuality, and linked to recent scholarship on nationalisms and postcoloniality.[18] There still remains a great need for a feminist critique in visual culture that establishes racial, ethnic, national, and postcolonial concerns since much of the current feminist work in the field does not address feminist participation in these discourses, and how race/ethnicity as a specific category of analysis operates within them. On the other hand, the work that does address feminist and racial concerns does not necessarily focus on questions of white ethnicity. A case in point in the visual arts is the important 1994 book *The Power of Feminist Art: The American Movement of the 1970s, History and Impact.*[19] The anthology presents a wide array of works from this period including the work of Adrian Piper, Faith Ringgold, Ana Mendieta, and other women of color who were active during that period. However, what is noteworthy is how the anthology is the first in recent years to begin to bring back to scholarly attention the work of many Jewish artists from the period, such as Judy Chicago, Miriam Schapiro, Carolee Schneeman, Joyce Kozloff, and others who have been neglected in recent accounts. As strong and refreshing a revisionist history this represents, nonetheless, the terms of exclusion still presuppose a feminist sisterhood that cannot account for racial and white ethnic differences. The relative absence of white ethnicity as a category in the book, and Jewishness in particular, over and against the visibility of African Americans and Latina artists as women of color, is quite striking and points to perhaps the limits of this kind of revisionist project that attempts new inclusions but also reinstates long-standing invisibilities and visibilities dating from the very period it chooses to study. Thus, there still remains a great need for an examination of how different white ethnic women's identities are tied to other social identities and mediated through institutional discourses of art history.

This anthology, in contrast to *The Power of Feminist Art,* deals with questions of race, ethnicity, class, sexuality, nationalism, as well as gender and has been particularly informed by the shift in feminist consciousness that has taken place within the past fifteen years, prompted by recent writings and art by women of color on race and lesbianism as well as recent work on whiteness and Jewishness. Since the beginnings of the current feminist movement, and with particular insistence since the early 1980s, women finding themselves outside the frame of dominant feminism—lesbians, black women, other women of color, Third World women, white ethnic women—have contested the terms of its discourse, pointing out the limits of gender as the sole emphasis and the need for feminists to recognize the claims of other forms of difference besides sexual difference. For example, feminist art critics such as Michele Wallace, among others, have pointed not only to the inadequacies of the prevailing concept of woman as heterosexual and white but also to white feminism's own consolidation of Western, middle-class culture. In the afterword to the anthology on *Black Popular Culture,* Wallace writes:

> The key problematic among feminist theorists of color in our debates around identity and "otherness" has been this notion of "and blacks too." The insight of the most recent genera-tion of feminists of color has been that blacks (or black women or women of color or black men) cannot be tacked onto formulations about gender without engaging in a form of con-ceptual violence. In no theoretically useful way whatsoever are blacks like *women*.[20]

Not only can one not simply add black women to feminist categories but also, according to Wallace, one must develop a theory that takes into account the complicity of construc-tions of gender with ideologies of race, sexuality, and class. Wallace's emphasis on the need for a complex understanding of the way that the categories of gender and race are interarticulated is important, but I would extend her categories to include not only women of color but white ethnic women who might have also had an uneasy allegiance to feminism that would erase a consideration of other differences.

Unfortunately, neither has taken place fully within the debates on postmodernism and feminism in the arts, given the monocultural and assimilationist tendencies in art and art history departments.[21] But without these debates the story would be even more dismal than it is now. With the rise of performance and body art in the past two and a half decades have come unavoidably gendered and racially specific representations of the body in art. Because of these and other specifically feminist and queer practices, postmodernist theory has had to make space for the consideration of the construction of the gendered, the racialized, and the queered subject since the late 1970s, when body-oriented practices in the art world split off into a separate discipline that is largely discussed within perfor-mance studies or theater departments rather than art history. It is in part due to the sup-port of these other institutional spaces that feminism, postmodernism, and more recently queer theory have emerged as three of the most important intellectual movements in the arts of the past two decades: all three have offered a challenge to the notion of represen-tation and its address. All have tried to transform art practice by challenging both the humanist notion of the artist as romantic individual "genius" and the modernist domina-tion of two particular art forms, painting and sculpture. But there are differences, too. Postmodernists offered new forms as well as a new self-consciousness about representa-tion, but unlike the feminists and/or queer artists their focus was not necessarily overtly political, in the sense that they did not have strong ties to political projects. In this regard, feminist and queer artists/theories were not really fully compatible with or even an example of postmodern thought even though many were very influenced by postmodernism. However, together with women of color they became the most powerful force in changing the direction in which postmodernism was heading and continue to be to this day.

Yet despite the groundbreaking importance of these shifts, many postmodern feminists and queer theorists who see the value of postmodernist theories in the arts are still somewhat Eurocentric in their perspective, in the sense that they don't always acknowledge the different forms that feminism takes as a critical practice. According to Inderpal Grewal and Caren Kaplan, two contributors to this anthology and the editors of *Scattered Hegemonies*,

> In fact, many postmodern feminists in the United States see postmodernism as a movement toward ambivalence, the decentered subject, and so on, rather than as a thorough critique of modernity and its related institutions. . . .
>
> What gets left out of such considerations are the concerns of many women across the world regardless of whether or not they choose to describe themselves as "feminists": the place of women in the nation-state, resistance to revivals of "tradition," the complex issue of fundamentalism, the situation of workers in multinational corporations, and the relationship between gender, the nation-state, and mobile, transnational capital.[22]

Kaplan and Grewal want to expand the understanding of feminist postmodernism to one that takes into account the workings of gender in new forms of multinational domination. They believe that it is only by addressing the relationship of gender to global economic structures, patriarchal nationalisms, as well as local structures of domination within and outside the United States that it is possible to construct a less exclusionary feminism that considers the cultures and traditions that a diverse group of women negotiate in their everyday lives and their art. Such innovative approaches are especially important in art history since dominant regimes of visual representation say nothing about the historical differences of women as such. Indeed, the framework of feminist theory initially developed in relationship to cinematic representation by Laura Mulvey that claims that men look and women are looked at doesn't on its own challenge or complicate the prevailing Euro-American terms of feminist art history.

Following Grewal and Kaplan's attempt to flesh out more innovative theories and strategies that offer a place for more complex categories of female identity and sense of belonging that are not solely about U.S. cultures and situations, the essays in the anthology are examples of how recent work coming out of a subfield of cultural studies called feminist colonial discourse studies has much to offer, especially in terms of putting into practice the writing and teaching of a different kind of art history or art criticism. Some of the scholars working in this area include Grewal, Haraway, Kaplan, Anne McClintock, Trinh T. Minh-ha, Kum Kum Sungari, Ella Shohat, and Gayatri Spivak.[23]

The term *feminist colonial discourse studies* designates feminist critical discourses that thematize issues emerging from postcolonial relations and their aftermath (including a wide range of diasporic circumstances from the late nineteenth century to the present). One of the ways this anthology intervenes institutionally in these debates is by making available writings by Third World women and U.S. women of color as well as lesser-known ethnic white women who are involved in interdisciplinary feminist work. Since there are very few women of color with Ph.D.'s in art history, but many seeking interdisciplinary degrees in humanities disciplines who write about visual culture, it is important that their scholarship be made available, all the more so in that it is this kind of scholarship that is most likely to redefine in the near future what art and art history departments and women's studies programs, and so on will be.[24]

What *With Other Eyes* accomplishes is to show that these new changes are already happening. However, the stakes of what it means to intervene in the field of art history are not uniform for all the authors in this anthology, since only a few of the contributors teach in art history departments. Given that many of the writers in this anthology are coming from other, more interdisciplinary fields, their stakes in the culture wars in the arts are not as high as those who are doing this kind of work within the field, where a se-ries of local battles around hiring, promotion, funding, and curricula has taken place, as evidenced by a set of articles highlighting the antagonism between art history and visual cultural studies, with the most recent aptly titled "Art History's Anxiety Attack" by Eloy J. Hernandez in 1997. Hernandez's article "Questionnaire on Visual Culture," published in the summer 1996 issue of *October,* and the three articles written in 1996 by Scott Heller for the *Chronicle of Higher Education* and *Art News* that occasioned Hernandez's piece have not only given visibility to the polarizations and tensions in the field but also have shown the existence of an audience of students, artists, scholars, and journalists whose interest in our work is wider than what the generally narrow public polemics suggests.[25] This an-thology is written for that broader audience.

The book has two parts: part 1 is called Gender, Race, and Nation: Histories and Discourses. Part 2 is titled Contemporary Visual Discourses: Postnational Aesthetics. The premise be-hind part 1 is that in order to understand and deal with contemporary visual culture, it is important first to examine how historical racism and sexism have affected the very consti-tution of the disciplines themselves and what gets excluded from their purview. Though all the authors in both sections are women, this is not meant to conflate feminism with female authorship. For many of the authors a feminist approach does not mean they will be writ-ing exclusively about women artists, critics, or historians. Thus, the inclusion of only female authors in this anthology is less a statement about the exclusivity of feminism and its scholarship and more a programmatic response to a discipline that is notoriously sexist and racist.

Given the current debates that seem to polarize visual culture and art history, I must point out that the anthology does not argue for a priority of feminist cultural studies over art history. Rather, it demonstrates some of the ways that this new scholarship falls be-yond the scope of some of art history's long-held assumptions. For example, in my essay "Ghosts of Ethnicity: Rethinking Art Discourses of the 1940s and 1980s" I historicize the emergence of the New York School's critical hegemony and its transnational Jewish history to offer an example of how even the most well-known formalist aesthetic posi-tions are inescapably imbricated by the politics of identity. At the same time that the essay argues that the experience of ethnicity has been at the heart of U.S. modernism all along, it also takes issue with ways of seeing black and Jewish experiences that underestimate the differences and hybridities among these groups. Inderpal Grewal's chapter, "Constructing National Subjects: The British Museum and Its Guidebooks," might also fall outside what is ordinarily considered art history because her ideological analysis of spectatorship at the British Museum refuses to focus solely on the museum's objects. Instead, she puts her attention on the working classes who came to the museum and how mid-nineteenth-century British Museum guidebooks constructed a discourse of spectatorship through a discourse of colonialism, nationalism, gender, and class. According to Grewal, this discourse suggests that bringing the working classes into the museum was not simply a way to "educate" them, but also a way to negotiate rigid class differences, by producing national pride in the exploits of the aristocracy and thus establishing an "imagined national community" seemingly based not on stringent class lines, but on national and postcolonial ones that were gendered.

In the case of Francette Pacteau's chapter, "Dark Continent," her interest in examining certain gendered and racialized constructions and expressions of French and American feminine beauty and the persistence of this legacy in the present historicizes the notion of beauty in terms of different national traditions. Starting with the Hottentot Venus, she examines a wide range of discursive constructions of black femininity including Pablo Picasso's *Les Demoiselles d'Avignon*, Josephine Baker, and Jean Paul Goude's image of Grace Jones. Drawing on the theoretical writings of Julia Kristeva, Hélène Cixous, and Homi K. Bhabha, among others, Pacteau complicates a psychoanalytic discourse on (white) femininity and beauty by taking into account the workings of colonial discourse. As Pacteau's article indicates how a discourse of visual culture on beauty is already interdisciplinary by nature, Shawn Michelle Smith's "Photographing the 'American Negro': Nation, Race, and Photography at the Paris Exposition of 1900" brings together scholarship from various disciplines—history of photography, literature, women's studies, postcolonial studies, and American studies. Smith examines the ways in which photographs participated in the construction of contested American identities by analyzing two sets of photographs presented at the "American Negro" exhibit at the Paris Exposition of 1900. Reading the images produced by Frances Benjamin Johnston, a white woman photographer, against the photographic albums collected by W. E. B. Du Bois, Smith demonstrates how to differing degrees both sets of images contested national and racial identifications posed by eugenicists and white supremacist nationalists at the turn of the century and posed competing notions of what constitutes a multicultural nation.

This more historically based section sets up the context for part 2, which examines how current conceptualizations of the disciplines are being refurbished in ways to accommodate new kinds of artists, critics, and historians who are not unmarked as white or male. However, the difference between the two sections should not be simply read as historical versus contemporary. To do so would miss the contemporaneity of the concerns in a diachronic sense in the first section and how they prepare us for some of the thematic issues that the whole volume raises, even though essays such as the ones by Grewal and Smith are more specific about period and argument.

Both sections address the persistence as well as the changing connotations of binary oppositions—such as First World versus Third World, colonizer versus colonized, dominant versus dominated, modern versus primitive—that are inadequately theorized, as in the case of women. The privileging of white in the binary also needs to be rethought since it assumes that whiteness is a monolithic entity devoid of multiple ideologies and ethnicities (see, for example, the chapters by Ann Pellegrini, Irit Rogoff, and me). It is important to examine how these binaries signify differently to diverse subjects when they are applied to contemporary visual culture within subcultures in the United States, the United Kingdom, France, or Israel.

The second part also attempts to move outside of such paradigms of colonial discourse and destabilize the segregation reproduced in the traditional disciplines by focusing on new kinds of feminist writing and feminist artwork that call into question these oppositions. There is a growing scholarship by critics, artists, and filmmakers that in the words of filmmaker and writer Trinh T. Minh-ha "challenge[s] the West as authoritative subject of feminist knowledge, while also resisting the terms of a binarist discourse that would concede feminism to the West all over again."[26] These more interesting developments are exciting and need greater exposure, especially in fields that tend not to see gender and colonial discourse as relational terms in tension with one another but as strictly hierarchical ones, with feminism's being exclusively equated with the West alone. In this section, the contributors' multiple points of departure complicate questions regarding a gender-, ethnic-, and race-based notion of location and what it means to imagine the United States, the United Kingdom, France, or Israel as a nation that one unproblematically belongs to.

In "Daughters of Sunshine: Diasporic Impulses and Gendered Identities," Irit Rogoff uses categories of gender and Eurocentricity to critique the limits of the discourses within which "High Culture" with a capital *C* gets practiced in Israel. Drawing from both popular and high culture (the work of Israeli artist Sigal Primore), Rogoff points to the contradictions that Israeli feminist artists and critics face in challenging restrictive nationalist notions of acceptable Israeli femininity as white, European, and socialist. Caren Kaplan's "'A World without Boundaries': The Body Shop's Trans/National Geographies" is a departure from the anthology's emphasis on visual artists, critics, and museums but is significant in broadening its terms to include work done currently in women's studies departments that combines discourses of transnationalism, feminism, and popular culture with those that deal with circuits of consumption in an era of globalizing advertising narratives. Kaplan's analysis of gendered visions of colonial discourse in Ralph Lauren Safari ad campaigns and the Body Shop's corporate representations reveals how women are represented in mainstream advertising narratives as traveling in a world without boundaries through ads that associate the practices of consumer culture with the glorification of travel.

In "Making Art, Making Citizens: Las Comadres and Postnational Aesthetics," Aida Mancillas, Ruth Wallen, and Marguerite Waller trace specific histories of colonial discourse in their own region to show both the importance as well as the difficulty of constructing viable feminist alliances across racial, ethnic, and national lines. This essay focuses on the autobiographical work of practicing women artists and writers in the San Diego/Tijuana region and examines the politics of gender and race relations within different psychic spaces associated with women's daily lives in this border region.

"The Fae Richards Photo Archive" makes the issues of lesbian representation, feminist politics, and race in the United States central. The work, a collaboration between Zoe Leonard and filmmaker Cheryl Dunye for Dunye's film *The Watermelon Woman* (1996), is a fictional photographic archive of an African American lesbian woman who lived from 1908 to 1973. The archive draws on photographic tropes from the period to give the pictures a "reality effect" in order to make us see precisely what we have not been allowed to notice about other African American women. Richards is represented not only as a servant and a performer, but also as a lesbian involved in an affair with a prominent white female director. Thus, Leonard and Dunye's construction of Richards's works is a commentary on the absence of the representation of such figures resulting from the historical prohibition in U.S. culture of cross-racial looking and the prohibition accorded to lesbianism and cross-racial sex during that period.

In "Archaeological Devotion" Jennifer A. González writes about the installation pieces of Amalia Mesa-Bains, Renée Stout, and Jenni Lukac to emphasize a visual overlap of institutional domains to include other social affinities and communities outside of U.S. avant-garde art communities as critical sites for female resistance. Through a rhetorical analysis of these artists' works she examines how powerful a practice it is to bring reconstructed notions of home and religion into the public art gallery or museum space, in terms of enabling a generationally and ethnically diverse female community to be portrayed in the context of the artists' own self-agency. Each artist's visual display of collected artifacts, she argues, needs to be understood for both its interrogation of a modernist legacy and for the way such visual displays map an alternative and complex conception of women's histories not reducible to nostalgic signs of an "outside" other.

Griselda Pollock in her article "Tracing Figures of Presence, Naming Ciphers of Absence" shows how Sutapa Biswas's work replaces unitary notions of "woman" and "Britishness" with plural, complexly constructed conceptions of social identity. In addition to examining the figurative paintings and multimedia works and performances of Sutapa Biswas; Pollock also credits her role in effecting curricular change in the Leeds Department of Fine Arts away from an exclusive focus on Marxism and feminism to a program that makes colonial discourse more central to its examination of art and theory. The institutional particularity of Pollock's essay is significant in the sense that it documents a specific instance in which questions of nation, postcolonialism, and feminism are currently transforming the hierarchical order of scholarship and feminist art practices.[27]

All the articles in this anthology are reevaluating traditional discourses and viewing practices about art and culture to acknowledge the diversified differences at work in the field of feminist visual culture as well as in contemporary art practices. Rather than posit final readings of particular cultural products, most of the articles question the writer/interpreter as arbiter of cultural value, by pointing to his or her specific investments motivating a reading. The emphasis is indeed on shifts in critical viewing in relation to questions of nation, transnationalism, citizenship, and gender. The first section examines a genealogy of modern art history and how its very constitution as a discipline is rooted in nation-states and constituted through racism and sexism. This more historically based section contextualizes part 2, which challenges the current conceptualization of the disciplines by focusing on new kinds of feminist writing in visual culture and feminist artwork. Many of the essays in this section focus on issues that are still not discussed within the discipline. In particular, the section foregrounds the visual work of white ethnic cultures, immigrant cultures, and Third World populations as a way to emphasize transnational visual production as well as just national ones. The impact of gender, race, and sexual politics of imperialisms and nationalisms on contemporary visual culture and its practices has not been much examined in the traditional disciplines. I hope these essays have much to offer in terms of enabling a new form of dialogue to take place that acknowledges the complexity of what is actually happening in feminist visual culture at this moment.

NOTES

1. Lucia Moholy was a photographer closely associated with the Bauhaus in Weimar, and then Dessau. She was married to Lázlo Moholy-Nagy in 1921 and worked closely with Moholy-Nagy in the creation of photograms and photomontages. She continued her photographic work throughout her life and combined her photography practice with her teaching, which emphasized the social history of photography.

2. Franz Roh was not a conventional art historian but a photo historian and one of the foremost spokesmen for the formalist/modernist model of photography. He was known for dispelling the notion of the unique, hand-printed art photograph in favor of a kind of modernist photography that self-consciously emphasized its very reproducibility. He wrote a well-known article on the photographer Moholy-Nagy titled "Mechanism and Expression: The Essence and Value of Photography" and published two books in 1929, *Foto-Auge* (a selection of photographs from the *Film und Foto* exhibition edited with Jan Tschichold [Tübingen: Wasmuth, 1973]) and *Moholy-Nagy: 60 Fotos* (Berlin: Klinkhardt and Biermann, 1930).

3. See Amelia Jones, ed., *Sexual Politics: Judy Chicago's "Dinner Party" in Feminist Art History* (Berkeley and Los Angeles: University of California Press, 1996).

4. Mark Roskill, *What Is Art History?* 2nd ed. (Amherst: University of Massachusetts Press, 1989), 9.

5. Ibid.

6. Laura Mulvey, "Visual Pleasure and Narrative Cinema," *Screen* 16, no. 3 (1975): 6–18; John Berger, *Ways of Seeing* (Middlesex, England: Penguin Books, 1972). More recently, the interventions of the Guerrilla Girls, an anonymous group of feminist political artists formed in 1985 to specifically critique racist and sexist institutional practices of the art world, have also put an emphasis on looking relations. For further information regarding their posters and activities, see *Confessions of the Guerrilla Girls* (New York: HarperCollins, 1995).

7. See Laura Mulvey, "Afterthoughts on 'Visual Pleasure and Narrative Cinema' Inspired by *Duel in the Sun,*" in *Feminism and Film Theory,* ed. Constance Penley (New York: Museum of Contemporary Art, 1984), 360–74.

8. Abigail Solomon-Godeau, "Going Native," *Art in America* 77, no. 7 (1989): 118–29.

9. See Jane M. Gaines, "Competing Glances: Who Is Reading Robert Mapplethorpe's *Black Book?*" and Kobena Mercer, "Skin Head Sex Thing: Racial Difference and the Homoerotic Imaginary." Both appear in *New Formations* 16 (Spring 1992).

10. bell hooks, "The Oppositional Gaze," in *Black Looks: Race and Representation* (Boston: South End Press, 1992), 115–32.

11. In this volume, see the chapter by Ann Pellegrini, "You Make Me Feel (Mighty Real): Sandra Bernhard's Whiteface."

12. See among other books on this issue bell hooks, *Art on My Mind: Visual Politics* (New York: New Press, 1995); Ann Pellegrini, *Performance Anxieties: Staging Psychoanalysis, Staging Race* (New York and London: Routledge, 1997).

13. There seems to be a return in recent years to using positivist histories and chronologies on the part of U.S. curators to reestablish the neutral gaze of the art historian, as evidenced in the recent exhibition and book by Paul Schimmel at the Museum of Contemporary Art at the Geffen Contemporary, Los Angeles, titled *Out of Action: Between Performance and the Object, 1949–1979* (London: Thames and

Hudson, 1998). See also Linda Nochlin, "The Imaginary Orient," in *The Politics of Vision: Essays on Nineteenth-Century Art and Society* (New York: Harper and Row, 1989), 33–59; Lucy Lippard, *Mixed Blessings: New Art in a Multicultural America* (New York: Pantheon, 1990); Joanna Frueh, Cassandra L. Langer, and Arlene Ravn, eds., *New Feminist Criticism* (New York: HarperCollins, 1994); Michele Wallace, "Why Are There No Great Black Artists? The Problem of Visuality in African-American Culture," in *Black Popular Culture* (Seattle: Bay Press, 1992), 333–46.

14. See Donald Preziozi's *Rethinking Art History: Meditations on a Coy Science* (New Haven, Conn.: Yale University Press, 1989); and Michael Ann Holly's "Wölfflin and the Imagining of the Baroque," in *Visual Culture: Images and Interpretation* (Hanover, N.H.: Wesleyan University Press, 1994), 347–64.

15. Donna Haraway, "Situated Knowledges: The Science Question in Feminism and the Privilege of Partial Perspective," in *Simians, Cyborgs, and Women* (New York: Routledge, 1991), 188.

16. Roland Barthes, "The Death of the Author," in *Image Music Text* (New York: Hill and Wang, 1977), 142–48.

17. Edward Lucie-Smith, *Race, Sex, and Gender in Contemporary Art* (New York: Harry N. Abrams, 1994); Horst de la Croix, Richard Tansey, and Diane Kirkpatrick, *Gardner's Art through the Ages,* 9th ed. (New York: Harcourt Brace Jovanovich, 1991).

18. *Postcolonialism* generally refers to the effects of colonization on cultures and societies. The term was originally used by historians after the Second World War to designate the postindependence period, as in terms such as "the postcolonial state." Since the late 1970s the term *postcolonialism* has been used by cultural critics to discuss the various cultural effects of colonization.

The term *colonial discourse* derives from the interdisciplinary area of contemporary postcolonial studies. It is a formulation of recent currency that can best be understood as designating a conceptual area first marked out by Edward Said's *Orientalism* and his use of Michel Foucault's notion of discourse as a strongly bounded area of social knowledge.

19. Norma Broude and Mary D. Garrard, eds., *The Power of Feminist Art: The American Movement of the 1970s, History and Impact* (New York: Harry N. Abrams, 1994).

20. Michel Wallace, "Why Are There No Great Black Artists?" 342.

21. Often the concerns of postmodernists are seen as opposed to those of the multiculturalists, as evidenced by the split between postmodern theorists (often white) and multicultural theorists (often critics and artists of color). In an attempt to account for this racial divide, bell hooks, who has been something of a mediator in this debate, suggests that part of the problem seems to be the way that gut-level experience has always been opposed to critical thinking in the arts in the United States. See bell hooks, "Postmodern Blackness," in *Yearning: Race, Gender, and Cultural Politics* (Boston: South End Press, 1990), 23–32.

22. Inderpal Grewal and Caren Kaplan, eds., *Scattered Hegemonies: Postmodernity and Transnational Feminist Practices* (Minneapolis: University of Minnesota Press, 1994), 21–22.

23. See, among others, Rey Chow, *Writing Diaspora: Tactics of Intervention in Contemporary Cultural Studies* (Bloomington: Indiana University Press, 1993); Ruth Frankenberg, *The Social Construction of Whiteness: White Women, Race Matters* (Minneapolis: University of Minnesota Press, 1993); Deborah Gordon, ed., "Feminism and the Critique of Colonial Discourse" (special issue), *Inscriptions* 3/4 (1988); Inderpal Grewal and Caren Kaplan, eds., *Scattered Hegemonies*; Inderpal Grewal, *Home and Harem: Nation, Gender, Empire, and the Cultures of Travel* (Durham, N.C.: Duke University Press, 1996); Donna Haraway, *Primate Visions: Gender, Race, and Nature in the World of Modern Science* (New York: Routledge, 1989); D. Emily Hicks, *Border Writing: The Multidimensional Text* (Minneapolis: University of Minnesota Press, 1991); Trinh T. Minh-ha, *Woman Native Other* (Bloomington: Indiana University Press, 1989); Chandra Mohanty, Ann Russo, and Lourdes Torres, eds., *Third World Women and the Politics of Feminism* (Bloomington: Indiana University Press, 1991); Aihwa Ong, *Spirits of Resistance and Capitalist*

Discipline: Factory Women in Malaysia (Albany: State University of New York Press, 1987); Andrew Parker, Mary Russo, Doris Sommer, and Patricia Yaeger, eds., *Nationalisms and Sexualities* (New York: Routledge, 1992); Ella Shohat and Robert Stam, *Unthinking Eurocentrism: Multiculturalism and the Media* (New York: Routledge, 1994); Gayatri Chakravorty Spivak, *In Other Worlds: Essays in Cultural Politics* (Minneapolis: University of Minnesota Press, 1987).

24. For a partial list of works already published in the arts on feminist theory and colonial discourse, see Jesús Fuenmayor, Kate Haug, and Frazer Ward, *Dirt and Domesticity: Constructions of the Feminine* (New York: Whitney Museum of American Art, 1992); Coco Fusco, *English Is Broken Here: Notes on Cultural Fusion in the Americas* (New York: New Press, 1995); Saidiya V. Hartman, "Excisions of the Flesh," in *Lorna Simpson: For the Sake of the Viewer* (Chicago: Museum of Contemporary Art, 1993), 55–67; bell hooks, *Art on My Mind: Visual Politics* (New York: New Press, 1995); Abigail Solomon-Godeau and Constance Lewallen, *Mistaken Identities* (Seattle: University of Washington Press, 1992); Gilane Tawadros, "Beyond the Boundary: The Work of Three Black Women Artists in Britain," *Third Text 8/9* (Autumn/Winter 1989): 121–50; John Taylor, *A Dream of England: Landscape Photography and the Tourist's Imagination* (Manchester: Manchester University Press, 1994); Lydia Yee, *Division of Labor: "Women's Work" in Contemporary Art* (New York: Bronx Museum of Art, 1995).

25. Eloy J. Hernandez, "Art History's Anxiety Attack," *Afterimage* (May/June 1994): 6; "Questionnaire on Visual Culture," *October 7* (Summer 1996); Scott Heller, "Rochester Is Only University Offering Ph.D. in Visual Culture," *Chronicle of Higher Education,* July 19, 1996, A15; Scott Heller, "Visual Images Replace Text As Focal Point for Many Scholars," *Chronicle of Higher Education,* July 19, 1996, A8; Scott Heller, "Changing Course: Art Historians Replace Traditional Surveys with New Approaches," *Chronicle of Higher Education,* May 3, 1996, A19. Also see letter from David S. Andrews, professor of art history, University of New Hampshire, in "Letters to the Editor, The Role of 'Visual Culture,'" *Chronicle of Higher Education,* September 13, 1996, B7.

26. Trinh T. Minh-ha, *Woman Native Other* (Bloomington: Indiana University Press, 1989), 106.

27. The Leeds Department of Fine Arts is a unique art program in which art practice and cultural and feminist theory are taught together rather than being separated into distinctive schools or disciplines of art history and studio art.

PART I

GENDER, RACE, AND NATION

Histories and Discourses

GHOSTS OF ETHNICITY

Rethinking Art Discourses of the 1940s and 1980s

Lisa Bloom

*[Eastern European jews] have been and still are the most particularist people on earth;
yet they have been accused of making it their particular mission to destroy particularity,
to internationalize, to create the brotherhood of man.*
    —Clement Greenberg, "The Jewish Dickens: Review of the
    World of Sholom Aleichem by Maurice Samuel"

The epigraph, from the late New York art critic Clement Greenberg, emphasizes the contradictions and paradoxes of a certain U.S. modernist jewish dilemma as it was understood in the 1940s.[1] Taking the perspective of the informed jewish insider, Greenberg praises the Eastern and Central European jew's predilection for a contradictory set of local and global attachments, as well as a discomfort with the national, particularly the historical European nationalism that assumes only a superficial recognition of jews as authentic citizens of the nation. To circumvent the national, Greenberg celebrates a discourse of universal humanism that "produce[s] the supreme example of the gratuitous and disinterested man."[2] He is referring to the lack of self-interest on the part of jews who advocated a discourse of universal humanism that worked for the erasure of all differences rather than just their own.

Greenberg's interest in the contradictions of a certain jewish subjectivity appears within the larger context of his critique of the (anti-Semitic) outsider view that jews have a hidden language and manner of thinking that make them "devious."[3] One of the ways in which Greenberg tackles this stereotype is by delineating the complexity of the idea of the jew and the jewish response to this projection of difference:

> The last thing the Jew is, is tricky, and the last thing he thinks of is his front to the world. The ostentatious Jew—that myth of the Anglo-Saxon world—is ostentatious only about his wealth, and unlike maharajas and Vanderbilts, makes no other claim by his ostentation than that of his wealth. And when he loses it he does not bother to keep the lace curtains hanging in the front parlor.[4]

Greenberg's emphasis on the Eastern European jews' abhorrence of hypocrisy and their impatience with etiquette and decorum, present in this passage, is also important in understanding the epigraph. Just as he suggests that as a people Eastern European jews do not bother to keep up appearances, he also notes that when jews are threatened with marginalization or exclusion from nationally imagined communities, they will not abide by nationalist sentiments for the sake of propriety.

The paradox of Greenberg's dualistic thinking, in which he sets particularism against internationalism as a way to transcend the national, has quite a powerful legacy in the present. However, I would argue that his ideas, though they might have enabled a certain way of thinking that was effective at the time they were written, no longer provide us with an accurate map of social relations in the 1990s. The discourse of the devious jew is no longer as widespread as it was during World War II, nor is the pure internalization of a negative image of "jewishness" as prevalent for my generation as it was for Greenberg's. (I will address this later when I analyze Greenberg's own admission in 1955 of being "a self-hating jew.") Another major change that has taken place is that an earlier generation's predilection for the universal is now being replaced by a more contemporary notion of the global and the transnational. The latter is not as tied in with a discourse of imperialism as the forms of "globalism" and "universalism" championed in the 1940s. In addition, new conceptions of locality and connectedness are also emerging, which are not so bound up with a discourse that sees ethnicity as distinct from a spectrum of other identities and differences. Contradictory and constantly shifting relations can now define a given community; as Ella Shohat writes, "The intersection of ethnicity with race, class, and gender discourses involves a shifting, relational social and discursive positioning, whereby one group can simultaneously constitute 'norm' and 'periphery.'"[5]

I conceived this essay as a way to rethink Greenberg's early binarisms for the purpose of dealing with the multicultural, feminist, and queer debates of the present. It is worth noting that these newer ways of imagining identities provided an impetus for me to connect in a more engaged way my own Ashkenazi jewish identity to my cultural politics of race and gender. This perspective is only beginning to be addressed in contemporary art history, since jewish ethnicity as a positionality in these debates has been absent until recently.[6] Strong opposition from conservative critics to expanding the traditional art historical curriculum beyond the binaristic hierarchy of high/low art world as well as a culturally conservative political climate in general—marked in part by the rise of the Christian Right, the attempt to close the National Endowment for the Arts, and the return of a subtle anti-Semitism that still permeates U.S. culture—have shut down a complicated discussion of jewish identities in relation to other political issues, including feminism and colonial discourse. By making connections between various debates in this essay, however, I am not intending to privilege such a perspective but, rather, to suggest that it has informed my presence and point of view in what follows.

This essay rethinks the relationship between art discourses of the 1940s and 1980s to imagine a more complicated relation between the discourses of modernism, nationalism, cosmopolitanism, masculinities, and jewish identities in the 1940s. The second half of the chapter deals with the legacy of a U.S.-based modernist art criticism established in the forties and the way it continues to reassert itself today in altered form in the critical art discourses of the 1980s and early 1990s. The quotation I began with deals specifically with the paradoxes of jewish identities in the forties. The idea of universalism it articulates is relevant to the changing debates in the arts in the United States, especially since the notion of universality on which aesthetic judgments depended was itself constructed out of discussions in which racial and ethnic differences were central issues.

The first section focuses on the writings of Clement Greenberg, Harold Rosenberg, Meyer Schapiro, and some of the abstract expressionist painters of the 1940s. In the second section I examine the reception of a shift in art criticism that took place in the 1980s and 1990s around the work of two late contemporary artists of some renown, Robert Mapplethorpe, an openly gay white photographer, and Jean-Michel Basquiat, an artist of Puerto Rican and Cuban descent. This section focuses on the different terms by which each of these artists has been accepted into the canon of "great" universal art. In particular, it considers how an older modernist discourse treats the discourses of ethnicity, gender, and homosexuality differently from that of race.

My rationale for making some connection between the 1940s and 1980s is not to overdraw the similarities between them, since there are important and obvious distinctions between the forms of globalism, cosmopolitanism, and universalism championed in 1940s and 1980s art discourses, respectively, but to map the ways that cultural and political dialogues in the arts have taken place across different immigrant art communities in New York at specific historical moments. To examine in further depth the politics of location of a history of art, the cultural identities of artists and art critics need to be taken into account, especially when analyzing in retrospect a discourse of modernism, which was conceived by its proponents to dislodge the notion of identities altogether.

NEW YORK ART DISCOURSES AND UNIVERSALISM: 1930S AND 1940S

In the growing field of visual cultural studies, there has been interest in inflecting a discourse of contemporary art history with a much more self-conscious and critical analysis of how power relations work—most notably those of gender, sexuality, race, ethnicity, and nationalism—as opposed to what one finds within the discourse of market institutions of New York art galleries, museums, and magazines of the 1980s and 1990s. One of the ways this is currently being done is by deconstructing the notion of the New York art world as monolithic and unchanging. Critics, such as Irit Rogoff, working in the area of visual culture explain how the New York art world is "a world unto itself, with a distinct cultural and linguistic tradition and a vehement sense of territoriality."[7] Rogoff proceeds to formulate this particular art world much the way that historian Benedict Anderson theorizes the nation as "an imagined community" or as a performative space where roles and relationships of both belonging and foreignness are acted out. In some key ways, the New York art world and the nation in Anderson's sense operate analogously. Both are mythic yet very powerful and effective communities that are built on shared fictional narratives. Both have key performers (artists, critics, curators, art dealers in the case of the art world) who have the discursive power to define how they situate themselves as well as Others within this community that they interpret and control, and both arouse in Anderson's words "deep attachments" of belonging and "command profound emotional legitimacy."[8]

Despite the similarities between the two terms I have outlined, what is paradoxical about the concept of the New York art world is its simultaneous attachment and detachment from the U.S. nation, and how this ambivalent connection to the United States actually authorizes its universalizing image of itself. It is fitting that the genealogy of the term *New York art world* and its cosmopolitan aspirations can be traced to the beginnings of the Cold War and the development of a New York art market. As Serge Guilbaut argues in his intellectual history of the period titled *How New York Stole the Idea of Modern Art,* this also was a moment when New York began to have dreams of replacing Paris as the presumed imperial cultural center of the so-called West.[9] Like the formulation "New York art world," abstract expressionist painting that characterized this period was embraced by New York intellectuals not merely as a New York school of painting or as American painting, but as a universalist cultural style that transcended the geographically specific. In 1943, the *New York Times* art page launched this art movement with the headline "'Globalism' Pops into View."[10] This media recognition coincided also with the way that New York jewish artists Adolph Gottlieb and Mark Rothko defined themselves that year, writing as members of the cultural committee of the Federation of American Painters and Sculptors:

> The current 3rd annual exhibition of the Federation . . . prompts us to state again our position on art, and the new spirit demanded of artists and the public today. At our inception we stated "We *condemn artistic nationalism* which negates the world tradition of art at the base of modern art movements." . . . As a nation we are being forced to outgrow our narrow political isolationism. Now that America is recognized as the center where art and artists of all the world must meet, it is time for us to accept cultural values on a truly global plane.[11]

The insistent globalism that defined the terms by which these painters authorized themselves reappears in the writings of both jewish and nonjewish art critics of the time, although for the purposes of this essay I will concentrate on the writings of Clement Greenberg and Harold Rosenberg, who were key to constructing an identity for the New York group.[12] One way in which Greenberg could convince outsiders of the international significance of these mostly New York painters was to explain how a real culture, an avant-garde, was possible in a nation imagined as a cultural vacuum. Greenberg accomplished this by discursively transforming the abiding limitation of American culture—its putative isolation—into an asset:

> Isolation is, so to speak, the natural condition of high art in America. Yet it is precisely our more intimate and habitual acquaintance with *isolation that gives us our advantage* at this moment. Isolation, or rather the alienation that is its cause, is the truth—isolation, alienation, naked and revealed unto itself, is the condition under which the true reality of our age is experienced. And the experience of this true reality is indispensable to any ambitious age.[13]

In Greenberg's formulation, modernity, alienation, and what it means to be American went hand in hand. Greenberg turned a previously unacceptable way of being in the United States (alienation) into cultural capital. Ironically, he used America's greatest weaknesses—its geographical isolation, its so-called lack of culture, and its alienation—and turned them into an advantage.

Harold Rosenberg's discursive strategy was similar to Greenberg's.[14] He also saw the proverbial alienation that artists experienced in America as beneficial:

> Attached neither to a community nor to one another, *these painters experience a unique lone-*
> *liness of a depth that is reached perhaps nowhere in the world.* From the four corners of their
> vast land they have come to plunge themselves into the anonymity of New York, *annihilation*
> *of their past being not the least compelling project of these aesthetic Legionnaires. . . .* The very
> extremity of their *isolation forces upon them a kind of optimism,* an impulse to believe in their
> ability to dissociate some personal essence of their experience and rescue it as the beginning
> of a new world. [15]

For Rosenberg, it was precisely because American artists were alienated that they were antiprovincial, and thus he saw them capable of imagining the creation of a "new world," a world without alienation. However, the two critics disagreed sharply about how this would come about. Writing in 1947, Greenberg states:

> In the face of current events painting feels, apparently, that it must be epic poetry, it must be
> theater, it must be an atomic bomb, it must be the rights of Man. But the greatest painter of
> our time, Matisse, preeminently demonstrated the sincerity and penetration that go with the
> kind of greatness particular to twentieth century painting by saying that he wanted his art to
> be an armchair for the tired business man.[16]

For Greenberg, this new world could not be obtained unless artists returned to purely visual formal values. In his desire to preserve high culture by cutting it off altogether from the social, Greenberg wanted art to be an "armchair" for the exhausted capitalist, whereas critics like Rosenberg disagreed with this art-for-art's-sake prescription. In his famous manifesto of abstract expressionism titled "The American Action Painters" (1952), Rosenberg saw that abstract expressionist art embodied this formalist ideal by bringing art and life closer together. This collapsing of life into art was seen as an absolute heroic task compared to which any other form of engagement would pale by comparison: "The lone artist did not want the world to be different, he wanted his canvas to be a world."[17]

Despite the disagreements between the two critics, what linked their work was the way each made the claim that great aesthetic experiences occur most profoundly in a cultural vacuum. Such an argument, perhaps, was effective in giving a new cosmopolitan prestige to American art that it previously lacked in the 1940s and 1950s. But, as I will later suggest, it also set the stage for the continuing belief in the dissident artist as an alienated modernist, unable to engage in any form of political art not based on the notion of the outsider. Furthermore, the notion of the alienated and autonomous artist/intellectual as it emerged in the 1940s and 1950s has a complex relationship to notions of masculinities, jewish identities, socialism, and the political climate between 1936 and 1945.

The pre–World War II generation of New York intellectuals and artists saw themselves as much more autonomous from an American business culture than the generation that followed them. They directed their energies not toward promoting an aggressive international art market in which modern art played a leading role, but toward a more populist agenda, politically creating a local culture in which the working class could represent themselves as participants in power.[18] This socialist project that involved a number of writers as well as other artists in the United States also valorized a cosmopolitan ideal, but one that was linked to social revolution in Russia and the Marxist notion of a revolutionary international class struggle. This political project was eventually challenged and, in some cases, redefined when Soviet policy itself moved away from its original purpose. This shift began in July 1935 when the Seventh World Congress set a new Soviet policy of the Popular Front, which was an attempt to unite a broad group of intellectuals in a common campaign against fascism. Similarly, in the United States, in discussions held in 1936 by the First American Artists' Congress, artists and intellectuals joined forces also to fight fascism and tried to widen their political base by recruiting nonaligned Marxists and liberals so as to play a more significant role in a more broadly based American cultural politics. Worried that fascism could spread to the United States, the Artists' Congress saw a parallel between the new emphasis on nationalism in the arts in the United States and the way that the Nazis and Italian fascists were using the arts as a means to build group identities centered on the myths of nationalism and racial superiority. These fears were especially pronounced among jewish critics, who brought to their work a strong sense of coming from elsewhere, of standing outside the white American mainstream at a time when there was general uneasiness about artists and critics of jewish descent. As Lynd Ward and Meyer Schapiro suggest in a speech given at the congress in 1936 titled "Race, Nationality, and Art":

> We have many appeals for an "American Art" in which the concept of America is very vague, usually defined as a "genuine American expression" or "explicitly native art" and sometimes includes a separation of American painters into desirable and undesirable on the basis of Anglo-Saxon surnames . . . finally the word "American" used in that way has no real meaning. It suspends a veil of fictitious unity and blinds our eyes to the fact that there can be no art in common between the Americans who own Rockefeller Center, the Americans in the Legion in Terre Haute, and the Americans in, as a symbol, Commonwealth College in Arkansas.[19]

Harsh words were directed toward an ideology of a national "American art," since it assumed only a perfunctory recognition of ethnic and racial differences in favor of a common culture that Ward and Schapiro evidently felt ambivalent about. The limitations of the cultural pluralist agenda were evident to Schapiro and Ward, who might be perceived as "undesirable" themselves, given their jewish surnames. It is worth noting that although they were uneasy about the idea of a "genuine American expression," both were also equally skeptical about an essentializing notion of a jewish cultural expression:

> But even if there is no ground for a structure of racial differences in Europe, the theorists of blood chemistry will still point to the Jewish race as evidence of the persistence of unique qualities that can be traced to blood alone. They hold it to be self-evident that the Jewish race has definite physical characteristics and equally characteristic cultural qualities, and the one stems from the other. . . . In our time we have the same lack of evidence as regards a common blood and culture. Rothenstein is English; Pissarro, French; Soutine, Russian; Pechstein, German; Modigliani, Italian. Who can point to anything in the work of these men that can be said to be common to all of them, . . . and therefore a Jewish characteristic? (116–17)

Any mapping of art by jewish artists according to racialized categories was obviously suspect, since the last thing jewish critics wanted was for jewish American artists to be reduced to their very "un-American" religious background. According to Ward and Schapiro,

> the import of this has a direct bearing on our problems as American artists, for if there is not one iota of evidence acceptable to scientists that will support a claim of uniqueness in the Jewish blood stream, then we must read out of court all propositions based on it, such as the condemnation of Alfred Stieglitz's place in American art because he is a Hoboken Jew. (117)

This was a moment when individual artists such as Stieglitz had to live with the threat that they might be called to account not for their art or their writing, but for their jewishness, and it was necessary for critics not to tie these identities together. Anti-Semitism was on the rise in the United States prior to America's entry into the war, and in this climate an attempt was made to discredit Stieglitz's authenticity as an American artist solely on the basis of his ethnicity. In 1934, Thomas Craven, a conservative U.S. art critic, wrote:

> Stieglitz, a Hoboken Jew without knowledge of, or interest in, the historical American background, was—quite apart from the doses of purified art he had swallowed—hardly equipped for the leadership of a genuine American expression; and it is a matter of record that none of the artists whose names and work he has exploited has been noticeably American in flavor.[20]

Stieglitz's jewishness made him a so-called inauthentic American, according to Craven, and thus disqualified him from a leadership position in constituting a "genuine" American art.[21] While individual artists might have been targeted in the United States because of their jewishness, modern art in general was rarely made synonymous with jewishness to the extent it was in Hitler's Germany. The 1937 Degenerate Art exhibition in particular functioned as a broad condemnation of all modern art, which was seen by Nazis as "Jewish."[22]

After the war, when the full dimensions of the European Holocaust became known, there was a move on the part of jewish writers and art critics to assert their ethnic identity as evidenced by the following pronouncement in 1944 made by the organizers of the Under Forty symposium, which was printed in the *Contemporary Jewish Record:* "American Jews have reached the stage of integration with the native environment. They are spectators no longer but full participants in the cultural life of the country."[23] Despite the celebratory rhetoric of the *Contemporary Jewish Record,* the ability of U.S. jews to pass as fully white was nowhere a foregone conclusion, especially since the ethnic category white constantly shifts at different historical moments in U.S. culture. As Donna Haraway explains:

> The point makes it easier to remember how the Irish moved from being perceived as colored in the early nineteenth century in the United States to quite white in Boston's school busing struggles in the 1970s, or how U.S. Jews have been ascribed white status more or less stably after W.W. II, while Arabs continue to be written as colored in the daily news.[24]

Haraway's point is important to take into account, even if she herself is not attentive enough to the diversity of the jewish diasporic community in the United States, especially the marked differences between German and Eastern European jews (many of whom did not speak English in the mid-1940s). Nor does she note the complicated status of, for example, a jewish Iraqi in the United States today. Indeed, it is the heterogeneity of identities among jews that made the shift toward jewish assimilation in postwar America anything but uniform. For instance, various religious sects are operative within Judaism and make for large differences in what it means to be a jewish man or jewish woman. Nevertheless, given the supposed historical shift in jewish ethnic identity in the postwar United States, it seems important to question how the significant art criticism of this period, written mostly by jewish men (Greenberg, Schapiro, and Rosenberg), emerges through and against historical discourses of ethnicity, race, nationalism, as well as gender. Despite the inordinate amount of writing on Greenberg within the past two decades, by postmodernists (Victor Burgin) and by Marxists (Griselda Pollock, Serge Guilbaut, Michael Fried, T. J. Clark) among others, the relative silence on this issue was not broken until the mid-1970s by Max Kozloff. [25] Writing a review in 1976 in *Artforum* on the Jewish Museum exhibit curated by Avram Kampf titled "Jewish Experience in the Art of the Twentieth Century," Kozloff explains the enormous influence of jewish art criticism: "From that old-time jewish sect called American art criticism, many unsuspecting Gentiles picked up their broadest, most governing ideas of modern art."[26] Despite Kozloff's important article, the issue was dropped and not taken up again until the multicultural debates of the late 1980s and early 1990s by art historians such as Matthew Baigell, Catherine Soussloff, Kenneth E. Silver, Milton Brown, Norman L. Kleeblatt, Susan Chevlowe, Bradford R. Collins, and Susan Noyes Platt, as well as by intellectual historians writing more generally on the New York intellectuals involved in the journal *Partisan Review*. Of the few articles on this topic, Collins's "Political Pessimism, Jewish 'Self-Hatred' and the 'Dreams of Universalism': The Origins of Greenberg's Purist Aesthetics, c. 1930–1940" is the most relevant for this essay because it provides a systematic and detailed analysis of the impact of ethnicity and race on Greenberg's early ideas on art.[27] However, although I found Collins's piece immensely valuable in the inclusion of ethnicity in its biographical approach to Greenberg, my perspective is somewhat different from that of Collins. Drawing from Michel Foucault's analysis of historical writing, discursive formations, and their practical institutionalization, I am more concerned with the "discourse" of his writing and its powerful legacy than with evaluating what Collins refers to as the "personal care and concerns" of Greenberg the person.[28]

CLEMENT GREENBERG AND JEWISH HEGEMONY: LEGITIMIZING A FORM
OF DECULTURATION IN THE ARTS

In 1955, Greenberg scripts himself in terms of his ethnic identity in the following biographical entry that appeared in *Twentieth Century Authors*:

> I was born in the Bronx, in New York City, the oldest of three sons. My father and my mother had come, in their separate ways, from the Lithuanian Jewish cultural enclave in northeastern Poland, and I spoke Yiddish as soon as I did English. When I was five we moved to Norfolk, Va., but moved back to New York—Brooklyn this time—when I was eleven. My father had by that time made enough money to change over from storekeeper (clothing) to

manufacturer (metal goods). However, I can't remember there ever having been any worrying about money in our family, or any one in it lacking for anything. Which is not to say that we were rich.

I attended public school in Norfolk and Brooklyn, took the last year of high school at the Marquand School, and went to Syracuse University for an A.B. (1930). For two and a half years after college I sat home in what looked like idleness, but did during that time learn German and Italian in addition to French and Latin. The following two years I worked in St. Louis, Cleveland, San Francisco and Los Angeles in an abortive left-handed venture of my father's into the wholesale drygoods business; but I discovered that my appetite for business did not amount to the same thing as an inclination. During the next year I supported myself by translating. . . . At the beginning of 1930 I went to work for the federal government, first in the New York office of the Civil Service Commission, then in the Veterans Administration, and finally (in 1937) in the Appraiser's Division of the Customs Service in the Port of New York. Until then I had been making desultory efforts to write, but now I began in earnest, in my office-time leisure—of which I had plenty—and fairly soon I began to get printed.[29]

This rather lengthy biographical statement in which he makes his jewish origins part of his persona suggests among other things that he is somewhat at ease with his jewish background. This entry thus offers a very different self-presentation from the one he earlier scripted in 1950 in which he casts himself in the role of "a self-hating jew." The article "Self-Hatred and Jewish Chauvinism: Some Reflections on 'Positive Jewishness'" starts out as a bitter and acrimonious indictment of his own inability to deal with his self-criticism:

The Jewish self-hatred in myself, . . . its subtlety and the devious ways in which it conceals itself, from me as well as from the world outside, explains many things that used to puzzle me in the behavior of my fellow Jews. It is only reluctantly that I have become persuaded that self-hatred in one form or another is almost universal among Jews—or at least much more prevalent than is commonly thought or admitted—and that it is not confined on the whole to Jews like myself.[30]

Greenberg's confession casts his successful career and secure reputation in a different light and as such is a significant piece of writing in Greenberg's oeuvre. Despite the gesture to universalize his personal experience and connect it to that of all American jews, it is noteworthy in its frank interrogation of his own ethnic anxiety and his willingness to narrate the unspeakable about himself.

This 1950 article also inscribes him in a more complex relationship to his jewishness than his 1944 comments for the Under Forty symposium suggest. In this earlier piece he presents himself as caught within the restrictive injunctions his parents have internalized, including the way that they downplayed their ethnicity in public in favor of an identification with socialist politics:

This writer has no more of a conscious position toward his Jewish heritage than the average American Jew—which is to say, hardly any. His father and mother repudiated a good deal of the Jewish heritage for him in advance by becoming free-thinking socialists who maintained only their Yiddish, certain vestiges of folk life in the Pale, and an insistence upon specifying themselves as Jews.[31]

This inscription of himself within a familial narrative in private nevertheless permits him to reject a self-conscious quality of jewishness in public, but to acknowledge at the same time some aspect of his ethnic identity that he associates with "heredity": "I believe that a quality of Jewishness is present in every word I write. . . . It may be said that this quality . . . is very informal, being transmitted mostly through mother's milk and the habits and talk of the family" (177). What comes through most clearly in this short essay is not only his sense of familial loyalties in private but his allegiance to an elitist-tinged socialism and to cosmopolitan values over and above his ethnicity, equating the latter with conventional notions of identity and narrow bourgeois values:

> Jewish life has become, for reasons of security, so solidly, so rigidly, restrictedly and suffocatingly middle-class. . . . No people on earth are more correct, more staid, more provincial, more commonplace, more inexperienced; none observe more strictly the letter of every code that is respectable; no people do so completely and habitually what is expected of them. (178–79)

Greenberg's act of writing frees him from a "suffocatingly middle-class" jewish identity and enables him to become a member of the cosmopolitan cultural elite. Still, what he most wants to escape is not his ethnicity, but the constraints of a certain U.S. ethnic particularism:

> Flight—as well as its converse, pursuit—is of course a great American theme, but the Jewish writer sets himself off by the more concerned and more immediately and materially personal way he treats it. His writing becomes essentially a career which provides him with the means of flight. This writing is my wings away. (178)

In the international world of letters and art criticism, of Anglophone high culture, Greenberg finds a space of flight that is seemingly neutral. What is ironic, though, is that writing and the history of jewish culture have always been intertwined—most specifically, rabbinic, Eastern European culture, for instance, as well as early-twentieth-century Viennese culture, in which jews had a strong presence in publishing. While Greenberg doesn't acknowledge the connection between writing and jewish culture, he does work to salvage the modernist notion of the jew as outsider and Other. He emphasizes "the Jew's chronic conception of himself as a wanderer even when has lived in the same place all his life. . . . Centuries of existence as an insecure minority make people conceive of themselves as always coming into the world from outside it" (177). Most significantly, he values what he takes as the jewish ability to theorize and analyze. Greenberg's valorization of abstraction can also be seen in his 1943 book review of Maurice Samuel's *The World of Sholom Aleichem,* in which he suggests that the tendency to conceptualize, to think abstractly, was a mode of self-protection for the jew from the excruciating realities of the ghetto. Interestingly, in his 1944 essay, in which he asserts himself in the privileged role of the writer and cosmopolitan firmly removed from life in the ghetto, he sees himself also energized by the powers of abstraction, which he essentializes as a jewish quality:

> There is a Jewish bias towards the abstract, the tendency to conceptualize as much as possible, and there is a certain *Schwärmerei,* a state of perpetual and exalted surprise—sometimes disgust— at the sensuous and sentimental data of existence which others take for granted. (177)

His emphasis on the abstract is significant. It authorizes his assignment of a negative valence to the sensuous and the everyday, and it sets the terms of his construction of oppositions between the categories of the general and the particular, the abstract and the detail.[32] Greenberg's hostility toward the incursions into high art of the detail is most fully articulated in his famous 1939 essay "Avant-Garde and Kitsch," in which he places the blame on

> that thing to which the Germans give the wonderful name of *Kitsch*: popular, commercial art and literature with their chromotypes, magazine covers, illustrations, ads, slick and pulp fiction, comics, Tin Pan Alley music, tap dancing, Hollywood movies, etc. etc.[33]

Whereas to Greenberg, kitsch seems tied to the constraints of ethnic particularism and the everyday, high art by contrast does not have any identifiable referent, and is thus "valid solely on its own terms" (8). Even though Greenberg's theories of abstract art—in which the decorative or the illustrative have no place—seem on the surface to have nothing to do with the question of cultural identity and sexual, ethnic, and racial difference, their privileging of the abstract as the only authentically avant-garde art worked to ensure the reading of art so it consistently favored the assimilation and integration of mostly New York white male artists such as Jackson Pollock (of Scotch-Irish descent) as well as artists of Eastern European and European jewish origins (Adolph Gottlieb, Barnett Newman, Mark Rothko) over and above those nonwhite artists and women artists who did not feel drawn to nonrepresentational art. Thus, implicit in his theory was a certain selective privileging of a particular ethnicity and gender stated in new terms that valorized a nonethnic cosmopolitanism. This position can be seen in his reviews of artwork by nonwhite artists. Writing in 1942, Greenberg claims that Wilfredo Lam's Afro-Cuban work suffers from "a straining after bravura effects, by showy motions, . . . obsessive rhythms, and the inability to be more than decorative."[34] On the prints of the Mexican artist José Guadaloupe Posada, he concludes: "Posada's art was after all limited in its range. The same points are made again and again. The patterns in which the picture rectangle is organized are unerring yet repetitious."[35] And finally, Rufino Tamayo's "error," according to Greenberg, "consists in pursuing expressiveness and emotional emphasis beyond the coherence of style. It has led Tamayo . . . into an academic trap: emotion is not only expressed, it is *illustrated.*"[36]

In some ways his art criticism stands in contrast to his theory that despite its underlying positivism abstract art can be presumed to be egalitarian in the sense that nowhere in his writings does he explicitly condemn women, for instance, as unable to produce anything but inferior works of art because of their gender. Nor does he consider nonwhite artists as incapable of producing "great" art. For Greenberg, just as he was able to escape his "suffocatingly middle-class jewish identity" by writing art criticism, any artist regardless of ethnicity, gender, and race can aspire to greatness as long as he or she admits to the superiority of abstract art. Greenberg's dogmatism regarding abstract purism is likened to another romantic myth, that of romantic love, in a rather ironic collage made in 1946 by Ad Reinhardt (fig. 1). In this image a young girl helplessly standing on the railroad tracks is equated with "art" and is rescued just in time from "sin, money-grubbing, corruption, inferiority complexes, drink, linguistic stereotypes, prejudice, and banality" by her male suitor and hero who is likened to "abstract art."

Figure 1. Ad Reinhardt, "The Rescue of Art," collage drawing published in *Newsweek*, August 12, 1946. Copyright 1998 Estate of Ad Reinhardt/Artists Rights Society (ARS), New York.

In Greenberg's art critical practice, abstract expressionism becomes a white, ethnic, masculinist aesthetic designed to check the rise of a literal emotionalism or a decorative-ness. Greenberg's emphasis on abstract purity, the sublime, and a timeless and placeless definition of art, at the expense of the illustrative and the everyday, worked to include certain jewish and Irish male artists, at least in a reshaped intellectual art culture, and left out many others/Others who did not share these aesthetic priorities. It could be argued that the emphasis of modernist art theory on the abstract, despite its claims of neutrality, re-asserted the priority of one axis of identity over another, as the very gendered terms of Rienhardt's rescue image suggests. In 1944 if a discourse of modernism provided protection against the charges of being different, the acceptable modernist aesthetic criteria were too prescriptive, rigid, and even alienating to those who were not of European descent, or who could not pass as white or as men. The embrace of high culture in the discourse of universalism by jewish art and literary critics such as Greenberg can be seen as a critique of narrow nationalist and chauvinist agendas and the conservative traditional bonds of a provincial realist American art and literature. Today, in very changed historical circumstances, many now reject European universalism, since its schema, despite its purported inclusiveness, now seems too parochial.

In the 1970s and 1980s a number of important critiques of modernism appeared by such art critics as Eva Cockcroft, Serge Guilbaut, Max Kozloff, Fred Orton, Griselda Pollock, and David and Cecile Schapiro, among others.[37] They took issue with canonical accounts of American art, particularly the understanding of abstract expressionism as epitomizing "alienation," "individualism," and revolutionary avant-gardism. These writers opened up questions that were neglected by an earlier generation of art historians and critics. They examined among other issues the ways that Greenberg, and other intellectuals of his generation, moved from leftist positions associated with Trotskyism in the late 1930s and early 1940s to anti-Communism during the 1950s and after (Guilbaut); the similarities between "American cold war rhetoric" and the way that many abstract expressionists articulated their "individualist" existential experiences (Kozloff); how Greenbergian modernism became institutionalized at the Museum of Modern Art and turned into modernist ideology and dogma (Cockcroft); and the political implications resulting from the transformation of aesthetic modernism from a mere style to a Cold War weapon (Cockcroft).

The work done by Guilbaut, Cockcroft, and others mapped out a critical history of modernism and opened a debate that was instrumental in unraveling a certain Cold War consensus on the arts. In an important way, these critical writings made it no longer acceptable to look at modern art as autonomous or disengaged from the work's conditions of production and reception. As a result of these critics' resistance to modernist dogma, and despite ongoing attempts by neoconservatives to maintain a commitment to a tradition of high art and a purist notion of Western culture, a younger generation of curators, art critics, and historians are not speaking so smugly or unconsciously about an insulated and value-free tradition of "quality art." Although these revisionist critics of the 1970s and 1980s did not concern themselves with questions of multiculturalism, postmodernism, feminism, or queer theory, they nevertheless did help displace the idea of a perfect norm or correct visual standard, and in this way they set the stage for a critical art discourse that has become more multiple, more complex, and more paradoxical. Since the late 1970s, the detail and the emphasis on the everyday have received a new cultural currency in the arts. I would argue that as a result the range of "imagined communities" in the arts has tremendously expanded. This has not happened by virtue of some essentialist artistic style that particular distinct identities are to embody or emulate, but as a result of the proliferation of critical dialogues across political communities and constituencies. However, this process has not happened smoothly or effortlessly; the complex field of antagonisms brought into play by the multiple discourses of multiculturalism, queer theory, feminist theory, and postmodernism in the arts is indicative of the tensions that have been set in motion.

Despite these changes, some basic assumptions of Greenberg's art criticism continue to reassert themselves today in altered form. This raises questions about why, despite this new range of imagined communities in the arts, there is a perpetuation of an older discourse of modernism that still remains hostile to an art that doesn't meet the required modernist aesthetic norms. This older modernist discourse can be seen in the defense's legal strategy behind the obscenity charges brought against Robert Mapplethorpe's photographs exhibited in 1990 at the Contemporary Arts Center in Cincinnati. The testimony by curators and art historians in support of Mapplethorpe invoked a traditional system of beliefs and values of older modernist art history and art criticism to defend a so-called radical artist. Though this could be regarded simply as a savvy strategy to win a legal case, the testimony of the defense deserves attention because it demonstrates a popularly held view of contemporary art. Much has been written about the Mapplethorpe case, but surprisingly little has been written about the compromised terms of this supposed "victory."[38]

Janet Kardon, the organizer of the Mapplethorpe show when she was the director at the Institute of Contemporary Art in Philadelphia and the defense's first witness, focused her testimony solely on defending the quality of Mapplethorpe's work, stating that it was "good" art with aesthetic value that addresses a universal art audience. For example, in her formalist description of the artist's self-portrait with a bullwhip she recalls the rescue scenario played out in the 1946 Reinhardt collage in her emphasis solely on the abstract quality of the photograph. The twist is that this time it is a female critic and curator saving a male artist:

> The human figure is centered. The horizon line is two-thirds of the way up, almost the classical two-thirds to one-third proportions. The way the light is cast so there's light all around the figure. It's very symmetrical which is very characteristic of his flowers."[39]

Her use of binary logic enables her to push the terms of a formalist analysis to extremes. This same binary thinking is evident in her emphasis on the importance of the liberal aesthetic experience, which she opposes to a "closed" reading of Mapplethorpe's work that would be exclusively content driven. This either-or construction also informs her bizarre formalist analysis of the "action" in Mapplethorpe's photograph *Man in a Polyester Suit,* which she oddly likens to a tennis match: "The action cannot be perceived unless the eye constantly darts in opposite directions as in a tennis match, or, in this instance, between the mundane polyester suit and what outrageously protrudes from its trousers."[40]

Whereas Kardon's construction of Mapplethorpe's photographs sets up an arbitrary schism between so-called content and so-called form, between a multiplicity of readings and a single correct reading, Robert Sobieszek, then senior curator of the George Eastman House International Museum of Photography, evokes other aspects of Greenbergian modernism. He emphasizes Mapplethorpe's "alienation" and his special access to transcendence and creative subjectivity:

> I would say they [the homoerotic photographs] are works of art, knowing they are by Robert Mapplethorpe, knowing his intentions. They reveal in very strong, forceful ways a major concern of a creative artist . . . a troubled portion of his life that he was trying to come to grips with. It's that search for meaning, not unlike Van Gogh's.[41]

Through emphasis on Mapplethorpe's "troubled" life, Sobieszek constructs him as the paradigm of the suffering modern artist-genius. However, here the retrieval of Van Gogh in relation to Mapplethorpe and the implication of both genius and madness serve to secure that subjectivity as the revealed meaning of the work of art. At the same time, this reading effectively masks the specificity of that subjectivity (Mapplethorpe's homosexuality) while still alluding to it as pathological or as a mental disorder. Sobieszek, in his attempt to help the defense by countering the charge of "obscenity" with "art," deploys the trope of the artist-genius, close to the way in which Greenberg did almost fifty years earlier. Greenberg had revived the trope of the romantic alienated artist in order to give a new cosmopolitan prestige to American art.

The mythic notion of the artist-genius is a flexible trope. Whereas it enabled Greenberg and Rosenberg as critic-geniuses to sidestep the issue of how it was possible to produce culture in a "cultural vacuum" in the 1940s, here it allows Sobieszek to strategically avoid altogether the more controversial issue of sexuality in relation to Mapplethorpe's work and substitute the more familiar, abstract notion of alienation in its place. In choosing this strategy, Sobieszek ensures that Mapplethorpe's homoeroticism becomes authorized as solely the expression of the creative personality of the artist. Doubtless, had he not been considered a "great" male modernist artist, his homoeroticism would not have been acceptable.

Arguments made by Kardon and Sobieszek enabled the defense to win under the conditions set by the obscenity ruling in *Miller v. California,* since the Mapplethorpe verdict hinged on whether or not his photographs should be considered works of art. Yet despite the contribution of such arguments to the defense's victory, it is important to point out the contradictions and the limitations of a position that salvages Mapplethorpe within the terms of a traditional modernist art history. For, to put emphasis solely on Mapplethorpe as a worthy artist who demonstrates exceptional special individuality also authorizes a homophobia-based view that legitimates homosexuality only for great artists. This is why the power of Jesse Helms's more accessible populist argument against Mapplethorpe, dealing directly with his homosexuality, needs to be reexamined, not only in relation to its obvious puritanism and homophobia, but also for the way it calls into question the elitism of an older discourse of art history. Such a reexamination could provide the beginnings of an effective strategy to counter the force of a Jesse Helms–style antielitism. Andrew Ross's work in *No Respect* and Linda Williams's book on pornography, *Hard Core,* have paved the way with their insistence on the importance of having frank public discussions on many forms of sexuality in culture, including, for Williams, conversations "beyond the question of whether these texts should exist to a discussion of what it means that they do."[42]

The court case around censorship and Robert Mapplethorpe's photographs couches a debate about sexuality and contemporary art in a discourse on modernist aesthetics and the trope of the artist-genius, which vehemently opposes the turns toward disruptive content, especially homosexual content, and toward detail. The art discourse around the work of Jean-Michel Basquiat and his rise as an '80s "minority" art star is different, since the racial content of his work is only assimilated as "great" art on the basis of its "primitivism," not on its formal qualities alone. Though Basquiat was accepted within the parameters of modernism, somehow the rules changed; his ethnic and racial identity were *always* structured into the very reception of his art in spite of his presumably abstract idiom. What is new and somewhat awkward in the discourses on Basquiat and Mapplethorpe is the way that certain liberal art curators and critics are following in the footsteps of neoconservatives such as Greenberg in making arguments about aesthetic quality, artistic genius, and the importance of "authentic" cultural styles to defend new artists whose work doesn't quite fit these older terms.

Aspects of this new alliance can be seen in the early critical art discourse on Basquiat in that he is denied the ability to create truly symbolic art that is not literally about his own life on the streets. Such a notion of abstraction, using terms set by the abstract expressionists, placed Basquiat in an inferior position to white artists (fig. 2). For an artist is not supposed to descend to the level of everyday life and reproduce the filth of life on the streets; as Barnett Newman explains in 1940 in the introduction to the catalog of a show held by Polish artist Teresa Zarnover:

> Art must say something. . . . It is this concern with abstract subject matter rather than abstract disciplines that gives her work its strength and its dignity. The truth here is mutually inclusive, for the defense of human dignity is the ultimate subject matter of art. And it is only in its defense that any of us will ever find strength.[43]

According to Newman, art must convey an abstract thought as its subject matter and narrate something about the dignity, not the debasement, of universal man/woman. The horror of the modern condition could not be described graphically, since that would be too close to not transcending it. In this context one needs to understand why Basquiat would not be considered an acceptable artist, given that the abstract aspect of his work was seen as not removed enough from his own personal circumstances. This lack of critical distance, while intolerable for a white artist, was evidently understood by these critics as the best a black artist could be expected to achieve. It is not surprising that when curators such as Richard Marshall later decided to upgrade Basquiat's status from a *street artist* to a *great modernist* they used the terms set by the abstract expressionists. This shift in his position entailed segregating him from the host of other black graffiti artists and placing him instead next to Cy Twombly, Jean Dubuffet, Robert Rauschenberg, Jackson Pollock, Pablo Picasso, and African high art and culture.[44]

Despite attempts by Marshall and others, Basquiat's paintings were mostly seen by art critics and art dealers as about being a poor American minority living on the streets. This is in part why there was such a condescending fascination with his life as a street artist

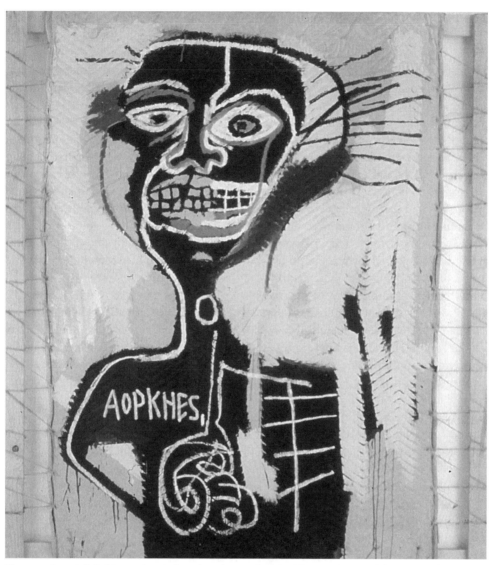

Figure 2. Jean-Michel Basquiat, *Cabeza* (1982). Reprinted with permission of the Estate of Jean-Michel Basquiat. Courtesy Robert Miller Gallery, New York. Copyright 1998 Artists Rights Society (ARS), New York/ADAGP, Paris.

making graffiti, presumably outside the realm of "civilized" sensibilities, as, for example, in Rene Ricard's 1981 essay titled "The Radiant Child."[45] This fixation on Basquiat's street authenticity served to mark him as unmistakably different from white artists. Unlike their treatment of white graffiti artist Keith Haring, critics fabricated a myth about Basquiat's street origins that ranged from fanciful statements by Rene Ricard, such as, "If Cy Twombly and Jean Dubuffet had a baby and gave it up for adoption, it would be Jean-Michel" to other racist allusions that constructed him as a foundling, such as the comment by Jeffrey Deitch that Basquiat was "the wild boy raised by wolves" and "a freak of nature."[46]

It is also telling that Basquiat's reputation among white critics suffered when the mystique of his exoticism evaporated. This happened in the mid-1980s when people learned that he was not a poor black ghetto kid but an upper-middle-class, private-school boy of Haitian and Puerto Rican parentage. Though the prices of his paintings dropped, the voyeurism never completely died out. Instead, the interest in his mythical street origins shifted to his paintings. Those works with original graffiti tags, cartoon crowns, and notary seals remained highly desirable collector's items.[47] So did those in which the methods and materials used reflected the street and its debris, such as Basquiat's paintings on discarded doors or canvases in which the wood support is revealed. Anxieties about Basquiat's loss of authenticity were evident everywhere, but perhaps most acute among his dealers. So concerned was Bruno Bischofberger in 1984 with Basquiat's authenticity that he worried that the artist's use of visual technologies, such as xerography, would in Bischofberger's words "ruin his 'intuitive primitivism.'"[48]

Even some of the recent writings on Basquiat by the critic Adam Gopnik perpetuate in a somewhat altered form assumptions about the relationship between modernism and the tradition of so-called Others that one can find in the writings of Greenberg from the late 1930s. For example, the presumption of Gopnik's 1992 piece on Basquiat, fittingly titled "Madison Avenue Primitive," is that Basquiat is not an authentic enough black; he doesn't conform to Greenberg's notion that true blacks adore kitsch, as stated in his famous 1938 essay "Avant-Garde and Kitsch," in which he writes that an epidemic of kitsch is responsible for "crowding out and defacing native cultures in one colonial country after another, so that it is now by way of becoming a universal culture."[49] According to Diana Trilling, in the initial draft of the essay Greenberg wrote: "Unable to resist the oncoming tide of kitsch the first thing these marvelous native tribesmen in Africa and Australia, who do such wonderful abstract work, demand of the explorer is not the works of Picasso but picture postcards, gaudy, horrible."[50] But the twist here is that Basquiat asks for Picasso *and* picture postcards and doesn't play by the modernist Greenbergian script. So Basquiat "failed" not because he liked kitsch but because he liked modern art over folk art; he is faulted for not conforming to the most available stereotypes concerning blacks. For Gopnik, Basquiat's work is not "an authentic vernacular folk expression" but "ersatz primitivism"—a calculated stylization. He was not "native" enough and therefore couldn't produce what Gopnik wanted: "a genuinely original 'wildstyle.'"[51]

THE FACT AND EFFECT OF AFRICAN AMERICANNESS

The more recent writings on Baquiat by Greg Tate and bell hooks present a counter to these earlier discourses. One of the ways this has been done is through the production of a new genre of multicultural art criticism in which contemporary narratives of blacks are now funneled through a newer discourse of the artistic genius. But this approach differs from an earlier one in the sense that it doesn't privilege an older diasporic discourse of the alienated and autonomous artist-intellectual as outsider to the United States in the same way as Greenberg's criticism. The concept of the artist-genius has been an issue long debated by feminist art historians. For example, in her article "Here Today, Gone Tomorrow? Some Plots for a Dismantling," Eunice Lipton observes that "one of the most powerful ways that art history produces insiders and outsiders is through its notion of 'artist-geniuses.'"[52] African American art critics, such as Michele Wallace, frame the discourse of the artist-genius in a way that is both strategic and more institutionally grounded than Greenberg's or Gopnik's by tying the "problem of a white-dominated art world that does not usually conceptualize blacks as visual producers" to the question "Why are there no great black artists?" (a reframing of Linda Nochlin's famous 1971 essay "Why Are There No Great Women Artists?").[53] This approach represents a significant departure from earlier writing on the arts and is strategic in Gayatri Spivak's sense of "a strategic use of positivist essentialism in a scrupulously visible political interest."[54] The concept of "strategic essentialism" suggests that it is possibile to use an older and more conservative discourse of art history, such as a discourse of the artist-genius, in order for black artists to be accepted into the canon of "great art."

Another essentialist strategy is to address how race provides the very conditions that enable and shape creative work. This tactic allows critics such as Wallace, hooks, and Tate to both contest the racism of the New York art world as well as disrupt the way that certain white art gets elevated alone to the realm of "good taste." For Wallace, however, the simple fact of being a person of color isn't in itself definitive, especially if a critic's writing or an artist's work performs the privileges and entitlements afforded by affluent backgrounds and educations at elite universities in Great Britain or the United States. In her eyes such writing or artwork runs the risk of erasing the specificity of blacks' experience in the United States in favor of an abstract postmodern or postcolonial subjectivity:

> And yet finally there is only an implied entry way here for the artist or the critic of color who is not a member of a postcolonial intellectual elite, because we who are subject to internal colonization, we who are called "minorities" suffer the problem of the modern and of cultural identity perhaps more than anyone, and the unified, unmarked subject of this and so far most other analyses of the Postmodern, never mind the Modern, continues to render us "invisible" and silent.[55]

Referring to the "new" mutual influence and transformation of Europe and non-European cultures by each other in the New World (America), Wallace concludes: "While the most concrete sign of that something new is generally referred to as Postmodernism, unfortunately this move usually carries along with it the reinscription of Modernism's apartheid."[56] According to Wallace, the so-called postcolonial elites' distance from or unfamiliarity with U.S. blacks makes them perpetuate a Eurocentric discourse of modernism, a cultural form and category that she sees as aesthetically and materially at odds with U.S. culture, which she in turn sees as rooted in a discourse of black popular culture.

Greg Tate's position further enriches Wallace's, but referring specifically to Basquiat he finds significance in Basquiat's mixture of high and low aesthetic references in his paintings and the important influence of U.S. hip-hop culture (street talk, rap, etc.) in his article "Nobody Loves a Genius Child: Jean-Michel Basquiat, Flyboy in the Buttermilk":

> Though we can certainly point to racism for the refusal in certain quarters to consider Basquiat a serious painter, we shouldn't overlook the fact that Basquiat, like Rauschenberg and Warhol, his brothers in canvas-bound iconoclasm, *made paintings that are unrepentantly*

about American culture. There is a strain of Europhilia among our art historians and critics that is as uncomfortable with American artists looking to this culture for subject matter and vernacular as they are with artists holding the celebrity of household names. Looking to the uncertainty and reticence that abounded—and still abounds. . . . it seems that the surest way to be consigned dilettante-hick status, ruining your chances for fawning art historical hagiography, is to act as if you thought the United States was spilling over with the stuff of Art.[57]

Tate's parallel references to Rauschenberg and Warhol, two white artists who fascinated Europeans, suggests that like these artists Basquiat, too, is doing something specifically about American culture, rather than subsuming American materials into European forms, which is what U.S. art criticism has written out of Basquiat's oeuvre. Thus, Tate's observation that some critics' "Europhilia" is to blame for the refusal to consider Basquiat a serious painter is an important insight if one thinks of Gopnik's article and the way he refuses to acknowledge Basquiat's work except as a sign of his failure to be a "real primitive," as evidenced by the title "Madison Avenue Primitive." However, Tate's other assertion that only an insider like himself could understand Basquiat's particular references to black American experience perhaps is not the last word on this question: "If you're Black and historically informed there's no way you can look at Basquiat's work and not get beat up by his obsession with the Black male body's history as property, pulverized meat, and popular entertainment" (238). Here Tate marks a crucial difference—the fact of Basquiat's African Americanness and his use of popular culture—but the way he does it also perhaps runs the risk of overstating the case by simplifying Basquiat's complex identities and his intellectual influences.

For other writers such as bell hooks with other strategies in mind, Basquiat's mixed cultural background may lead to other tactical considerations:

Basquiat's work holds no warm welcome for those who approach it with a narrow Eurocentric gaze. . . . That gaze which can value him only if he can be seen as part of a continuum of contemporary American art with a genealogy traced through white males. . . . Even when Basquiat can be placed stylistically in the exclusive, white male art club that denies entry to most black artists, his subject matter—his content—always separates him once again, and defamiliarizes him. . . .

Basquiat was in no way secretive about the fact that he was influenced and inspired by the work of white artists. It is the multiple other sources of inspiration and influence that are submerged, lost, when critics are obsessed with seeing him as solely connected to a white Western artistic continuum.[58]

Hooks grapples with the homogeneous representations of the black male body in the United States, the black body that is commodified and appropriated. The colonization and anguish of such a body and mind are understandably anything but exotic to hooks. Yet how close did Basquiat adhere to either Tate's or hooks's conception of him and his work? In accepting the terms—form is "European and white" (high art) and content is "American and black" (popular culture)—both of these critics inadvertently perhaps overlook the diversity of the black diasporic community in the United States out of which

Basquiat came. For example, to what degree could Basquiat be considered a Caribbean or even a Latino artist? What would happen to our understanding of Basquiat's work if it were read in terms of the diversity of these communities rather simply in terms of a putative blackness? I'm not arguing for either position but, rather, for the fact that any racial category will be marked by diversity and overlap with other categories because race, like ethnicity, is a multiple construct and a social product. This is why earlier I put the ethnic designation *jewish* in lowercase throughout to signal a shifting set of historically diverse experiences rather than a unified and monolithic notion of jewishness.

It is significant, then, that my discussion here has begun with a critique of Clement Greenberg as a way to historicize the emergence of the New York School's critical hegemony and its transnational jewish history in order to highlight how the most well-known formalist aesthetic positions themselves are inescapably imbricated by a complex politics of identity. I then argue how the aura of high art and the myth of the artist-genius remain in certain circles and are used to posit either a development that erases one's cultural past (Greenberg) or one's sexual persuasion (Mapplethorpe), but never seemingly one's race (Basquiat). In a similar way to how conservatives make blacks, Latinos, women, and so forth prisoners of their race, ethnicity, gender, or sexuality, a U.S. discourse of formalist art criticism makes race and Americanness the most limiting of subject positions to occupy, in contrast to what Tate, hooks, and Wallace would argue.

At the same time that I argue how the fact and effect of race and ethnicity have been at the heart of U.S. modernism all along, I also take issue with ways of seeing black and jewish identities that underestimate the differences and hybridities among these groups. A rethinking of the tropes of art history and criticism is indeed long overdue. Yet it is also important that such new writing—in its attempt to diversify its practices by including a more heterogeneous group of artists—also deals more openly with the differences of race, ethnicity, sexuality, and nation rather than presuming "natural" similiarities in order to ensure that the essentialisms we seek to disempower in the dominant discourse of art history will not be reproduced in its critique. In the late 1990s, despite the numerous conservative backlashes in the arts, it is important to acknowledge the ways that cultural and political dialogues in the arts are taking place across different immigrant art communities, in the ongoing work to transform the way the discipline of art history is taught.

NOTES

An earlier version of this article was published in *Socialist Review* 94, nos. 1–2 (1995): 129–64, a special double issue titled "Arranging Identities." Note that the conclusion has been substantially altered from the earlier published version thanks to the perceptive criticism I received from an anonymous reader of this anthology's manuscript. I am greatly indebted to Stanford University's Mellon Postdoctoral Fellowship Program and Brown University's Pembroke Center for Women for providing me with the space and time to formulate my ideas on this topic. I especially want to thank Linda Brodkey, David Halperin, Francette Pacteau, Lydia Matthews, Alex Nemerov, Robert Jensen, Dan Selden, and David Trend for pointing out the strengths and weaknesses of my argument; Max Kozloff and Peter Selz for allowing me to interview them, and for sharing some of their insights on this topic; my graduate students in my fall 1993 visual culture seminar at Stanford, especially Evelyn Hankins; and Bradford Collins for sending me the English translation of his article "Le pessimisme politique et 'la haine de soi' Juive: Les origines de l'esthétique puriste de Greenberg" (Political pessimism, Jewish "self-hatred" and the "dreams of universalism": The origins of Greenberg's purist aesthetics, c. 1930–1940), which appeared in *Les Cahiers du Musée national d'art modern* (Fall/Winter 1993): 61–83. Finally, I owe special thanks to Roddey Reid and Elissa Weintraub for reading the manuscript several times and giving me thoughtful and thorough advice, criticism, and editorial assistance.

This article is part of a larger book project that I am currently working on titled *Ghosts of Ethnicity: Rethinking Ethnicity and Feminist Art Practices in the United States,* which considers my thesis in relation to other historical periods besides the '40s and '80s as well as gives more detail to my arguments on the periods discussed. In my book I further investigate how terms such as *internationalism, universalism,* and *globalism* evolved in a U.S. context. I discuss the different applications of these terms in relation to jewish and nonjewish identities and how they were attached to both high and so-called low art forms as disparate as abstract expressionist painting, photojournalism, and feminist installation art, among other cultural forms. Sections from the book soon to be available in published form include "Ethnic Notions and Feminist Strategies of the 1970s: Some Work by Judy Chicago and Eleanor Antin," in *Jewish Identity in Art History: Ethnicity and Discourse,* ed. Catherine Soussloff (Berkeley and Los Angeles: University of California Press, 1999); "Contests for Meaning in Body Politics and Feminist Art Discourses of the 1970s: The Work of Eleanor Antin," in *Performing the Body/Performing the Text,* ed. Amelia Jones and Andrew Stephenson (London: Routledge, 1999); and Lisa E. Bloom, "Rewriting the Script: Eleanor Antin's Feminist Art," in *Eleanor Antin,* ed. Howard Fox (Los Angeles: Los Angeles County Museum, 1999).

1. I have put the ethnic designation *jewish* in lowercase throughout to emphasize that *jewishness* can also stand for a cultural identity rather than only a strictly defined religious one, and to signal a shifting set of historically diverse experiences rather than a unified and monolithic notion of jewishness.

2. Clement Greenberg, "The Jewish Dickens: Review of *The World of Sholom Aleichem* by Maurice Samuel," *Nation,* October 16, 1943. Reprinted in *Clement Greenberg: The Collected Essays and Criticism,* ed. John O'Brian, vol. 1 (Chicago: University of Chicago Press, 1986), 158 (hereafter abbreviated as *Collected Essays*).

3. For more on the stereotype of jewish deviousness, see Sander Gilman, "The Jewish Voice: Chicken Soup or the Penalties of Sounding Too Jewish," in *The Jew's Body* (New York: Routledge, 1991), 10–37.

4. Greenberg, "The Jewish Dickens," 156.

5. Ella Shohat, "Ethnicities in Relation: Toward a Multicultural Reading of American Cinema," in *Unspeakable Images: Ethnicity and the American Cinema,* ed. Lester D. Friedman (Urbana and Chicago: University of Illinois Press, 1991), 216.

6. For other recent examples of this new scholarship that became available after this article was published in *Socialist Review,* see Linda Nochlin and Tamar Garb, eds., *The Jew in the Text: Modernity and the Construction of Identity* (London: Thames and Hudson, 1995); and Margaret Olin, "C[lement] Hardesh [Greenberg] and Company: Formal Criticism and Jewish Identity," in *Too Jewish: Challenging Traditional Identities,* ed. Norman Kleeblatt (New York: Jewish Museum and Rutgers University Press, 1996), 39–59.

7. Irit Rogoff, "The Empire of Art: Ana Mendieta," unpublished paper, 1992, 1.

8. Benedict Anderson, *Imagined Communities: Reflections on the Origin and Spread of Nationalism* (London: Verso, 1983), 16, 14.

9. Serge Guilbaut, *How New York Stole the Idea of Modern Art* (Chicago: University of Chicago Press, 1983), 1.

10. Edward Alden Jewell, "'Globalism' Pops into View," *New York Times,* June 13, 1943, 9.

11. Guilbaut, *How New York Stole,* 222 n. 81 (my emphasis). According to Guilbaut, this quotation originally appeared in a letter sent to the papers by the federation on the occasion of another show at the Wildenstein Gallery, June 2–26, 1943.

12. Greenberg started by valorizing the work of single artists beginning with Jackson Pollock in 1943,

whom he wrote about six times through 1948. He followed with David Smith, Willem de Kooning, Hans Hofmann, Robert Motherwell, William Baziotes, Adolph Gottlieb, Clyfford Still, Mark Rothko, and Barnett Newman.

13. Clement Greenberg, "The Situation at the Moment," *Partisan Review* 5 (January 1948). Reprinted in *Collected Essays*, vol. 2, 193 (my emphasis).

14. For an extended discussion of the connection between Rosenberg and existentialist thought, see Erica Doss, *Benton, Pollock, and the Politics of Modernism: From Regionalism to Abstract Expressionism* (Chicago: University of Chicago Press, 1991), 378–87.

15. Harold Rosenberg, Maeght show catalog, cited in *Possibilities* 1 (Winter 1947–48): 75. Reprinted in Guilbaut, *How New York Stole*, 159 (my emphasis).

16. Reprinted in *Collected Essays*, vol. 2, 133–34. Originally appeared as "Review of Exhibitions of the Jane Street Group and Rufino Tamayo," *Nation*, March 8, 1947.

17. Harold Rosenberg, "The American Action Painters," *Art News* (December 1952): 23.

18. The study of worker narratives of a native U.S. culture was taken on by Farm Security Administration photographers James Agee and Walker Evans in their *Let Us Now Praise Famous Men* (Boston: Houghton Mifflin, 1941), Erskine Caldwell and Margaret Bourke-White's *You Have Seen Their Faces: A Folk History of the Negro in the United States* (New York: Modern Age Books, 1937), and Richard Wright's *12 Million Black Voices* (New York: Viking, 1941), among others.

19. Meyer Schapiro is acknowledged by Lynd Ward as contributing part of the material contained in the paper. Lynd Ward, "Race, Nationality, and Art," *Art Front* 2 (March 1936). Reprinted in *Artists against War and Fascism: Papers of the First American Artists' Congress,* ed. Matthew Baigell and Julia Williams (New Brunswick, N.J.: Rutgers University Press), 119–20. For further historical information regarding this period see Matthew Baigell's chronology of the lives and careers of jewish American artists in New York City in his essay "From Hester Street to Fifty-Seventh Street: Jewish American Artists in New York," in *Painting a Place in America: Jewish Artists in New York 1900–1945,* ed. Norman L. Kleeblatt and Susan Chevlowe (New York: Jewish Museum, 1991), 28–88. For an extended discussion on Meyer and Schapiro and the Popular Front, see Patricia Hill, "1936: Meyer Schapiro, *Art Front,* and the Popular Front," *Oxford Art Journal* 17, no. 1 (1994): 30–41.

20. Thomas Craven, *Modern Art* (Garden City, N.Y.: Halcyon House, 1934), 312.

21. I am currently working on a chapter for my forthcoming book *Ghosts of Ethnicity* that further examines the complex stakes in the shift to modern art in the 1940s. I focus on how this change had a tantalizing relationship with right-wing U.S. cultural nationalism, anti-Semitism, and a form of virile white masculinity of the 1930s, as it was expressed in the writings of Craven and the work of the artist most promoted by Craven, Thomas Benton.

22. Stephanie Barron, ed., *Degenerate Art: The Fate of the Avant-Garde in Nazi Germany* (New York: Abrams, 1991). Modern art was not directly equated with jewishness, but this was implied when it was connected with Bolshevism in 1921. When the Metropolitan Museum reluctantly recognized modern art, a group of anonymous supporters of the museum issued "A Protest against the Present Exhibition of Degenerate 'Modernistic' Works in the Metropolitan Museum." See Edward Abrams, *The Lyrical Left: Randolph Bourne, Alfred Stieglitz and the Origins of Cultural Radicalism in America* (Charlottesville: University of Virginia Press, 1986), 169.

23. Adolph S. Oko, ed., "Under Forty: A Symposium on American Literature and the Younger Generation of American Jews," *Contemporary Jewish Record* 7, no. 1 (February 1944): 3.

24. Donna Haraway, *Primate Visions* (New York: Routledge, 1989), 401–2.

25. Victor Burgin, "Modernism in the Work of Art," *The End of Art Theory: Criticism and Postmodernity* (Atlantic Highlands, N.J.: Humanities Press International, 1986), 1–28. See the following articles in Francis Frascina, ed., *Pollock and After: The Critical Debate* (New York: Harper and Row, 1985); Fred Orton and Griselda Pollock, "Avant-Gardes and Partisans Reviewed," 167–84; Serge Guilbaut, "The

New Adventures of the Avant-Garde in America," 153–66; T. J. Clark, "Clement Greenberg's Theory of Art," 47–64; Michael Fried, "How Modernism Works: A Response to T. J. Clark," 65–80; Max Kozloff, "American Painting during the Cold War," 107–24; Eva Cockcroft, "Abstract Expressionism, Weapon of the Cold War," 125–34; David and Cecile Schapiro, "Abstract Expressionism: The Politics of Apolitical Painting," 135–52. See also Barbara M. Reise, "Greenberg and the Group: A Retrospective View" (originally published in *Studio International* 175, no. 901 [May 1968]: 254–57 [part 1] and 175, no. 902 [June 1968]: 314–16 [part 2]; reprinted *Art in Modern Culture,* ed. Francis Frascina and Jonathon Harris [New York: HarperCollins, 1992], 252–63); Kay Larson, "The Dictatorship of Clement Greenberg," *Artforum* 25 (Summer 1987): 75–79; Saul Ostrow, "Avant-Garde and Kitsch, Fifty Years Later: A Conversation with Clement Greenberg," *Arts Magazine* (December 1989): 56–64.

26. Max Kozloff, "Jewish Art and the Modernist Jeopardy," *Artforum* 14, no. 8 (April 1976): 44. Thanks to Max Kozloff for giving me the reference to this intriguing article.

27. Kleeblatt and Chevlowe's *Painting a Place in America* includes the following articles: Baigell, "From Hester Street to Fifty-Seventh Street," 28–88; Milton Brown, "An Explosion of Creativity: Jews and American Art in the Twentieth Century," 22–27; Norman L. Kleeblatt and Susan Chevlowe, "Painting a Place in America," 89–149. See also Sidney Tillim, "Criticism and Culture: Greenberg's Doubt," *Art in America* (May 1987): 122–27, 201. Kenneth E. Silver and Romy Golan, *The Circle of Montparnasse: Jewish Artists in Paris 1905–1945* (New York: Jewish Museum, 1985) includes the following articles: Kenneth E. Silver, "The Circle of Montparnasse: Jewish Artists in Paris 1905–1945," 12–59; and Romy Golan, "The *Ecole Française* vs. the *Ecole de Paris*: The Debate about the Status of Jewish Artists in Paris between the Wars," 80–87. See also Susan Noyes Platt, "Clement Greenberg in the 1930s: A New Perspective on His Criticism," *Art Criticism* 5, no. 3 (1991): 47–64; Bradford Collins, "Le Pessimisme Politique et 'La Haine de soi' Juive: Les origines de l'esthétique puriste de Greenberg" (Political pessimism, Jewish "self-hatred" and the "Dreams of Universalism": The Origins of Greenberg's Purist Aesthetics, c. 1930–1940), *Les Cahiers du Musée national d'art modern* (Fall/Winter 1993): 61–83. I am grateful to Bradford Collins for sending me a copy of the English translation. His excellent article gave me the foundational history that I needed to build my own argument. For discussion of the *Partisan Review,* see Terry A. Cooney, *The Rise of the New York Intellectuals: Partisan Review and Its Circle, 1934–1945* (Madison: University of Wisconsin Press, 1986), 229–45; Alan M. Wald, *The New York Intellectuals* (Chapel Hill: University of North Carolina Press, 1987), 27–50.

28. Michel Foucault, "What Is an Author?" in *Perspectives in Post-Structuralist Criticism,* ed. Joseph V. Harari (Ithaca, N.Y.: Cornell University Press, 1979), 27–50.

29. Reprinted in John O'Brian, "Introduction," in *Collected Essays,* vol. 1, xix–xx.

30. Clement Greenberg, "Self-Hatred and Jewish Chauvinism: Some Reflections on 'Positive Jewishness,'" *Commentary* (November 1950). Reprinted in *Collected Essays,* vol. 3, 45.

31. *Collected Essays,* vol. 3, 176.

32. Robert Jensen has rightly pointed out to me how derivative Greenberg's ideas were concerning his critique of the illustration and the detail. However, since I am not concerned in this essay with authorship but discourse analysis, Greenberg's lack of originality doesn't weaken my argument critiquing his social and cultural assumptions.

33. Greenberg, "Avant-Garde and Kitsch," *Partisan Review* (Fall 1939). Reprinted in *Collected Essays,* vol. 1, 11.

34. Greenberg, "Review of Exhibitions of Corot, Cézanne, Eilshemius, and Wilfredo Lam," *Nation* 12 (December 1942). Reprinted in *Collected Essays,* vol. 1, 131.

35. Greenberg, "Review of an Exhibition of José Guadaloupe Posada," *Nation* 30 (September 1944). Reprinted in *Collected Essays,* vol. 1, 232.

36. Greenberg, "Review of Exhibitions of the Jane Street Group and Rufino Tamayo," *Nation* 8 (March 1947). Reprinted in *Collected Essays,* vol. 2, 133.

37. See the following articles: Max Kozloff, "American Painting during the Cold War"; Eva Cockcroft, "Abstract Expressionism, Weapon of the Cold War"; David and Cecile Shapiro, "Abstract Expressionism: The Politics of Apolitical Painting"; Fred Orton and Griselda Pollock, "Avant-Gardes and Partisans Reviewed"; Serge Guilbaut, "The New Adventures of the Avant-Garde in America." All appear in *Pollock and After: The Critical Debate,* ed. Francis Frascina (New York: Harper and Row, 1985), 107–84.

38. The exceptions include Douglas Crimp, "Introduction: Photographs at the End of Modernism," in *On the Museum's Ruins* (Cambridge: MIT Press, 1993), 2–31; Peggy Phelan, "Censorship," talk delivered to University of California, Davis, art department, Spring 1994.

39. Quoted in Jayne Merkel, "Art on Trial: Report from Cincinnati," *Art in America* (December 1990): 47.

40. Janet Kardon, "The Perfect Moment," in *Robert Mapplethorpe: The Perfect Moment,* ed. Janet Kardon (Philadelphia: Institute of Contemporary Art, 1988), 11. Though I do not address the complex question of Mapplethorpe's images of the black male nude as a racialized object of desire, this has been an important part of the discussion around his work, including the following: Kobena Mercer, "Imaging the Black Man's Sex," in *Photography/Politics: Two,* ed. Pat Holland, Jo Spence, and Simon Watney (London: Comedia Publications Group, 1986); Kobena Mercer, "Skin Head Sex Thing: Racial Difference and the Homoerotic Imaginary," in *How Do I Look: Queer Film and Video* (Seattle: Bay Press, 1991), 168–222; and Jane Gaines, "Competing Glances: Who Is Reading Robert Mapplethorpe's *Black Book*?" *New Formations* 16 (Spring 1992): 24–39.

41. Quoted in Markel, "Art on Trial," 47.

42. Andrew Ross, *No Respect: Intellectuals and Popular Culture* (New York: Routledge, 1989); Linda Williams, *Hard Core: Power, Pleasure and the Frenzy of the Visible* (Berkeley and Los Angeles: University of California Press, 1989), 8.

43. John P. O'Neill, ed., *Barnett Newman: Selected Writings and Interviews* (New York: Knopf, 1990), 105.

44. Richard Marshall, "Repelling Ghosts," in *Jean-Michel Basquiat* (New York: Whitney Museum, 1993), 15–27. Thanks to Robert Jensen for remarking on this important distinction.

45. Rene Ricard, "The Radiant Child," *Artforum* 20 (December 1981): 35–43.

46. Ibid., 35; Jeffrey Deitch, *Flash Art* 16 (May 1982): 50.

47. David D'Arcy, "Basquiat Case," *Vanity Fair,* November 1992, 124–46.

48. Quoted in *The Andy Warhol Diaries,* ed. Pat Hackett (New York: Warner Books, 1989).

49. Greenberg, "Avant-Garde and Kitsch," 13–14.

50. Diana Trilling, "Interview with Dwight Macdonald," *Partisan Review* (1985): 806.

51. Adam Gopnik, "Madison Avenue Primitive," *New Yorker,* November 9, 1992, 38.

52. Eunice Lipton, "Here Today, Gone Tomorrow? Some Plots for a Dismantling," in *The Decade Show: Frameworks of Identity in the 1980s* (New York: Museum of Contemporary Hispanic Art, 1990).

53. Michele Wallace, "Afterword: Why Are There No Great Black Artists? The Problem of Visuality in African-American Culture," in *Black Popular Culture* (Seattle: Bay Press, 1992). Linda Nochlin, "Why Have There Been No Great Women Artists?" in *Women, Art, and Power and Other Essays* (New York: Harper and Row, 1988), 145–78.

54. Gayatri Chakravorty Spivak, "Subaltern Studies: Deconstructing Historiography," in *Other Worlds* (New York: Routledge, 1988), 205.

55. Michele Wallace, "Modernism, Postmodernism and the Problem of the Visual in Afro-American Culture," in *Out There: Marginalization and Contemporary Cultures* (Cambridge: MIT Press, 1990), 48.

56. Ibid., 49.

57. Greg Tate, "Nobody Loves a Genius Child: Jean-Michel Basquiat, Flyboy in the Buttermilk," in his *Flyboy in the Buttermilk: Essays on Contemporary America* (New York: Simon and Schuster, 1992), 241 (emphasis mine).

58. bell hooks, "Altars of Sacrifice: Re-membering Basquiat," *Art in America,* June 1993, 70.

CONSTRUCTING NATIONAL SUBJECTS

The British Museum and Its Guidebooks

Inderpal Grewal

In his landmark work *Imagined Communities*, Benedict Anderson includes a section on museums, showing how the "museumizing imagination" enables the iconography of the nation to be infinitely reproducible and thus concretized in innumerable settings.[1] What he does not ask is how various groups that supposedly comprise the nation read or interpret this iconography, nor how different readings construct the national imaginary. An important question becomes how various readings of the iconography of the nation interpellate social divisions such as class and gender. Furthermore, the museumizing imagination does not only represent itself, it represents many others. How it represents others is an important part of nationalism, as are the ways in which diverse readerships are created around this iconography. In examining the representation of objects from different countries in Victorian museums, I will focus on guidebooks to the British Museum not only to answer how objects are read and interpreted but also how gendered and classed subject positions are formulated through an aesthetic education. I will explore both the commonalities and the divergent locations from which the spectacle of the museum is read.

GUIDEBOOKS TO THE BRITISH MUSEUM (1800–1826): NEOCLASSICISM AND THE COLLECTOR

For museum-goers, guidebooks worked to sublimate the alienating practices of the museum, an institution formed by collections given by the aristocratic patrons and named after them, such as the Hamilton, Elgin, Towneley collections. They contributed to the consolidations of a larger section of the middle classes and to the reduction of working-class radicalism that occurred by mid- and late-nineteenth century. The guidebooks mediated between those with "taste" and those that were "vulgar," a mediation central to both class and gender formation, and therefore they reveal the role of aesthetics in the class conflicts of nineteenth-century England.

For the casual visitor, the museum guidebook did not aim at inculcating specific knowledge; it aimed at inculcating general ideas, creating general sensations—all within a short time period. It propagated a generalized idea of the new and unknown world; for easy and quick consumption of British Self and Foreign Other, it provided easy stereotypes and homogenized ideas; it suggested, above all, the availability of the treasures displayed within it. Within the British Museum, the public was "civilized" by means of an aesthetic education that involved showing the non-Western world as uncivilized. Thus, while the East was civilized by a colonial venture that resulted in its commodification, the British public was disciplined through a knowledge that involved the reification and domestication of the non-Western Other; such a process involved also the misrecognition of such a binary within England itself. Everything in the museum, as well as in stores and exhibitions, created a distance between viewer as spectator and display as object.[2]

In 1808 the first *Synopsis* of the contents of the British Museum was published by order of the trustees. This was also the year in which the practice of issuing admission tickets was abolished, for admission had earlier been through applications in writing that had to be approved by the museum officials. Museum officials recognized that they must cater to all classes of people. Compiled by the museum staff, the *Synopsis* was its first official publication that was meant for the general public and could be bought for a few shillings.

Thus guidebooks to libraries and museums had been published before 1836, when the first *Murray's Travel Guide* appeared. The methods of museum guidebooks were the same as those of the travel guides, for all these works posited a homogeneous discursive community where the reader/user was treated as the perfect reader, receptive to the assumed transparency of a text that proposed to lay out an objective geography. These guidebooks catered to the casual visitor and pointed out the highlights of the museum, leaving the specialized scholar to pour over the more detailed catalogs. A number of these general guidebooks were printed, some by the New Library of Useful Knowledge, one of the many societies for disseminating knowledge to the middle as well as working classes. For instance, there was *A Guide to the Beauties of the British Museum* (1826, 1838) and *The British Museum in Four Sections; or, How to View the Whole at Once* (1852).[3] Many more of these guides were printed, and some went through multiple editions. The price of these books averaged two shillings, and therefore would not have been read by the working class. As Richard Altick points out, working-class readers, who often worked sixteen hours a day for two shillings or less, were only willing to spend a few pence at most for reading material; thus this guidebook would have been bought by a member of the middle class, or perhaps the lower spectrum of it such as the prosperous artisan or clerk, those that Altick calls the "modestly circumstanced booklover."[4] This reader of modest income who constituted a huge market by the middle of the nineteenth century certainly did not include most of the industrial workers who lived in constant fear of starvation.

Catering to a wider public, the 1826 *Guide to the Beauties of the British Museum* valorizes the discourse of labor that was so essential to Victorian bourgeois, industrial culture. The labor of collecting and describing was described as enabling the guidebook; this labor also defined the emerging class of professional scholars, constituting new knowledges and constructing new forms of masculinity, that became a part of imperial power. Ed Cohen has pointed out that whereas the 1841 census listed only the ancient professions such as law, medicine, and the church, the 1861 census included schoolmasters, professors, civil engineers, actors, authors, journalists, and musicians.[5] The 1881 census added even more professions to the list.

This new professionalizing, however, retained for its own authority upper-class aesthetic and economic values. The writer of the Underwoods guide replicates the endeavors of the male travelers and collectors who obtained the artifacts in the first place, since he claims he has searched assiduously in the museum for the beauties that he now brings to the reader's notice. The writer will, we are told, "convey some of the impressions which he himself received, during a search, diligent at least, and often repeated, without which search the beauties here pointed out may have remained undiscovered" (1826, preface). This labor of exploration within the museum mimics but also compensates for the labor of the collector (since women had few rights of ownership of property, this collector was also a masculine subject), whose work in creating the collection includes the obliteration of the use value of the objects and the substitution of aesthetic value—the value that Susan Stewart defines as "the value of manipulation and positioning."[6] The guidebook thus disguises the fact that the collection comes into being by the abstraction of labor within the cycle of exchange; it substitutes, instead, a masculine aesthetic labor that masks the alienation of labor within the process of producing commodities.

The new visitor to the museum absorbed alien histories and cultures within the historical context of his own history, whose referent was, as Stewart puts it, the interiority of his own self.[7] The primacy of the self was suggested by the aesthetic that was disseminated by the guidebooks. Greek art, for instance, was interpreted as validating and inscribing English values. The neoclassicism of the first half of the nineteenth century was visible in the valorization of Greek art and in its participation in creating an ideal "English" subject, unquestioningly masculine, but one who was receptive to a "moral" art and who immediately recognized the "purity" of classical forms. Classicism was believed to be the apotheosis of all art forms, one that was seen as part of the European heritage. It stood as proof of the superiority of the West over the barbaric East; as such, it presented one more reason for the civilization of the East through European colonization.[8]

Erotic or sensual interpretations were suggested and negated; what was stressed was the purity and the transcendent value of classical art. A binary aesthetic, positive purity versus negative sensuality, was offered. The division between purity and sensuality conformed to the gendered binary of virgin and whore, while the museum-goer occupied the position of a masculine, normative spectator/consumer of such aesthetic objects. The white marble of the statues was utilized to suggest a racialized conjunction of purity and whiteness. The transformation did double duty in attempting to elevate both the disciplined, pure female body and the sculpture of Greece. The fact that these statues had been painted in their original state was ignored; the weathered historicity of the paintless, broken statues was emphasized instead.[9]

In the British Museum, Greek art functioned as a signifier of purity/transcendent value, while Egyptian art signified materiality. Greek art was thought to have, according to the 1826 guide, an "intrinsic merit," which "speak[s] for itself" (38). Egyptian art, on the other hand, was suggested as being given value by the collector, a value emerging only because it was displayed. Believed to have display value and to lack intrinsic, transcendent value, Egyptian sculptures were thought to lack any elevating moral effect. They functioned, instead, as signifiers of materiality. Egyptian statues were described as repositories of erotic, sexual, and animalistic qualities—qualities that were shown to be the opposite of the sexual normativity of Greek statuary. Figures of Egyptian sculpture were thought, according to the guidebook, to represent "a phantasm and a dream" and not a reality and were similar to those "which haunt us in that nervous affection called the nightmare" (1826, 30). According to the 1826 guidebook, "We do not feel the least degree of human sympathy with the face [of an Egyptian statue], because there is nothing individualized about it"; instead of uplifting the viewer toward what is sublime, such art supposedly "exercises an almost painful and oppressive effect on the imagination" (33).

Not surprisingly, the 1826 guidebook suggested that England could itself be ancient Greece reborn; "classical" art, supposedly the highest achievement of art, became a representation of England. The virtues represented by classical sculpture were believed to be replicated in the people of England; the likenesses of the statues were the men and women of England. While Egyptian sculpture was believed to have nothing that could be called "natural," statues of Jupiter and Apollo supposedly were "actual likenesses of men and women that most of us have seen in the course of our own lives" (1826, 13). Consequently, England was thought to embody this ideal and contain these "divine" forms; "classical" England was further differentiated from the "barbaric East."

Such a rebirth was part of the neoclassicism of the early nineteenth century. It soon was incorporated into the very body of the British Museum. Its architecture, which was modified by 1852, was in the classical style, according to a plan created in 1823 by the Tory architect Sir Robert Smirke.[10]

WORKING-CLASS EDUCATION AND UPPER-CLASS HEGEMONY (1832–1850)

Peter Bailey has argued that popular culture was increasingly subject to various forms of control from many directions, but that this control was by no means uncontested, nor were the emerging forms of working-class leisure conforming to bourgeois ideals.[11] Yet the attempts at pacification, evident in the British Museum and its guidebooks, represented the increasing hegemony of an upper-class definition of a "national culture." The attempts at pacification led to a consolidation of a cultured class with the negotiated participation of a section of the working class bent on improving itself. No doubt other sections of the working class opposed this notion of a national culture; yet their participation in empire has been addressed by other scholars such as Penny Summerfield, who has examined the jingoism and imperialist discourses of music-hall entertainment toward the end of the century.[12] Imperialism was interpreted, disseminated, and negotiated through specific class interests even while the ideology of the superiority of the English race and nation was ubiquitous.

Admission to the museum had become far easier than it had been in the eighteenth century, when it could only be obtained by tickets applied for in advance with references.[13] By the year 1810, when the second edition of the *Synopsis* for the public was published, admission had become open to all persons on Monday, Wednesday, and Friday. In 1835, when the House of Commons ordered a committee of inquiry into the museum, the Principal Librarian was still resistant to the committee's recommendations to open the museum for public holidays and more days during the week. The librarian, Sir Henry Ellis, opposed more public days because he believed that the museum should also cater to men of rank and scholars, and he felt they should not mingle with the working class. He was against the opening of the museum on Easter, for then "the most mischievous portion of the population" could enter the museum.[14]

While museum officials and its trustees believed their public to be the men of "rank and wealth," parliamentary committees presumed it to be the "vulgar class." Consequently, at the same time that the House of Commons was interested in bringing the working class into a museum that was being supported, in large part, by parliamentary grants, the officials of the museum were interested in making it a more exclusive institution. Such a contradiction was apparent in the guidebooks written by the museum officials, which, while claiming that their audience was the section of society that needed to be educated, created a culture in which the aristocracy became increasingly idealized. Thus, even though the increase of power of the middle class in Victorian England cannot be denied, the aristocracy still was quite influential in the values of collecting and capitalism that it represented. "Men of rank and wealth," as Josiah Forshall called them, were enshrined as preservers of culture and as persons who placed national interest and national education before their personal needs.

For instance, in a guide to the collection called *Elgin and Phigaleian Marbles,* Sir Henry Ellis discusses the controversy surrounding the obtaining of the marbles, suggesting that Elgin did so out of concern that England had no classical models that could teach its artists and students.[15] Furthermore, Ellis supposedly had to rescue these artifacts since he had heard of the "almost daily injury which the originals were suffering from the violent hands of the Turks" (1846, 3). Ellis ends the chapter by saying that Elgin's perseverance and taste have helped establish England's reputation as a repository of art: "The possession of this collection has established a national school of sculpture in our country, founded on the noblest models which human art has ever produced" (1846, 10). The aristocratic collector of the seventeenth and eighteenth centuries is here recast as a patriot, one who collects not for his own power but for the power of the state, and for the disinterested improvement of art and taste in its population. National pride becomes pride in the power of the aristocracy and results in the valorization of class difference.

The education disseminated by the guidebooks thus emphasized the importance of the wealthy collector and was reiterated by the museum's displays. Such an emphasis was evident by the titles given to exhibits: the Towneley Marbles, the Elgin Marbles, the Payne-Knight Collection, the Christy Collection, the Sloane Collection. Each object in the museum came to be a mark of those who funded the travelers and collected the objects. As Joseph Mordaunt Crook reports in his book on the British Museum, "the age of the great private patron overlapped with the age of municipal enterprise," for the private patron was still a crucial factor in the development of the museum.[16]

IMPERIALISM AND CONSUMERISM: CLASS AND GENDER DISTINCTIONS WITHIN A NATIONAL CULTURE

"Do you mean to say, that the behavior of the public, generally, is such as it ought to be in viewing the Museum?"

"Yes, the ignorant are brought into awe by what they see about them, and the better informed know, of course, how to conduct themselves. We have common policemen, soldiers,

sailors, artillerymen, livery servants, and, of course, occasionally mechanics, but their good conduct I am very much pleased to see, and I think that the exhibition at the Museum will have a vast influence on the national character of Englishmen in general."
   —Mr. Samouelle, assistant in the Department of Natural History, from the
   Minutes of Evidence (1835)

In the nineteenth century, committees set up by the House of Commons, such as the one that interrogated Mr. Samouelle, investigated whether the museum was endeavoring to educate all classes and how it was going about this task. While there is no clear evidence of how many working-class men and women went to the museum, it is well known that they flocked in large numbers to fairs and exhibitions. Like the British Museum, these fairs exhibited objects and goods from many countries. The Great Exhibition, that collection of the spoils of empire displayed in the Crystal Palace, was a monument of consumption. It was a museum and a market, which signaled the era of the spectacle and from which advertisers and retailers learned that, as Thomas Richards puts it, "the best way to sell people commodities was to sell them the ideology of England."[17]

Excursion clubs were set up in 1841 so that the less affluent could save up to take package tours to these fairs, testifying to their popularity.[18] These clubs were originally a reform measure for the cause of temperance, since it was hoped that wages would be spent on edifying travel rather than on alcohol. James Cook, a temperance worker, took 165,000 people to the Great Exhibition in 1851 and set in motion mass tourism.[19] The number of visitors to the British Museum increased rapidly that year, when almost two million people visited it, more than the entire residential population of central London.[20] By visiting museums and fairs, a larger portion of the population was able to see objects and collections from remote parts of the world. These exhibitions were to have a great impact on Victorian life and culture, marking the "home" as domestic space to replicate the power of empire and creating a female consumer who in turn domesticated empire in new ways. In such a space, Victorian interior design emerged, which in its crowded style simulated the juxtapositions of imperial objects in museums and exhibitions. Even in working-class homes, Jubilee souvenirs of Victoria's reign had a place.

The Museums Act of 1845 and the Public Libraries Act of 1850 enabled local authorities to build libraries and museums out of the public rates. Whereas in 1800 there had been less than a dozen museums, by 1850 there were nearly sixty, and by 1887 there were at least 240.[21] The British Museum had grown immensely as well. A number of famous collections, from the royalty, the aristocracy, as well as other collectors, had expanded such that in 1823 Montagu House, the first building to house the original collections, had to be rebuilt. The museum added new buildings, a reading room, and another wing between 1838 and 1882, and subsequently the natural history collections were removed to South Kensington.

Advances in public participation in libraries, fairs, and museums and the ascendancy of the department store occurred within the context of the decline of working-class radicalism after 1850, as well as the emergence of new forms of gendered consumption. Nationalism, as the misrecognition of class difference, contributed to this decline. Richard Johnson has suggested that after 1850 the alternative system of "really useful education" for the working class, supported by radicals such as William Cobbett and by the Owenites and the Chartists, was replaced by working-class demands for education provided by the state. Such demands came from popular liberal politicians and, much later, from the Labor Party. As Johnson puts it, while radicals, Chartists, and Owenites had all opposed state education except as the work of a transformed state, later socialists actually fueled the growth of state schooling by their own agitations.[22] Whereas the radical publication *Black Dwarf* had opposed the setting up of national libraries on the ground that learning should support itself, and other radicals had opposed state education on the Godwinian grounds of opposition to authoritative education, the acceptance and even the demand for state education signaled that the incorporation and the pacification of the working class had begun. After 1851, all classes were visiting the British Museum, although the numbers did not reach the peak of almost two million a year that occurred during the Great Exhibition.

It has been suggested that one reason for the rise in visitors was that the Great Exhibition contained displays of manufactured goods, which were relevant to the social life of factory workers.[23] Yet this view does not explain why the British Museum became more popular when its exhibits did not change in any significant way. While other museums such as the South Kensington Museum (created by the planner of the Great Exhibition, Henry Cole) exhibited the products of industry and science, the British Museum did not alter its displays to include popular objects. Though the increase of interest in museums in general created by Cole's exhibits may have brought in more people to the British Museum, other factors that contributed to the popularity of all museums may also have helped. The increase in earning power of all classes, in leisure time, and in literacy must be cited, as well as the greater acceptance of state interventions and institutions.

An important factor may be the continuity between museum and the department store, as new forms of classed and gendered consumption, based on a shared ideological aesthetic, came into existence. Commodity culture was evolving through the transformation of high style.[24] The Victoria Jubilee ushered in a gendered commodification, where Victoria became at once the prototype of the female consumer, asserting the hegemony of the upper classes while creating a shared consumer culture, much as the British Museum had done. Regardless of the class she represented, she contributed to gendering the consuming subject.[25] The empire became gendered through having Victoria as a symbol that signified a racialized heterosexual nuclear family within which the role of the woman as the bearer and upholder of English "tradition" was recast in imperial terms. What Thomas Richards calls a "jingo kitsch"—the objects manufactured in commemoration of the Jubilee—connected "home" and harem, nation, and empire, by removing empire from the domain of political struggle and moving it into the home (134). Yet it was not only the objects in the home that inscribed the domestic space with imperial ideology, but also the clothes women wore, new foods influenced by colonial tastes and colonial goods, and the ability of the middle and upper classes to buy these goods, which was the result of money made through the colonies. Judith Walkowitz has suggested that the new public space for women, a "heterosocial space" that emerged during this time, included the music hall as well as the theater, department store, museum, library, and public transport.[26] The specularity of these spaces no doubt brought about a sense of an urban, mass, commodified culture as a characteristic of the imperial metropolis, within which classed and gendered subjects could exist as consumers.

To claim the necessity and the success of the museum and library laws, the Select Committee on Public Libraries was told by museum officials in 1849 that the character of the working man had improved in recent years both "in a moral and literacy point of view."[27] By 1852, it was believed that the British Museum had become successful in educating the public. The preface to the 1852 guidebook, published by the New Library of Useful Knowledge, another series of books aimed at educating the middle and lower classes, begins with an enthusiastic counting of the steady increase in the number of visitors to the museum, a tally that reinscribed the participation of the working class in the dominant culture. It is "wonderful" that 53,912 people came to the museum in one week; what is even more a matter of wonder and jubilation is their "perfect propriety and decorum," which is "highly creditable to their good taste and feeling"(1852, 13). It was felt that the "mob" had been disciplined by seeing and acquiring knowledge and information. To indicate the success of the museum, the guidebook of 1852 continues:

> Formerly the English populace was a mere mob—a mischievous assemblage, incapable of appreciating the beautiful or the good, or of behaving with common decency in public places; and upon this plea they were virtually excluded from inspecting not only the mansions of the nobility . . . but our noblest national treasure. (13)[28]

While suggesting that it was merely a lack of proper behavior that prevented the mob from participation in the glories of the nation, the writer states also that increased participation can come about now that the lower classes have shown civilized behavior in the Crystal Palace during the Great Exhibition of 1851. The mob has behaved with propriety in viewing the "houses of the aristocracy, several of which have been liberally thrown open to their admission" (1852, preface):

> It comes as no surprise, therefore, that the guidebook of 1852 concludes happily: Verily this is an age of progress, and the conviction of this truth . . . [is] that the sympathies of the rich and the poor are identical. . . . That we are all of one common nature, let us still further show (by acting on) the maxim of universal love. (1852, 13)

Thus the union of rich and poor is believed to have taken place only through the much greater wealth, learning, and condescension of the wealthy.

The guidebook suggests, furthermore, that with its help the objects in the museum are now accessible to all visitors, much as the Exhibitions, presenting objects without price tags, suggested as well. The guidebook proposes to give visitors "a general idea of the nature and amount of the treasures that lie within their reach" (1852, 5). The guidebook points to a world of objects "within the reach" of the visitor, offering the possibility of ownership even when the separation of viewer from artifacts kept in glass cases, of visitor from the collectors whose names were enshrined in the museum displays, negated such a possibility. The objects were only "at a glance," for they could be viewed, but not "within reach"; in other words, they could not be owned. The promise of democratic ownership connected the museum with the exhibition and the department store.[29] The museum displayed realms of knowledge that had earlier been hidden from the general public and provided the proximity of valuable objects that, without any possibility of possession, aroused the pride of national ownership.

The advances made by women included also their presence not only in the streets and stores but also in the previously male sanctum of the British Museum Reading Room (which became a trysting place between heterodox men and women).[30] The viewing public, both male and female, felt pride in the collections, without realizing that they were looking upon products that exemplified their own alienation, for the products included in the collection would be property created by the division of the worker from the product of his labor (1852, 16). Such a lack of alienation would be central to a imperial, nationalist, consumer culture. The guidebook of 1852, by pointing out the harmony and unity in the nation, collapsed the difference between capital and labor. It thus seemed to reunite the workers with the product of their labor. Yet the reconciliation was proposed through the promise of ownership, which, though national, suggested that all people could own property, a relationship very different from the reconciliation of labor value with use value wished for by early nineteenth-century radicals. This new form of ownership promised, to all visitors to the museum and to the greatly increasing audience that included the working class, the breakdown of class divisions through the creation of a new homogeneous class of the consumer. Thus one important factor within English nationalism was the emergence of the consumer.

The consumer was a product of the collection because, as Susan Stewart argues, the consuming self constituted not by the production but the consumption of goods is the result of alienation. This alienation emerges from the abstraction of labor from the process of production of the collection.[31] The separation of labor from product, and of object from production, resulted in the creation of a self that could only overcome alienation by consumption. Gender difference could, for example, be sublimated by shopping, which emerged as a female activity in the 1870s.[32] The existence of the public collection, in which objects seemed to be produced magically, signified the subjects who were not the producers but the "inheritors" of value. And because the labor of the consumer was the labor of "magic" and not of production, the collection came to signal the economy of consumption. Such a relation is suggested in the 1852 guidebook, signaling the decline of working-class agitation and the rise of state education as well as the increased commodification of social relations, which signals the emergence of the consumer. While guidebooks before 1850 carefully included narratives of the labor of collecting and writing to mediate the radical disjunction of the object from its origin and production, even though what was produced was not use value but display value, the guidebook of 1852 contains no such narrative.

What it provides instead is a narrative of magic and transformation—the consumer's labor. There are no accounts of the acquisition of objects, as in Ellis's books. What is mentioned is that when objects arrived at the museum—and we are not told how they arrived there since the writer merely quotes from the most current edition of the *Synopsis*—the museum had to be made bigger. If a narrative is given, and this occurs in the description of the Lycian room, it is one of accident and chance, and not of labor or hard work. Sir Charles Fellowes, we are told, made the "discovery" as a "result of mere accident," for while traveling in Asia Minor he "happened to alight upon the ruins of an ancient city." Being "struck with the beauty of the sculptured remains," he made drawings of these and took them back to England. There it became "immediately apparent" that these were the ruins of the ancient capital of Lycia (1852, 27). In contrast to earlier narratives of learning and acquisition, all of Fellowes's responses are unpremeditated, easy, not sought or worked for. The Lycian collection thus becomes a narrative of chance, of a magical transformation of ruins stumbled onto by chance into beautiful remains that have value.

The narrative of transformation becomes also the narrative of the process by which the museum educates. This education does not occur by the conscious mental labor of the viewer, but by the effect of the proximity of objects. By the visit to the museum, according to this guidebook,

> the mind of the visitor will become gradually the recipient of an invaluable variety of infor-
> mation and knowledge, and will find itself qualified, in a superior degree, for historical, artis-
> tic and antiquarian pursuits, should inclination and circumstance prove favorable. (1852, 5)

The public would be "civilized" by viewing the objects in the museum, objects that suggested their own commodification.

While working-class agitation decreased by the end of the century, movement for women's rights and equality became increasingly vociferous. Working-class women had always been seen as threatening to upper-class male conceptions of the domestic space. For instance, the strike of fifteen hundred female card-setters in West Riding, taken as an indication of female independence, was seen to be "more menacing to established institutions than the education of the lower orders."[33] Yet suffrage movements became predomi-
nantly middle class, even though gendered and classed forms of resistance in terms of agitations by laboring women continued.

Whereas empire, nation, and race provide the site of enunciation for feminist sub-
jects, consumer culture, also producing imperial subjects, presented another public space for middle-class women, along with philanthropy, which was aimed at reducing the aliena-
tion of the poor.[34] The gendered consumer, predominantly the middle- and upper-class woman, was the target for goods displayed in exhibitions and stores. Department stores provided a series of services and comforts for women that would re-create a home-like at-
mosphere,[35] domesticating the public space of the market. Liberty's Eastern Bazaar was the first to market the romance of the East to Londoners, a romance that in earlier decades had been sold by returning memsahibs in the forms of shawls and jewelry to middle-class women.[36] Philanthropy, aimed at the poor in England and unfortunate "sisters" in the colonies, was seen by middle-class women to be an equivalent recreational activity to shopping.[37]

Just as socialist women's groups and women's labor groups continued to struggle against capitalism and consumerism, there remained some working-class agitation in the latter half of the nineteenth century, for there were champions of the working-class causes such as William Morris and John Ruskin. Morris was against what he called "keeping art vigorously alive by the action, however energetic, of a few groups of specially gifted men and their small circle of admirers amidst a general public incapable of understanding and enjoying their work."[38] He was also aware of the danger that the working class would strive for this elitism. In an 1885 essay called "Useful Work versus Useless Toil," he warns against what he sees around him—an economic system in which the working class did not strive for socialism but for participation in capitalism: "Civilization has bred desires which she forbids us to satisfy, and so is not merely a niggard but a torturer too."[39] Thus

Morris was opposed to the inclusion of art and its knowledge as one of the goods of a consumer civilization.

Yet Morris did suggest, perhaps as a way to turn the alienation implicit in the museum and the elitism implicit in classical art into oppositional tools, that workers should visit museums in order to learn of the time when art and work were one and thus gave pleasure. He believed that great works of art, such as Greek sculpture from the Parthenon, could teach the working class to know of that great time and to become discontent with the present. For Morris, therefore, the museum could inculcate revolutionary awareness. Yet even when he recommended that workers visit museums, he acknowledged the problems of the museum, that is, that it decontextualized art and presented it as alienated from labor by placing it in an artificial medium far from where it was produced: "Nor can I deny there is something melancholy about a museum, such a tale of violence, destruction, and carelessness, as its treasured scraps tell us."[40]

Such a contradiction indicates that working-class movements in the second half of the nineteenth century were less powerful than those of the early nineteenth century since they were more intertwined with the power structures of the dominant classes. Women's movements also continued to struggle with large fractures within them; the conflicts of the Pankhurst sisters, with Christabel as apologist of empire and Sylvia in a missionary, benevolent opposition to it, symbolize some of the struggles going on at the time. Yet despite such struggles, the education of the working class by means of institutions such as the British Museum and department stores continued and furthered the rise of imperialism, another function of nationalism. The British subject, alienated and made into a consumer by her/his own commodification, saw other races and other peoples also as commodities. The British Museum had shown the world to be a storehouse of goods, and imperialism and the acquisition of artifacts for the museum became synonymous processes. When guidebooks from the end of the century mention how objects are acquired through military conquest, they elide the labor and cost of acquisition by suggesting its ease. The preface of the 1899 museum catalog describing antiquities from Benin contains a narrative of their acquisition in which the reader/viewer is told that the objects have been obtained "by a recent successful expedition sent to Benin to punish the natives of that city for a treacherous massacre of a peaceful English mission."[41] The destruction of Benin City is shown to be a punishment to its natives that "made accessible to students of ethnography the interesting works of native art which form the subject of the following pages."[42] The ease of this acquisition, the erasure of labor are suggested when the cost of the acquisition, in human lives, time, and money, is not mentioned. An 1890 guidebook, after a preface that lists the museum's entire collections, adds that the main part of the Egyptian collection was laid "by the acquisition in 1802 of the antiquities which passed into the possession of the British army on the capitulation of Alexandria in the previous year."[43] In these catalogs of the late nineteenth century, the military might of a colonial power is given credit for enabling the collection and preservation of objects. Since display value in the collection comes from the transformation of goods into artifacts and art, military conquest becomes a source of aesthetic value, one that is easily converted into economic value. The history of the museum is therefore revealed as the history of colonization.

The British Museum was an imperial project because it embodied a love of order, and an attempt to domesticate the unknown through this ordering. The world was re-assembled in the museum as an ordered construct. The love of variety—that function of the power of capital through the acquisition of goods—was the aesthetic of the imperial-ist collector; it enabled the collecting of objects that could be put in order within a famil-iar taxonomy. The British Museum collected objects that were believed to have obtained value only by being placed in the museum collections. Taken out of circulation in their original economic spheres where they had use value, they were placed in another symbol-ic system. However, what was suggested was that they had been transformed into use when they were made objects of knowledge; without this new use value they were merely the dirt that awaits transformation into gold.[44] The East and the Other, made into inter-changeable entities, were spatially and temporally frozen into artifacts within the museum.[45]

The unmoving, frozen spoils of travel showed the mobility of the English collectors. Armed with the guidebook, the visitor who perambulated through the museum, past the atemporalized, stilled artifacts, imaginatively traversed the geography of Euro-imperial travel. A visit to the museum was like a guided journey to foreign lands.[46] Here lay the ivories from many Dark places; the spoils of travel, like the novel, the travelogue, narra-tivized the Other. The "rescue" of personal fragments, which for Walter Benjamin gave the private collection its ability to provide rebirth and renewal, was on a public and national level an imperial ordering.[47]

NOTES

A longer version of this essay appears in my book *Home and Harem: Nation, Gender, Empire and Cultures of Travel* (Durham, N.C.: Duke University Press, 1996).

1. Benedict Anderson, *Imagined Communities,* rev. ed. (New York: Verso, 1991), 178–85.

2. Timothy Mitchell, "Orientalism and the Exhibitory Order," in *Colonialism and Culture,* ed. Nicholas Dirks (Ann Arbor: University of Michigan Press, 1992), 299.

3. *A Guide to the Beauties of the British Museum* (London: Thomas and George Underwood, 1826, 1838); *The British Museum in Four Sections; or, How to View the Whole at Once* (London: Cradock and Co., 1852); further references to this book appear in the text as 1852.

4. Richard Altick, *The English Common Reader* (Chicago: University of Chicago Press, 1957), 266.

5. Ed Cohen, *Talk on the Wilde Side* (New York: Routledge, 1993), 20.

6. Susan Stewart, *On Longing* (Baltimore: Johns Hopkins University Press, 1984), 164–66.

7. Ibid., 158.

8. See Martin Bernal, *Black Athena* (New Brunswick, N.J.: Rutgers University Press, 1987).

9. It is important to consider how new ways of objectifying bodies, especially female ones, emerge with the aesthetic of the fragments of these statues.

10. Joseph Mordaunt Crook, *The British Museum* (London: Lane, 1972).

11. Peter Bailey, *Leisure and Class in Victorian England: Rational Recreation and the Contest for Control, 1830–1885* (London: Routledge, 1978).

12. Penny Summerfield, "Patriotism and Empire: Music-Hall Entertainment," in *Imperialism and Popular Culture,* ed. John Mackenzie (Manchester: Manchester University Press, 1986), 17–48.

13. Kenneth Hudson, *A Social History of Museums* (London: Macmillan, 1975), 10.

14. *Minutes of Evidence Taken before the Select Committee on the Condition, Management and Affairs of the British Museum* (1835), P-99.

15. Sir Henry Ellis, *Elgin and Phigaleian Marbles of Classical Ages* (London: Charles Knight, 1846).

16. Crook, *The British Museum*, 90–91.

17. Thomas Richards, *The Commodity Culture of Victorian England: Advertising and Spectacle, 1851–1914* (Stanford, Calif.: Stanford University Press, 1990), 3–5.

18. Robert Rydell, *All the World's a Fair: Visions of Empire at American International Expositions, 1876–1916* (Chicago: University of Chicago Press, 1984).

19. See Edmund Swinglehurst, *The Romantic Journey* (New York: Harper and Row, 1974). Swinglehurst comments that this tour fulfilled James Cook's best ambitions: "To bring travel to people, to stimulate desire for learning and to make them aware of the glorious future which the Great Exhibition presaged" (35).

20. Crook, *The British Museum*, 196.

21. Ibid., 90.

22. Richard Johnson, "Really Useful Knowledge: Radical Education and Working-Class Culture," in *Working-Class Culture*, ed. J. Clarke, C. Critchen, and Richard Johnson (New York: St. Martin's Press, 1979), 95.

23. Hudson, *A Social History*, 42.

24. Richards, *Commodity Culture*, 54.

25. Ibid., 108–9.

26. Judith Walkowitz, *City of Dreadful Delight: Narratives of Sexual Danger in Late-Victorian London* (Chicago: University of Chicago Press, 1992), 45.

27. *Minutes of Evidence Taken before the Select Committee on Public Librairies* (1849).

28. The 1985 BBC Series (also an exhibition at the National Gallery) called *The Treasure Houses of Britain* does exactly the reverse. It reeducates the British public about the glories of the English aristocracy by taking the viewers back into the houses of the wealthy and showing them the art and artifacts within.

29. Richards, *Commodity Culture*, 19.

30. Letters complaining of such an intrusion appeared in the *Pall Mall Gazette*. See Walkowitz, *City of Dreadful Delight*, 69.

31. Stewart, *On Longing*, 156.

32. Walkowitz, *City of Dreadful Delight*, 47.

33. Comment by John Wade, recorded in E. P. Thompson's *The Making of the English Working Class* (New York: Vintage, 1963), 416.

34. Walkowitz, *City of Dreadful Delight*, 46.

35. Ibid., 48.

36. Nupur Choudhury, "Shawls, Jewelry, Curry, and Rice in Victorian Britain," in *Western Women and Imperialism*, ed. Nupur Choudhury and Margaret Strobel (Bloomington: Indiana University Press, 1992), 231–46.

37. Walkowitz, *City of Dreadful Delight*, 53.

38. William Morris, *News from Nowhere and Selected Writings and Designs* (Harmondsworth: Penguin, 1984), 143.

39. Ibid., 123.

40. Ibid., 96.

41. Charles Hercules Read and Ormonde Maddock Dalton, *Antiquities from the City of Benin* (London: British Museum, 1899), 4.

42. Ibid.

43. E. Maude Thompson, *A Guide to the British Museum* (London: British Museum Trustees, 1890), xi.

44. John Russell (chief art critic of the *New York Times*) writes in the *Times Magazine* of June 2, 1985, that "art is everywhere in India, if we know how to look." Rejecting any Indian idea of art or beauty,

Russell appreciates India in moments of epiphany when he can see "a private India, a confidential India and an alternative India." Proving that he still thinks he can turn dust to gold, Russell writes that art "is just there [in India], in the air, on the ground, all over the place, for the taking, and no name attached to it."

45. The Victoria and Albert Museum even now vividly brings back England's imperial past.

46. The British Museum is now a journey into the past of all the cultures of the world. As one popular guidebook (*Let's Go: The Budget Guide to Britain and Ireland* [New York: St. Martin's Press, 1985], 115) says: "It is the closest thing this planet has to a complete record of its civilizations." The British Museum is popularly considered the historian of the world.

47. Walter Benjamin, "Unpacking My Library," in *Illuminations,* ed. Hannah Arendt (New York: Schocken Books, 1969), 59–67.

PHOTOGRAPHING THE "AMERICAN NEGRO"

Nation, Race, and Photography at the Paris Exposition of 1900

Shawn Michelle Smith

In "The Conservation of Races," published in 1897, W. E. B. Du Bois asks: "What, after all, am I? Am I an American or am I a Negro? Can I be both? Or is it my duty to cease to be a Negro as soon as possible and be an American?"[1] As Du Bois attempts to plot a course through the "doubleness" of racial and national identities facing African Americans at the turn of the century, he asserts that distinct racial cultures must be maintained, even as different groups come to coexist as citizens of the same nation.[2] His essay is titled, after all, "The *Conservation* of Races," and Du Bois asserts that African Americans must resist the ethnic erasure that assimilation into a dominant white culture would entail, while simultaneously fighting for political, economic, and social equality in Jim Crow America.

Du Bois affirms that the African American must struggle to be both an "American" and a "Negro" in his 1897 essay, and he helps to define the position of the African American further with his prominent participation in the American Negro exhibit at the Paris Exposition of 1900. Du Bois assisted in preparing many of the displays for the American Negro exhibit, and he also assembled hundreds of photographs of African Americans into a series of three albums (four volumes) for the presentation. Frances Benjamin Johnston, a professional white woman photographer, provided another collection of photographs for the exhibit, a series of images of the Hampton Institute commissioned expressly for the 1900 Paris Exposition. Reading Du Bois's photograph albums against Johnston's images of the Hampton Institute, this essay investigates how racial and national identities were posed and negotiated in the terrain of visual culture at the Paris Exposition of 1900. Proposing that the American Negro exhibit itself was deeply invested in defining the place of the "Negro" in America, I examine how such positions were established in the visual codes of turn-of-the-century photography.

While most studies of the nation and of national identity have focused on the printed word as the medium through which a national community could be imagined in the nineteenth century, this essay demonstrates the role that photography, another medium of mass reproduction, played in envisioning a racially codified American identity.[3] In order to understand fully the ways in which the photographs displayed in the American

Negro exhibit participated in the formulation of visual codes of national belonging, we must situate the images within the historical legacy of representations that they both draw on and significantly challenge. Johnston's and Du Bois's photographs of the American Negro entered a visual terrain already mapped in terms of both race and nation over the course of the nineteenth century. The American Negro exhibit itself, the frame in which Johnston's and Du Bois's photographs were presented, signified the nexus of scientific discourses defining both "race" and "national character" at the turn of the century. Further, the images that Johnston produced and those that Du Bois assembled circulated within a redefined field of photographic representation. Situating Johnston's and Du Bois's images within a changing historical context, this essay reads photographs not simply as signs that represent real-world referents, but as signs with a distinct visual genealogy—signs that enter into conversation with and contest other photographs. My argument proposes that visual culture is not a mere reflection of an imagined community, but one of the sites in which narratives of belonging are produced and propelled. In other words, I suggest that the nation is not simply the referent of photographic images, but also the product.[4]

Johnston's photographs and Du Bois's albums initiated new visual strategies for representing both race and national character at the turn of the century. Both sets of images challenged the essentialized discourses of race and national identity dominant during this period, although they did so to varying degrees. While Johnston's photographs forwarded the American identity of Hampton students over their racial identities, Du Bois's albums suggested that the African American could indeed be both an "American" and a "Negro." This essay illustrates how the photographs displayed in the American Negro exhibit marked a new and internally contested moment in the history of visual culture and inaugurated a legacy of representational strategies still manifest today, in the visual culture of the 1990s.

RACIALIZED BODIES, NATIONAL CHARACTER,
AND PHOTOGRAPHIC DOCUMENTATION

The American Negro exhibit itself participated in a new era in the history of race representation, both for the United States and for international expositions in general. Following a trend initiated with the "Negro Building" at the Cotton States and International Exposition of Atlanta in 1895, Paris Exposition organizers invited African Americans to present their history, cultural achievements, and social advances to the world in their "own terms" at the Paris Exposition of 1900.[5] A very few years after African Americans were denied official participation in the Columbian World Exposition of 1893, they were invited to contribute as self-defining agents to the Atlanta Exposition of 1895, the Nashville Centennial Exposition of 1897, and the Paris Exposition of 1900.[6] As Du Bois describes the American Negro exhibit at the Paris Exposition, it was "planned and executed by Negroes, and collected and installed under the direction of a Negro special agent, Mr. Thomas J. Calloway."[7] Unlike the exoticized displays of African villages that reinforced white European estimations of their own "civilized" superiority in relation to "Negro savages," the American Negro exhibit of the Paris Exposition represented African Americans as thoroughly modern members of the Western world. Through a series of maps, charts, models, photographs, and detailed descriptions of work in African American education, as well as hundreds of examples of African American literary production, the American Negro exhibit presented the progress made by African Americans in the terms of white Western culture. The exhibit was considered one of the most impressive in the Palace of Social Economy and was honored with an exposition grand prize.[8]

While it is important to underscore the unique nature of the American Negro exhibit, it is also important to note that this was by no means a utopian moment. Housed in the U.S. section of the Palace of Social Economy, the exhibit was framed by international notions of social progress. According to Du Bois, the exhibits in the Palace of Social Economy did not portray sociology, the "science of society" per se, but instead, various systems of social reform. Included in national exhibits were the "mutual aid societies of France," "the state insurance of Germany," as well as "the Red Cross Society."[9] The U.S. section presented models of tenement houses, maps of industrial plants, and the work of factory inspectors. Within the Palace of Social Economy, amid displays expounding treatments for social ailments, the American Negro exhibit provided a social success story, but it was compelled to deliver that story within the implicit context of solutions to national problems, in this case, no doubt, the ubiquitous white-coined American "negro problem." Thus, while the American Negro exhibit provided an opportunity for African Americans to visualize complex racial and national identifications, it remained confined within a white-dominated system of social surveillance.

The very term *American Negro* would have registered as a kind of oxymoron to particularly strident Anglo-Saxon American nationalists at the turn of the century. Since the Civil War, many white Americans had attempted to define *American* as an exclusively Anglo-Saxon denomination, and by the turn of the century their white-supremacist nationalism was backed by the scientific discourse of eugenics.[10] Eugenicists and biological racialists[11] in the United States were intent on establishing much less permeable national borders than those configured through the reading practices enabled by the expansion of print capitalism, and they sought to delineate the borders of the "imagined community"[12] through discourses of essentialized racial characteristics. Francis Galton, the founder of eugenics, or "science of race," claimed that national character was an effect of race, a kind of racial attribute. Further, Galton believed that the racialized properties of national character could be enhanced and controlled through monitored breeding. Conversely, Galton claimed that national character might be enfeebled through both unmonitored procreation of the "weak" and interracial reproduction. In Galton's universe races were measured according to a hierarchical scale in which the ancient Greeks represented a lost ideal, nineteenth-century Anglo-Saxons claimed the modern pinnacle, and "Negroes" occupied the lowest link. According to Galton, improvement might be bred within a race, but cross-breeding between the races would always result in tragically weakened stock. Further, while he argued explicitly against amalgamation, his work also implicitly buttressed antiassimilationist policies. Cultural equality among the races—a sharing of "essential" national character—was inconceivable according to Galton's notion of biological difference. In Galton's terms, nations of races were by definition separate and not equal.[13]

Galton's eugenics provided a scientific basis for the arrangement of racialized Others commonly presented at international expositions around the turn of the century.

Even as African Americans were represented as successful participants in white Western "progress" in the American Negro exhibit at the Paris Exposition, other "Negroes" were hired to people the living displays that represented an exoticized "sliding scale of humanity" popular at international expositions since their introduction at the 1889 Paris fair.[14] As Thomas J. Schlereth describes the racialized spatial logics of such exhibits on the Midway Plaisance at Chicago's Columbian Exposition of 1893, "ethnic" displays were arranged along the periphery of the fairgrounds, around the center of the exposition, which celebrated Western European triumphs in science, industry, and art. At the Chicago Columbian Exposition, the imagined Western whiteness of the exposition center was dramatically represented by architect Frederick Law Olmsted's literally white stuccoed buildings, modeled after ancient Greek and Roman architecture. Outside this Greek- and Roman-inspired Anglo-Saxon "White City," ethnic displays in the Midway Plaisance were arranged according to their imagined proximity to Anglo-Saxon culture. The Teutonic and Celtic races, represented by German and Irish exhibits, occupied the Midway territory closest to the "White City" center of the exposition, while the Mohammedan and Asian worlds stood farther away, and the "savage races," including Africans and North American Indians, remained at the farthest reaches of the Midway.[15] A similar structure, in which a city center celebrating Western industrial, social, and artistic achievements, replete with educational exhibits, was surrounded by a relatively chaotic zone filled with new forms of entertainment and exotic displays of non-Western peoples (many the "trophies" of Western imperialism), dominated international expositions throughout the early twentieth century. It is within this context that one notes the most radical and, indeed, perhaps the most contained critique of turn-of-the-century notions of race and culture forwarded by the American Negro exhibit. Contesting the colonialist and imperialist logics advanced by living racial and ethnic displays, the American Negro exhibit disrupted the essentialized narratives that depicted nonwhite peoples as the uncivilized infants of human evolution. The exhibit dissociated "race" from a single set of cultural practices and progressive potentialities.

While the space in which Johnston's photographs and Du Bois's albums were presented was the already unique and contested domain of the American Negro exhibit, the photographs themselves were also imbedded in changing conceptions of photographic documentation. Unlike Mathew Brady's daguerreotype portraits of "Illustrious Americans," which received the most prestigious awards at the London Crystal Palace Exposition of 1851, Johnston's and Du Bois's photographs were not presented as art objects in a separate photographic salon.[16] Instead, the images were meant to *document* and to *illustrate* the "progress and present conditions" of the American Negro. Johnston's and Du Bois's photographs signified in photographic registers developed outside the auratic domains of both the sentimental portrait keepsake and the photographic work of art.[17] Displayed in the Palace of Social Economy, alongside model tenement houses and the reports of factory inspectors, the photographs included in the American Negro exhibit functioned as evidence, just as the many charts and graphs included in exhibits served as scientific documentations of progress. Unlike the photographic portraits that dominated popular and professional photography in the United States throughout the nineteenth century, Johnston's photographs did not aim to emulate an individual but to capture the imagined essence of an entire group, namely, the "American Negro." Johnston rarely photographed solitary individuals, and the majority of her Hampton photographs depict entire classes concentrating on lessons staged for the camera. The students in Johnston's photographs are not named or in any other way identified as individuals. They are not memorialized as relatives, lovers, or glamorous stars; in short, they are not sentimentalized. In Johnston's images Hampton students become examples, samples of the disciplined, successful "American Negro." Even Du Bois's photographs, the large majority of which are portraits, do not name or identify individuals but instead present portrait photographs as the unnamed evidence of African American individuality.

Presented within the context of both sociology and reform, Johnston's and Du Bois's images may have resonated with the contemporary sensationalist images that Jacob Riis produced of the "other half," even as they foreshadowed the social documentary photography of Lewis Hine.[18] However, unlike Riis's dramatic images of tenement squalor and Hine's detailed images of child laborers, the photographs Johnston and Du Bois brought to the American Negro exhibit aimed not to document social problems but to record the progress made by African Americans at the turn of the century. Johnston's photographs in particular do not attempt to illustrate a need for social reform but instead demonstrate the success of a social reform already in place, namely, the Hampton Institute's program of manual training.[19] Rather than attempting to incite public furor at social ills, the exhibit as a whole proclaimed to present the work of "a small nation of people, picturing their life and development without apology or gloss."[20] While the celebratory tone of the American Negro exhibit certainly marked a well-deserved source of African American pride, it may also have communicated a much more problematic message to Anglo-American viewers. The congratulatory nature of the exhibit may have demonstrated to white viewers that they no longer needed "to be afraid of black people or [to feel] guilty at what had happened to them after Reconstruction."[21] To white American viewers schooled in the rhetoric of the "negro problem," the exhibit may have indicated that segregation, disfranchisement, and poverty were not debilitating social forces and that, in fact, the so-called negro problem itself could be socially segregated.

Functioning as a kind of visual testimony or evidence, Johnston's and Du Bois's images dovetailed not only with the photographs of social science, but also with the photographs that circulated in the registers of biological science. By the turn of the century photographs were being used in the United States to map "deviant" bodies in prisons, medical treatises, and scientific explorations into the nature of both gender and race.[22] Within the field of eugenics, photographs were used to illustrate the biological roots of social structures. Francis Galton devised two photographic techniques for recording what he believed to be the physical indices of essential biological difference, both composite portraiture and a strictly standardized system of family photography. I describe both of Galton's strategies at length here, as they exemplify the scientific representations of racialized bodies that Johnston's and Du Bois's photographs implicitly contest.

Galton believed that his system of composite photographic portraiture would enable one to document the common physical features of a predetermined racial group. As Galton maintained that physical features indexed the intellectual and creative potential of a race, he felt corporeal signs could legitimately be said to demarcate one's appropriate position in a hierarchical society. Faithful to the purported objectivity of the photographic image, Galton held that the abstract, "perfected" signs of common physical characteristics could be determined by overlaying a series of standardized frontal and profile mug shots of any given group. Exposing each of the individual images on top of one another for an equally proportionate time, Galton was able to make his single, layered, and eerily abstract composite portraits.[23] These portraits were traced in the soft, blurred lines of overlapping facial features, and they revealed ghostly hints of the physical "anomalies" particular to each face. Galton claimed that such images enabled one "to obtain with mechanical precision a generalized picture; one that represents no man in particular, but portrays an imaginary figure possessing the average features of any given group of men."[24] In his composite portraits Galton claimed to capture "the central physiognomical type of any race or group."[25] Galton imagined that his composite photographic records would serve as a kind of key for (presumably white) viewers, as a map of the racialized body, allowing one to study abstract, "pure" racial characteristics, and later to discern the racial identity of individuals according to that model, to assess their corresponding intellectual attributes, and to situate them "appropriately" along a sliding social scale stratified by biological difference.

While Galton aimed to identify the salient characteristics of predetermined biological groups with his composite portraiture, he hoped to monitor the reproduction of racial attributes with his scientific "family albums." In 1884, Galton designed both the *Record of Family Faculties* and *The Life History Album*.[26] The *Record* served as a chronicle of one's ancestry (a kind of detailed family tree) and was intended to aid individuals in predicting their own, and their children's, future abilities and ailments. Galton suggested that photographic portraits would provide important illustrations of family members, augmenting verbal descriptions and medical histories. The photograph played a more central role in *The Life History Album,* as Galton proposed a system of thorough, standardized photographic documentation. The *Album* was designed to record the growth and maturation of an individual child (functioning as a precursor to the modern "baby book"), and Galton called on parent contributors to make a standardized set of photographs of the child, "an exact full-face and a profile" every five years.[27] In each of his records, Galton treated the photograph as a transparent document of the body, which was in turn regarded as the physical record of an essential racial character transmitted through the blood. By standardizing family photograph albums, Galton hoped to open to scientific scrutiny a vast colloquial resource, namely, the sentimental family archive.

While systems of photographic documentation were being designed to record and to codify the body as the ultimate sign of racial essence at the turn of the century, representing the more elusive national character that supposedly corresponded to racialized physical features (the very core of racial identity in Galton's terms) proved a more difficult task. It is at this juncture, between the photographic documentation of race and of nation that Johnston's and Du Bois's photographs for the American Negro exhibit enter public visual culture. While the photographic work of Frances Benjamin Johnston and W. E. B. Du Bois represents an important moment in the history of building national photographic archives, they were not the first to attempt to portray "American character" in photographs. Mathew Brady, a famous forerunner in the history of visualizing American identity, sought to emblematize national character in his portraits of "Illustrious Americans," which he made throughout the 1850s and 1860s.[28] Brady was one of the first and one of the most famous photographers in nineteenth-century America, making a name for himself and his portraits in the early days of daguerreotypy, the first photographic process. Adhering to a long-standing aesthetic tradition that positioned the eminent individual of the formal portrait in the larger-than-life posture of Roman busts, in three-quarter profile, looking loftily up and away from viewers, Brady photographed an extraordinary number of famous American politicians, artists, and authors.[29] Brady showcased his portraits of Illustrious Americans in his popular New York galleries, no doubt intending to heighten his own public renown, and also, as he himself explicitly contended, to provide salient examples of American character for the praise and emulation of others. Brady also selected twelve of his many portraits to be reproduced and circulated in a printed "Gallery of Illustrious Americans." Each of Brady's daguerreotype portraits, reproduced as a lithograph for printed form, was accompanied by a written biographical text that expounded the particularly American character of each representative individual. Brady's Illustrious Americans were not "typical," but model Americans, the embodiment of abstract ideals, and their biographies attested to the specific achievements that could not be read in their faces. Unlike Galton, who attempted to represent in abstract form the "typical" physical features of a "national race," Brady aimed to depict the equally abstract spiritual and moral characteristics of individuals who emblematized abstract national ideals. While Galton looked to the lowest common physical denominator as the definitive sign of a racialized national identity, Brady heralded the highest spiritual denominator as the signal of true American character.

While his aim was quite distinct from Francis Galton's later "scientific" attempts to document a racialized national identity, Mathew Brady's portraits of Illustrious Americans also, if only implicitly, forwarded a distinctly racialized notion of national character. As Alan Trachtenberg has argued, Brady's "Gallery of Illustrious Americans," produced in 1850, placed "national heroes" from opposing sides of a dissolving nation on the same patriotic landscape.[30] A portrait of Zachary Taylor, the Whig President, joins a portrait of John Calhoun, outspoken Democrat, on the patriotic horizon of Brady's gallery.[31] In this way, Brady's images extricate national character from the tense political conflicts developing over slavery and racial difference in the pre–Civil War era, reproducing (white, male) Americanness as an exalted quality removed from and unmarred by divisive politics rooted in racial conflicts. Half a century later, Johnston's and Du Bois's photographs delineate national character after the Civil War, and decades after Reconstruction, in a period of heightened racial tension, continuing debate over the so-called Negro question, Jim Crow segregation, African American disfranchisement, and increased lynching. By representing the American character of peoples excluded from many levels of legal and cultural American privilege, namely, African and Native Americans at the turn of the century, Johnston and Du Bois situate national identity within the terrain of racial identity and racial conflict at the turn of the century. In this later period, as evidenced by Galton's eugenics, racial divisions actually fueled the definition of national character, as this once ephemeral, interiorized quality was harnessed to a racially inflected biology. Indeed, reading Brady's earlier images of Illustrious Americans from this turn-of-the-century vantage point, the implicit, albeit unmarked signs of a racialized white national identity become (if not already) apparent in Brady's portraits.

While not the first photographs to attempt to portray American character, Johnston's and Du Bois's images represent new visual strategies for representing an explicitly racialized version of national identity (unlike Brady's implicitly racialized Illustrious Americans). Responding to new notions of national and racial identities, Johnston and Du Bois present new means of visually codifying American identity. At the time of the Paris Exposition, Galton's theories of racial difference were gaining wide acceptance among physical and social scientists in the United States, and it is against an increasingly dominant discourse of a racialized national essentialism that one must read Johnston's and Du Bois's efforts to visualize competing versions of the "American Negro" at the turn of the century. As I will demonstrate, Frances Benjamin Johnston's Hampton photographs and W. E. B. Du Bois's photograph albums contest the racist biological determinism of Galton's particular national paradigm, even as the two projects work toward different ends.

MAKING AMERICANS

Frances Benjamin Johnston's views of the Hampton Institute may have been slightly anomalous in what Du Bois described as an exhibit produced and executed exclusively by African Americans. Indeed, in his review of the exhibit, Du Bois praises Johnston's work, which won a gold medal at the exposition, but as he evaluates the images, he completely effaces Johnston as photographer: "From Hampton there is an especially excellent series of photographs illustrating the Hampton ideas of 'teaching by doing.'"[32] In Du Bois's account, Johnston's images are important because they "illustrate" Hampton ideas, and the photographs themselves come "from Hampton," not from Johnston. Du Bois emphasizes the discursive formulation of Johnston's subject matter, the pedagogical philosophy of the Hampton Institute, but he fails to comment on the codified construction of the photographs themselves. In his review, Du Bois draws on discourses of documentary and scientific photography that erase the ideological underpinnings that inform photographic images and styles. Putting Johnston back into a reading of the Hampton photographs, one can begin to tease out her ambiguous position as photographer, if only, finally, to heighten the conundrum of her role as white woman photographer for an African American exhibit. It is important to underscore the ways in which this exhibit was implicitly tied to a complexly gendered and racialized system of white social surveillance at the turn of the century, in order to explain some of the tensions and conflicting racial ideologies apparent in Johnston's photographs.

The Hampton Institute was an industrial arts and teachers' training school founded in 1868 by Colonel Samuel Chapman Armstrong, and originally designed to educate former slaves after the Civil War. Toward the latter part of the nineteenth century, the institute began to admit Native American, as well as African American students. In 1899, the second president of Hampton, Hollis Burke Frissell, invited Johnston to photograph the school specifically for the 1900 Paris Exposition.[33] Johnston produced dozens of images at Hampton, including landscapes; group portraits of bands, teams, and graduating classes;

and a couple of family portraits taken in homes. By far her most common views, however, were those made in classrooms, depicting students "in action" working on a project or paying exaggerated attention to the day's lesson. All of these classroom images are marked by a certain stiffness, the result of long camera exposures combined with a staginess aimed at illustrating a particular skill, idea, or theme for later viewers. Messages written on the board and visual spaces constructed to privilege the camera's point of view mark the intended presence of a later viewing audience. However, this future audience (and indeed, the photographer herself) is not acknowledged directly by the student subjects in Johnston's images. In the photographs, Hampton students never meet the camera with curious, approving, or challenging eyes; instead, they are depicted as the objects of a scrutinizing gaze, one that has been invited to evaluate their "progress and present conditions." The omission of any recorded interaction between Hampton students and Johnston (the photographer standing in for later viewers), and the absence of even a documented glance in the direction of the camera pose Hampton students as the willing objects of an outside investigation, the test subjects of an external study.

Johnston's unquestioned role as observer, as practitioner of a dominating, unreturned gaze at the Hampton Institute may at first surprise contemporary viewers schooled in a tradition of psychoanalytic feminist film theory. After Laura Mulvey's groundbreaking analysis of the "male gaze" posed and propelled by the film industry, how can one explain a white woman's visual mastery over African American and Native American students at the turn of the century?[34] Does Johnston adopt a masculine position from which to represent her subjects as the feminine objects of a male gaze? Must Johnston perform a kind of "transvestism" in order to visually represent her desire in these images?[35] And what is the nature of the desire that Johnston's photographs project? The answers to these questions are not readily available within a field that poses the visual representation of desire as strictly gendered and invisibly white. Scholars such as bell hooks, Jacqueline Bobo, Jane Gaines, Richard Dyer, Manthia Diawara, Isaac Julien, Kobena Mercer, and Mary Ann Doane, who are revising Mulvey's influential work by addressing race and ethnicity as discourses central to the development of modern visual culture, have problematized understandings of desire and of the gaze that have been dominated by gender categories, reading the history of visual culture (and specifically the history of Hollywood film) as a trajectory bound by white Western ethnocentrism.[36] In addition, artists and scholars such as Trinh T. Minh-ha and Coco Fusco, and cultural critics such as Timothy Mitchell, Mary Louise Pratt, and Deborah Willis are beginning to identify what bell hooks has called a "white supremacist gaze"[37] as a key constituent of Western colonial and imperial power.[38] Bound to a mythology of scientific objectivity and a system of increasing social surveillance, an invisible white gaze functioned as the arbiter of biological and cultural difference in Jim Crow America. While one cannot discard the terms of gender in assessing Johnston's gaze, it is important to rearticulate her visual practice according to the *racialized* discourses of gender and sexuality dominant at the turn of the century.[39]

In the post-Reconstruction South, the gaze functioned as a powerful threat within the racist discourse of sexual assault. According to one cultural historian who assesses the spread of lynching at the turn of the century: "If a black man so much as looked a white woman in the eye he risked being accused of lechery or insolence, and in some cases this was as good as committing an actual assault."[40] Given this racist dynamic, Johnston's inability to photograph students looking at the camera, looking at her, takes on profoundly disturbing connotations. Photographing the Hampton Institute during the height of racial terrorism in the South, at a time when African American men were lynched in the name of protecting the sexual (and racial) purity of white womanhood, Johnston may have posed a dangerous threat to her Hampton subjects.[41] Indeed, while Johnston was pursuing another photographic project six years later, one of her African American male hosts was attacked for his audacity in accompanying a white woman alone at night. In this cultural context, the downcast eyes depicted in Johnston's photographs signify doubly the charged power dynamics out of which the images were produced. As a white woman, Johnston represented both a threat and a potentially powerful advocate for young African Americans. African American feminist activists like Ida B. Wells and Anna Julia Cooper recognized the white woman's singular power to dismantle the mythology of rape that fueled post-Reconstruction lynching.[42] However, Johnston's photographs do not forward the radical defense of African American virtue heralded by Wells but instead ambiguously skirt the "challenging" gaze, thereby subtly reproducing a legacy of racial hierarchy in the turn-of-the-century South.

Johnston's position as photographer was embedded within a particularly troubling sexual discourse, a cultural logic sexualized primarily according to a racist paradigm of white supremacism. As a white woman, Johnston was able to scrutinize African American bodies because, according to the logics of white supremacist lynching, a white woman's sexual desire for a black man (or woman) was posed as unimaginable. While the white woman's sexual desire itself was marked as a disruptive perversion of "natural" white womanhood in turn-of-the-century U.S. culture, her willing alliance with an African American man could be attributed only to the perversity and moral depravity of her doubly unnatural white womanhood. Indeed, a patriarchal white discourse of lynching erased this "anomaly" by representing a white woman's alliance with an African American man as the result of a single destructive force, namely, black male aggression.[43] Given the racist mythologies specific to this era, the potentially gendered or sexualized nature of Johnston's gaze cannot be separated from her racialized position as a white woman in an increasingly white supremacist nation. Her role as subject, gazing upon nameless African American bodies, is a position privileged not in terms of gender but in those of race. As an Anglo-Saxon woman, Johnston represented the very lifeblood, the potential reproduction, not only of the Anglo-Saxon race but also of the "American character" delineated by white supremacists and eugenicists in the United States. Her inability to represent an exchange of looks or glances between herself and Hampton students not only construes her images as the "natural" documents of an unobtrusive assessment but also points to the social distance maintained between Johnston and her photographic subjects. As photographer, and as white woman, Johnston has not "mixed" with her subjects; her photographs remain "objective" and her (white, female) person remains "pure."[44]

The Hampton photographs attest to the social progress of African Americans in several different registers. A set of six family portraits comprise a before-and-after series that demonstrates the upward class mobility of Hampton graduates. Run-down shacks turn into sparkling white mansions through the Hampton metamorphosis depicted by

Johnston. Representing the middle-class success of Hampton's graduates, these photographs ideologically frame Johnston's images of classroom activities, setting the terms—modern, mechanical, and economic—in which the achievements of the Hampton Institute's program of rigorous discipline and manual training are to be measured. Inside this frame of upward economic mobility, photographs of classroom activities depict students mastering geography, arithmetic, sewing, welding, agriculture, and a remarkable focus and self-discipline, as well as the explicit codes of an American identity. I am particularly interested here in the images that illustrate Hampton students engaging in American rituals, as these images begin to formulate one version of the "American Negro" at this time. Taken as a whole, Johnston's photographs would seem to propose that much of the progress made by African Americans after the Civil War was rooted in the process of Americanization itself.

Unlike Brady's "Illustrious Americans," Johnston's photographs of African American Hampton students do not single out famous individuals but, instead, depict anonymous groups of African American schoolchildren and young adult students simply as Americans.[45] Further, Johnston does not necessarily assume the American identity of her subjects, as Brady does, and she is at pains to demonstrate the American character of Hampton students to the later viewers of her photographs. While Brady may have been eager to specify the exemplary characteristics of his model Americans, Johnston worked hard simply to delineate the American character of Hampton students. In a political climate increasingly dominated by eugenicist white nationalists, Johnston had to establish the American identity of her African American subjects for the resistant portion of her white audience.

In several of her most salient photographs, Johnston represents African American students, even the very young, as preeminently patriotic. The image titled "Saluting the Flag at the Whittier Primary School" is almost impossible to read as anything other than a performance of national pride (fig. 1).[46] In this photograph the young students are packed so tightly into a square formation that it is very difficult to distinguish their individual characteristics; they are presented as one entity, performing one act. Thus, the image appears to be less about Whittier students than it is about the act they are performing, namely, "saluting the flag." A guiding adult presence is difficult to discern in the photograph, making the image read as the documentation of a self-compelled performance on the part of these African American children. With its visual emphasis on a patriotic performance that appears to be self-directed, this photograph subtly forwards a vision of assimilation that contests scientific definitions of racial difference and national character at the turn of the century. If eugenicists believed in biologically distinct races, and in national characteristics specific and exclusive to each race, then this image presents American patriotism as one of the natural dispositions of young African American students. In other words, Johnston's image naturalizes the *performance* of national identity. It highlights performance in order to demonstrate the "nature" of an essentialized national character, if not of an essentialized racial identity.[47] With this image Johnston would seem to cleave American national character from an essentialized Anglo-Saxon identity, countering eugenicists' coterminous delineation of nation and race with a potentially multiracial nation.

Figure 1. Frances Benjamin Johnston, "Saluting the Flag at the Whittier Primary School" (1899). Reproduced from the collections of the Library of Congress.

In another image taken at the primary school, "Thanksgiving Day Lesson at the Whittier," several young students construct a log cabin as their classmates watch conscientiously (fig. 2). Despite the rather exaggerated attention of the seated classmates, it is clear that the set for this photograph has been constructed to privilege exclusively the gaze of the viewer. The ring of students around the table opens up on the side closest to the photographic plane, allowing the photographer and later viewers to observe the activity with ease. The view of the children on the far side of the room (farthest away from the camera) is almost surely blocked by the group of students and teachers. The center stage has been shifted away from the students for the benefit of outside viewers. Nevertheless, most of the seated students pretend to watch the scheduled activity with great attention. Their poses are utterly rigid; they sit with hands folded on top of their desks, disciplined into postures of gratitude, as in prayer. The obedient manner of these students in the background, not watched by the teachers in the room, is perhaps a "reassuring" performance conducted for the (white) viewer of the photograph. The official, explicit classroom activity is contextualized by words written on the blackboard: "The Landing of the Pilgrim Fathers." These words literally frame the young builders, and, further, they point to the ideological framework that is being formulated around the performers. These young black children are taught new American histories, and they are given (symbolically) new

Figure 2. Frances Benjamin Johnston, "Thanksgiving Day Lesson at the Whittier" (1899). Reproduced from the collections of the Library of Congress.

"fathers." Whittier students become heirs to a patriarchal national lineage, learning where to anchor an official American identity. Their *national heredity,* if not their *racial origin,* is reinvented as they are taught to forget the boats that brought many of their forebears to North America in chains and relocate their roots on the pilgrim ships.[48] They are being symbolically reborn as Americans of an Anglo-Saxon tradition.

One of the most profoundly disturbing and revealing of Johnston's Hampton photographs is her image titled "Class in American History" (fig. 3). In this photograph, a Native American man, in fully codified ethnic regalia including feather headdress, beaded leather, and braided hair, joins the stuffed American bald eagle behind him as a symbol of the American nation. The photograph functions as a before-meets-after image, in which Native and African American Hampton students observe a Native American from the past. The Native American most explicitly on display is studied as part of American history—as an object, an ancient relic, but not as a subject of that history. The other Native Americans, also on display for the viewer in Johnston's image, are to look on him as part of their American, but not their ancestral past; they are to substitute a national narrative, one now shared with their African American colleagues, for a racialized hereditary bloodline. The Native American students in this image bear no apparent relation to the historic display; like their African American colleagues, they stand in military uni-

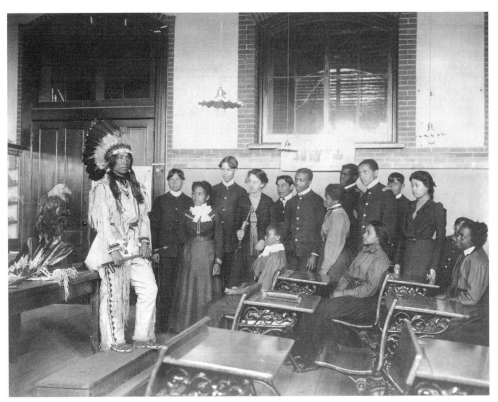

Figure 3. Frances Benjamin Johnston, "Class in American History" (1899). Reproduced from the collections of the Library of Congress.

forms and Victorian dresses, with hair worn short or pulled back in a single knot. In this photograph, racially specific ethnic identities have been erased in a narrative of national belonging. The image constructs a lesson in which "Americans" learn about the past of "Indians."[49]

Circulating in a period of vast immigration in the United States, Johnston's assimilationist images do not anchor national identity in the land of one's ancestors but instead in a specific set of cultural codes. Indeed, if the photographs did root American identity in ancestral land, there would be no need to Americanize Hampton students, whose ancestors had resided in the territories of the twentieth-century United States for hundreds (in the case of African Americans) and thousands (in the case of Native Americans) of years. If land occupation were the measure of national inclusion in Johnston's photographs, her own American identity might prove more tenuous than that of her subjects. Instead, the Hampton photographs forward a narrative of assimilation in which national identity is first untangled from and then reintegrated into the visual codes of racial identity.[50] Johnston's Hampton photographs show students actively engaged in the process of learning national histories and performing national rites. The photographs would seem to separate national character from a racially encoded discourse of blood, marking American identity as a set of performative rituals. However, despite this seeming rupture between an essential and a performative national identity, the rituals of turn-of-the-century Americanness posed in Johnston's photographs are rooted, ultimately, in a history delineated by Anglo-Saxon bloodlines—the blood of the "founding" "Pilgrim fathers." Thus, while Johnston's photographs first de-essentialize the markers of American identity, they then reessentialize those performances by anchoring them in a distinctly Anglo-Saxon lineage. Johnston's images forward the beginnings of Anglo-Saxon heritage on North American soil, celebrating the ethnically specific national identity that was founded with the "landing of the Pilgrim fathers." The unmarked signs of whiteness are visualized through patriotic performances; Anglo-Saxon identity is consolidated in a specific discourse of national American identity. In Johnston's photographs the American character of African American students is measured by the success with which those students can adopt and perform Anglo-Saxon-inspired national rituals. At best, this assimilating erasure of racial identity in favor of a common national character is tenuous and readily recuperated in the terms of racial essentialism. Johnston's Americans are easily reinterpreted in the separate-but-equal terms of turn-of-the-century segregation.

CONSERVING RACE IN THE NATION

While Johnston's photographs of the Hampton Institute forward a narrative of assimilation, tenuously erasing racial difference under the signs of a national identity, W. E. B. Du Bois's photograph albums recuperate a sense of racial autonomy and self-determination. The photograph albums that I discuss here constitute one of three displays supervised by Du Bois for the American Negro exhibit at the Paris Exposition of 1900. In addition to the albums, other exhibits included a series of charts and graphs documenting the social and economic progress of African Americans, and a three-volume set containing the complete legal history of African Americans in Georgia.[51] As the photographers who produced the images for Du Bois's albums remain unidentified, the focus of authorship is transferred to Du Bois himself, the person most conspicuously associated with the albums, as collector, organizer, and presenter of the images. Thus, while he may not have produced the photographs for his albums, this essay poses Du Bois as the archivist who framed the images both materially and ideologically.

Du Bois's photograph albums, titled *Types of American Negroes, Georgia, U.S.A.* (vol. 1–3) and *Negro Life in Georgia, U.S.A.* (vol. 1), include formal studio portraits of African Americans as well as informal snapshots of groups outdoors, children playing, people working, homes and business establishments, and interior views of elaborately decorated middle-class parlors. Unlike Johnston's formal photographs, Du Bois's snapshots convey a sense of spontaneity and immediacy. The subjects and scenes of these images are diverse, and many of the photographs suggest an interaction between unnamed photographers and subjects, through the variously questioning, surprised, laughing, and smiling faces that greet later viewers. Signifying in the context of Johnston's professional group portraits, the snapshots collected in Du Bois's albums may have functioned in ways similar to those images preserved in African American family archives throughout the twentieth century, as described by bell hooks:

Photographs taken in everyday life, snapshots in particular, rebelled against all of those photographic practices that reinscribed colonial ways of looking and capturing the images of the black "other." Shot spontaneously, without any notion of remaking black bodies in the image of whiteness, snapshots posed a challenge to black viewers. Unlike photographs constructed so that black images would appear as the embodiment of colonizing fantasies, these snapshots gave us a way to see ourselves, a sense of how we looked when we were not "wearing the mask," when we were not attempting to perfect the image for a white supremacist gaze.[52]

Hooks's sense of snapshots "rebelling" against institutionalized racist representations is important to bring to a reading of the images collected in Du Bois's albums, as he proposed that many of his images of "typical Negro faces" "hardly square with conventional American ideas."[53] However, while the spontaneity of the snapshot may have enabled a form of African American self-imaging outside the dominant domain of racist representation, it is also important to remember that Du Bois's snapshots were viewed not only privately but also publicly, by a racially and ethnically mixed international audience. Read against Johnston's photographs, and in the context of the American Negro exhibit, Du Bois's images pose a challenge to black *and* white viewers. They are offered up explicitly, self-consciously as images that contest racist "American ideas" and representations, as photographs that ask white viewers to rethink dominant American "conventions."

While the presumed spontaneity and informality of the snapshots Du Bois gathered for his albums may have situated them somehow beyond racist imagery, the more profoundly contestatory images in Du Bois's albums are those that both adopt and subvert turn-of-the-century imaging conventions. The images that differentiate Du Bois's collection from Johnston's work most powerfully are the formal, individual portraits that introduce each volume of *Types of American Negroes*. The portrait series presents individuals posed for two photographs each, one a frontal image, the other a profile or semiprofile image (figs. 4 and 5). Each pair of photographs is presented on a separate page, and the first two volumes of *Types* consist almost entirely of such portraits (there are more than two hundred). Unlike Johnston's group photographs, constructed uncannily around the unnoticed presence of the camera, these images mark their subjects' intentional interaction with the camera, and as the viewer flips through the albums, she is met with the gaze and the likeness of one individual after another. The subjects of these formal portraits engage the gaze of photographer and later viewer, forcing white viewers to recognize what hooks has called a resistant, "oppositional gaze," a gaze that confronts and challenges the privileged position of the white viewer, a gaze that makes that position apparent.[54]

While Johnston's Hampton photographs, framed by before and after images, mark the Hampton Institute's notion of advancement, Du Bois's series of portraits does not produce a narrative of teleological development. In Du Bois's albums there is no explicit activity performed to demonstrate a particular ideology of race progress for later viewers. Further, signs of Americanness are utterly absent from Du Bois's albums. Du Bois assumes the Americanness of his subjects and indicates no need to demonstrate the American character of the "Negroes" of "Georgia, U.S.A." Articulating such a position in "The Conservation of Races," Du Bois delineates the collateral boundaries of "Negro" and American identity as follows: "We are Americans, not only by birth and by citizenship, but

Figure 4. From *Types of American Negroes, Georgia, U.S.A.*, compiled by W. E. B. Du Bois (1900). Reproduced from the collections of the Library of Congress.

Figure 5. From *Types of American Negroes, Georgia, U.S.A.*, compiled by W. E. B. Du Bois (1900). Reproduced from the collections of the Library of Congress.

by our political ideals, our language, our religion. Farther than that, our Americanism does not go. At that point, we are Negroes, members of a vast historic race."[55] The African Americans in Du Bois's albums need not prove their right to be included in an American Negro exhibit; because they are Americans by birth, they need not assimilate. Further, while Du Bois defines the national ties of Americanism in the cultural terms of *political ideals, language,* and *religion,* he also defines racial identity primarily in cultural terms that transcend theories of physical difference founded in blood. Rejecting "the grosser physical differences of color, hair and bone" as the definitive determinants of racial identity, Du Bois identifies "subtle, delicate and elusive" forces as the foundation on which distinct races develop: "While these subtle forces have generally followed the natural cleavage of common blood, descent and physical peculiarities, they have at other times swept across and ignored these."[56] In other words, for Du Bois "race," like "national character," is not an essential property, and it does not always follow the reproduction of a single bloodline.

Given Du Bois's assertions regarding the inessential nature of racial identity, it is disturbing the way in which the title of his albums—Types *of American Negroes*—echoes the terms of turn-of-the-century scientific "race" taxonomies.[57] Even the repetition of poses and props evident in his collection of portraits marks a consistency in formal representation roughly congruent with the mathematical evenness of scientific photographic archives that sought to map the racially codified body of ethnic Others. Further, the very style in which Du Bois's portraits are made and presented, the combination of frontal and semiprofile poses, marks a striking formal parallel to the photographs Galton hoped parents would collect of their children in *The Life History Album*: "An exact full-face and a profile should be obtained" (5). As noted previously, Galton's *Album* was designed to document the maturation of a single child by creating a standardized archive of images of the child. The archive allowed a reader to compare later documents to earlier documents, and to measure change, valued in terms of "growth" or "progress," by way of apparent physical alteration over time. While Galton's albums set up a comparison of various representations of a single individual, Du Bois's albums structurally invite a comparison of one individual to another. Like Galton, Du Bois keeps the terms of his archive consistent: Du Bois's images adhere to a singular format that limits the factors of difference to the individuals photographed. Assembled as they are, individuals posed in parallel, Du Bois's portraits encourage viewers to read one image against the next, comparing the aspect of one individual to another. What one finds after a comparative scrutiny of the individuals represented in Du Bois's albums is a vast diversity in the physical characteristics generally held to determine racial identity at the turn of the century. In Du Bois's albums, blond and blue-eyed "Negroes" take their place beside brunette and brown-eyed "Negroes."

Reproducing the variations of "color, hair and bone" that were legally encompassed by "one drop of blood" identity laws at the turn of the century,[58] Du Bois's albums confront white America's obsession with the color line in two ways. First, the albums dismantle the stereotyped and caricatured images of African Americans reproduced in American popular culture. To that end, Du Bois's portraits construct a kind of composite image in reverse. Instead of blending individual portraits or likenesses into a single, abstract "type," Du Bois's albums undo the notion of a unifying image, filtering difference back into the picture, decomposing the "American Negro" into diverse, multiple "Negro Types." Second, the albums point toward the dual nature of "colonial desire," the white supremacist's simultaneous repulsion from and fascination with interracial reproduction.[59] Du Bois's albums of "types" reproduce the biracial subjects of the unions so powerfully repressed by lynching and antimiscegenation laws, challenging the very social dictates that forbade Frances Benjamin Johnston's black male subjects to return her gaze.[60] The portraits dispute the notion of racial purity upheld by eugenicists and white supremacists, and the antimiscegenation laws that prohibited legal, mutually desired unions between whites and blacks, but not the rape of African American women by white men.[61] Looking back at the images of African American men, women, and children procured by Du Bois, this essay hopes to participate in his antiracist project by transforming the trajectory laid out for the white woman scholar, namely, the position culturally delimited for Frances Benjamin Johnston at the turn of the century. To that end, I suggest that Du Bois's images do not purport to represent "real" blackness, to invite white (or black) viewers of the early or late twentieth century to gaze upon blackness revealed. Du Bois's images do not lift "the Veil" that distorts images of African Americans by projecting them through a lens of colonial desire.[62] Instead, the photographs begin to enable white viewers to see the Veil itself, to see the cultural logics and privileged practices that reproduce racism. Consequently, it is toward an investigation of the visual structures of white supremacy, and of resistance to those forms, that I have directed my reading of Du Bois's images, situating the photographs in the context of the visual legacies produced by the converging discourses of eugenics and white supremacist nationalism at the turn of the century.

Du Bois's photographs signify somewhere between the images collected in scientific archives of race at the turn of the century and Mathew Brady's earlier portraits of Illustrious Americans. Formally similar to Galton's frontal and profile portraits standardized to meet the needs of scientists, Du Bois's albums of "types" present a kind of evidence but not proof of the essential, physical racial identity sought by eugenicists and white supremacists. If in style and even title Du Bois's albums evoke a history of racist photographic documentation, they do so only to undercut that scientific register of naked, dehumanized bodies with formal portraits of African Americans elegantly dressed in middle-class trappings. Further, Du Bois's profile and semiprofile portraits formally approximate not only Galton's scientific photographs but also Brady's celebratory images. Many of Du Bois's near-profile portraits represent individuals posed not at exact right angles but, instead, positioned like Brady's subjects, in a three-quarter turn, with eyes directed slightly upward out of the photographic frame, perhaps focused on political ideals. Unlike Brady's model portraits, however, Du Bois's pairs enact both the visual tropes of illustriousness and those of engagement and recognition. Within the codes of late-nineteenth-century U.S. visual culture, Du Bois's portraits represent African Americans as both illustrious Americans contemplating shared ideals, and as distinct individuals. Du Bois's frontal portraits meet and engage the eyes of later viewers, individualizing and particularizing American identity, placing a lofty American character squarely back on the terrain of negotiation, conflict, and "race."

While Du Bois's "American Negroes" are Americans both legally and philosophically, their fundamental identity remains racial within the nation. Du Bois's albums contest a program of assimilation by portraying not the "American Negro" but the "Negroes" of America. Du Bois subtly challenges the exclusive authority of white Americans—assimilationists and eugenicists alike—to represent, signify, and embody the boundaries of national identity. Unlike Galton's racially essentialized notion of American character, Du Bois's sense of national identity is cultural, philosophical, and legal. Yet while Du Bois's version of American character corresponds to a set of ideals, his vision of national identity, unlike Brady's, does not erase or conceal racial identity. Unlike Johnston's assimilationist images, Du Bois's photographs do not harness patriotic performance to a single racialized bloodline. In the power-laden struggles to define *nation, race,* and *America* at the turn of the century, W. E. B. Du Bois envisions a nation of multiracial Americans.

EPILOGUE: NATION AND RACE IN THE VISUAL CULTURE OF THE 1990S

Attempts to represent, define, and codify racial and national identities, as well to determine where and when those constructs converge, intersect, and remain distinct, certainly did not end with the American Negro exhibit of the 1900 Paris Exposition. Indeed, the terms with which Frances Benjamin Johnston and W. E. B. Du Bois wrestled as they attempted to envision a place for African Americans in a white-dominated American nation remain entrenched in U.S. culture today. As the recent popularity of *The Bell Curve* indicates, many members of this contemporary "imagined community" are still intrigued by the idea of essential racial attributes, and specifically by the notion of "hereditary genius," as defined by Francis Galton more than a hundred years ago.[63] Further, as debates concerning multiculturalism demonstrate, the United States still has not come to terms with what it might mean to be a multiethnic and multiracial nation. And finally, as a relatively recent special issue of *Time* magazine, titled "The New Face of America: How Immigrants Are Shaping the World's First Multicultural Society," makes clear, the United States is an imagined community still fascinated with what racial and national identities might look like.[64]

Both the abstract images of racial "types" and the narratives of biological reproduction that Francis Galton sought to represent with his composite portraits and family albums have resurfaced in a computer morphing program designed by *Time* imaging specialist Kin Wah Lam (fig. 6). Using the Gryphon software package Morph 2.0, Lam created an interracial reproduction grid that aimed to entertain viewers with visions of biracial progeny. To make this grid, Lam began with fourteen images of models, seven men and seven women, representing a curious mix of racial, ethnic, national, and regional groups: Middle Eastern, Italian, African, Vietnamese, Anglo-Saxon, Chinese, and Hispanic. Lam then paired these seven types together in fifty-fifty ratios, producing a pattern that purports to predict the physical features that would be inherited by the offspring of interracial reproductions. In a sense, Lam's computer graphics program begins where Galton's composite photographic portraiture ended, by envisioning distinct racial "types" to then project the representation of race in a direction Galton himself did not want to proceed, namely toward mixture.

Time's visual grid works on the assumptions that racial "types" can be measured and itemized mathematically, divided into fractions, and combined with other racial compo-

Figure 6. *Time* cover illustration, by Kin Wah Lam for *Time* 142, no. 21 (special issue, "The New Face of America," Fall 1993). Copyright 1993 TIME Inc. Reprinted with permission.

nents. These assumptions become even more salient in Lam's creation of a "new Eve" designed to represent "the future, multiethnic face of America" (2). The new "ideal" image that emerges from Lam's calculations and combinations, this new Eve, is "15% Anglo-Saxon, 17.5% Middle Eastern, 17.5% African, 7.5% Asian, 35% Southern European and 7.5% Hispanic" (2). The new Eve is part this and part that, but she is always the sum of statistically equivalent pieces. Thus, while racial and ethnic groups may mix in a multicultural American nation at the turn of a new century, one can see that the "type"remains (at least ideologically) discrete. In other words, a code of visual distinctions remains intact, if ever more meticulously codified, even as racial mixture is imagined. In short, multicultural identity is configured as the sum of "separate but equal" parts.

While *Time*'s grid attempts to plot the physical characteristics of imagined interracial offspring, it is framed by other articles that demonstrate that the United States is still an ideologically white-dominated nation fascinated, and yet concerned, like Galton, by the "coloring" of America. In the editorial that inaugurates this special issue, titled "America's Immigrant Challenge," the editors assert that "the U.S. before long will have to redefine just who its minorities are" (3), predicting that African Americans will soon be outnumbered by Latinos in the United States. Further, according to the editors, and "even more startling," "sometime during the second half of the 21st century the descendants of white Europeans, the arbiters of the core national culture for most of its existence, are likely to slip into minority status" (5). Quoting Martha Farnsworth Riche, the director of policy studies at Washington's Population Reference Bureau, the editors note: "We have left the time when the nonwhite, non-Western part of our population could be expected to assimilate to the dominant majority. In the future, the white, Western majority will have to do some assimilation of its own" (5). In *Time*'s multicultural issue, the "origins" of an American nation delineated by an image of Anglo-Saxon whiteness are mourned, as Anglo-Saxon identity becomes one racial and ethnic statistic among many. In their new Eve, the editors of *Time* see a present and future in which the conflation of "American" with "Anglo-Saxon" may be contested. With the new Eve they imagine a new racial origin story for America, a legacy no longer founded by Pilgrim fathers. However, while this image seems to problematize the dominance of Anglo-Saxon inheritance in the demarcation of American identity, we must remember that *Time*'s "new Eve" remains the latest apparition of a national imagination obsessed with visually representing racial identities defined according to bloodlines. As we face the turn of another century, we must see that the image of the new Eve does not reproduce the racial legacy from which it was made.

NOTES

I would like to thank Phel Steinmetz, Michael Davidson, Roddey Reid, Nicole Tonkovich, Wai Chee Dimock, Eric Breitbart, Molly Rhodes, and Carolyn Haynes for the comments and encouragement they offered while I was working on earlier versions of this argument, and Lisa Bloom and Joe Masco for their careful suggestions during the final revisions.

1. W. E. B. Du Bois, "The Conservation of Races," in *Writings* (New York: Literary Classics, 1986), 821.

2. In *The Souls of Black Folk*, published in 1903, Du Bois asserts that "double consciousness," the "twoness" of living as both a "Negro" and as an "American" (8), is central to "the strange meaning of

being black" (3) in the United States at the dawn of the twentieth century. W. E. B. Du Bois, *The Souls of Black Folk* (New York: Vintage, 1986, 1990).

3. Studies of the nation that focus on the printed word generally follow the influential work of Benedict Anderson. Benedict Anderson, *Imagined Communities: Reflections on the Origin and Spread of Nationalism* (London: Verso, 1983).

4. Vicente Rafael has begun the important task of investigating the role photography played in nation building. See Vicente Rafael, "Nationalism, Imagery and the Filipino Intelligentsia in the Nineteenth Century," *Critical Inquiry* 16:3 (Spring 1990): 591–611; and "White Love: Surveillance and Nationalist Resistance in the U.S. Colonization of the Philippines," in *Cultures of United States Imperialism*, ed. Amy Kaplan and Donald Pease (Durham, N.C.: Duke University Press, 1993) 185–218.

5. See the section titled "The Negro Building" in the *Report of the Board of Commissioners Representing the State of New York at the Cotton States and International Exposition Held at Atlanta, Georgia, 1895* (Albany: Wynkoop Hallenbeck Crawford, 1896), 197–99. This text also reproduces Booker T. Washington's famous "Atlanta Compromise" speech delivered at the opening ceremonies of the Atlanta exposition.

6. For discussions of racism at the Chicago World's Columbian Exposition of 1893, see Hazel Carby, "'Woman's Era': Rethinking Black Feminist Theory," in *Reconstructing Womanhood: The Emergence of the Afro-American Woman Novelist* (New York: Oxford University Press, 1987), 3–19; and Robert W. Rydell, "The Chicago World's Columbian Exposition of 1893: 'And Was Jerusalem Builded Here?'" in *All the World's a Fair: Visions of Empire at American International Expositions, 1876–1916* (Chicago: University of Chicago Press, 1984), 38–71.

The exclusion of African Americans from official participation in the fair was protested by both Ida B. Wells and Frederick Douglass. See Ida B. Wells, *The Reason Why: The Colored American Is Not in the World's Columbian Exposition* (Chicago: Ida B. Wells, 1893).

7. W. E. B. Du Bois, "The American Negro at Paris," *American Monthly Review of Reviews* 22:5 (November 1900): 576.

8. The success of the exhibit is reported by Morris Lewis in "Paris and the International Exposition," *Colored American Magazine* 1:5 (October 1900): 295.

9. Du Bois, "The American Negro at Paris," 575.

10. For studies of the extended impact that eugenics had on late-nineteenth and early-twentieth-century U.S. culture, see Richard Hofstadter, *Social Darwinism in American Thought,* rev. ed. (Boston: Beacon, 1944), especially 161–67; Daniel J. Kevles, *In the Name of Eugenics: Genetics and the Uses of Human Heredity* (New York: Knopf, 1985); Donald K. Pickens, *Eugenics and the Progressives* (Nashville: Vanderbilt University Press, 1968).

For a discussion of various forms of white racism in the United States throughout the nineteenth century see George M. Fredrickson, *The Black Image in the White Mind: The Debate on Afro-American Character and Destiny, 1817–1914* (New York: Harper and Row, 1971).

11. "Biological racialism" is the category Kwame Anthony Appiah uses in order to describe the various sciences of "race" that developed over the course of the second half of the nineteenth century. See Kwame Anthony Appiah, "Race," in *Critical Terms for Literary Study,* ed. Frank Lentricchia and Thomas McLaughlin (Chicago: University of Chicago Press, 1990), 274–87.

12. Anderson, *Imagined Communities.*

13. Francis Galton, *Hereditary Genius: An Inquiry into Its Laws and Consequences* (London: Macmillan, 1892); *Inquiries into Human Faculty and Its Development* (London: J. M. Dent and Sons, 1907; London: Macmillan, 1883); *Memories of My Life* (London: Methuen, 1908); *Natural Inheritance* (London: Macmillan, 1889).

14. Fatimah Tobing Rony describes such exhibits in her fascinating essay on anthropology and early

ethnographic film, "Those Who Squat and Those Who Sit: The Iconography of Race in the 1895 Films of Felix-Louis Regnault," *Camera Obscura* 28 (January 1992): 262–89. Robert W. Rydell uses the image of a "sliding scale of humanity" to describe the racialized spatial logics that organized "ethnic" displays at the World's Columbian Exposition of 1893. See "The Chicago World's Columbian Exposition of 1893," especially 64–65.

15. Thomas J. Schlereth, "The Material Universe of American World Expositions, 1876–1915," in *Cultural History and Material Culture: Everyday Life, Landscapes, Museums* (Ann Arbor: University of Michigan Press, 1990), 284–85. See also Rydell, "The Chicago World's Columbian Exposition of 1893."

16. Alan Trachtenberg, "Illustrious Americans," in *Reading American Photographs: Images as History, Mathew Brady to Walker Evans* (New York: Hill and Wang, 1989), 38.

17. According to Walter Benjamin, the photograph does not lose what he sees as a negative, "parasitic" dependency on "aura," a spiritualized notion of art tied to the cult of the original masterpiece, until the portrait ceases to dominate the potentially revolutionary medium of mechanical reproduction. According to Benjamin, Eugene Atget was the first to produce photographs that were not sentimentalized documents but, instead, pieces of "evidence." Walter Benjamin, "The Work of Art in the Age of Mechanical Reproduction," in *Illuminations,* ed. Hannah Arendt (New York: Schocken, 1969), 217–52.

I regard such distinctions between the "auratic" and the "evidential" photograph as chiefly the result of the discursive contexts in which images are viewed and consumed. I certainly do not mean to claim that Johnston's or Du Bois's images were more "objective" than any other images, but simply to underscore that these images were imbedded in new discursive contexts, new institutional paradigms that sought to claim the photograph as objective evidence for social science.

The notion of the objectivity of the photograph and photographic processes has been thoroughly critiqued by photography scholars. For a review of these critiques, see *Thinking Photography,* ed. Victor Burgin (London: Macmillan, 1982), especially Allan Sekula's "On the Invention of Photographic Meaning" (84–109), and John Tagg's "The Currency of the Photograph" (110–41). See also *The Contest of Meaning: Critical Histories of Photography,* ed. Richard Bolton (Cambridge: MIT Press, 1989); Martha Rosler, "In, Around, and Afterthoughts (on Documentary Photography)," in *Martha Rosler, 3 Works* (Halifax: Nova Scotia College of Art and Design, 1981); Allan Sekula, *Photography against the Grain: Essays and Photo Works, 1973–1983* (Halifax: Nova Scotia College of Art and Design, 1984); John Tagg, *The Burden of Representation: Essays on Photographies and Histories* (Amherst: University of Massachusetts Press, 1988).

18. For an analysis of the ways in which Lewis Hine and Jacob Riis were posed as the "fathers" of documentary photography in the United States by photography historians working in the 1940s, see Sally Stein's essay "Making Connections with the Camera: Photography and Social Mobility in the Career of Jacob Riis," *Afterimage* 10:10 (May 1983): 9–16. First detailing how many historians have conflated the work of Hine and Riis, Stein then goes on to analyze important political and aesthetic differences in the work of these two men. For more on the invention of documentary photography see Alan Trachtenberg, "Camera Work/Social Work," in *Reading American Photographs,* 164–230. For more on the work of Lewis Hine and Jacob Riis, see Verna Posever Curtis and Stanley Mallach, *Photography and Reform: Lewis Hine and the National Child Labor Committee* (Milwaukee: Milwaukee Art Museum, 1984); Judith Mara Gutman, *Lewis W. Hine and the American Social Conscience* (New York: Walker, 1967); Jacob Riis, *How the Other Half Lives* (1890) (New York: Dover, 1971).

19. Booker T. Washington, Hampton's most famous graduate and founder of Tuskegee, has come to be regarded as one of the most important advocates of manual training for African Americans at the turn of the century. Washington argued that manual training and strict self-discipline would provide economic independence for African Americans, a resource he viewed as more important than political power. Washington advocated slow, gradual economic and social advancement for African Americans,

arguing that manual, as opposed to professional, white-collar labor, was a necessary first stage in "the natural law of evolution" (202) for any race: "In a word, we have got to pay the price for everything we get, the price that every civilized race or nation has paid for its position, that of beginning naturally, gradually, at the bottom and working up towards the highest civilization" (202). See Booker T. Washington, "The Storm before the Calm," *Colored American Magazine* 1:4 (September 1900): 3, 200–213; "Industrial Education: Will It Solve the Negro Problem?" *Colored American Magazine* 7:2 (February 1904): 87–92; *The Successful Training of the Negro* (New York: Doubleday, 1903); and *Up from Slavery* (New York: Penguin, 1986; Doubleday, Page, 1901).

For counterarguments to an educational system focused exclusively on manual labor, see Du Bois, *The Souls of Black Folk*; and his "The Training of Negroes for Social Power," *Colored American Magazine* 7:5 (May 1904): 333–39.

20. Du Bois, "The American Negro at Paris," 577.

21. This is how James Guimond describes Johnston's photographs at the Paris Exposition of 1900. I am suggesting that the entire exhibit may have communicated this sense of moral and political reprieve or reconciliation to white viewers. James Guimond, "Frances Johnston's *Hampton Album*: A White Dream for Black People," in *American Photography and the American Dream* (Chapel Hill: University of North Carolina Press, 1991), 39.

22. For a fascinating study of photographic "archives" and the body as constituted by its imagined place within (or outside of) those archives, see Allan Sekula, "The Body and the Archive," *October* 39 (Winter 1986): 3–64.

23. Francis Galton, appendix A, "Composite Portraiture," in *Inquiries,* 221–41.

24. Ibid., 222.

25. Ibid., 10.

26. Francis Galton, *The Life History Album* (London: Macmillan, 1884); and *Record of Family Faculties* (London: Macmillan, 1884).

27. Galton, *The Life History Album,* 5.

28. For more on Brady's Illustrious Americans, as well as a history of the celebrity photographic portrait in nineteenth-century U.S. culture, see Barbara McCandless, "The Portrait Studio and the Celebrity: Promoting the Art," in *Photography in Nineteenth-Century America,* ed. Martha A. Sandweiss (Fort Worth, Tex.: Amon Carter Museum, 1991), 48–75.

29. Alan Trachtenberg describes the formal style of Brady's daguerreotype portraits in relation to a tradition of Roman sculpture in "Illustrious Americans," 46.

30. Ibid., 50, 51.

31. Ibid., 50.

32. Du Bois, "The American Negro at Paris," 577.

33. Frances Benjamin Johnston, *The Hampton Album,* ed. Lincoln Kirstein (New York: Museum of Modern Art, 1966). For more background information see also James Guimond, "Frances Johnston's *Hampton Album*"; and Laura Wexler, "Black and White and Color: American Photographs at the Turn of the Century," *Prospects* 13 (Winter 1988): 341–90.

34. Laura Mulvey, "Visual Pleasure and Narrative Cinema," in *Art after Modernism,* ed. Brian Wallis (New York: Museum of Contemporary Art, 1984), 360–74.

35. In a piece titled "Afterthoughts on 'Visual Pleasure and Narrative Cinema' Inspired by *Duel in the Sun*," Mulvey explains a woman's pleasure in the scopophilic process of film viewing as the result of a kind of "transvestism" through which the female viewer adopts a masculine viewing position. The film Mulvey reads in order to come to this conclusion, *Duel in the Sun,* follows the life course of a mixed-blood female protagonist who is exoticized, feared, and desired primarily in the terms of a racialized identity. Mulvey's analysis of transvestism fails to account for the power of racialized identities and

racialized identifications in this film, and it is into this interpretive space that my own reading of Johnston's photographs enters a history of visual theory. I read Johnston's work, and her position as photographer, not only through the terms of gender, but also through the terms of race posed at the turn of the century in the United States. Laura Mulvey, "Afterthoughts on 'Visual Pleasure and Narrative Cinema' Inspired by *Duel in the Sun*," in *Feminism and Film Theory*, ed. Constance Penley (New York: Museum of Contemporary Art, 1984), 360–74.

36. bell hooks, "The Oppositional Gaze: Black Female Spectators," in *Black Looks: Race and Representation* (Boston: South End Press, 1992) 115–31; Jacqueline Bobo, *Black Women as Cultural Readers* (New York: Columbia University Press, 1995); Jane Gaines, "White Privilege and Looking Relations: Race and Gender in Feminist Film Theory," *Screen* 29:4 (Autumn 1988): 12–27; Richard Dyer, "White," *Screen* 29:4 (Autumn 1988): 44–64; Manthia Diawara, "Black Spectatorship: Problems of Identification and Resistance," in *Black American Cinema*, ed. Manthia Diawara (New York: Routledge, 1993), 211–20; Isaac Julien and Kobena Mercer, "Introduction: De Margin and De Centre," *Screen* 29:4 (Autumn 1988): 2–10; Mary Ann Doane, "Dark Continents: Epistemologies of Racial and Sexual Difference in Psychoanalysis and the Cinema," in *Femmes Fatales: Feminism, Film Theory, Psychoanalysis* (New York: Routledge, 1991), 209–48.

Discussing the "characteristic aesthetic and political problems of postmodernism" in their "Introduction," Isaac Julien and Kobena Mercer note: "It is ironic that while some of the loudest voices offering commentary have announced nothing less than the 'end of representation' or the 'end of history,' the political possibility of the *end of ethnocentrism* has not been seized upon as a suitably exciting topic for description or inquiry" (2). Julien and Mercer call for critical theorists of visual culture to "recognize and reckon with the kinds of complexity inherent in the culturally constructed nature of ethnic identities," and they assess the "implications" such complexity "has for the analysis of representational practices" (3).

37. bell hooks, "In Our Glory: Photography and Black Life," in *Picturing Us: African American Identity in Photography*, ed. Deborah Willis (New York: New Press, 1994), 50.

38. Trinh T. Minh-ha, *Woman, Native, Other: Writing Postcoloniality and Feminism* (Bloomington: Indiana University Press, 1989). Coco Fusco, *English Is Broken Here: Notes on Cultural Fusion in the Americas* (New York: New Press, 1995); Timothy Mitchell, *Colonizing Egypt* (Berkeley: University of California Press, 1988); Mary Louise Pratt, *Imperial Eyes: Travel Writing and Transculturation* (New York: Routledge, 1992); Deborah Willis, "Introduction: Picturing Us," in *Picturing Us*, 3–26.

I find hooks's "white supremacist gaze" useful as a means of making explicit the ways in which the cultural privilege of looking has been racially coded in the United States. Playing on Richard Dyer's notion that "white" generally functions as an invisible cultural category, while as Mercer and Isaac note, the "colored" is made all too visible (6), I would claim that "white" is rarely the object of the Western gaze because it is almost always behind (not in front of) that gaze, imbedded in the viewing position, structuring the reception and the evaluation of Other bodies represented.

39. In my analysis of Johnston's racially encoded viewing privilege, I have tried to follow the lines of analysis suggested by Mary Ann Doane in her individual response for the Spectatrix special issue of *Camera Obscura*: "Consideration of race ought to transform the entire framework of the questions posed to the media rather than simply initiating an extension of existing feminist categories (such as the female spectator) to include other, neglected differences. Racial difference and sexual difference are not parallel modes of differentiation that are equally accessible to the same theoretical apparatus. Neither are they totally unrelated: there is a densely intricate history of relations between the two which requires analysis. What is needed is a theorization of the relation between racial and sexual differences, particularly with respect to questions of visibility and invisibility, power and sexuality" (146). Mary Ann Doane, *Camera Obscura* 20, 21 (May-September 1989): 142–46.

According to bell hooks, such a space is opened up by the critical black female spectator: "Black female spectators, who refused to identify with white womanhood, who would not take on the phallocentric gaze of desire and possession, created a critical space where the binary opposition Mulvey posits of 'woman as image, man as bearer of the look' was continually deconstructed" ("The Oppositional Gaze," 122, 123).

In my reading of Johnston's position as photographer/viewer I am trying to tease out the "densely intricate" relations posed between race and gender at that time. I am trying to read Johnston's position as one inscribed by a racial hierarchy of access to the gaze, not simply by a heterosexual, binary gender hierarchy.

40. Vron Ware, *Beyond the Pale: White Women, Racism, and History* (London: Verso, 1992), 182. Bell hooks also discusses this powerful cultural prohibition against the African American gaze in her analysis of an oppositional gaze, specifically the critical gaze of the African American female spectator who interrogates filmic representation in order to protest the negation of African American women in Hollywood films ("The Oppositional Gaze"). Jane Gaines also notes that there is a need for work that analyzes "the social prohibitions against the black man's sexual glance" (21), in order to demonstrate the ways in which "racial difference structures a hierarchy of access to the female image" (17) ("White Privilege and Looking Relations").

41. Lynching, legally defined as murder committed by a mob of three or more persons, increased dramatically in the 1890s. See Fredrickson, *The Black Image in the White Mind*; and Paula Giddings, *When and Where I Enter: The Impact of Black Women on Race and Sex in America* (New York: William Morrow, 1984), 18.

For further analyses of the racialized and sexualized nature of lynching at the turn of the century as well as the economic factors that fueled such actions, see Bettina Aptheker, *Woman's Legacy: Essays on Race, Sex, and Class in American History* (Amherst: University of Massachusetts Press, 1982); Hazel Carby, "'On the Threshold of Woman's Era': Lynching, Empire and Sexuality in Black Feminist Theory," in *"Race," Writing, and Difference,* ed. Henry Louis Gates Jr. (Chicago: University of Chicago Press, 1985, 1986), 301–16, and *Reconstructing Womanhood*; Frederick Douglass, "Why Is the Negro Lynched?" *A.M.E. Church Review* (Bridgewater, Mass.: J. Whitby and Sons, 1895), 1–38; Ida B. Wells, *Crusade for Justice: The Autobiography of Ida B. Wells,* ed. Alfreda M. Duster (Chicago: University of Chicago Press, 1970), and "Southern Horrors: Lynch Law in All Its Phases," in *Selected Works of Ida B. Wells-Barnett* (New York: Oxford University Press, 1991) 14–45.

42. Ida B. Wells, "Southern Horrors," in *Selected Works;* Anna Julia Cooper, *A Voice from the South* (New York: Negro Universities Press, 1969). Cooper's *A Voice* was originally published in 1892.

43. According to Karen Sanchez-Eppler, in the discourse of lynching, the white wife's or white daughter's desire for a black man must become the unimaginable in order to ensure the perpetuation of the white patriarch's cultural privilege. See "Bodily Bonds: The Intersecting Rhetorics of Feminism and Abolition," *Representations* 24 (Fall 1988): 28–59.

44. My discussion of Johnston's relative social privilege in relation to African American students at Hampton is not meant to suggest that her visual mastery of African American bodies was not itself subject to a more comprehensive white male social prerogative. Indeed, the discourse and practice of lynching worked to protect the interests of the white male body and the reproduction of a patriarchal white bloodline. See also Ware, *Beyond the Pale.*

45. I wish to distinguish both the aim and the signifying context of Johnston's Hampton photographs from Brady's earlier portraits of Illustrious Americans. However, the terms of these distinctions might become much subtler if one were to compare Johnston's presidential portraits to those of Brady's. In addition to her extensive work photographing the Hampton and Tuskegee Institutes, Johnston also ran a successful portrait business, and she established herself as a kind of court photographer for several presidents, including Theodore Roosevelt. For biographical information on Johnston, see Pete Daniel

and Raymond Smock, *A Talent for Detail: The Photographs of Miss Frances Benjamin Johnston, 1889–1910* (New York: Harmony, 1974); Olaf Hansen, "Johnston, Frances Benjamin," in *Notable American Women: A Biographical Dictionary,* vol. 4, ed. Barbara Sicherman, et al. (Cambridge: Belknap, Harvard University Press, 1980), 381–83.

46. Whittier was the primary school affiliated with the Hampton Institute.

According to Eric Hobsbawm, "the educational system was transformed into a machine for political socialization by such devices as the worship of the American flag, which as a daily ritual in the country's schools, spread from the 1880s onward" (280). Eric Hobsbawm, "Mass-Producing Traditions: Europe, 1870–1914," in *The Invention of Tradition,* ed. Eric Hobsbawm and Terence Ranger (Cambridge: Cambridge University Press, 1983), 263–307.

47. My reading of the way patriotic performance establishes an essentialized Americanism for Hampton students in Johnston's images is informed by Judith Butler's innovative work on gender. Butler reads gender as an endlessly repeated performance that fabricates an interiorized, "essentialized," sexual identity. Judith Butler, *Gender Trouble: Feminism and the Subversion of Identity* (New York: Routledge, 1990), especially "Subversive Bodily Acts" (79–141) and "Conclusion: From Parody to Politics" (142–49). While I find Butler's work particularly useful because her analysis denaturalizes the notion of "essence," I do not mean to suggest that gender identities and national identities (or ethnic identities) are culturally coextensive, or even parallel. I am chiefly interested here in noting the ways in which "essences" of various kinds are inscribed on the body through ritualized and repeated performances.

48. According to Laura Wexler, "The students she [Johnston] photographs are the sons and daughters of 'freedom's first generation,' but nothing about their appearance reveals this fact. Instead, the invisibility of the marks of slavery seems to be part of the point." "Black and White and Color," 369.

49. My reading of this image is inspired by Laura Wexler's insightful interpretation of this image and other of Johnston's Hampton photographs in ibid., especially 381–83. For another important reading of this image, see Guimond, "Frances Johnston's *Hampton Album,*" 35.

50. In a lecture he delivered at the University of California on March 4, 1992, titled "Nationalism and Ethnicity," Benedict Anderson argued that ethnic identities were maintained in the modern age of international migrations through the family photograph album. According to Anderson, before modern mass migrations, ethnic and national identities were considered almost coextensive, subsumed under the single category of nationality. In premodern days, one knew "who [and what] one was" because his or her ancestors were buried in the local graveyard, in the earth, where one would someday join them. Families and identities were tied to the local, to the land of one's "patria." After the mass migrations of the nineteenth and twentieth centuries, ethnic identities ceased to be isomorphic with national identities. In the new social context of the late twentieth century, Anderson claims that the photograph album replaces the graveyard as the site of ethnic identifications. Grandmother and grandfather are no longer buried in one's own local graveyard: they are buried in the family photo album. Thus, the photograph album enables one to formulate and maintain an ethnic identity distinct from one's national identity.

In this essay, I am examining the intersection of racial (Anglo-Saxon) and national identifications in the construction of "American" identities at the turn of the century and view photographs as the site of racially inflected *national* identities.

51. This collection of Du Bois's papers is housed in the prints and photographs division of the Library of Congress.

52. hooks, "In Our Glory," 50.

53. Du Bois, "The American Negro at Paris," 577.

54. hooks, "The Oppositional Gaze."

55. Du Bois, "The Conservation of Races," 822.

56. Ibid., 816, 817.

57. For a detailed analysis of how nineteenth-century white supremacists came to use the category of "type" in order to describe what they considered permanent racial differences, see Robert J. C. Young, *Colonial Desire: Hybridity in Theory, Culture and Race* (New York: Routledge, 1995), especially 13–18, 129–33.

58. In her fascinating study of how the law was employed to perpetuate a "broad-reaching ideology of white supremacy" at the turn of the century, Susan Gillman demonstrates how "for purposes of racial identification, the color line was more stringently and narrowly defined" in legal terms in the early twentieth century. She also notes that "the legal fraction defining blackness was still one thirty-second 'Negro blood'" in Louisiana as late as 1970. Susan Gillman, "'Sure Identifiers': Race, Science, and the Law in Twain's *Puddn'head Wilson*," *South Atlantic Quarterly* 87:2 (Spring 1988): 205.

59. See chapter 6, "White Power, White Desire: The Political Economy of Miscegenation" in Young, *Colonial Desire*, 142–58.

60. Du Bois's biracial "types" problematize the notion that race is visible in physical characteristics by demonstrating that "Negroes," legally defined as such by "one drop" of African American blood, may nevertheless bear the stereotypical features of whiteness (blond hair, blue eyes, and pale skin). Du Bois's photographs of "types of Negroes" thus function in ways similar to the typecasting of white actresses to play mulatta characters in mid-twentieth-century Hollywood films that Mary Ann Doane describes in "Dark Continents." According to Doane, the practice of employing white actresses to represent mulatta characters "tends to demonstrate inadvertently the quiescent discordance between ideologies of racial identity (defined by blood) and cinematic ideologies of the real (as defined by the visible)" (235).

61. Ida B. Wells makes this critique in "Southern Horrors," 26–28.

62. I am drawing on Du Bois's well-known image of the Veil that he employs to introduce *The Souls of Black Folk* and that he purports to lift for white readers (3). I am also borrowing the notion of "colonial desire" from Robert J. C. Young's *Colonial Desire*.

63. In their recent, overwhelmingly popular book, Richard Herrnstein and Charles Murray make a case for the innate intellectual capabilities of different races, an argument disturbingly reminiscent of Francis Galton's nineteenth-century studies of "hereditary genius" and eugenics. Richard J. Herrnstein and Charles A. Murray, *The Bell Curve: Intelligence and Class Structure in American Life* (New York: Free Press, 1994).

64. *Time*, special issue, 142:21 (Fall 1993). Since my initial interest in *Time*'s "new Eve," several intriguing and important examinations of this image have been published. See Lauren Berlant, *The Queen of America Goes to Washington City: Essays on Sex and Citizenship* (Durham, N.C.: Duke University Press, 1997), 200–209; Victor Burgin, *In/Different Spaces: Place and Memory in Visual Culture* (Berkeley and Los Angeles: University of California Press, 1996), 258–64; Donna J. Haraway, *Modest Witness @ Second Millennium. FemaleMan Meets OncoMouse* (New York: Routledge, 1997), 259–65.

DARK CONTINENT

Francette Pacteau

Where is she?
Activity/Passivity
Sun/Moon
Culture/Nature
Day/Night
Father/Mother

Head/Heart
Intelligible/Palpable
Logos/Pathos
Form, convex, step, advance, semen, progress.
Matter, concave, ground—where steps are taken, holding—and dumping-ground.
Man
Woman

. . . Thought has always worked through opposition. . . . Night to his day—that has forever been the fantasy. Black to his white. . . .
—Hélène Cixous, "Sorties," in *The Newly Born Woman*

Hélène Cixous's set of binary oppositions makes clear the position of the feminine in a patriarchal system of difference, a system in which femininity is always defined as the secondary, subordinate term. In a repetitious replay of the creation, *woman* is granted meaning from the stuff of a fully realized, perfectly complete sign. As such, *woman* comes into signification as a supplement to the prior term *man* (a supplement often reconceptualized as complement in the service of an ideology of heterosexual plenitude). It is a dangerous supplement (after all, it was the cause of the Fall of man), which ever threatens to corrupt the "natural" state—that ideological state of nature in which culture is presented *as* nature, or the "natural *order*." The system of difference that posits *man* as the primary term from which *woman* derives cannot signify her alterity. She can only ever be a man with a difference, a man with a deficiency.

If woman's entry into signification is through the term *man*, the black woman's access to intelligibility, in a Western order of difference, is through the modified term *white man*. Black to his white; that is, not man, not white. In an essay on racism, Victor Burgin writes:

> "White" . . . has the strange property of directing our attention to colour while in the very same movement it ex-nominates itself *as* a colour. For evidence of this we need look no further than to the expression "people of colour," for we know very well that this means "not White." We know equally well that the colour white is the higher power to which all colours of the spectrum are subsumed when equally combined: white is the sum totality of light, while black is the total absence of light.[1]

Western discourse construes blackness as palpable, entirely visible, and yet empty, null—the presence of an absence. It opposes the reflective "power" of white—black does not reflect—to the absorptive property of black. Blackness, thus defined in a parasitic role, feeds off light, ever threatening its luminosity with total absorption and extinction. In 1840 Alexander Walker wrote:

> That, independent of any association blackness is naturally disagreeable, if not painful, is happily determined by the cause of the boy restored to sight by Cheselden, who tells us that the first time the boy saw a black object, it gave him great uneasiness; and that some time after, upon accidentally seeing a negro-woman, he was struck with great horror at the sight. This appears to be perfectly conclusive.[2]

He then cites Richard Payne Knight, scholar and connoisseur, who proposes the following explanation of the boy's reaction:

> As to the uneasiness which the boy, couched by Cheselden, felt at the first sight of a black object, it arose either from the harshness of its outline, or from its appearing to act as a partial extinguisher applied to his eyes, which, as every object that he saw, seemed to touch them, would, of course, be its effect.[3]

The opposition between white and black becomes, in Walker's discourse on the aesthetic of the woman, an opposition between beauty and ugliness.[4] Walker's account moves, in a semantic *crescendo,* from the "great uneasiness" experienced at the sight of the dark object, to the downright "horror" felt at accidentally seeing the Negro woman. In order to assert the inherent unattractiveness of blackness, Walker calls on the "immaculate" vision of the blind boy, newly born out of a state of purported innocence—an existence supposedly outside of the symbolic order. Walker's very schematic and decontextualized account of the event does not allow us to test the validity of Payne Knight's interpretation. It is not really this, however, that interests me here; it is, rather, that Walker chooses to tell a tale of the fear of loss, here the loss of the power to see, in which the principal actors are the (threatening) black woman and the taintless (frightened) white male subject.[5]

"Black to his white," writes Cixous, and nature to his culture. The positioning of the black woman on the side of nature is overdetermined by her being both black and female. In the colonial discourse of the West, Africa has historically been associated with nature and femininity, a femininity that was expressed, alternatively, as domesticated sensuality or uncontrollable lasciviousness. Written between 1853 and 1855, Joseph Arthur de Gobineau's influential *Essai sur l'inégalité des races humaines* formulates racial difference in terms of gender difference. Blacks and Jews, considered to be very sensual, are defined as feminine and are credited with aesthetic superiority. The masculine races, on the other hand, possess "a more precise, abundant, and richer language than the female races."[6] Thus Gobineau restates a thesis already present in, for instance, Gustave Eichtal and Ismayl Urbain's *Lettres sur la race noire et la race blanche,* which was published fourteen years earlier:

> The black appears to me to be the female race in the human family, while the white is the male race. Just like the woman, the black is deprived of political and scientific faculties; he has never created a great state, he is no astronomer, mathematician, or naturalist; he has done nothing in industrial mechanics. But, on the other hand, he possesses to the highest degree the qualities of the heart, the feelings, and the domestic virtues; he is the man of the house. Like the woman, he also loves with a passion adornment, dance, and singing; and the few examples I have seen of his native poetry are charming idylls.[7]

The discursive construction of a feminine Africa, like Paul Gauguin's quest for a native, unchanging world peopled by languid pleasure-seeking girls, is, in Abigail Solomon-Godeau's words, a "fantasmatic construction of a *purely feminized geography.*"[8] Within that imaginary geography, the black woman comes into signification as *extremely* other. It is this polarization that I wish to address here, and more particularly the negotiating of desire within this structure of exclusion. Confronted with an excess of difference, the white male subject will excel at defensive ingenuity, making her blackness becoming to his light, brightening up his day with her night.

> *Mountains and abysses, such is the relief of the grotesque body; or speaking in architectural terms, towers and subterranean passages.*
> —Mikhail Bakhtin, *Rabelais and His World*

In 1810, in London, an African woman was exhibited to the public, stark naked, so as to allow the viewer to observe "the shape and frame of her body."[9] Her name was Saartjie Baartman, Saat-Jee for short; she became known as the "Hottentot Venus." After having been exhibited for a period of five years all over Europe, she died in Paris at the age of twenty-five. Her body was whisked away and promptly cut open, cut into pieces. We can, to this day, examine Saartjie Baartman's anatomical particularities at the Musée de l'Homme in Paris. Alive, she was simply a shape, a breathing silhouette, displaying the outline of her protruding buttocks; dead, she is reduced to a couple of cuts of flesh— buttocks and genitalia—preserved in glass jars. The titillating fascination with Saat-Jee's "formidable" posterior was greatly heightened by the widespread knowledge of her "exceptional" genitalia (which she never exhibited to the public). Saartjie Baartman's elongated labia and nymphae, obtained through manipulation of the genitalia, were a sign of beauty among certain African tribes. To the nineteenth-century anatomists and pathologists they represented a "hypertrophy," an "anomaly," which was promptly enrolled in the service of a theory in which the "primitive" genitalia were taken as the external sign of a primitive sexual appetite. Such a theory was not entirely original: the purported particularity of the black woman's genitalia had been invoked before to argue for the distinct nature of all black peoples. In 1829, another Hottentot woman also known as the Hottentot Venus was displayed, naked but for a few ornaments, for the amusement of the Duchesse du Barry's jaded guests.

The salient buttocks of the Hottentot woman, a physical characteristic of all the Hottentot people, were pathologized as an "abnormal accumulation of fat" and were given a Greco-Latin name, "Steatopyga." The Hottentot woman's genitalia became known as the "Hottentot Apron." This appellation evokes at once the domestication and disavowal—the apron protects by concealing—of a sexuality to which medicine had assigned a nature different to the point of abnormality. The Hottentot Apron was classified as a malformation, alongside other genital malformations supposedly caused by concupiscence and other sexual excesses such as lesbian love. The Hottentot woman became associated, in the discourse of physical anthropology, with "deviant" sexuality and most particularly with the purported lasciviousness of the prostitute. Nineteenth-century physiologists, physiognomists, and phrenologists were busy scrutinizing the prostitute's body for external signs of her deviancy and immorality. Such signs they found in the configuration of the bumps of her head, the asymmetry and masculinity of her facial features, the *embonpoint* of certain regions of her body, and the unusual size of her genitals.[10] In his analysis in 1870 of the external form of the genitalia of no less than eight hundred French prostitutes, the dedicated researcher Adrien Charpy comments on the "characteristic" elongation of the labia majora of the prostitute and likens it to the apron of the "disgusting" Hottentots. In Cesare Lombroso's 1893 study of the criminal woman, subtitled *La Donna delinquente, la prostituta e la donna normale,* two of the plates carry drawings of the Hottentot Apron and the Steatopyga. In a 1905 publication by a student of Lombroso, *Staetopigia in prostitute,* the Italian prostitute is depicted quite literally as a Caucasian version of the Hottentot woman. Nineteenth-century physical anthropology was firmly grounded in an evolutionist ideology. Within that ideology, the prostitute's deviancy was interpreted as degeneracy. Her physical particularities, whether genetically acquired or developed, were signs of her descent; they were "atavistic throwbacks" to an archaic nature, long forgotten, which the Hottentot woman with her "grotesquely" protruding buttocks and elongated labias had come to represent.

Drawing on Mikhail Bakhtin's analysis of the carnivalesque, Allon White and Peter Stallybrass describe the grotesque body and its bourgeois Other—the Classical body—in the following terms:

> To begin with, the classical statue was always mounted on a plinth which meant that it was elevated, static and monumental. In the one simple fact of the plinth or pedestal the classical body signaled a whole different somatic conception from that of the grotesque body which was usually multiple (Bosch, Bruegel), teeming, always already part of a throng. By contrast the classical statue is the radiant centre of a transcendent individualism, "put on a pedestal," raised above the viewer and the commonalty and anticipating passive admiration from below. We *gaze up* at the figure and wonder. We are placed by it as spectators to an instant—frozen yet apparently universal—of epic or tragic time.... The classical statue has no openings

or orifices whereas grotesque costume and masks emphasize the gaping mouth, the protuberant belly and buttocks, the feet and the genitals.... The grotesque body is emphasized as a
mobile, split, multiple self, a subject of pleasure in processes of exchange; and it is never
closed off from either its social or ecosystemic context. The classical body on the other hand
keeps its distance.[11]

The grotesque body, then, is the sensuous, material body signified as excessive and transgressive. In Bakhtin's words, it is "the body that fecundates and is fecundated, that gives
birth and is born, devours and is devoured, drinks, defecates, is sick and dying."[12] It is the
body that bears and ostentatiously displays the inscriptions of its physical needs as "defor-
mities." This clamoring affirmation of physicality represents a transgression of the limits
of the social; the domesticated body reverts to a state of nature, "primitiveness." The
grotesque body is a disarticulated body, whose internal chaos threatens to violently exter-
nalize itself in the form of contagious symbolic disorder. Stallybrass and White enumerate
the discursive norms of the grotesque body: "impurity (both in the sense of dirt and
mixed categories), heterogeneity, masking, protuberant distention, disproportion, exorbitancy, clamour, decentred or eccentric arrangements, a focus upon gaps, orifices and symbolic filth..., physical needs and pleasures of the 'lower bodily stratum,' materiality and
parody."[13] "Protuberant distentions," excess of matter pushed, expelled to the surface of
the body; "gaps and orifices," passages between the inside and the outside, zones of pleasure, excretory sites though which the body wastes itself. The social body seems to burst at
the seams under the pressure of a recalcitrant physicality, which breaks out, out of place,
as dirt, as disease. Coming into being at the edges of our existence, straddling the dividing
line of formative binary oppositions, threatening to infect, pollute the sanitized zones of
our subjectivities, the grotesque body partakes of the abject.

Sociality and subjectivity are premised on the exclusion of the disorderly, the unclean, the improper—an exclusion that defines them, in Julia Kristeva's words, as *non-
objet du désir*. However, what would be excluded "hovers at the edges or borders of our
existence, haunting and inhabiting regions supposedly clean and free of any influence or
contamination."[14] It is the recognition of the impossibility of an uncontaminated site of
subjectivity that elicits the response that Kristeva terms "abjection." In the pre-Oedipal,
abjection is the condition of the emergence from undifferentiation, the distinction between inside and outside, the precondition of identity. Abjection becomes manifest in the
movements of ingestion and evacuation, at the various sites of transition between inside
and outside—mouth, anus, genitals—through which the objects—food, vomit, spit, feces,
urine (later semen and blood)—are ingested and evacuated. In a prototypical instance,
the infant vomits the mother's milk; like all trauma, this visceral movement of expulsion
leaves its mark, the inchoate marking of a boundary between inside and outside, between
infant and mother. In the double movement of ingestion and evacuation, however, the
objects of abjection can never be *fully* separated from the body. Indeed, it is precisely this
indeterminate status that will mark them as abject. Here, the first intuition of a subjective
boundary is both the convulsive expulsion of the "self" and the vomiting of the archaic
mother. In the post-Oedipal, abjection is in the impossibility of maintaining clear boundaries between inside and outside, clean and unclean, proper and improper—lines of demarcation that are constitutive of, and constituted by, the Symbolic order. That which

provokes abjection, the abject, is "necessarily and undecidably both inside and outside (like the skin of milk); dead and alive (like the corpse); autonomous, yet engulfing (like infection and pollution)."[15]

Kristeva speaks of the abject in terms of three main categories: food, bodily wastes, and signs of sexual difference. The most archaic form of abjection is oral disgust: "Food is the oral object (this ab-ject) which founds the human being's archaic relation to the other, his mother, who enjoys a power as vital as it is formidable."[16] The infant vomits the mother's milk. Kristeva speaks of the retching as the lips touch the skin of the milk, the nausea that separates her from she or he who offers it. The refusal of the food is the rejection of maternal/parental love; more fundamentally, it represents the expulsion of the body of the archaic mother. As the subject only exists in the desire of the (m)other—since the subject only exists through the body of the mother—the subject violently *expels itself* in the very movement through which it would define itself: "In this trajectory where 'I' become, I give birth to me in the violence of sobbing and vomit."[17]

Bodily fluids, wastes, and refuse constitute the second main category of the abject—corporeal by-products that are both internal and external. When inside the body, they are the condition of its regeneration, the very stuff of life. When externalized, expelled, they come to signify the unclean, the filthy. However, wastes are never completely external to the subject, as they are part of the subject. In expelling its bodily wastes, therefore, the subject expels part of itself. Kristeva writes: "It is not then an absence of health or cleanliness which makes something abject, but that which perturbs an identity, a system, an order; that which does not respect limits, places or rules. It is the in-between, the ambiguous, the mixed."[18] The corpse is the most sickening of bodily wastes, intolerable because "in representing the very border between life and death, it shifts this limit into the heart of life itself."[19] Here, in the presence of the dead body, the subject confronts the most extreme and complete form of expulsion: "It is no longer I who expel, 'I' is expelled."[20]

The corporeal signs of sexual difference constitute the third category of the abject. Kristeva speaks of the cultural horror of menstrual blood. We may recall here Plotinus's repudiation of the materiality of the woman's body: "Now what is the beauty here? It has nothing to do with the blood or the menstrual process."[21] What is at stake here is not just sexual difference, but the differentiation between men and mothers. Like all other bodily wastes, menstrual blood partakes of a cyclical crossing of the border between inside and outside. In this case, however, the waste is the internal food that may sustain a nascent life; it is the expelled link between the fetus and the mother. Disgust toward menstrual blood is the refusal of that original corporeal link.

The abject, then, is simultaneously the precondition of subjectivity and its greatest threat. Kristeva speaks of abjection as a *crise narcissique*—a testimony to the ephemeral nature of the narcissistic state, to its status as semblance. In reminding the subject of its relation to animality, corporeality, and death, the abject asserts the facticity of a disembodied, unified subjectivity:

> The abject confronts us, on the one hand, with the fragile states where man wanders in the territories of the *animal*. . . . On the other hand, the abject confronts us in our personal archeology, with our most original attempts to mark ourselves out from the maternal entity even before existing outside it thanks to the autonomy of language.[22]

From these early visceral movements of rejection and demarcation, to the later repetitive reassertions of identity in abjection, the subject remains caught up, in Kristeva's words, in a perpetual *"corps à corps."*

In Pierre Loti's novel, *Le Roman d'un saphi,* the white protagonist's sexual intercourse with a black woman is perceived as a fatal passage, a process of defilement from which he will tentatively purify himself by breaking off the relationship: "It seemed to him that he was about to cross a fatal threshold, to sign with this black race a sort of mortal pact"; later, "He had recovered his dignity as a white man, soiled by the contact with this black flesh."[23] Symbolic defilement shades imperceptibly into medical disease. Sander L. Gilman writes that "medical tradition has a long history of perceiving this skin color as the result of some pathology. The favorite theory, which reappears with some frequency in the early nineteenth century, is that the skin color and attendant physiognomy of the black are the result of congenital leprosy."[24] It was in this same period that Africa was declared to be the homeland of syphilis, from which the infectious disease had spread into Europe during the Middle Ages. We are told that the threat of syphilitic contagion was originally to have been inscribed in Pablo Picasso's painting of *Les Demoiselles d'Avignon,* celebrated for purportedly introducing African art into Western painting. According to Phyllis Rose,

> When he finished *Les Demoiselles d' Avignon* in July 1907, the faces of the two prostitutes on the right and one on the left resembled African masks. . . . People have begun to realize that the African masks were painted in for their emotional impact—to express the terrifying aspects of female sexuality. Thus the painting in its final form expresses the contradictory attraction and repulsion which was handled narratively and somewhat conventionally (through the images of sailor and medical student—the latter presumably warning about disease) in the first version.[25]

Before painting *Les Demoiselles d'Avignon,* Picasso visited the Musée du Trocadéro:

> Picasso had seen African masks and figures before this, in the studios of some of his friends, but they were isolated objects held up for aesthetic contemplation. In the Trocadéro, he encountered a jumble of objects whose ethnographic interest and ritual purpose was paramount. . . . They were not tastefully displayed on black velvet or in glass boxes or against neutral carpeting. They were jammed together on hastily constructed tables and in cases. The place was badly lit and evil-smelling. There was something horrifying about the setting. . . . It was a shock, a revelation. He was repelled by the place, but couldn't leave. "It was disgusting. The Flea Market. The smell . . . I wanted to get out of there. I didn't leave. I stayed."[26]

In another account, Picasso recalls his first visit to Le Troca: "When I went for the first time, at Derain's urging, to the Trocadero Museum, the smell of dampness and rot there stuck in my throat. It depressed me so much I wanted to get out fast, but I stayed and studied."[27] It was then that Picasso decided to depict the faces of his *Demoiselles* as African masks, or so goes the legend. Whether or not Phyllis Rose's version of Picasso's words, punctuated by an ellipsis full of menace, is an accurate representation of what Picasso meant to say, the myth of the painting's origin appears to be founded on the association of the stench of decay with the image of black femininity, which in turn in the painting is assimilated into a dangerous sexuality. If we are to take Kristeva at her word, it is doubtful whether the abject can ever be absent from the relation to the Other. Disgust is an ever-present undertow in the otherwise adulatory discourses on feminine beauty. The black woman however, doubly marked with difference—as woman, as black—throws the role of the abject in the attribution of beauty into a particularly sharp relief. The difference between the white woman and the black woman, in the characteristic reaction of the white heterosexual man, is not one of kind, but one of degree.

In the 1920s the Charleston swept Europe. The Vicar of St Aidan's, in Bristol, commented: "Any lover of the beautiful will die rather than be associated with the Charleston. It is neurotic! It is rotten! It stinks! Phew, open the windows!"[28] The Charleston was strongly associated with black "jazz" music, and Josephine Baker was its incarnation. The image of Josephine Baker's dislocated and mobile nakedness appeared to the commentators of the time as both grotesque and beautiful. A reviewer for *Vogue* wrote: "She brings to her dancing a savage frenzy inherited from distant African ancestors, and the result is a masterpiece of grotesquerie and beauty unlike anything previously seen in Europe."[29] The dance critic André Levinson:

> Certain of Miss Baker's poses, back arched, haunches protruding, arms entwined and uplifted in a phallic symbol, had the compelling potency of the finest examples of Negro sculpture. The plastic sense of a race of sculptors came to life and the frenzy of African Eros swept over the audience. It was no longer a grotesque dancing girl that stood before them, but the black Venus that haunted Baudelaire.[30]

Baker's commentators construe her well-rehearsed moves as a spontaneous "savage frenzy," the disjointed movements of a body out of control, gone "wild." They invoke the influence of "distant African ancestors" in order to explain away, far away, the deliciously threatening possibility of a body unrestrained by symbolic laws. Aroused, they freeze her movement in the familiar discourse of an aesthetic of the static. Josephine Baker is a statue; her ancestors, "a race of sculptors."[31] They watch her, poised between contempt and idolatry.

In a catalog essay for the 1990 exhibition Envisioning America, John Czaplicka cites a German critic writing about Josephine Baker's appearance in Berlin in 1926: "Her dance is instinct against civilization, is uproar of the senses. She reveals the unconscious which overthrows our whole world view."[32] At the Los Angeles County Museum of Art, Envisioning America was housed under the same roof as The New Vision, an exhibition of the Ford Motor Company photographic collection that was compiled during the 1920s and 1930s. The 1990 explanatory text to a 1930 photograph of Josephine Baker unselfconsciously speaks of the primitive sensuality that Baker embodied. The Hottentot Venus had been the object of the pseudoscientific "anthropological" gaze of the nineteenth century, which scrutinized the body of the sexual and racial other for signs of its difference, its deviance. As the explicit reference to the Classical body of Greek statuary indicates, the Hottentot Venus, with her physical exorbitancies, came to represent the other of beauty in its Classicist insistence on rules of symmetry and proportion.

Josephine Baker was the representative of an imaginary Africa, come to Europe by way of America; she was the embodiment of a primitivism inflected by a view of American culture as dominated by technology and the machine.[33] Josephine Baker's dynamic body moved against the Classicist notion of a static, statuesque beauty to the rhythm of the urban jungle of modernity. Her "impossible anatomy," disjuncted body echoed the formally controlled fragmentation of the object in Cubist art. The Other of Classicism, the other of the West, became conflated in the legend of the painting of *Les Demoiselles d'Avignon*. The modernist challenge posed to the statuary beauty of the Greek Venus in the visual arts—a challenge brought about in part by the influence of non-Western cultures—left beauty without its specific cultural and historical grounding. And yet this modernist challenge did not lead to the assertion of a different beauty, but to the abandonment of the concern with the beauty of the object, and the eventual renunciation of the object as modernism moved toward the highly abstract beauty of the form of the work itself. While the body triumphs on the stage of the Folies Bergères, it is evacuated from "high art," which celebrates the beauty of abstraction. This is really a reassertion of the Ideal by another route, prefigured by the masterpiece imagined by Honoré de Balzac—the most beautiful portrait of a woman that could ever be, which showed nothing of the woman but encrusted layers of paint.

The body celebrated in the graphic manipulations of artist/publicist Jean-Paul Goude—most particularly, that of singer/performer Grace Jones—is an abstract body in that it displays an impossible female anatomy reminiscent of Velázquez's Rokeby Venus (with her famous extra vertebrae).[34] It is abstract also, in that what first appears to be a singular body proves to be an assemblage of citations. The question of beauty here refers us to an infinity of identities without depth, quotations that do not so much point us to a history as they remain caught up in the one-dimensionality of Goude's luscious airbrushed spaces. However, as the black female body spreads itself thinly across the synchrony of paper-cut identities, it takes on an omniformity that, as we shall see, often translates into omnipotence. History, evacuated from the one-dimensionality of the image, returns by another route. In the pages of Goude's *Jungle Fever* we find a discourse of Otherness in which blackness is still essentially "bestial" and "primitive," but this primitivism is now transposed to the sleek orderliness of Jean-Paul Goude's constructions. Of Grace Jones, Goude writes: "The strength of her image, then as now, is that it swings constantly from the near grotesque—from the organ grinder's monkey—to the great African beauty. You are constantly looking at her and wondering if she's beautiful or grotesque, or both and how can she be one if she is the other."[35] The object of Goude's ambivalent fascination is a truly *hybrid* construction, which, brilliantly displayed in the refined minimalism of his designs, clearly speaks of the idealization of a *different* body, the fantasy of an Other beauty that is multiple, excessive, exorbitant.[36]

> *So for Radiah, I devised the complete African look, with removable scars. This made the papers.*
> —Jean-Paul Goude, *Jungle Fever*

Goude says that Grace Jones's face is "something more than just pretty. It was more like an African mask."[37] The mask serves the double function of displaying and concealing; it is at once surface and depth. Writing about the racial stereotype, Homi Bhabha observes: "Colonial discourse produces the colonised as a fixed reality which is at once an 'other' and yet entirely knowable and visible."[38] Seen in this light, the conversion of living features into a mask becomes a particularly apposite instance of, and metaphor for, the discursive petrifaction of another culture into a set of idées fixes. The stereotype, Bhabha writes, is "an arrested and fixated form of representation" that denies "the play of difference."[39] As such, Bhabha argues, it is structurally and functionally analogous to the fetish. Like the fetish, it is the corollary of a defensive strategy of disavowal: the acknowledgment of Otherness and its reduction to one specific characteristic, culturally intelligible, familiar. Like the fetish, it is the certainty to which the subject repeatedly returns when the threat of difference forces the reassertion of identity. Indeed, always delivered as if it were an informed statement, the stereotype functions to reassure the subject confronted with difference, with the possibility of lack, of the integrity of its *own* identity. Bhabha begins his argument by stating that "within the apparatus of colonial power, the discourses of sexuality and race relate in a process of functional overdetermination," to eventually conflate sexual and racial difference in his formulation of the "stereotype *as* fetish."[40] For my purposes here, I wish to retain the idea of a relation of *overdetermination,* which produces the black woman as "excessive" while also retaining the strictly Freudian specificity of the notion of fetish—a substitute for the absent penis in the defensive process of disavowal of sexual difference. Bhabha's analogy between the fetish and the stereotype is most useful *as* an analogy, one that allows us to formulate the ambivalent nature of the racial stereotype as *disavowal.* To say that Grace Jones's face is like an African mask is to suggest, however subliminally, that these features and this color could be removed, like a mask; and, like a mask, they could be put on and worn for the excitement of a temporary transgression. The racial particularity of the woman is conceptualized as a masquerade. "Her face . . . was more like an African mask," says Goude; in other words, "I know very well that this woman is black, but nevertheless, under her African mask she is just like me." The disavowal of racial difference duplicates and reinforces the fetishistic structure (erected to fend off the threat posed by the recognition of sexual difference). In the process of fetishization, Jones loses her specificity to the stereotype; she becomes the generic African mask.

The African mask speaks of distant rituals to the Western subject. More generally, the mask worn at festivities permits the wearer to assume another identity, to transgress for a day, a night, the boundaries of gender, class, and race. Goude imagines a black identity that would be worn like a mask and thus invests blackness with an inherent transgressive value. Richard Dyer discusses such a scenario of transgression, taken from the 1938 film *Jezebel* (a literally and figuratively black-and-white film) in which blackness is assumed by the white woman in the form not of a mask, but of a dress: "The most famous scene in the film is the Olympus Ball, at which all the unmarried women wear white. Julie, to embarrass Pres [her fiancé] and to cock a snook at outdated convention ('This is 1852, not the Dark-Ages—girls don't have to simper about in white just 'cos they're not married'), decides to wear a red dress."[41] The red dress, described by Julie as "saucy"—"Vulgar," says her aunt—is the dress that Julie's black maid, Zette, most covets; after the ball, Julie gives it to her. Dyer remarks that "the red dress looks merely dark in this black and white film."[42] The white woman exudes sensuality and will be punished for it. She will shed the colored skin of the dress and expiate in luminous white. When the black woman takes on the burden of this sensuality in the form of the red dress, sensuality ceases to be a problem: the dress is returned to its *natural* owner, whom it fits like a second skin.

Jean-Paul Goude had a brown dress made for Radiah, a previous lover, "exactly to match the color of her skin, skintight" (31). The black skin is here seen as mask or dress: it is a detachable object, the function of which is to conceal by displaying itself—a fetish. This discursive insistence on the surface is made manifest in Goude's manipulations of Jones's image. He often depicts Grace Jones in a one-dimensional space, against a light background, where she appears flattened and sharp like a cardboard cutout. In these epidermal spaces, Goude displays her skin, airbrushed into a darker shade of blue-black-brown, sleek, shiny as if oiled, not in the manner of the bodybuilder to show off the muscles underneath, but to turn the skin into a reflective surface. Grace Jones can never be "just naked." Her skin is endowed with a presence that eclipses any perception of the absence of clothes: the white viewer sees not her nudity but her black skin. What Frantz Fanon has called the "epidermal schema"—the reduction of another identity to its corporeal surface, the color of which is further equated with negativity—is emphatically re-presented here,[43] no longer in terms of deficiency or lack, but in terms of plenitude: blackness, no longer a signifier of the total absence of light, is endowed with luminosity. Black reflects.

Plenitude turns into excess in Goude's work: "When I described her [Grace] to friends, I couldn't help exaggerating, making her appear bigger than life in every way" (104). To make her bigger than life in every way is precisely and literally what Goude applied himself to doing. He had already made Radiah into a seven-foot-tall "giant African beauty" by having her wear very high platform shoes concealed under a long brown dress. He had given Toukie a "race-horse's ass." He retouched the photographs he took of her; he remodeled plaster replicas—twelve-inch-high white Toukies that he then colored—so as to "exaggerate her proportions": "There she was, my dream come true, in living color." (41). Then he turned Grace Jones into an elongated anatomical anomaly:

> First I photographed her in different positions—to get all my references, which I combine, as you can see in the cut-up version of the picture. I cut her legs apart, lengthened them, turned her body completely to face the audience like an Egyptian painting. . . . Then I started painting, joining up all those pieces to give the illusion that Grace Jones actually posed for the photograph and that only she was capable of assuming such a position. . . . If you really study it, the pose is anatomically impossible.[44]

Grace Jones called this image of her impossible self "Nigger Arabesque." Charles Baudelaire, who wrote of a "bizarre deity, brown as the nights," spoke of *bizarrerie* as the condition of beauty, rhetorically asking, "Try to conceive of a beauty that would be commonplace!"[45] Whatever *bizarrerie* comes to mean, it always hovers at the extremities of our existence, while banality occupies the middle ground (the banality of the "predictable, gray, middle-class, boringly normal" suburb of Paris, the "nowhere" where Goude grew up, or the sense of banality that inevitably assails us when we are confronted with difference, with the exotic). Goude turns his black lovers into unique creatures, whose difference he stresses to the point of exorbitancy, lifting them out of the normal, the everyday, and displaying their particularities to a white public, who more than a century ago might have been ogling, with fearful fascination, at the protuberant buttocks of Saartjie Baartman, wishing to catch a glimpse of her "exceptional" genitalia.

To the European of the time, the Hottentot body was an impossible body that could only be conceptualized as malformed or even diseased. Goude's aesthetic of the excessive and the impossible invokes the distensions and scarifications of a native African aesthetic, and the possibility of a totally different anatomy. It also recalls the angular and dislocated form of Josephine Baker's dancing body, or the impossible anatomy depicted in Ernst Ludwig Kirchner's painting of the *Tapdancing Negro,* whose body has been "turned and twisted into an angular cipher of the syncopated motion and speed of tap dance."[46] In positioning his "impossible objects" within familiar spaces, Goude emphasizes the unsettling moment of the white subject's encounter with difference. In a 1979 image titled "Grace and Fashion Crowd, Imagined," the homogeneous space occupied by two symmetrically positioned groups of seated white spectators is ripped asunder by the eruption of Grace Jones, who appears, like a tall shiny winged insect, emerged from another dimension, from behind luxuriant green draperies, suggestive, perhaps, of the edge of a jungle.

Grace Jones is transgressive to the point of transcendence: "She has become a creature whose unique beauty transcends both the gender of her sex and the ethnicity usually associated with the colour of her skin. She looks barely human. She is more like a strange alien, blue-black, in black" (106). Difference is here emphasized to the point where the black woman crosses over into another register of being and meaning. Grace Jones is "barely human." Her difference is disavowed. Excluded as she might be from the order of the human, her difference would no longer make any difference. Indeed Jones is barely human, even unequivocally bestial in Goude's depiction of her, naked, on all fours in a cage that bears the sign DO NOT FEED THE ANIMAL. On the ground scattered morsels of raw meat and bloody bones echo the red lips of her growling mouth; in the foreground, the back of the heads of an audience. Goude recalls going to the *Foire du Trône* as a small child:

> This is where I saw the fire-eaters. They were chained inside a cage. I remember they were four or five black wild men. But there was one who was my favorite—one with a bone in his nose. He would hold the bars and shake them like a gorilla. There was a rattling of chains and the savage would spit out enormous flames over our heads. It was very dramatic. (4)

In 1980, Helmut Newton photographed Jones, crouching in profile, holding a black leather whip with a red lash; she is naked but for the red and black makeup, the brilliant red on her nails and lips, the slash of yellow on her forehead, the ring around her finger, the bracelet around her forearm, the lash of the whip around her neck, and the chains around her ankles. She glances over her shoulder back at the viewer, with the hint of a smile.[47] Encaged by Goude, enslaved by Newton? In Newton's photograph the instruments of enslavement do not tear the flesh; they are worn like fashion accessories. The chains, loosely draped around her ankles, do not seriously restrain her; she wraps the lash around her neck in the same way that she might a scarf or a tie. Her hands are free. She holds the whip as if to lead, to restrain herself, or to control someone else. Is this Grace Jones as the black slave of a white master's erotic fantasies, actively engaged in her own subjection? Or Grace Jones as the black *Maitresse*? The image is uncertain: Jones appears neither submissive nor threatening. Her look toward the camera is irresolvably ambivalent; it leaves me with the impression of a performer who has not yet quite entered her role, who is perhaps unconvinced by the act she is required to play out for the camera: "You mean like this...?"

Jean-Paul Goude's growling Grace is definitely menacing. No longer the subjected bestiality of the organ grinder's monkey, but the raw animality of the carnivorous wild beast threatening to break loose. The live performance, designed by Goude, on which this image is based involves the enactment of a fight between Grace Jones wearing a tiger costume and a real tiger. She wins and is shown, still in her furry outfit, chewing on the bloody remains of her victim. A small photograph showing the fight between Jones and the tiger is reproduced on the side of Goude's airbrushed image of Grace Jones naked in the cage. Were we to carry over the symmetry of one image—tiger fighting tiger—to the other, the bloody remains would be human remains, and Grace a cannibal. On the other hand, were we to interpret the shedding of the tiger costume as the passage to another level of condensation, the black skin would now *be* the tiger skin. While the awkwardness in Newton's photograph suggests the self-consciousness involved in the production of the stereotype, Jean-Paul Goude creates a seamless image of femininity and blackness *as* animality in the simple play of condensation.[48] However, this is not a simple reiteration of a colonial stereotype, but the re-presenting of that stereotype in the present context of post-colonialism: as the microphone held by the hand of a white man (off-frame) indicates, the encaged woman (the personification of black Africa in certain colonialist allegories)—no longer mere spectacle—is now to be heard, loud and clear, by the silent white spectators. The fairground barker has had to surrender his megaphone.

Goude plays up to the anxieties of whites who fear the retribution of history, who fear that they will be in their turn colonized, invaded by an army of "strange, alien creatures." Through the use of masks, he creates a multiplicity of Grace Joneses in black suits, their gaze obliterated by dark glasses: "I made an army of marching Grace Joneses—soldiers, same size, wearing perfect masks of her face, goose-stepping in formation across the stage" (107). A dark phalanx, without even the breach of a white smile (the ever-present smile of the "good Negro," the smile of Josephine Baker). When, as a child, Goude drew pictures of cowboys and Indians, he would lavish all his attention on the detailed depictions of the Indians: "The good guys, the Indians, were all different." The white men he drew as an undifferentiated throng of generic "cowboys," "to help you understand that [they] were all crummy guys" (5). Goude creates an army of similarly identical Grace Joneses—"Whatever Grace couldn't do, a clone was made by me to do it for her"—in a replay of his childhood war games (107). But there is a difference: he endows Grace Jones with omnipotence—Jones can do anything. He multiplies the image of his obsession, drumming her particular features into our head: "They all look like Grace." At the same time, and in the very movement of multiplication, he denies Grace Jones her specificity; she becomes a mask among masks, a dark figure among dark figures who now "all look alike"—just as, subsumed under their common difference, all blacks may "look alike" to the distant white.

She became the threatening, blue-black, male-female, erotic menace I wanted her to be,
crashing cymbals and chanting to music, breaking out of my frozen stop-time drawings
through my direction to surges of gesturing rage.
    —Jean-Paul Goude, *Jungle Fever*

Grace Jones as a wild beast, a boxer who "throws jabs and hooks, just like a pro," a samurai, a demolition man whose brow is pearled with sweat, a dark, domineering deity, a force to be reckoned with, the imaginary embodiment of the threatening animality and corporeality that hovers at the limits of our existence.[49] However, the menacing physicality that Goude attributes to his creation—from the "savagery" of the beast to the choreographed force of the professional fighter—is represented with meticulous formalism. There is no cluttered jungle, battlefield, or ring, but the orderliness of sanitized spaces, straight-lines minimalism, in which Jones stands, trimmed, geometrized, and polished into a glorious *objet.* Homi Bhabha speaks of the chain of signification of the racial stereotype as being

> curiously mixed and split, polymorphous and perverse, an articulation of multiple belief. The black is both savage (cannibal) and yet the most obedient and dignified of servants (the servant of food); he is the embodiment of rampant sexuality and yet innocent as a child; he is mystical, primitive, simple-minded and yet the most worldly and accomplished liar, and manipulator of social forces.[50]

Of Toukie, Jean-Paul Goude writes: "She was a combination of innocence and aggressive sexuality" (40). Of Grace Jones, he says, "Grace is modern because she is all new and yet reflective of what she has been all along" (106). Is she the organ-grinder's monkey or the black and shiny "demi-Goddess"? Is she the growling beast or the *Bête Humaine* of modernity, "blue-black, shiny, aerodynamic in design"?[51] The subject's ambivalence, articulated in the discursive chain of binary oppositions, marks its object as either good or bad. However, from the space of discourse to the space of the book *Jungle Fever,* from the fixity of binary dualism to the multiplicity of identities, the object of Goude's fascination becomes endowed with that polymorphous perversity that marks it as both omnipotent and transgressive. By virtue of her difference, the black woman can be all that the white male subject has had to give up in his "ascent" to subjectivity.

Kristeva writes of the encounter with *l'étranger*:

> First, it is his singularity that arrests me: those eyes, those lips, those cheekbones, this skin unlike other skins, distinguish him, and remind me that there is *somebody* there. The difference of this face reveals that which all faces should disclose to the attentive gaze: the inexistence of banality in humans. And yet it is banality that constitutes a community for our everyday habits. But this captivating seizure by the foreigner's features both attracts and repels me: "I am as singular as he and therefore I love him," "I prefer my own singularity and therefore I kill him," he could conclude.[52]

In 1925, artist Paul Colin was commissioned to design the poster for *La Revue Nègre.* At Colin's request, Josephine Baker posed for him at least three times, naked but for her underpants. The finished work, which was posted all over Paris, includes the image of a thick-lipped, pop-eyed Baker that, as Phyllis Rose observes, "barely rises above the stereotypes of Sambo art."[53] The triumph of representation over the real—here, of stereotype over individuality—could not have been more complete. Jean-Paul Goude turned Grace Jones into a product of his imaginary, "a vision entirely my own." But, again, the "private" vision emerges by way of a public preconscious that is heavily invested with the historical accretions of representations. The conflicting impulses (to annihilate or to love) find expression in the very structure of these representations of black femininity—a femininity whose difference is stressed to the point of excess. Identifiable as the subject's "own" construction, without ever totally losing its identity as other, as singular, the racial and sexual other is thus able to fulfill its role as mirror image of the white subject's own desired singularity.

NOTES

1. Victor Burgin, "Paranoiac Space," in *In/Different Spaces: Place and Memory in Visual Culture* (Berkeley and Los Angeles: University of California Press, 1997), 131.

2. Alexander Walker, *An Analysis and Classification of Beauty in Woman* (New York: J & H. G. Langley, 1840), 82.

3. Quoted in ibid.

4. Tzvetan Todorov reads the encyclopedist Georges-Louis L. Buffon's *De l'Homme* (1749), citing the litany of oppositions in which black is associated with ugliness and white with beauty. See Tzvetan Todorov, *Nous et les autres—La réflexion française sur la diversité humain* (Paris: Editions du Seuil, 1989).

5. We may recall here that the biblical myth of the origin of blackness is centered on the dialectic of seeing and not seeing. Ham, having looked on the naked body of his father, Noah, and failed to cover it as propriety required, was punished for his indiscretion. God willed that Ham's son and his descendants would be born black and thus would be banished from his sight. Blackness equated here with invisibility is made to bear the burden of the son's guilty desire for the paternal phallus. See Joel Kovel, *White Racism: A Psychohistory* (New York: Pantheon, 1970), 51 ff.

6. Joseph Arthur de Gobineau, quoted in Christopher L. Miller, *Blank Darkness: Africanist Discourse in French* (Chicago: University of Chicago Press, 1985), 122.

7. Gustave Eichtal and Ismayl Urbain, quoted in ibid: "Le noir me parait être la race femme dans la famille humaine, comme le blanc est la race mâle. De même que la femme, le noir est privé des facultés politiques et scientifiques; il n'a jamais créé un grand état, il n'est point astronome, mathématicien, naturaliste; il n'a rien fait en mécanique industrielle. Mais, par contre, il possède au plus haut degré les qualités du coeur, les affections et les sentiments domestiques; il est l'homme d'intérieur. Comme la femme, il aime aussi avec passion la parure, la danse, le chant; et le peu d'exemples que j'ai vus de sa poésie native sont des idylles charmantes" (my translation).

Kobena Mercer writes of the feminization of the black male body in the works of late photographer Robert Mapplethorpe: "While images of gay S/M rituals represent a sexuality that consists in 'doing' something, black men are defined, confined and reduced in their 'being' as sexual and nothing more or less than sexual, hence 'super-sexual.'" K. Mercer, "Imaging the Black Man's Sex," in *Photography/Politics: Two,* ed. Patricia Holland, Jo Spence, and Simon Watney (London: Commedia/Photography Workshop, 1986), 64.

8. Abigail Solomon-Godeau, "Going Native," *Art in America* (July 1989): 123 (my italics).

9. Unattributed quotation (1810) in Sander L. Gilman, "Black Bodies, White Bodies," in *"Race," Writing and Difference,* ed. H. L. Gates Jr. (Chicago: University of Chicago Press, 1986), 232.

10. It was in 1830 that Philadelphian doctor Samuel George Morton delivered a lecture on the internal

capacity of the five skulls of Blumenbach's classification—Caucasian, Mongolian, Malay, American, Ethiopian—in which he concluded that whites had the biggest brains and blacks the smallest, thus explaining the differences in the "capacity for civilization." Morton's table of measurements was copied by German racial theorist Carl Gustav Carus in 1849, and later by Joseph Arthur de Gobineau in his influential *Essai sur l'inégalité des races humaines.* See Michael Banton, *Racial Theories* (Cambridge: Cambridge University Press, 1987).

11. Peter Stallybrass and Allon White, *The Politics and Poetics of Transgression* (Ithaca, N.Y.: Cornell University Press, 1986), 22.

12. Mikhail Bakhtin, *Rabelais and His World* (Cambridge: Harvard University Press, 1968), 319.

13. Stallybrass and White, *The Politics and Poetics of Transgression,* 23.

14. Elizabeth Grosz, "Language and the Limits of the Body: Kristeva and Abjection," *Futur Fall* (1987): 108.

15. Ibid., 111–12.

16. Julia Kristeva, *Powers of Horror* (New York: Columbia University Press, 1982), 75–76.

17. J. Kristeva, "Approaching Abjection," *Oxford Literary Review* 5, nos. 1–2 (1982): 127.

18. Ibid.

19. Elizabeth Grosz, "Julia Kristeva: Abjection, Motherhood and Love," in *Sexual Subversions: Three French Feminists* (Sydney: Allen and Unwin, 1989), 75.

20. Kristeva, "Approaching Abjection," 127.

21. Plotinus, *The Enneads,* V, eighth tractate, "On the Intellectual Beauty" (Cambridge: Harvard University Press, 1988), 486.

22. Kristeva, "Approaching Abjection," 134.

23. Pierre Loti, *Le Roman d'un saphi,* quoted in Todorov, *Nous et les autres,* 354: "Il lui semblait qu'il allait franchir un seuil fatal, signer avec cette race noire une sorte de pacte funeste." "Il avait retrouvé sa dignité d'homme blanc, souillé par le contact avec cette chair noire." (my translation).

24. Gilman, "Black Bodies, White Bodies," 250.

25. Phyllis Rose, *Jazz Cleopatra: Josephine Baker in Her Time* (London: Doubleday, 1989), 42.

26. Ibid.

27. Quoted in James Clifford, *The Predicament of Culture: Twentieth Century Ethnography, Literature, and Art* (Cambridge: Harvard University Press, 1988), 135.

28. Quoted in Carolyn Hall, *The Twenties in Vogue* (New York: Harmony Books, 1983), 80.

29. A reviewer for *Vogue,* quoted in ibid.

30. André Levinson, quoted in Rose, *Jazz Cleopatra,* 31.

31. Phyllis Rose adheres to a similar discourse when she writes: "She went down and up; she slid; she turned sideways; she faced the audience; she crossed her eyes; she twirled, putting her finger on her head as though she herself were a top she was spinning; she sang in a man's voice. The next moment she dropped the contortions, the mugging, and reverted to beauty," ibid., 25.

32. John Czaplicka, "Jungle Music and Song of Machines: Jazz and American Danse in Weimar Culture," in *Envisioning America* (Cambridge, Mass.: Busch-Riesinger Museum, Harvard University, 1990), 98.

33. See Frank Costigliola, *Awkward Dominion: American Political, Economic, and Cultural Relations with Europe* (Ithaca, N.Y.: Cornell University Press, 1984).

34. Jean-Paul Goude was commissioned by the Socialist government to design the 1989 parade for the Bicentenary of the French Revolution. The result was a splendid display of witty multicultural clichés often condensed and displaced into new, unexpected forms. The parade was led by the silent formations of Chinese men and women slowly pushing their bicycles as they rang the bells on the handlebars— a powerful echo of the repressive force that had silenced so many on Tiananman Square earlier that

summer. Had the bloody repression not occurred, Red Guards would have been marching down the Champs-Elysées in military formations, their orderly ranks suddenly erupting into break-dancing.

35. Jean-Paul Goude, *Jungle Fever* (New York: Xavier Moreau, 1981).

36. One of my fears, here, is that I may be misperceived by some as a woman pointing the finger at "bad" men. Here, as elsewhere, I would emphatically distinguish between analysis of the author and analysis of the effect. *Authorial intent is not at issue.* Anyone familiar with the past twenty-five years of theories of representations knows this: the meanings of the codes escape the control of the "author" who assembles them. What follows, then, is not about the real author, Jean-Paul Goude. It is about the historically and psychically overdetermined *meanings* of the collage of images (advertising, books, and so on) and utterances (interviews, and so on) that are in the public domain and that bear his signature.

37. Goude, *Jungle Fever,* 102 (hereafter cited parenthetically by page number in the text).

38. Homi K. Bhabha, "The Other Question—the Stereotype and Colonial Discourse," *Screen* 24, no. 6, (November–December 1983): 23.

39. Ibid., 27.

40. Ibid., 26.

41. Richard Dyer, "White," *Screen* 29, no. 4 (Autumn 1988): 56.

42. Ibid., 57.

43. Frantz Fanon, *Black Skin, White Masks* (New York: Grove Press, 1967).

44. Goude, *Jungle Fever,* 103. In an essay about *Jungle Fever,* Ted Colless and Paul Foss relate the ideal of physical perfection in fascist art to Goude's concern with correct proportions, thus choosing to ignore the less sensational fact that representations of the body in fascist art were inherited from ideals that have dominated, and still dominate, Western representations of the body since Classical times. See Ted Colless and Paul Foss, "Demolition Man," *Art and Text* 10 (Winter 1983).

45. Charles Baudelaire, "Sed Non Satiata," *Les Fleurs du Mal* (XXVIII), in *Oeuvres complètes de Charles Baudelaire* (Neuilly sur Seine: Editions de Saint-Clair, 1974), 148: "Bizarre déité, brune comme les nuits"; "tâchez de concevoir un beau banal!" (my translation). See *The Flowers of Evil* (Fresno, Calif.: Academy Library Guild, 1954), 91.

46. Czaplicka, "Jungle Music and Song of Machines," 88.

47. Helmut Newton, *Portraits* (New York: Pantheon, 1987), plate 160.

48. See "Condensation," in Jean Laplanche and Jean-Bertrand Pontalis, *The Language of Psycho-Analysis* (London: Hogarth Press, 1973), 82–83.

49. Goude, *Jungle Fever,* 105. The masculinization of Grace Jones is effected here through what Kobena Mercer describes as "the most commonplace of media stereotypes of the black male; the black male as athlete and sportsman, endowed with a 'natural' muscular physique with a capacity for strength and machine-like perfection." K. Mercer, "Imaging the Black Man's Sex," 65.

50. Bhabha, "The Other Question," 34.

51. Goude, *Jungle Fever,* 106. See Emile Zola, *La Bête humaine* (Paris: Gallimard, 1984), translated as *The Monomaniac* (London: Hutchinson, 1901).

52. J. Kristeva, *Etrangers à nous-mêmes* (Paris: Fayard, 1988), 12: "D'abord sa singularité saisit: ces yeux, ces lèvres, ces pommettes, cette peau pas comme les autres le distinguent et rappellent qu'il y a là *quelqu'un.* La différence de ce visage révèle en paroxyme ce que tout visage devrait dévoiler au regard attentif: l'inexistence de la banalité chez les humains. Pourtant, c'est le banal, précisement, qui constitue une communauté pour nos habitudes quotidiennes. Mais cette saisie, qui nous captive, des traits de l'étranger à la fois appelle et rejette: 'Je suis au moins aussi singulier et donc je l'aime,' se dit l'observateur; 'or je préfère ma propre singularité et donc je le tue,' peut-il conclure" (my translation).

53. Rose, *Jazz Cleopatra,* 7.

PART II

CONTEMPORARY
VISUAL DISCOURSES

Postnational Aesthetics

MAKING ART, MAKING CITIZENS

Las Comadres and Postnational Aesthetics

Aida Mancillas, Ruth Wallen, and Marguerite R. Waller

Las Comadres was a multinational women's collective of artists, educators, and critics who studied, taught, and created art in the San Diego–Tijuana region during the years 1988 to 1992. The group included more than fifteen women from the United States, Mexico, Britain, and Argentina, of diverse racial, ethnic, and economic backgrounds. Initially, we met together as a study group to discuss theory, art, and politics in relation to our experiences in/of the increasingly polarized U.S.-Mexico frontier. Fundamentally, we were committed to perceiving the border experience as a bridge rather than a barrier to dialogue, a foundation on which to build a discussion of art making and activism. The group viewed itself as part of a new and evolving paradigm for the region—a cross-cultural, multidisciplinary, feminist cooperative devoted to understanding and communication across the many existent cultural, linguistic, artistic, and political divisions.

In 1990, the newly named Las Comadres[1] took an activist position in response to the increased violence against undocumented Mexican laborers and the rise of nativist feelings along the San Diego-Tijuana border. Witnessing the growing numbers of San Diegans participating in anti-immigrant demonstrations, and the increasingly inflamed rhetoric directed against Mexican immigrants, Las Comadres joined the voices of counterprotest by distributing a Border Handbook that provided contextual information about the relationship between the United States and Mexico. We also contributed to the visual expression of counterprotest and participated in the ensuing dialogue among all those who laid claim to the border.[2]

Concurrently, Las Comadres became interested in how both artists and the media represented the Other, notably our Mexican neighbors but also women, the poor, and people of color. The group deconstructed examples of representational strategies used to disempower or objectify those groups and discussed how artists and arts organizations often perpetuate strategies of misrepresentation and misinformation. The photographic exhibition *Los Vecinos/The Neighbors* commissioned by the San Diego Museum of Photographic Arts in 1990, which represented the "neighbors" largely as poor, desperate, shadowy aliens trying to scale the border fence, was closely studied as an example of how visual representation can work as a negative, polarizing stereotype of Tijuana.[3]

The result of Las Comadres' border activism, theoretical studies, and ongoing analysis of the responsibilities of the art maker was La Vecindad/The Neighborhood, a multimedia, multidisciplinary exhibition. The installation featured three principal spaces representing not so much different places as different frameworks. A bright, multicolored kitchen contrasted with a completely black and white "conflict room" (fig. 1). A third space, actually two small rooms, included a border feminist library and video viewing room. A performance, *Border Boda (Border Wedding)*, which was staged in the installation, centered on the differences between written and oral, as well as "First World" and "Third World" histories. We explored what it meant to create border culture, a culture that instead of highlighting the alien and destitute celebrated the diversity of the entire neighborhood.[4]

La Vecindad was installed originally at the Centro Cultural de la Raza, San Diego, California, in 1990 and subsequently opened at the Bridge Center for Contemporary Art in El Paso, Texas, in 1991. In 1993 a new version of the library was included in a large traveling exhibition, *La Frontera/The Border*.[5] By this time Las Comadres no longer existed as such, the same tensions that motivated our collaboration contributing to our breakup. Still trying to understand the many reasons for our "divorce *fronterizo*," we have continued our conversation, providing each other with an important ground for addressing the ongoing polarizations of border politics.

As we write, the tensions along the U.S.-Mexico border that first prompted Las Comadres to respond have, in fact, greatly intensified. In California, both Democratic and Republican politicians are fetishizing the fence, blaming the state's economic woes on a flood of "aliens" seeping through a leaky border. Paradoxically, multinational corporations are extolling the benefits of a border publicly defined as "open" by the North American Free Trade Agreement (NAFTA). Both characterizations are based on maintaining a binary ideology, fixated on a literal, linear border that is more than ever defined within the frame of privilege. While money and those who have it may legally cross, the poor are reminded of their place.

But new paradigms of subjectivity and citizenship are also taking shape. Gloria Anzaldúa, who strongly influenced our work, reenvisions the border not as the locus of nationalistic sentiments or as a barren wasteland far from centers of economic and cultural importance, but as a self-defining territory, a fertile zone in constant transition. The borderland could be conceptualized as an "ecotone," an area that is particularly rich in resources between two ecosystems.

In the following pages, three members of the group present their readings of the ongoing significance of the work of Las Comadres for the development of a nondualistic (postnationalist, postpatriarchal) border subjectivity. We write as three distinct voices influenced by a common collaborative experience. The essay as a whole can be read as illustrative of a border dialogue, with multiple perspectives—at moments harmonious, or at least resonant, at other moments cacophonous, but always challenging singular truths, fixed locations, and rigid identities.

The passage of NAFTA itself demands an international constituency, a public to

Figure 1. Las Comadres, "The Kitchen," from the installation *La Vecindad* at the Bridge Center for Contemporary Art, El Paso, Texas, 1991. Photograph by Ruth Wallen.

which to be accountable. A nation-state has such a public that can respond, with greater or lesser efficacy, to economic developments. But apart from a small environmental movement, the only transnational constituency along the U.S.-Mexico border has been the multinational corporations themselves.[6] The development of border culture provides a basis for the creation of a postnational citizenry responsible to, but not bound by, legacies of gender, ethnicity, and territory.

Consistent with our earlier practice of not attributing work to individuals, we do not intend the selection of materials discussed here to be read as evaluative. Our choices have been governed instead by theoretical concerns and the availability of work or its documentation.

THE ARTIST AS CITIZEN

In the turbulent years between 1909 and 1914 my mother's family, the Oviedos, moved freely and frequently between the United States and Mexico as part of the cross-migration engendered by the Mexican Revolution, and internal and external economic forces propelling workers toward a rapidly growing U.S. economy. Mexicans entered or reentered the United States to take jobs in agriculture, forestry, railroads, and, in the Oviedos' case, mining. Their route north was circuitous, involving several return trips to Mexico. Children were born in both countries along the way at a time when entry into what had formerly been Mexico (the present U.S. Southwest) amounted to placing a dollar in a box at the border crossing. The family, like other families, was reunited with extended clan members who had continuously resided in what were once the northern provinces of Mexico (California, Arizona, New Mexico,

*Texas, Colorado, Nevada). Only when the carnage in the South reached unbearable propor-
tions did the family commit themselves forever to the United States. Some of the Oviedo children were already U.S. citizens by right of birth, while others were citizens of Mexico.*

The line that divides Mexico and the United States has a tenuous feel to it, alarming to nationalists of both countries.[7] No significant land barriers exist to divide the two peoples,
although the political barriers are significant, often denying social, historical, and economic realities. In the introduction to his book *The Power of Maps*, Denis Wood writes:

> National boundaries are not sensible. If variations in land use (as between Haiti and the
> Dominican Republic), or the gauge of railroad track (as between Russia and China), or the
> orientation of mailboxes (as between Vermont and Quebec), indicate the presence of an
> otherwise insensible border, no less often there is no difference to mark such a boundary
> through the rain forest (between Bolivia and Brazil), or across the desert (between Oman
> and Saudi Arabia), or in Los Angeles (between Watts and Compton). Or, the opposite situa-
> tion, there *is* a chain link fence dripping with concertina wire and guard posts establishing
> the rhythm of a certain paranoia, and this border, which is more than sensible, *is not the bor-
> der*, the border is contested, the neighbors disagree, there are binding United Nations' resolu-
> tions that are ignored, atlases show the border . . . *somewhere else.* Here the stretch between
> the sensible and the mapped is close to the breaking point: what *is* being mapped?[8]

The sensible border between Mexico and the United States bears little resemblance
to the mapped border grafted onto the landscape by the 1848 Treaty of Guadalupe
Hidalgo, the treaty that ended the Mexican-American War. The mapped border is an artificial and shifting line, argued over incessantly since the original 1848 border commission
set out to survey and establish the new boundary between the two countries. This border,
in spite of the physical barriers erected along its perimeter, is not so much a line drawn
through a geographic landscape as it is a line drawn through a territory of fear and suspicion. Sustained by the tragedy of American historical amnesia, the southern border wall
declares itself, albeit naively, an inviolable mechanism for keeping apart people, cultures,
and histories. The sensible border, conversely, resembles an organic membrane, permeable in both directions, through which people, materials, ideas, and culture pass, combine, split, give off energy, and recombine in innumerable variation. In the San Diego–
Tijuana region, artists, including members of the women's art group Las Comadres, have
been experimenting for many years with visual and performance strategies that identify
characteristics of mapped and organic borders, revealing the complex belief systems that
underlie both border concepts.

During the 1980s and early 1990s a series of related political events in California
launched Las Comadres into the struggle over the representation of the border and its
residents. In the late 1980s Californians began to grow uneasy at the numbers of non-
European immigrants settling in California from all over the world. Media reports indicated that the state would have a nonwhite majority by the early twenty-first century. In
1986, as the reality of their shaky economic situation became evident (a condition brought
about by the passage of Proposition 13, the so-called taxpayers' revolt; the loss of defense-
related industries with the collapse of the Cold War; and changes in the global economy),

California voters responded to growing numbers of immigrants in the state and the necessity of providing bilingual services by passing an English-only initiative making English the official language of the state.[9] The 1990s ushered in a tidal wave of xenophobic activities, some of which echoed earlier examples of racism in California in the twentieth century.[10] In 1990, a series of nativist demonstrations against undocumented workers, titled Light Up the Border and American Spring,[11] created a climate of hostility that gave tacit encouragement for vigilantism to the radical right fringe.[12] San Diegans were stirred into a racist frenzy by the talk-radio ravings of former San Diego mayor Roger Hedgecock, a supporter and organizer of Light Up the Border activities.

In the supercharged atmosphere of the San Diego–Tijuana social and political scene of the late 1980s and early 1990s, Las Comadres met the challenge of transforming their ongoing critical and theoretical discussions into direct political action. Working collaboratively with human rights groups, students, educators, and cultural organizations, Las Comadres added our participation to a transnational, critical dialogue examining Mexico–U.S. border culture, advancing new perspectives on "the border," "community," "citizenship," and "nationalism" in the public arena. Although the group has disbanded, we continue to participate in the creation of a humane, public life for all border citizens. A review of the group's challenges and accomplishments may help direct the invention of new metaphors for our region, cross-cultural dialogue, and citizenship "not bound by legacies of gender, ethnicity, and territory."[13]

From its inception Las Comadres operated anonymously within the arts community and community-at-large, a move that strengthened our resistance to the contemporary art world focus on individual celebrity rather than on the collaborative models being explored in the group. The anonymity of group members also helped divert the media and others from attaching hierarchies of "expertness" or "leadership" to individual members, creating instead the possibility for multiple nonhierarchical structures in which every Comadre could take on leadership and decision-making tasks. Beginning with the 1990 Light Up the Border counterdemonstrations, in which group members circulated among demonstrators and the press, to the interactive aspects of *La Vecindad/The Neighborhood,* which invited the viewer literally into the work, Las Comadres functioned as anonymous facilitators or "neighbors," attempting to break down barriers of Otherness and provide spaces of exchange and education. Anonymity assured a leveling of the relationship between artist and audience/community. Rejecting the traditional hierarchical categories of artist as genius, special, or exotic, we could position ourselves as citizens among fellow citizens. This action, in turn, opened up the possibility of innovative partnerships between the arts and the community, two groups not generally viewed as having anything substantive in common. Allan Kaprow describes such work as "lifelike art," artwork that is inseparable from the context in which it has been created, whose genre, frame, public, and purpose do not resemble what we have come to recognize as art.[14]

Street art and street performance, anonymous by nature, had been significant in prior work by members of Las Comadres. These temporary and unexpected works tweaked our notions of recognizable art still further. Occurring on both sides of the mapped border, the artworks dealt with a variety of border issues including racism, civic life in all its contradictions, the media, and sociopolitical and economic power relationships between the so-called Third and First Worlds. Especially noteworthy were the works of Emily Hicks and Rocio Weiss as the "Wrestler Bride and Santa Frida"; Berta Jottar's recording of herself in her various border-crosser personae, as well as her street performances in Tijuana with artist/journalist Maria Eraña (among others);[15] and Cindy Zimmerman and her downtown San Diego performance titled *Cool Waters*. Each woman used performance as a tool to expose, if only temporarily, the controlling mechanisms imposed by the dominant political structure of both the United States and Mexico, tolerated or barely noticed by the majority. Border checkpoints, the lack of human interaction possible through the design and maintenance of public space, and the official uniforms or behaviors that signal approval or disapproval from mass culture all became the subject and context of these women's street interventions in ephemeral but highly charged urban vignettes.

These pre-Comadres performances were comic, even slightly surreal, and designed to turn heads, creating public space in which the unexpected, the humane, the spontaneous, the unresolved, and the ambiguous might be encountered. Emily Hicks's exploration of sexuality and border contradictions took on an extreme theatricality as she appeared in public in her guise of a masked wrestler, an important popular Mexican icon. Her persona (singly and in collaboration with Rocio Weiss as Santa Frida), moving through the U.S.-Mexico border checkpoint, was a critical visual representation of ideas that would be formalized as written border theory. Cindy Zimmerman's *Cool Waters* installation/performance piece redeemed downtown San Diego civic space by establishing a small humane oasis amid the concrete and office buildings where the lives of white-collar professional workers, blue-collar workers, artists, and the unseen urban disenfranchised might intersect over a glass of "cool water."[16] Discussion of these works, their strategies, and outcomes was an important cornerstone in the foundation of Comadres' thinking and subsequent work. If anonymity had liberated Las Comadres from the high visibility and closed, circular economic system of the art world,[17] performance proved to be the map through a new territory of active participation in community events and public life. Performance in the public sphere introduced a disordering of the status quo. In the resultant space there was an opportunity to call attention to the structure of everyday reality, to awaken the sleepwalker whose feelings and experiences are dulled by prevailing mass culture and mass information systems.

Although women artists had worked for years on border issues in a variety of media, generally in association with male artists or male-controlled art groups, Las Comadres represented one of the first all women's group committed to challenging the status quo, including the art establishment, on all levels with the introduction of feminist critical tools. Within the so-called progressive or multicultural arts movements, male support for the often groundbreaking intellectual and philosophical work of women artists was scarce. Chicana artist Yreina Cervantez, speaking at a forum highlighting the first wave of important Chicana artists (held at the University of California, Santa Barbara, 1991), asked the obvious question as she looked out across the auditorium, "Where are the men, and why are they consistently absent when the subject is the work of women?" The perception that culture (including the arts and the arena of ideas) is a territory to be claimed and defended, as well as the perception, real or imagined, of scarcity (of money, jobs, and critical attention), proved to be as debilitating and divisive in the art world as in the larger community. The political implications of male control of the local art dialogue, whether orchestrated by artists or critics, were clear. The introduction of new voices was not seen as contributing to the realm of ideas, but as an incursion into territory mapped and defined by men with the assistance of male and female critics. Comadres members found their position as women to be painfully familiar—as necessary but (preferably) invisible contributors. Occurring in the context of the serious deconstruction of colonial structures underpinning the Columbus Quincentenary advanced by local "progressive" artists and artists of color, the attacks on individual Comadres and the group as a whole were painfully ironic. The border of gender and sexism proved as resistant to crossing as the new steel fence being installed at the border.

Internationally, in contrast to the local activities of Light Up the Border, the destruction of the seemingly inviolable Berlin Wall offered nightly displays of spontaneous performance as hundreds of ordinary Germans did the extraordinary—bringing down the wall with hammers and pocketknives. The spectacle held out the possibility that even the most dualistic structures might be dismantled. Seizing the energy and hope of the moment, we hired a plane to fly above the second Light Up the Border demonstration with a banner posing "1,000 Points of Fear: Another Berlin Wall?" (fig. 2). The impact was immediate, as demonstrators gasped at the message. The dislocation of the viewer, as the association between walls erected and walls dismantled resonated through the crowd, seemed to provide the possibility for dialogue—a window, as Maria Eraña described, through which real change could blow. As Light Up the Border demonstrations grew progressively uglier in tone with the greater participation of white supremacy groups, we began to look increasingly toward performance as a mechanism for disrupting the oppositional paradigm. Alternatives proposed included acting as silent witnesses at these demonstrations throughout 1990 and 1991; the organization of a binational *kermesse* or street fair along the border where neighbors might meet each other while sampling food, music, and products from each side of the conceptual line; and the collaborative production of *Border Boda* and *La Vecindad*. We continued to refine the concept of artists as active agents in the creation of public space and public life, both vital to a healthy and humane city and populace. Performance had led us to reenvisioning the artist's role in society, the artist as citizen.

Citizenship, as we were living it, involved participatory action. It called on us to engage the dominant culture over the metaphors and paradigms that shape our society. As women, women of color, intellectuals, and artists, we were uniquely positioned to illuminate the mechanics of the cultures we daily navigated and negotiated. Our daily lives were rich with multiple realities and instances of translations necessitated by our cross-cultural lives. Often we found our critical perspectives assigned to the margins of American culture and public discourse. Rather than seeing this position as one of weakness, however, we discovered the position outside the center to be essential in understanding the dominant culture in two areas: first, in the identification of the strategies and formal structures by which that culture marginalized large segments of its population; and second, in the identification of possible alliances forged with other marginalized people. The position "on the edges," as described by bell hooks, was a place of both resistance and strength, historically and self-consciously *chosen* by the members of Las Comadres.[18] In fact, it was not

Figure 2. Light Up the Border demonstration, April 1990. As demonstrators gathered along Dairy Mart Road, Las Comadres hired a plane to fly a banner, passed out Border Handbooks, and tried to engage press and demonstrators in dialogue. Composite photograph (actual size of banner is smaller) by Ruth Wallen.

a fixed position but a movement, similar to the natural ebb and flow we were observing in the reciprocity of daily border life. What might seem at any given moment to appear only at the margins of society was actually in constant movement toward and across the center, transforming and being transformed by the dominant culture in an increasingly complex and interactive dance. Our challenge, in the context of forging a new border citizenry, was to join fully in that dance, allowing a new sensibility to shape that concept of border citizenry while at the same time avoiding the mistake of duplicating the linear, hierarchical, exclusive structures that pervade every aspect of our lives.

The contradictions and ambiguities of life on the border (indeed, life in general) were our springboard to discussions of a reimagined citizenship. Linear, nationalistic models associated with traditional claims of citizenship demand the exact placement of cartographic marks and a muscular presence to police their observation. However, the historical reality of traditional citizenship has been anything but exact. For the disenfranchised it has proved to be a revolving process of citizenship granted, revoked, reinstated, and revoked yet again.[19] Another example of destabilized citizenship in the twentieth century came in the 1994 California elections. Proposition 187 and the xenophobic rhetoric of Governor Pete Wilson resuscitated the idea of stripping American citizenship from children born in the United States to undocumented workers. In recharging his failing campaign for reelection, the governor tapped into the deep historic roots of destabilized citizenship in California.[20] For Las Comadres the tenuous and ambiguous nature of citizenship in its static form (by birth within national boundaries, or by a systematic legal process), and the capriciousness of its determination, did not reflect the multiple realities of the border they were exploring: its fluidity, its reciprocity, its history, or the interrelatedness of its people. The concept of citizenship had to be reinvigorated, indeed, reinvented, to reflect those realities.

Primary to any redefinition of citizenship is the transformation of the individual from passive viewer to active agent. This had been Las Comadres' path as we moved from the studio and academy to the civic arena. In San Diego, former members of Las Comadres have directed citywide efforts to revitalize communities and empower a disenfranchised border citizenry. Through "lifelike art performances" in private and civic venues we continue to embrace the concept of a citizenship that is actively performed rather than ambiguously and capriciously granted. The resultant "art works" take the form of meetings, position briefs, budget analyses, community dialogues, workshops, and neighborhood festivals. Notable examples include the creation of policy resulting in the City of San Diego's Neighborhood Arts Program, which funds programs developed by artists and social service providers in at-risk communities, and the cofounding of the Fern Street Circus, a community-based organization that trains neighborhood youth in after-school workshops (Cindy Zimmerman); Project ArtNet, an arts and technology program for youth and their families with a special focus on community history (Aida Mancillas and Lynn Susholtz); ArtStreet, an arts and social service program for homeless youth (Lynn Susholtz in collaboration with San Diego Youth and Community Services); and Teens Against Racism, a forum for cross-cultural dialogue for young people (Eloise de Leon in collaboration with the America Festival and the Unitarian Church of San Diego). Other efforts to bring the citizen artist's perspective to civic discourse include the environmental work of writer/photographer Ruth Wallen, and the border dialogue and immigrant rights work of Kirsten Aaboe.

This list is by no means exhaustive and does not account for the many ways that all former Comadres daily call on the critical perspectives developed in the group. Border citizenship for us has meant taking a look at how the border really works, as a neighborhood with specific characteristics, a place of multiple levels of organization and meaning. Today the citizens within this border neighborhood are beginning to act as translators for each other, and as inventors of mutually beneficial and humane relationships—social, economic, and political. In the twenty-first century we hope they may operate unencumbered by ideologies or "official histories" that can function only by ignoring both the past and the present. Las Comadres found in both our successes and failures that the keys to a new citizenship involved the restructuring of power: creating horizontal or collaborative structures across zones of reciprocity, and the active self-agency of all citizens. It is also critical, as we discovered, to reexamine the metaphors we take for granted, evaluating their usefulness in describing and creating our reality. Metaphors of neighbor and neighborhood, bridge rather than fence, organism, ecosystem, and circle rather than ladder were some of the initial examples we allowed to direct our actions. And we began to visualize strategies—performances—that could initiate the kinds of disordering needed to break through the oppositional paradigms, the us-versus-them structures, that plague public discourse at the end of the twentieth century.

The citizen artist has many arenas and many audiences (constituencies) and can, indeed must, navigate multiple realities and multiple codes. She understands that the dominant culture is built on contradictions, that its institutions, even its arts institutions, are part of a colonial system that suppresses the history and value of the contributions of groups other than those of the dominant culture. At the same time, she knows that the ideas embedded in the psychology of the Americas—liberty, equality, tolerance, freedom, democracy, work, family, economic equity, invention—continue to resonate throughout both hemispheres. They are ideals worthy of people's allegiance. The challenge is to navigate through a sea of illusions, absurdities, inverted discourses, mass marketing, stereotypes, and other superficialities to touch a secure landfall where real dialogue and empowerment is possible.

I am the grandchild and niece of men and women who defined themselves and their citizenship in relationship to land, culture, family responsibility, civic authority and civic participation, and religion. The demarcation line that fell upon them in the nineteenth century did not change this fact. My aunt once told me that my grandfather had a card that he presented to show that he *was not a foreigner. And yet, I do not believe he was ever a citizen of the United States. His citizenship was like the line between Mexico and the United States as it was first sited down the middle of the Rio Grande River, a changeable proposition responding to a natural movement, navigated in arcs alternating north or south with every wet winter. So it is with those of us who live in a land without borders.*

Aida Mancillas
San Diego, California, 1995

THE AESTHETICS OF DETERRITORIALIZATION

The women who constituted the binational, bilingual art-making collective Las Comadres would agree (on this, if nothing else) that power politics and "multiculturalism" are inter-implicated up to their eyeballs.[21] We have been, and continue to be, turned inside out, unnerved, and violently refigured by the process of working across the borderlines scored in our universes by five hundred years (to speak of just the local contexts) of colonialisms, racisms, sexisms, homophobias, and other less nameable forms of violence. Symptomatically, installation and performance art, among the most category-free zones of exhibition, have emerged as primary forums for Comadres, whether working collectively or individually. Director and performance artist Laura Esparza stresses the centrality to her theater work of evading the classic Aristotelian injunctions of unity, and the voyeurism of conventional spectacle-spectator relations. She inserts a *carpa*, the nineteenth-century Mexican variety/vaudeville show, in the midst of her production of Alicia Mena's *Las Nuevas Tamaleras,* for example. The *carpa,* the traditional forum for community political discussions that could not safely take place more publically, fosters unforeseeable, nonhierarchical, nondualistic, nonlinear transactions, allowing audience members and performers together to explore issues that the script treats only tangentially. Riffing not only on explicit racism but also its more subtle expression in lingering Kantian insistences that "real art" be above (and apart from) politics, the Comadres' hired plane with its banner

Figure 3. Las Comadres, "Reading Room/Sala de Lectura" as reconstructed for *La Frontera/The Border* exhibition at The Museum of Contemporary Art, San Diego, 1993. Photograph by Lynn Susholtz.

("1000 Points of Fear: Another Berlin Wall?"; see fig. 2) at least physically turned heads at one of the anti-immigration demonstrations staged in the spring and summer of 1990 at the San Diego–Tijuana border. Our work, circuitously related to the fluxus movement of the sixties, attempts to maintain a flux of nonstabilizing relationships in a deterritorializing effort to "keep identity perpetually at bay."[22] "Home is where your toothbrush is," Yareli Arizmendi concludes, not, of course, without ambivalence, in her *Nostalgia Maldita* [Damned Nostalgia]: 1-900-MEXICO.[23]

Our conception of a border feminist library, one of the three principal "rooms" in our installation *La Vecindad/The Neighborhood*, relays the destabilization of subject-object, self-Other relations throughout all its levels and dimensions. Probably not coincidentally, this *Reading Room/Sala de Lectura* is one of our most completely collaborative ventures and represented us in the major traveling exhibition *La Frontera/The Border,* co-curated in 1993 by the Centro Cultural de la Raza and the Museum of Contemporary Art, San Diego. A highly interactive space, it situates spectators as simultaneously readers of, and figures in, its design, as they sit at a long multicolored table, reading through the collection of feminist and border-related materials that have been significant to us in recent years, supplemented now by new artist's books and essays created by some of us in response to the experience of the 1990 exhibition (fig. 3). Not only does reading in this way become an object, as well as a form, of perception, but in order to find in our texts the histories and theories underwriting this topologically complex space, visitors quite literally have to turn their backs on a rich assemblage of works and memorabilia mounted on the walls. They are encouraged to experience an awareness of their own position (and its limitations) in that space. Foiling the construction of neutral, transparent, unified subject/ viewers—ones who have only to look in order to see—this configuration of seer and seen also implies the coexistence of heterogeneous temporalities—none of them hegemonic— across which to read, see, think, and play. The piece itself seems to offer the opportunity to take time out from looking at art, to sit down and rest one's feet, while, by the same stroke, it confounds dichotomous terminology like *art* and *life* or *mind* and *body*. Binary behavior has deep roots in U.S. culture. By gently, restfully loosening the grip of this range of binarisms, of the imperative to control the field of vision, the *Reading Room/Sala de Lectura* invites the museum-goer to enact within his or her own person the preconditions of a less rigid, more multidimensional border subjectivity.

For the artists themselves to have sent their work through the looking glass of the *Reading Room/Sala de Lectura* likewise meant experiencing the splittings, loopings, and shiftings of border subjectivity. In the first *Sala,* banners that clearly announced a unitary political position in the context of a "real" border demonstration retained their historical significance but also became elements in a collage that challenged the demonstrators' categories. Artists' books on the walls still embodied women's personal testimonies and individual stories of mothers and grandmothers, but they were inserted by the context into a different ontology and a new community. "There" (not a localizable, geographical place), they could still challenge the hegemony of the printed pages of Anglocentric patriarchal history, while paradoxically lending authority—a nonreductive, experiential generality— to the printed pages, set out on the table, of Gloria Anzaldúa and bell hooks.

The controversial collaboration between the community-based Centro Cultural de la Raza and the MOMA-like Museum of Contemporary Art of San Diego (MCASD) that made possible the ambitious group show *La Frontera/The Border* raised the stakes and made more visible some of the risks of these antiracist, antisexist historiographical strategies.[24] Many of the new works on the table commented on these struggles, allowing the installation to contextualize the entire exhibition of which it was a part, giving it an uncanny mise-en-abîme effect that many of us have come to recognize as itself a distinguishing characteristic of life in the border region.[25] Was this collaboration (the word can cut two ways) what we had aspired to (our work had, in part, inspired it), or was it co-optation? Was the Centro being used to legitimate the MCASD? Was it looking to the MCASD for legitimation? What kind of collaboration (the pejorative sense insinuates itself especially here) can there be between two such socially and financially asymmetrical organizations? How might the collaboration intentionally or inadvertently denature either or both of the institutions, and would this be an irrevocable loss or a desirable gain? Such questions do not have codifiable answers but prove very useful in excavating the multiple layers of binary thinking that sustain individual and institutional identities. Whether the context of the new *Sala* either/both ratified or/and challenged Las Comadres' own artifacts of cultural collaboration, it left little room for the artists and visitors to avoid a powerful, nonreductive, "multicultural" experience, however momentary.

For the experience of standing in multiple places at once to be more healing than "swamping," the border citizen needs her or his own histories and communities.[26] With increasing intensity, in this and other works, members of Las Comadres are transforming "state-form" history into what French theorists Gilles Deleuze and Félix Guattari have called "nomadology"—a historiography that treats difference nonhierarchically and multiplicity nonquantitatively.[27] One of the new artist's books, for example, Frances Charteris's cardamum-impregnated, red-pepper-laced box of degenerate Polaroid studies of members of Las Comadres, holds traces of the processes rendered invisible by the pristine black-and-white photographs (for which the Polaroids were studies) made for the 1990 *La Vecindad/The Neighborhood* show. These stinging, stinking Polaroids, seductive and repellent as we were to one another, put process on the same footing with product, exposing the hegemonic effects of tropes like "development." It is also perfectly ambiguous whether the box of Polaroids constitutes an "earlier" or a "later" work. This box of fascinating but practically unapproachable images (not coincidentally, images of women who both constituted a community and have wildly divergent life histories) thus disrupts the habit of sequencing events as if they occurred in "homogeneous, empty time," exposing as yet another absurdly reductive trope the temporality that grounds the official histories of nationalist states.[28]

Pervading the performance *I DisMember the Alamo,* developed by theater director Laura Esparza, is a powerful awareness of the involvement of sexuality (as means of reproduction and as source of pleasure) and gender in creating and/or resisting such nationalist histories.[29] Esparza announces that she is "giving away the family jewels"—at once a euphemistic and off-color way of characterizing her rocky passage from Aristotelian tragedy to heteroglossic carnival.[30] She tells the bizarre tale of her great-great-grandfather's death on the *inside* of the Alamo, with the Anglo "heroes" fighting against the forces of the Mexican leader Santa Ana. Inside is, for once, the wrong place to be since the defenders of the Alamo were all killed. Her great-great-grandfather, though, had chosen to remain there out of loyalty to an Anglo Texan friend who had once saved the Mexican Texan's son from drowning. Later, of course, when the "sons and daughters" of the Alamo come to benefit politically and financially, the Esparzas as Mexicans are disenfranchised. In Esparza's performance, the flaws she finds lie not in the characters but in the narratives ("liestory") that cannot accommodate a Mexicano in the Alamo or a non-Spanish-speaking Chicana (herself) in modern San Antonio. These narratives, furthermore, leave out her great-great-grandmother, Anna, left with "four babies and a corpse." Looking through Anna's eyes suggests a double irony, a double disenfranchisement, that involves a binary gender system no less specious than the dualistic border that so reductively maps the complex history of the neighborhood in which her family has lived for four hundred years, changing nationality four times (Spanish, Mexican, Texan, and U.S.) without ever moving.

Wearing heals and fishnet hose with a man's shirt and bolo tie, Esparza "gives birth" to images of history—mostly family photos and newspaper articles—by having slides projected on a sheet through which she thrusts her open legs. These androgynously birthed images outflank the binary gender system's authority to enforce a univocal "reality," to exclude or simply occlude what does not fit. For example, she dissolves the linguistic (Spanish/English) and cultural (Mexican/American) binaries that have separated her from "real Americans" by discovering that, without exception, every member of the audience has also suffered the loss of ancestral lands and languages. As *pocha* (pejorative Mexican term for a U.S.-born Mexicana) or as "porkchop" (as her Anglo girlfriend hears it)—as both, in fact—she gains access to a global community of immigrants and refugees.

Her dismemory/dismembering of state-form history leads her not to an alienated (national/ethnic/sexual) identity but to carnivalesque citizenship in a serious but circus-like world whose energies flow with, rather than against, "Chicana" subjectivity.[31]

Three of Aida Mancillas's recent installation pieces refigure the patriarchs of state-form Spanish colonial history, not as heros or as villains, but as unstable, ambivalent hieroglyphs. Bishop de Landa first destroyed the codices of the Mayans, then spent the rest of his life trying, with the aid of Indian translators, to reconstitute (in Spanish, however) what he had destroyed (fig. 4). Bartolomé de las Casas championed the humanity of the Indians at a time when the church likened them to cattle. Coincidentally, he worked in Chiapas, which became (after the completion of Mancillas's piece) the site of a significant peasant uprising. Fernando Gonsalo de Oviedo, chronicler of the Americas and one of Mancillas's own ancestors, was profoundly disdainful of the native population, who now include hundreds of his own descendants. In all three of these sculptural portraits (combining image, text, a variety of different materials and scales, and directions for reading), the violently fixed points of authority, identity, and voyeuristic spectatorship betray their own fundamental *mestizaje*, disarticulating the blame, hatred, and terror they have so effectively constructed.[32]

As Aida, Ruth, and I collaborate on this essay, though, I see that I have left my own voice completely unspecified, an occupational hazard of working in academia, no doubt, and a habit marking me as "Anglo," too, perhaps. On the other hand, after four years as a member of Las Comadres, I find that the effort to locate positions may involve reifying some interpretive systems at the expense of others, reinscribing the framework and psychological effects, if not exactly the content, of cultural imperialisms. As a white, tenured, originally East Coast, literary-feminist-film theorist in her seventeenth year of teaching, I was, for example, not easy to talk to for anyone who had been marginalized by academic discourse, by the university, by Anglo feminists. As a recent arrival in San Diego who knew little about Mexican history and economics, Chicano culture, or contemporary visual art, however, I wanted to be (and thought of myself as) a willing student and ally. Until both these and our many other "positions" could be seen, felt, and lived as nonunitary and nonneutral, very little "multicultural" activity could take place. Only when we began to talk about how we defined one another and why, and where the resistances to redrawing those lines lay, could we even start to appreciate the degree to which we had been missing and miscommunicating with each other. I write, then, from a decidedly nonneutral, nonexpert position, in a language ill-equipped to encourage the discovery that positions, including my own, are multiply, even contradictorily, readable within an unforeseeable range of codes and frames.

Marguerite R. Waller
University of California, Riverside, 1995

BORDER CROSSING AS TRANSLATION

Growing up in California, of Eastern European Jewish ancestry, the word border *had various connotations for me. I was both fascinated and repulsed by my grandparents' stories about their early lives in Eastern Europe. Since the Holocaust, that border was closed, the lives they*

Figure 4. Aida Mancillas, "The Bishop Dreams," from the series "The History Lesson" (1992). Acrylic on Arches paper, approximately 24″ x 30″. Photograph by Lynn Susholtz.

had known utterly destroyed. They had made a new home here, in the United States. In the hazy fog of memory ravaged by ninety-plus years, my grandfather cried out that he would not speak Russian; he didn't want people to think he was a green horn. Yet he would ask, didn't I want to learn Yiddish? Instead, I learned Spanish. My father grew up in the same neighborhood as Aida's family. At the time East Los Angeles, where they both lived, was a Mexican American and Jewish ghetto/barrio. We discovered that her aunt and my father were in the same class in high school. But my father doubted that he had ever known Aida's aunt. He said that there were few Mexican Americans in his college-bound courses, though both Aida and I came from families that valued education. Even if her aunt had been in his courses, he didn't socialize much with non-Jewish women. Had he ever considered the possibility that while Aida's family were practicing Catholics, some of her ancestors were Ladino Jews? Years later I was pained to learn that my knowledge of Spanish created as much a separation as a bond with the Chicana women of Las Comadres. While I received a privileged education and was encouraged to learn other languages, they were told, in order to succeed: "Speak English only."

In Las Comadres' performance *Border Boda,* we explore the difficulties of negotiating borders—within ourselves, in intimate relationships, and as citizens of the borderlands. These conflicts are embodied in the character of the Chicana granddaughter. Not only must she translate between the kitchen, the room of matriarchal oral history, and the conflict room, the place of black-and-white reductive binarism, but she must also position herself within and between both of these multifaceted spaces. In the kitchen, she must relate not only to her grandmother but to her *tia* (aunt), who, though otherwise mute, sings Mexican folk songs that provide blunt and often painful commentary on the grandmother's perhaps idealized stories of the past. In the conflict room, the young woman responds to the reporters' use of various performative and postmodernist strategies that attempt to provide potent commentary without getting caught up in the very stereotypes and dichotomous categories they are deconstructing. The entire performance charges the granddaughter to assess critically both patriarchal and matriarchal legacies, to establish a relationship between the personal and the political.

Paradoxically, or perhaps appropriately, when we analyzed the performance we realized that the granddaughter persona, the character closest to our own experience and most charged with navigating border dualities, was the least fully delineated. Perhaps the specificity of her character would have occluded the multiple identities and varied lifestyles of members of the group. But her lack of development may also have signified our need for further growth. By resisting definition of her character, the performance took a significant step. Instead of suggesting a singular activist strategy, we delineated the terrain of growth to be negotiated. The border focus was not meant to appropriate the specificity of the Chicana experience but to acknowledge our residence in the borderlands and our involvement in intimate relationships that cross racial and heterosexist borders. Moving from theatrical recounting of oral history to disjunctive performance, from prerecorded video to live reenactment of events along the border, we used contemporary artistic strategies to begin to explore the multiple realities of the border region. Since the performance, many of us have continued to explore our position as multivoiced subjects and imperfect translators of multiple codes in the border regions. Here I briefly examine some of the recent work of fellow Comadres in an effort to understand how one can more effectively function as a border-crosser.

In Berta Jottar's sketch of a video script "Works en Progress: Intervenciones across d'Line," she alludes to many of the problems in creating activist art in and about the border region.[33] The loosely defined subjects of her piece are seven female characters working in the San Diego and Tijuana area. Each is described briefly, with mention of her activist role (matriarch of the artists, photographer, political activist, or reporter and reseacher of the Chicana movement) as well as individual idiosyncrasies: "She is a single mother, reads Latin, teaches literature, writes poetry, and sings the blues." Descriptions of particular characters and short scenes in which they appear are intercut with images and text about artistic/political events that have taken place in Tijuana, including a memorial for the undocumented, a commemoration of the twentieth anniversary of the Tlatelolco student massacre, and a protest against the Gulf War for which clothes with simulated gunshot wounds were hung on the border fence.

Jottar attempts to create a middle ground between a hip, deconstructive, relativistic reading and an equally reductive identity politics, which could result in reterritorialization—new rigidities, nationalisms, and fences.[34] To preclude snap judgments, or simplistic identifications, which essentially reinscribe the fence and all its attendant dualities, Jottar adopts postmodern strategies. She assiduously avoids concrete, linear readings. She includes only brief, fragmentary sketches of public activist events, refusing fuller documentary treatment. Her characters, though drawn from living people, are presented as personae. The work presents a multiplicity of voices, a cacophonous commentary about the events. The article describes a video of which only a short trailer will ever be made. Instead of master narratives she hopes to create "a bridge from where the spectator can see, jump, or enter into a dialogue with their own otherside."

I find her brief published sketch wonderfully clever, playful, and provocative. However, Jottar offers very fragmentary impressions. It is unclear whether she has offered enough information to create a bridge for a reader not already informed about what she is describing. Feminist critics have described the problematic use of postmodern theory by their peers.[35] They contend that while the critique of patriarchal master narratives is welcome, the relativity of postmodern theory also dampens the possibility of social critique. In response they suggest that the creator must continually position herself in multidimensional historical, cultural, and political contexts. These embodied positions, Donna Haraway argues, "allow us to construct a usable, but not innocent, doctrine of objectivity."[36] Jottar certainly locates herself geographically, but in her insistent desire not to overrepresent the border, so that "each participant and spectator" can draw "this line in the sand for themselves," she resists fully describing the dimensionalities of her position. For me, the most significant aspect of Jottar's experimental work is precisely the way in which it problematizes the issue of location in a constantly changing, never fully definable terrain. While Jottar's use of postmodern strategies destabilizes preconceptions of the border, her work presents the difficulty of establishing a middle ground, providing enough information for the reader to enter the work without smoothing over the disjunctions and the clash of cultures that the work was meant to elicit.

Bell hooks's examination of the usefulness and limitations of postmodern strategies in her essay "Postmodern Blackness" provides relevant insight. Hooks's argument would support Jottar's use of postmodern strategies to foil an overly rigid, static reading of border identity.[37] But hooks cautions that the facile deconstruction of identities and master narratives precludes the recognition that these narratives suppressed a voice yearned for by African Americans and other oppressed groups. Eloisa de Leon in a paper "Presente," about her role as performance curator at the Centro Cultural de la Raza in San Diego, echoes this need as she writes about the importance of voice: "I see my work primarily guided by one essential thing: a need for REPRESENTATION."[38] Unfortunately, however, the voice allowed to African Americans, to de Leon, and to others who have been silenced by the dominant culture is often a voice circumscribed by the very expectations of that culture. Deconstructive strategies can provide a useful critique of these essentialist expectations. However, hooks argues that this critique of essentialism should not be coupled with a blanket dismissal of identity politics but with a discussion of the specificity of individual legacies. Like other feminist critics she advocates an embodied position, stating that it is precisely "the authority of experience," that can lead to a developed, multifaceted, complex voice.[39]

As de Leon acknowledges, this "identity is as tricky as a coyote." For instance, when a Mexican filmmaker models a character after her and photographs her residence so that set designers can reconstruct a Chicana home, she worries about being stereotyped. On the other hand, when she sees the set she feels that they have gotten it all wrong, and together with Comadre Maria Kristina Dybbro Aguirre she intervenes to redesign it according to their specific ideal of a Chicana home. Though she and Dybbro Aguirre do not think they can speak for all Chicanas, they do have a sense of how they want to be represented.[40]

Perhaps the "authority of experience" can mitigate Jottar's fear that border art risks losing specific focus and becoming a hip commentary on appropriation and consumerist culture on the one hand, or becoming overly codified as a specific border identity on the other. For Las Comadres, the process of sharing specific experiences, of giving voice to memories often buried or silenced, precluded simplified notions of self. For many of us one of the high points of the collaboration occurred during the development of *La Vecindad* and *Border Boda,* when we sat around an open fire sharing our families' stories. The experience functioned as a way of beginning to explore the multiplicity of identities as well as the borders and dualistic prejudices that we had inherited. Trinh T. Minh-ha describes the efficacy of this response when she states that feminist consciousness is a process "by which one has come to understand how the personal—the ethnic me, the female me—is political. Subjectivity cannot therefore be reduced to a mere expression of the self. The identity question and the personal/political relationship is a way of rewriting culture."[41]

The retelling of stories by daughters or granddaughters in recent works by several members of Las Comadres involves this continuous reexamination and reinvention of (his)(her)story. To cite one example, Anna O'Cain's installation *There Are No Snakes in the Garden* is centered on two multi-image portraits of her grandparents, Harold and Madge, accompanied by four short audiotapes of stories about their lives in Mississippi (fig. 5). The first story presents the U.S.-Anglo monocultural viewpoint, as her grandmother admonishes her, "Lands alive Anna, there are no snakes in the garden." But Anna refuses

Figure 5. Anna O'Cain, "There Are No Snakes in the Garden" (1992), mixed-media installation with four audio recordings, in SITE, Tijuana, Mexico, 1993. Reprinted with permission of Anna O'Cain.

feigned innocence. She has seen the snake, the line dividing the garden, and uses this knowledge to examine the contradictions, the paradoxes of her southern heritage. The piece presents a series of dualities. Her conservative, fundamentalist grandmother is the only family member to give her a vote of confidence to go north; her courageous grandfather, who teaches her to hunt and fish, cowers in the face of integration. The work suggests that maturity involves learning to navigate these dualities. As O'Cain recognizes that racism is based on fear, she begins to deconstruct its hold. The recognition of the vulnerability of her grandparents also allows her to respect their warmth and nurturing. Instead of crossing the border north never to return, she can work with the ambiguities of her past. Had she made the decision simply to repudiate her southern heritage, she would have maintained the dichotomy between South and North. Instead, because she situates herself amid the dualities, they begin to loosen their hold.

As feminist citizen artists in the border region we are located in the midst of multiple codes. While recognizing "the authority of our experience" as ground, we also appreciate the diversity of border culture. I would argue that our function as translators is crucial. The border translator is able to establish relationships and create dialogue between differing cultural codes. In using the term *translator,* I am following the lead of Emily Hicks, who in her book *Border Writing* suggests that the border artist must function as translator because her position is multidimensional and deterritorialized, often requiring the reconstruction of events from the position of an outsider. She argues that there cannot be a strict division between original and translation. Instead, the border crosser as translator accepts the continuous parallax shifts, the fluidity of categories every time she changes tongues: "The border writer as translator understands that art is not a representation of reality that lies beyond itself but rather a nonlinear movement among the fragments that constitute it."[42]

Postmodernist deconstructive strategies may be useful to interrogate any tendency toward a more traditional monocultural or unilinear translation. But at the same time one must eschew disembodied, overly relativistic positions. Instead, one can function as an embodied translator, even a disruptive, politically engaged translator. To borrow a metaphor from Elspeth Probyn, the local can be seen as a nodal point: one can position oneself at the node of the border region and all of its attendant dualities, embrace the entire neighborhood, and dismember oppositional paradigms.[43]

In Yareli Arizmendi's two recent performances, *Penny Envy* and *Nostalgia Maldita: 1-900-MEXICO*, she playfully, passionately explores the problematics of both location and translation.[44] Though not rigidly autobiographical, the work draws on her experience living in both Mexico and the United States. She develops performance personae caught in the play of signifiers of the U.S.-Mexican border.

In *Penny Envy* Arizmendi playfully explores the tension between unidimensional characters with a singular national or cultural identity and multidimensional, multivoiced personae. In the beginning of the performance Arizmendi is introduced as Dra. Simona Ines de Boliva, author of the renowned *La Envidia del Penny* or, for English speakers only, *Penny Envy* (fig. 6). In this section she demonstrates the brilliant, fluid, and often hilarious function of the translator. Informing "English-only" audience members that *pene* is Spanish for penis, the twentieth-century female incarnation of Bolívar begins a complex multilayered, multilingual deconstruction of the free trade agreement (NAFTA), indulging in multiple referents and ruptured relationships between subjects and objects, the full impact of which is probably only apparent to someone equally bilingual/bicultural. At moments the argument sounds grounded in economics: the penny is the smallest element, the essence of the dollar. Freud's observations are simple common sense: women envy men's pennies because "of course the penny should belong to she who works it." But Dra. Boliva continually plays on the edge of sexual innuendo. The test for authenticity of the penny is its hardness. NAFTA in Spanish is Tratado Libre Comercio or TLC for short. One minute TLC seems to refer to the tendency for northerners to exoticize southern sensuality, the next moment it refers to U.S. paternalism. So just what is the "real thing"? The penny is passed around the room for tasting, to confirm that it is not a cheap imitation. Soon it appears that the subject of her scrutiny is not the penny but the nature of envy itself. As the performance proceeds, her translation becomes a potent decoding of the manipulation of desire by multinational corporations, the chief beneficiaries of NAFTA.

Dra. Boliva's ability to translate, to cross borders, is presented in contrast to two other strategies: reductive monolingual/monocultural identity and equally reductive cross-border cultural homogenization. Sergio Arau (coauthor of the performance) plays a distinctly Hollywood version of a monolingual Mexican, strumming an electric guitar while wearing Aztec or mariache costumes. In addition to Dra. Boliva, Arizmendi plays Chulis, "an authentic first-generation American born in Mexico" who does a hilariously believable San Fernando Valley girl imitation. While Chulis envisions the new border project as "one continent . . . one economy . . . under the flag of Coke-Colada," products appear to be as

Figure 6. Yareli Arizmendi and Sergio Arau in *Penny Envy*. Arizmendi, playing Chulis, demonstrates how to make Coke-Colada. Centro Cultural de la Raza, San Diego, 1992. Photograph by Becky Cohen; copyright Becky Cohen.

mobile as preconceptions of the North and South are fixed.[45] In Chulis's world, products gain their appeal precisely because of their reductive, "authentic" representation of the Other. In one mock commercial, Arau enacts an Aztec-style sacrifice, pulling a bright-red inflated heart from Arizmendi's chest. Hot, exotic love—the latest Mexican export. Dra. Boliva, who is able to read all of the codes, stands in stark contrast to both the stereotyped monoculturalism and pallid universalism represented by Arau and Chulis.

Arizmendi most fully examines the reductivist tendencies of free trade in her "Ode to Diet Coke," repeated in both performance pieces. Diet Coke is charged with the nationalization of hunger; this "official sponsor" will "take away hunger without adding a single pound." She begins the scene as if impaled on a cross, intoning, "Two great eras define Mexico—BDC and ADC, Before Diet Coke and After Diet Coke." Brilliantly doubling the signifieds, Diet Coke, the epitomy of consumerist culture, is also portrayed as offering spiritual redemption. Consumerism is the new religion, and Diet Coke will offer a palliative to the suffering of the poor. Mimicking marketing strategies, she appropriates clichés from both cultures but poignantly reveals internal contradictions as she reads the codes against each other. The slender, fit body will be achieved through the Catholic rhetoric of suffering and guilt. "Gracias, Diet Coke," she repeats, thankful for this antidote to materialism and carnal temptations, be they *carnitas* or pepperoni pizza. "Reduce, reduce, reduce," she intones. Arizmendi mocks the reductive, essentialist strategies of international consumerist culture. Diet Coke will lead the way to "pure essence." Drinking Coke will lead to the "sublime evaporation of the body," without getting older, without dying. If everything, reduced to its essence, evaporates, what is there left to envy?

In contrast to the reductive ideology represented by Diet Coke, *Penny Envy* ends with spectacle. While Arau, dressed in Aztec garb, reprimands Chulis that "the Cortez in you won't wash the Indian out," she covers her exercise outfit with an Aztec necklace and joins right in, cheerleading with feather dusters. Valley girl, maid, or Aztec maiden: la Malinche (mistress, translator for Cortez) or Bolívar (Latin American liberator), Arizmendi appears to be all of them at once. The closing scene of the performance provides a vivid vision of multiplicity.[46]

In the context of NAFTA, and now GATT (General Agreement on Tariffs and Trade), increasing globalization of trade is probably inevitable. *Penny Envy* raises the fear that multinational corporations will dictate the terms not only of economic but social and cultural exchange. But the performance also presents a distinctly different possibility. *Penny Envy* is replete with examples of the quasi-revolutionary type of appropriation described by Celeste Olalquiaga in *Megalopolis*. Olalquiaga argues that appropriation can be reciprocal and horizontal. Objects are transformed, hybridized, and Latin American cultures "participate in and overturn paradigms produced by First World."[47] Arizmendi as translator offers a particularly powerful form of appropriation, of cultural exchange, where differences remain visible.

The work produced by members of Comadres, both individually and collectively, suggests that increasing globalization need not be synonymous with increasing First World domination or cultural homogenization. Not only Arizmendi but those of us born north of the border, in the First World, can position ourselves as citizens of the border region. As border citizens we need not be "English onlys," knowing neither the languages of our ancestors, our neighbors, nor the first inhabitants of the region. The border fence need not continue to serve as a solid locus for the projection of fear but instead can function as a permeable reminder of the relativity of perception, the transitional nature of location. Instead of universalization, our work proposes another vision of the future: global trade can lead to a recognition of the multiplicity of codes we speak, the multiplicity of borderlands in which we all reside.

Ruth Wallen
San Diego, California, 1995

NOTES

1. In Latino culture a *comadre* (or *compadre*) is an important familial relationship between adults who are not necessarily related by blood. This relationship is structured around the ritual of baptism, at which time two significant adults are asked to be the godparents of a child to whom they often have no direct family connection. As friends (or often, family members), they are especially honored by the seriousness of this responsibility to the child and family. The baptism of the child brings all the adults into a special relationship of obligation to each other. The name *Las Comadres* was meant to convey that sense of obligation among the members of the group.

2. The members of Las Comadres, in no particular order, were Anna O'Cain, Carmela Castrejón, Maria Eraña, Lynn Susholtz, Emily Hicks, Cindy Zimmerman, Berta Jottar, Maria Kristina Dybbro

Aguirre, Kirsten Aaboe, Graciela Ovejero, Eloisa de Leon, Laura Esparza, Rocio Weiss, Frances Charteris, Yareli Arizmendi, Marguerite Waller, Aida Mancillas, and Ruth Wallen.

3. See Ruth Wallen, "Art in the Borderlands," in *Border Culture,* ed. Emily Hicks (Minneapolis: University of Minnesota Press, in press).

4. See Marguerite R. Waller, "Border *Boda* or Divorce *Fronterizo,*" in *Negotiating Performance: Gender, Sexuality, and Theatricality in Latin(o) America,* ed. Diana Taylor and Juan Villegas (Chapel Hill, N.C.: Duke University Press, 1994).

5. The Centro Cultural de la Raza and the Contemporary Art Museum of San Diego cocurated the traveling exhibition, which included a new version of the space/installation, *Reading Room/Sala de Lectura* from *La Vecindad. La Frontera/The Border* opened in February 1993 in San Diego and has traveled to Tijuana, New York, Washington State, and Northern California. See the catalog *La Frontera/The Border: Art about the Mexico United States Border Experience,* Patricio Chavez and Madeleine Grynsztejn, curators, and Kathryn Kanjo, exhibition and catalog coordinator (San Diego: Centro Cultural de la Raza and Museum of Contemporary Art, San Diego, 1993).

6. Daniel C. Hallin, "Free Trade and the Public Sphere," a lecture presented at the fourth annual conference of the Binational Association of Schools of Communication, Tijuana, Mexico, March 1994.

7. I wish to thank the women of the Oviedo matriarchy for their service as caretakers of both the family history and the history of the Mexican and American Southwest. They are Lucia Oviedo Dufoo, Jovita Oviedo Martínez, Elvira Oviedo, Consuelo Oviedo Mancillas, Velia Robles Byron, and Elisa Oviedo Baker (in memoriam).

8. Denis Wood, *The Power of Maps* (New York: Guilford Press, 1992), 8.

9. This law has been largely ignored as the practical matters of conveying important information in the political, health, education, and social service arenas take precedence over xenophobia. Note also that the original state constitution of California (1848) guaranteed that all public proclamations would be in both English and Spanish, assuring bilingualism in the public sphere.

10. An intractable state economic crisis contributed to the nasty mood of California voters who overwhelmingly passed Proposition 187 in November 1994, denying health and education services to undocumented immigrants.

11. These demonstrations were initiated by Muriel Watson, widow of a border patrol officer, and promoted by Hedgecock. Citizens were asked to drive to Dairy Mart Road, a road that runs parallel to the border, park their cards facing south, and turn on their headlights at dusk to "shine light on the problem of illegal aliens," as their supporters declared. The demonstrations provided the participants with a sense of civic accomplishment and had the flavor of a block party. Increasingly racist and xenophobic in rhetoric, the demonstrations were finally opposed by students, Chicano legal and cultural organizations, human rights activists, and artists' groups. During one demonstration Las Comadres joined other counterprotesters to reflect the wash of light back to the vehicles' owners with mirrors and Mylar- or aluminum-covered cardboard reflectors. Subsequently, Watson ran unsuccessfully for public office. Hedgecock, convicted of campaign irregularities and stripped of his office, saw his conviction overturned.

12. In the same year, the Southern Poverty Law Center reported that the highest concentration of white supremacy groups *nationwide* was in San Diego County. Also in 1990, an investigative television crew discovered that ROTC students from a local San Diego high school were dressing up in camouflage military gear and "hunting" Mexican men, women, and children along the border.

13. George Lakoff and Mark Johnson have written that new metaphors entering the conceptual system on which we base our actions alter both that system as well as the perceptions and actions that the system gives rise to. Las Comadres fully committed themselves early on to the examination of the metaphors that structure our daily lives. See Lakoff and Johnson, *Metaphors We Live By* (Chicago: University of Chicago Press, 1980), 145.

14. Allan Kaprow, "The Real Experiment," *Artforum* 12, no. 4 (December 1983): 37–43. Here he describes the work of conceptual artist Raivo Puusemp. Acting as a facilitator in a small town, Puusemp ran successfully for mayor with the specific purpose of helping his fellow citizens solve a seemingly intractable water-districting issue. His campaign never mentioned art, but his conceptual and philosophical re-structuring of the issues as aspects of a performance directed a course of action that broke through the gridlock and exhaustion of community members, allowing a resolution satisfactory to all.

15. A discussion of street performance in Tijuana, Mexico, is included in the unpublished manuscript by Maria Eraña titled "Streets as Stages: A Brief Description of Street Art in the Tijuana/San Diego Border Region." Tijuana artists were, and continue to be, leading exponents of visual and performance strategies that challenge the status quo.

16. *Cool Waters* was commissioned for *Streetsites,* an annual downtown installation event at a time when homelessness was at the height of visibility in downtown San Diego, and when high-stakes development was driving the future gentrification of the area. Sparkletts water company provided bottled water to be distributed by the artist to passing pedestrians. The installation also functioned as the site for a poetry reading by various local writers.

17. In this system the artists function as workers or producers of objects; museums and galleries serve as product containers; critics are product reviewers, and art patrons or collectors are the product consumers. Every aspect of this system is interrelated with nothing left to chance. In the art world, economics, marketing, and public relations replace talent as the most significant contributors to success in the field.

18. bell hooks, *Yearning: Race, Gender, and Cultural Politics* (Boston: South End Press, 1990), 151.

19. A new border and issues of citizenship for Mexicans residing in the ceded territories were critical negotiation points between the two nations after the Mexican-American War. Articles VIII and IX of the Guadalupe Hidalgo Treaty provided Mexicans located in what was now the United States to elect either Mexican or U.S. citizenship within one year of the exchange of ratifications. Those who chose to remain citizens of Mexico would be guaranteed title to their possessions and land "as if the same belonged to citizens of the United States" (whether they resided in Mexico or the United States). See *The Constitution of the United States and of the State of California and other Documents,* comp. C. F. Curry (Sacramento: Supt. State Printing, 1907), 70–71. I have not discussed the special circumstances of Native Americans, the group most affected by the imposition of maps, borders, and "foreign" culture. They are, for all practical purposes, truly exiled in their own country.

20. The nativist scapegoating of "foreigners" (citizens, legal alien residents, or undocumented), whether Mexican, Japanese, Chinese, or other nonwhites, is a cyclical phenomenon surfacing in times of economic downturn or sociopolitical insecurity since the mid-nineteenth century when California was first ceded to the Union by Mexico.

21. A number of important critiques of multiculturalism have been offered recently by artist/critics including Italian-Neapolitan-Canadian-Southern Californian Pasquale Verdicchio, whose "The Subaltern Written/The Subaltern Writing," *Pacific Coast Philology* 27, no. 1 (1992): 133–44, warns of the relationship between pedagogy and hegemony and discusses the significance of the commercial success of the sixty compositions by Neapolitan elementary school children, *Io speriamo che me la cavo* (I hopes that I'll make it); and Vietnamese, French, and U.S.-educated Northern Californian Trinh T. Minh-ha's equally passionate regard for unrecuperated diversification in all her films and essays. See, for example, "Outside In Inside Out," in her *When the Moon Waxes Red: Representation, Gender, and Cultural Politics* (New York: Routledge, 1991), 65–78.

22. See Diana Fuss's astute reading of Frantz Fanon's efforts to perform this decolonizing gesture in her "Interior Colonies: Frantz Fanon and the Politics of Identification," *diacritics* 24:2–3 (1994): 20–42.

23. Yareli Arizmendi, *Nostalgia Maldita: 1-900-MEXICO,* first performed at Cafe Cinema, San Diego, 1993.

24. The *La Frontera/The Border* catalog includes several excellent essays discussing the history and

some of the difficulties of this collaboration. I am also indebted here to my conversations with other Comadres who were involved in negotiating the relationship between the two museums.

25. Barbara Johnson describes the use of this device in Zora Neale Hurston's *Of Mules and Men*, Hurston's profoundly self-ironizing "ethnography" of African American culture in South Florida. See Johnson's "Thresholds of Difference: Structures of Address in Zora Neale Hurston," *in "Race," Writing, and Difference*, ed. Henry Louis Gates Jr. (Chicago: University of Chicago Press, 1985), 317–28. See also David Avalos's use of the Möbius strip to figure similar aspects of border art and politics in his essay "A Wag Dogging a Tale/Un meneo perreando una cola" in the *La Frontera/The Border* catalog, 59–63.

26. This is Gloria Anzaldúa's well-known metaphor for the sensation of *la mestiza* experiences: "Foundering in uncharted seas. . . . perceiving conflicting information and points of view" while still entrenched within rigid habits and patterns. See *Borderlands/La Frontera: The New Mestiza* (San Francisco: Spinsters/Aunt Lute, 1987), 79.

27. See particularly "Introduction: Rhizome" and "Treatise on Nomadology—The War Machine" in their volume *A Thousand Plateaus: Capitalism and Schizophrenia*, trans. Brian Massumi (Minneapolis: University of Minnesota Press, 1987).

28. "Homogeneous, empty time" is Benedict Anderson's term for the temporality that enables the birth and growth of the "imagined community" of the modern nation. See *Imagined Communities: Reflections on the Origin and Spread of Nationalism* (London: Verso, 1991), 22–26.

29. Laura Esparza, "I DisMember the Alamo," first performed as part of the *Counter Colonialismo* exhibition, Centro Cultural de la Raza, San Diego, 1991.

30. I refer here to Aristotle's description of dramatic tragedy in the *Poetics*. Plot, characterization, and audience relations all imply that there is a single, unified reality rather than a multiplicity of experiences and perspectives that do not necessarily reinforce one another. Esparza engages in the latter, which she characterizes as a "carnivalesque" theater. Emily Hicks, extending Mikhail Bakhtin's arguments about the internal difference, or "heteroglossia" of texts, has extensively theorized the carnivalesque reading and writing of the multidimensional border text in *Border Writing: The Multidimensional Text* (Minneapolis: University of Minnesota Press, 1991).

31. For the script of "I DisMember the Alamo" and an extensive commentary, see Alicia Arrizon and Lillian Manzor-Coats, *Latinas Onstage: Criticism and Practice* (Berkeley, Calif.: Third Women Press, 1995).

32. I am alluding here to Gloria Anzaldúa's brilliant description of "the many defense strategies that the self uses to escape the agony of inadequacy." She writes about how one internalizes oppressive structures in order to evade the threat of shame: "As a person, I, as a people, we, Chicanos blame ourselves, hate ourselves, terrorize ourselves" (*Borderlands/La Frontera*, 45).

33. Berta Jottar, "Works en Progress: Intervenciones across d'Line," *Video Networks* 16:4 (September 1992): 21–28. She has also produced the short video trailer titled "Border Swings" that is also mentioned in the article. Much of the discussion of the article would also be applicable to the video.

34. See Gilles Deleuze and Félix Guattari, *Kafka: Toward a Minor Literature* (Minneapolis: University of Minnesota Press, 1986), 16–27.

35. Nancy Fraser and Linda J. Nicholson, "Social Criticism without Philosophy: An Encounter between Feminism and Postmodernism," in *Feminism/Postmodernism*, ed. Linda J. Nicholson (New York: Routledge, 1990); and Donna J. Haraway, "Situated Knowledges: The Science Question in Feminism and the Privilege of Partial Perspective," in her *Simians, Cyborgs, and Women: The Reinvention of Nature* (New York: Routledge, 1991).

36. Haraway, "Situated Knowledges," 189.

37. bell hooks, "Postmodern Blackness," in *Yearning*, 23–32.

38. Eloisa de Leon, "Presente," unpublished manuscript, 4.

39. Note that Jacques Derrida, who is credited with founding the deconstructive strategies that are

referred to throughout this essay, was himself a border-dweller, born not in France but in Algeria as a Sephardic (dark) Jew.

40. Eloisa de Leon, "Presente," 14.

41. Trinh T. Minh-ha, "A Minute Too Long," in *When the Moon Waxes Red,* 113.

42. D. Emily Hicks, *Border Writing,* 67.

43. Elspeth Probyn, "Travels in the Postmodern: Making Sense of the Local," in *Feminism/Postmodernism,* 187. See also Caren Kaplan, "The Politics of Location as Transnational Feminist Practice," in *Postmodernity and Transnational Feminist Practices,* ed. Inderpal Grewal and Caren Kaplan (Minneapolis: University of Minnesota Press, 1994).

44. Yareli Arizmendi and Sergio Arau, *Penny Envy,* first performed at the Centro Cultural de la Raza, San Diego, 1992.

45. Yareli Arizmendi and Sergio Arau, *Penny Envy,* unpublished manuscript (1992), 9.

46. Emily Hicks's performance persona, La Marquesa de Casati, who was known for her turn-of-the-century decadence, "combining sex, politics and see-through gold pajamas," also creates lavish nonlinear overembellished spectacles. In her current performance piece, *Emily's Boxes,* she speaks of a tradition of decadence in a border region, a decadence that is best understood in response to the essentialist consumerist version of the borderless state, Coke-Colada, envisioned by Arizmendi's Chulis.

47. Celeste Olalquiaga, *Megalopolis* (Minneapolis: University of Minnesota Press, 1992), 91.

THE FAE RICHARDS PHOTO ARCHIVE

Zoe Leonard and Cheryl Dunye

Fae Richards is a fictional character conceived by Cheryl Dunye. A cast and crew staged events from Richards's life; Zoe Leonard photographed them and constructed this archive to tell Richards's story. The photographs were then used as source material for a "documentary" of Fae Richards's life in Dunye's film The Watermelon Woman *(1996).*

The Fae Richards Photo Archive, 1993–1996
Photographed by Zoe Leonard
Created for Cheryl Dunye's film *The Watermelon Woman* (1996)
78 black and white photographs, 4 color photographs, and notebook of seven pages of typed text on typewriter paper
Photographs range in size from 3⅜″ x 3⅜″ to 13⅞″ x 9⅞″; notebook is 11½″ x 9″
Installation at Whitney Biennial, March 1997
Edition of 3 (ZL 159 A DDDD PH)
Photography of installation by Geoffrey Clements
Courtesy of Paula Cooper Gallery, New York

Me and the girls at the "Hotspot"

"A WORLD WITHOUT BOUNDARIES"

The Body Shop's Trans/National Geographics

Caren Kaplan

For me Trade Not Aid also advanced the possibility that one day we would be able to go to the source for all our products—cut out the middlemen and trade directly with those people throughout the world who grew or harvested the raw ingredients we needed. That was my ambition. I wanted to be Christobel Columbus, going into little villages in Mexico or Guatemala or Nepal and seeing what they had to trade, instead of going to those boring old trade fairs where everyone buys the same mediocre products year after year.
　　—Anita Roddick, *Body and Soul*

Just how tempting and powerful is the notion of "a world without boundaries" at this historical juncture? A world without boundaries means many things in postmodernity—not only solace from nation-state terrorism at fraught borders or relief from the vast policing of citizenry through the computer data of everyday life but also the articulation of an economic order. For an entrepreneur such as Anita Roddick, the founder of the Body Shop, a world without boundaries signifies the freedom to imagine a link between European merchant/explorers and present-day multinationals; free trade without "middlemen" means liberation. As free trade zones proliferate and tariffs are dismantled, mobility, flexibility, and speed have become the watchwords of both the traders and the theorists in metropolitan cultures. The notion of a world without boundaries, then, appeals to conservative, liberal, and progressive alike: the multinational corporation and the libertarian anarchist might choose to phrase their ideal worlds in just such terms. But can the formation of free-trade zones and postmodern theories of diasporic subjects be equated?

I am interested in the representation of "the world" as it appears in several linked but distinct discursive formations. In particular, I am concerned with the resonances between contemporary cultural criticism and popular culture. Thus, articulations of theories of diaspora, for example, might be seen to be produced by some, if not all, of the same interests that produce a slogan for a Ralph Lauren perfume such as "a world without boundaries." Yet it would be reductionist, even purposeless, to confuse all sectors of society with one another. If a yearning for boundarylessness can be linked at all to the destabilization of the nation-state, I would argue that such a link must be carefully historicized and contextualized. More specifically, I would like to illustrate this methodological and political challenge by posing two related questions: how do Euro-American feminist discourses propose "worlds without boundaries," and what complicities with and resistances to transnational capital can be discerned in the practice of these feminist articulations?

"SAFARI": GLOBALIZATION THROUGH FEMINIST IMPERIALIST NOSTALGIA

Safari by Ralph Lauren. A world without boundaries. A world of romance and elegance.
A personal adventure and a way of life.
    —Advertising copy for Ralph Lauren

Although the imperial narrative is ultimately masculinist, the ambiguous role of European
female characters, as in the case of the harem, complicates the analysis. Here the intersection
of colonial and gender discourses generates a shifting, contradictory subject positioning.
Whether as traveler, settler, nurse or scientist, a Western female character can simultaneously
constitute "center" and "periphery," identity and alterity.
    —Ella Shohat and Robert Stam, *Unthinking Eurocentrism:*
    Multiculturalism and the Media

Postmodern engagements with the notion of boundarylessness are manifested in numerous ways, including the representational practices of popular culture and advertising. In fact, the phrase *a world without boundaries* constitutes the slogan of Ralph Lauren's very successful advertising campaign for his perfume Safari. The Safari ads, generated throughout the early '90s, are visually staged to evoke several different "imperial" locations. In all of the ads in the series, the same blond, lanky model is posed as a traveler during the Golden Age of Euro-American travel between the two World Wars, that period that Paul Fussell has celebrated in his well-known text *Abroad*.[1] Her baggage is extravagant and bulky, signaling extreme wealth, even as her demeanor suggests an impulsive tourist who is always already in transit—a chronic sightseer, a high-society nomad.

Playing on familiar cinematic and literary representations of wealthy white women in East Africa before formal decolonization, the Safari ad that most interests me here is the multiple-page evocation of the "great age of travel." In this soft-focus view of the Happy Valley set, white women lounge in harem pants, ride in jodhpurs, and pose next to planes, recuperating the popularity of Isak Dinesen's *Out of Africa* and its revival in film as well as the reissue of Beryl Markham's Kenyan memoir, *West with the Night*.[2] In the rather "pomo" confusion of colonial imagery that now marks some kinds of "postcolonial" discourse, the "African" elements of the ads tend to refer to external shots of landscape and wildlife while the interior depictions make direct reference to harem discourse through silky pillows and pajamas. Here, orientalism meets *The Flame Trees of Thika*—European settler society, military campaigns, and trade agreements merge with Islamic, African, and Asian cultural traditions.[3] Thus, many of the primary tropes of European colonization can be found in each ad that glorifies "travel": nostalgic placement of a white, female subject in the highly generalized site of the "colony," displacing indigenous residents and erasing political conflict.[4]

In recent years, an anti-imperialist feminist scholarship has contextualized the image of the white memsahib, identifying the political grounds that construct such mystified scapegoats. The white, Euro-American female in the colony is gaining a history that makes class differences between women travelers and settlers meaningful in the reproduction not only of racism but other forms of epistemic violence.[5] Blaming white women alone for empire, as the popular stereotype suggests, is no longer as widely practiced. Yet as new scholarship has made the white, female subject in the colony less unified and more historically contingent, a "Raj nostalgia" and renewed enthusiasm for the literature and imagery of travel has combined with ethnocentric feminist practices to produce newly gendered versions of colonial discourse in a supposedly *post*colonial era.[6] When the freedom to travel is held to be the sign of liberation for Euro-American women, it is inevitable that the terms and histories of modes of transportation, the production of "difference" for tourist consumption, and the social construction of class, race, and nation become mystified. Such literal and figurative travel enables and reproduces a dangerous "global-sisterhood" model that asserts similarities based on essentialized categories.[7]

I first noticed the advertising campaign for Safari and found myself musing on the slogan "a world without boundaries" when I was in the midst of writing the introduction to an edited book with my colleague Inderpal Grewal on transnational feminist critical practices.[8] As we struggled to formulate what we meant by juxtaposing "transnational" and "feminism" in the historical context of postmodernity, the liberal jingle of "a world without boundaries" rang in our ears. Along with *transnational,* other key terms in postcolonial studies and in cultural studies raise the question of how to represent the world and one's location in it; *diaspora* suggests a world without boundaries, perhaps, as do *cosmopolitan* and *nomad*. At the same time, theories of *location* have emerged to argue for historically specific boundaries and borderlines. The *politics of location* is only one recent phrase that argues for analysis of assertions of micropolitical resistances to globalized influences.[9] In the intellectual environment of Euro-American postmodernism, recourse to the *local* and *specific* over and against the *global* and the *general* often comes to seem like a theoretical panacea rather than a new articulation of the same old Western humanism.

As we worked on a theory of transnational feminist critical practices, we found ourselves searching for more nuanced ways to talk about connections and similarities without homogenizing or appropriating subjects. A notion of links between locations and subjects deconstructs the long-standing Marxist cultural hegemony model by demonstrating the impossibility of finding a pure position or site of subjectivity outside the economic and cultural dynamics that structure modernity. On the other hand, rather than opting for a "victim of capitalism" definition for either the subaltern or metropolitan subject, we would argue that it is through transnationality that feminists can resist the practices of modernity that have been so repressive to women—nationalism, modernism, imperialism, and so on.

In viewing the world as a series of unequal and uneven links between different subjects of transnational capital rather than simply the division between "us" and "them," we know that we are in danger of being seen as trying to slip the moorings of identity politics and the conventional terms of political struggle. That is, if we are not adhering to an oppositional consciousness model of resistance whereby all discourse and social practice fall only on one side or another of a central conflict, then we must be placed on one of those sides whether we like it or not. Arguing against nationalism in certain contexts can turn into a celebration of middle-class, Eurocentric feminist conventions—something that we would resolutely resist. Yet we must argue against many historical forms of nationalism if we view such modern political formations as structured through debates about gender as well as class, race, and ethnicity. For example, raising questions about nationalism and gender brings us to inquire into the relationship between "precolonial" and "colonial" cultures. As both Cynthia Enloe and Hazel Carby have pointed out in separate contexts, debates about "tradition" and the role of national culture in liberation struggles are often invested with contested notions of gender.[10] As a product of modernity, nationalism must be deconstructed and viewed as symptomatic of the master narratives of power and identity in late capitalism.

Nevertheless, living in the so-called First World, it is articulations of globality, specifically in Euro-American feminist contexts, that most concern us. Following both Gayatri Spivak and Rey Chow, who propose helpful theorizations of the complicities of metropolitan subjects, we are arguing that the humanist articulation of "global feminism" advances a new order of capitalist accumulation. For the exoticizations of other cultures and people, particularly indigenous women, found in the colonial and postcolonial discourse of Euro-American feminism produce what Chow identifies as "surplus value" in the production of "knowledge" about a seemingly neutral "world."[11] The commodification of Others enacted in the internationalizing of Euro-American feminist discourse can be linked productively to the more popularized manifestations that emanate from advertising, for example.[12] Taking potshots at Safari ads, then, is only meaningful if it does not give us a comfortable feeling of distance from the supposedly vulgar workings of low-brow culture. Making links between the "world" in advertising and the "world" in critical practices helps locate critics as subjects in formation—as consumers, producers, and ambivalent, even ambiguous, participants in contemporary culture.

TRANS/NATIONAL GEOGRAPHICS: MAPPING GENDER COMMODIFICATION IN A NEW WORLD ORDER

National Geographic's articles on travel offered the housewife an escape from reality to remote places of the globe and enabled her to enjoy the fantasy position of entering into situations completely different from her own life. The Geographic *made the housewife happy and productive. It refreshed, enlightened, and inspired her to prepare "something different for dinner that night," but most importantly, it did so without inspiring her to step out of place and upset the conditions of her everyday life.*
    —Lisa Bloom, *Gender on Ice*

Just as *National Geographic* magazine has promulgated gendered national interests throughout the twentieth century through representations of managed cultural difference, print and visual media today articulate contemporary versions of geopolitics and gender. If the "national" is increasingly destabilized in favor of more transnational modes of social and economic organization, then the "geographics" of that world order can be recognized as under construction in media and advertising. Inasmuch as this particular construct has much at stake in mystifying the globalization of capital and celebrating the national character of "authentic" cultural differences, I am terming it "trans/national"— that is, the representation of the world in these forms of advertising signals a desire for a dissolution of boundaries to facilitate personal freedom and ease of trade even as it articulates national and cultural characteristics as distinct, innate markers of difference. Enabled by transnational capital flows, these representations are heavily invested in signs of traditional, nonmetropolitan industries (marked as "native," "tribal," or "underdeveloped").

Such commodifications of cultural difference are profoundly gendered as well as imbricated in the production of other versions of alterity. To make such an assertion, however, is not to make claims for a unified subject of gender. *Different* women are formed through late capital's interpellations in different ways, often through the representation of travel and tourism.[13] I want to turn, then, to advertising that represents a certain kind of feminist project, constructing a Manichaean relationship between a feminist agent (consumer/entrepreneur) and her Other (the indigenous female producer/resource), forming a trans/national geographic. As Rey Chow has argued, the "production of the native is part of the production of our postcolonial modernity."[14] I would add that the Euro-American feminist production of the native is part of the production of postmodernity; that is, apparently progressive gender politics articulated through liberal discourses of equality and self-empowerment may participate in the *reobjectification* of the "gendered subaltern subject."[15] Euro-American "global feminism" homogenizes economic and cultural difference in favor of a universalizable female identity or set of sexual practices while simultaneously stressing cultural difference as a marker of value in an increasingly homogeneous world. That is, Euro-American, metropolitan feminism participates in the construction of cultural hegemonies even as it may also resist and strategize against such globalization. The questions become, who sets the terms of difference and similarity, who controls such representations, and, of course, at whose expense do these globalizations and resistances to globalization come?

It is a case of *whose* difference makes a difference. Critics from Fredric Jameson to bell hooks have been pointing out that an ahistorical or purely abstract emphasis on "difference" in Euro-American philosophical or psychoanalytic schools of thought ignores the impact of commodity capitalism on complex cultures of modernity. Hooks argues that such commodifications of difference promote

> paradigms of consumption wherein whatever difference the Other inhabits is eradicated, *via* exchange, by a consumer cannibalism that not only displaces the Other but denies the significance of that Other's history through a process of decontextualization.[16]

In popular culture, where hooks finds particularly effective examples of this mode of consumption, commodification brings difference into the mystified realm of "choice" as consumers insist on a spectacle of heterogeneity that can often be seen to be completely predictable and, even, homogeneous. Thus, Benetton offers us a "united world" of different, ethnically inflected models all wearing virtually the same product, while Banana Republic reappropriates the tropes of travel and adventure in marketing casual clothing for the Gap.[17]

In pointing out that "cultural difference *sells*," Jonathan Rutherford argues that the mediation of difference by way of consumer culture results in an erasure of visible power relations. "The power relation," he writes, "is closer to tourism than imperialism, an expropriation of meaning rather than materials."[18] Rutherford's comment reminds us that different historical moments offer us various versions of appropriation and exploitation as well as diverse opportunities to rework and reconfigure those instances. Putting history back into our consideration of difference neither erases nor simplifies our ambivalent relationship to the economic systems that we live with, by, and in spite of. Such historicization, in effect, sharpens our abilities to sort through the deadening multiplicities of consumer culture, to better articulate our desires and needs, and to understand the contradictory and productive powers of what Judith Williamson calls "*constructs* of difference." In her studies of colonial discourse and constructions of gendered desires in Western advertising, Williamson analyzes how difference is staged or set up to contain or manage any threatening or deeply subversive conflicts:

> The whole drive of our society is toward displaying as much difference as possible within it while eliminating where it is at all possible what is different from it: the supreme trick of bourgeois ideology is to be able to produce its opposite out of its own hat.[19]

Film, video, print, music, "high" art as well as "low"—all market differentiation and heterogeneity for contemporary consumption. Advertising, conversant in transnational markets and communications technologies, provides some of the most temptingly condensed messages about gender, global culture, and the relationship between local producers and global consumers. Producing local difference out of globalization is the hallmark of an interlocked series of advertisements for the Body Shop, a multinational corporation with a British accent, as it were, that markets products through appeals to a set of liberal political affectations. It is not insignificant that the Body Shop takes a principled stand *against* advertising, pointing to the absence of a "marketing" department in the corporation as part of a critique of mainstream business practices.[20] Yet the Body Shop, without "advertising," has managed since 1976 to achieve high visibility for its products and corporate identity through effective manipulation of news organizations that keep the corporation in the news and through visually striking displays in the shops, corporate packaging, shipping, and catalogs. Presenting itself as resolutely "counterculture," the Body Shop has reworked the conventions of publicity to achieve a spectacularly successful mode of representation.[21] Therefore, I will refer to the visual and textual representation of the corporation and its products as "ads" as a way of resisting corporate discourse and to call attention to important shifts in marketing practices in a transnational context.

Increasingly, such shifts construct female subjects in new ways. In examining the Body Shop's corporate representation, I am not arguing that mainstream advertising is monolithically constructed against women through the hegemonic deployment of sexist representations.[22] Current advertising is replete with references to bourgeois feminist concerns; middle-class and wealthy women are hailed as consumers with extremely significant buying power. Rather than interpret this state of affairs as the triumph of feminism, I view this process of ideological interpellation as one of a series of complex negotiations between Euro-American mainstream feminist efforts to consolidate subjectivity around raced, classed, and sexed bodies and the efforts of advanced capital to expand markets and construct new agents through cultural representation. And many of these ads depend on a postmodern, postcolonial situation; that is, the consumer knows about centers and peripheries in a number of contradictory ways and must be brought into a particular transnational logic, drawn through visual and financial consumption into a seemingly voluntary and historically specific relationship with global politics. Such a trans/national geographics advertises the downplaying of nation-state identities (except as ethnic or cultural "traditions") in favor of a generalized metropolitan or cosmopolitan site of consumption where women can travel in a world without boundaries through the practices of consumer culture.

BODY AND SOUL: TRAVELING TRADE AND THE ETHICS OF EXPLOITATION

I think all business practices would improve immeasurably if they were guided by "feminine" principles—qualities like love and care and intuition.
  —Anita Roddick, *Body and Soul*

What I am suggesting is that at the end of the kaleidoscopic tunnel of the postmodernist text (art-text or commodity-text) there still sits the figure of that most traditional moral authority—the Author/Producer.
  —Paul Smith, "Visiting the Banana Republic"

In his analysis of the corporate postmodernism of the Banana Republic throughout the 1980s, Paul Smith read the advertising copy of the successful catalog as the evacuation of history from its purposeful representation. That is, in advertising that makes appeals to a "history" (here of European imperialism), the complete mystification of histories of social relations results in "stories" that bolster the corporate image of maverick trader. In a liberal twist, "the multinational capitalist consumer is made to feel at home in the world" through the representation of that world as consumable difference.[23] That such a world has been produced through the appearance of adventure and the history of oppression is, of course, not news but still requires readings against the grain. If the Banana Republic catalog has vanished, the J. Peterman version has risen to take its place. And if the Zeiglers, who founded Banana Republic, sold out to the Gap, they have resurrected the entrepreneurial spirit of empire with a boutique mail-order company called the Republic of Tea. All of these companies rely on the "signature" of an "author" whose days spent roaming the globe signal the singular "trader/travel writer" who brings home the booty—information *and* goods. Value is accrued through the representation of personal travel, attested to by narratives of touring and discovery, and evidenced in the display of individually selected, "unique" items for sale.

The Body Shop has its own author and producer in the highly visible figure of Anita Roddick, the founder and current managing director. The corporate mythology of iconoclastic business against a heartless mainstream has found its literary articulation in the 1991 publication of Roddick's autobiography, *Body and Soul* (available through catalog and shop sales). As Shekhar Deshpande and Andy Kurtz have argued, *Body and Soul* represents Roddick as "undoubtedly vanguardist" yet promulgating a "*nostalgic* valorization of the petit-bourgeois subject-position where success is measured in terms of human perseverance, common-sense, and a suspicion of hermetic bureaucratic structures."[24] Embodying that ethos and claiming to be an idealistic, '60s flower child, Roddick has traded on her lack of conventional training in business to distinguish her company from others in an increasingly crowded field of green industries. She has also stressed her female-centered point of view, emphasizing that her choice of a business in soaps and scents came from her experience as a female consumer. Forceful, flamboyant, and feminist, as a spokesperson for environmentalism as well as for her company, Anita Roddick is, as John Kuijper puts it, "the best selling commodity at The Body Shop."[25]

The values of entrepreneurial individualism, hard work, independence, and corporate responsibility that reverberate throughout Roddick's memoir and all Body Shop texts and representations echo the fundamental precepts of Western autobiography as well as Western capitalism. Risk taking yields knowledge of self, and industry produces a community of responsible individuals. Travel (recalling an earlier era of capitalism) is required, both for the opportunities it affords for spiritual reflection and for the identification of new sources of materials and expansion of markets. In fact, Roddick often refers to both Christopher Columbus and Robinson Crusoe as models for her ideal entrepreneurial spirit. References to adventure abound, along with admonitions to be frugal and give something back to the community. The founder of the Body Shop, a company whose pretax profit rose 20 percent to $15.2 million in the six months ending August 31, 1993, claims that money means nothing to her:

> I am such a tramp, such a nomad. The accumulation of wealth has no meaning for me; neither has the acquisition of material riches. . . . I think the value of money is the spontaneity it gives you. There are too many exciting things to do with it right now to bother about piling it up, and in any case it is ennobling to give it away.[26]

Words to make Robinson Crusoe spin in his grave, perhaps. But then again, like Daniel Defoe's fictional protagonist, Roddick struggles with the spiritual meaning of life in the face of accumulating profits. This corporation *makes money,* and the imputation is that it is the founder's very puritan work ethic (mediated by '60s counterculture tastes) that makes it all work so brilliantly. Roddick's "origin story" includes Italian immigrant parents who settled in a seaside town in England, stints as a teacher and UN worker, early childbearing, a peripatetic husband, progressive politics, and a passion for hard work. Along the way, Roddick becomes a die-hard environmentalist *and* a millionaire, joining such companies as Ben & Jerry's in the vanguard of alternative, "ethical" corporations.

Even a company that grew phenomenally throughout a devastating recession in England and abroad will accumulate critics and ill will. The Body Shop has been under fire from the Left and the Right for some years, garnering lawsuits and attacks along with awards and homages.[27] The most recent, high-profile attack stems from an article by John Entine in *Business Ethics,* charging the Body Shop with hypocrisy in its stance against animal testing; other claims include misleading the public about the "natural" characteristics of its products and mishandling of franchises.[28] The entire Entine affair is a good example of the lucrative cross-referencing at work in transnational capitalism. The flurry of articles in newspapers and spots on television news that covered the rancorous exchanges between Entine and the Body Shop in effect superbly advertised his six-page text. *Business*

Ethics, a magazine with a relatively small circulation, published thousands of extra copies and issued press releases, thereby raising its visibility in a kind of piggyback publicity onto the Body Shop's outraged response. In the media frenzy that ensued there were ample signs that a fickle public (led by an even more fickle press) is ready to tarnish the saintly image of the Body Shop. That these more mainstream attacks occur just as U.S. and Japanese competitors rev into gear against the Body Shop's full-scale entry into their national markets (and as the Limited's Bath and Body Works begins direct competition with the Body Shop on its home ground in England) suggests that the *appearance*, if not the practice, of national trade interests has not yet been superceded.[29]

Embattled, but a significant multinational trader of continuing growth, the Body Shop's increasingly high profile in the United States in the past three years can be linked in part to a strategic alliance with transnational giant American Express. As Roddick notes in her memoir, the Body Shop's entry into the United States was planned for years in advance and very carefully orchestrated.[30] A number of newspaper articles and business writers expressed skepticism about a "no-advertising" policy in the mall-dominated U.S. market. For example, Harvard Business School professor Stephen A. Greyser was quoted in the *Wall Street Journal* as saying that the Body Shop's entry into the United States would fail without "major launch advertising."[31] Roddick, to prove that her business acumen is transgressive *and* successful, responded by printing up postcards that quote Greyser along with her response: "I'll never hire anybody from Harvard Business School. People are international. Ideas have wings. If we can manage in Chinese-speaking countries and in the Middle-East, why do they think America's going to be such a problem?"[32] Yet obviously the United States presented a unique set of challenges that required new strategies, including an agreement with American Express to produce both television and print advertisements for the well-known credit card that would "star" Anita Roddick.

The American Express–Body Shop ads can be read as the celebrity marriage of bourgeois feminist travel and adventure motifs to entrepreneurial capitalism. Hailing a gendered consumer, the ad presents the figure of Anita Roddick as a kind of environmentally responsible feminist-cum-explorer who will guide us in the adventure of shopping. In the hallowed format of many American Express ads before this one, we are asked, "Do you know me?" In the following text, Anita Roddick introduces herself to a broader U.S. consumer base through her corporate philosophy and practice:

> For me, the joy of selling bubblebath is to take that profit and do something with it. "Trade Not Aid" is a way of trading honorably with indigenous communities in disadvantaged areas—not changing the environment or the culture. Instead, we listen to what these people need and try to help them with it. What we bring back with us are stories—how they do things, the connections; the essential wisdom of indigenous groups. Stories are the soul of The Body Shop. Customers come into The Body Shop to buy hair conditioner and find a story about the Xingu reserve and the Kayapo Indians who collect Brazil nuts for us. We showed them a simple process for extracting oil from the nut, which consequently raises the value of the raw ingredient we use. The result is we pay them more for it, and that gives them an alternative to their logging income, which in turn protects the rain forest. That's what we mean by helping through "Trade Not Aid."[33]

In unpacking this text, I want to emphasize several key points. First, the ad copy refers to a site of consumption that can only be in a metropolitan location where information about the Xingu reserve and the Kayapo Indians will be pleasingly novel. It assumes that a customer in the metropole will enter a store to buy a mundane item such as hair conditioner only to procure simultaneously something "different." Second, it is implied that consumption leads not only to the pleasure of owning something but to the acquisition of a moral object lesson in Roddick's entrepreneurial philosophy, a set of practices she calls "Trade Not Aid." Trade Not Aid emits bits of '80s-style Thatcher/Reagan injunctions in the '90s, displaying a savvy, neoconservative message all wrapped up in environmentally sensitive packaging. Finally, Roddick mystifies the conditions of production through primitivism. The Kayapo, a tribe that is well known in anthropological and environmentalist circles for resisting both national and corporate domination by utilizing sophisticated media, are depicted as simple storytellers who convey an "essential wisdom."

The images that accompany the text include Anita Roddick embracing "native" women who are dramatically tattooed and painted, bargaining for goods in a colorful market, and looking thoughtfully into space while wearing a hat that suggests "ethnic" fashion. Roddick's memoir contains many more of these photographs—all emphasizing "going native" in her manner of dress and always marking the extreme cultural difference between "natives" and the entrepreneur from Littlehampton, England. *Body and Soul* is filled with examples of Roddick's search for authentic exotica and arcane beauty and bathing "secrets" based on "natural" ingredients (usually foodstuffs such as fruits and vegetables). The company is founded on the premise that its products are inspired by Roddick's interactions with locals as she travels ("about four months every year").[34] The American Express ad emphasizes this aspect of Roddick as world traveler and explorer, depicting her as fearlessly venturing among "indigenous communities in disadvantaged areas" in order to exchange First World assistance for Third or Fourth World products and labor. The presumption is that Anita Roddick is personally bringing economic aid to a periphery (here figured as "native women") and that the cosmetics marketed in the Body Shop are imbued with the moral and political value that such pull-yourself-up-by-your-own-bootstraps activity accrues.

Roddick appears to have reached the apotheosis of her desire to teach and make a difference in her invention of Trade Not Aid. Referring to this practice as an "international trading policy," Roddick differentiates Trade Not Aid from business as usual: "Most multinational companies don't give a damn about the Third World," she asserts.[35] Following her belief that the Third World needs "work rather than handouts," Roddick has trod on some complicated ground. For example, her first project, the production of wooden "footsie rollers" in a Boys' Town in India, went, in her words, "terribly wrong."[36] Completely bamboozled by local agents, rapturously embracing the "simple" way of life they thought they had "found," Roddick and her business partner and spouse, Gordon, raised funds among their franchises and affiliates to build another "town" for more unfortunate orphans. Meanwhile the local agents simply pocketed the money for the rollers and had the product made off-site in sweatshops. Once this deception came to light, the Roddicks, devastated by what they perceived as a betrayal, decamped to other locations including Nepal, Brazil, Mexico, and Indian reservations in the Southwestern United States.

While Roddick declares her papermaking project in Nepal to be one of her most successful Trade Not Aid ventures, I am most interested here in the Body Shop's excursion into the rainforest of Brazil. The Kayapo Indians have been the subject of numerous anthropological studies and, most interestingly, have developed syncretic, complex strategies of dealing with the destruction and usurpation of their land by government-sponsored development projects. The emergence of "indigenous media," cogently discussed in the work of Faye Ginsburg, Terence Turner, and Robert Stam and Ella Shohat, to name only a few, is conveniently ignored in Roddick's accounts of her visits to the Kayapo.[37] Instead, she muses about an appropriate gift in return for the hospitality she has received and decides that a camcorder for every village would allow the Indians to "record all their collected customs, legends and wisdom about the rainforest, its animals and plants."[38] Here, Roddick's urge to erase the "middlemen" means that the agency of the tribe has been undercut since there is no mention of an already flourishing video culture among the Kayapo or the existence of the *Centro de Trabalho Indigenista* (Center for Work with Indigenous Peoples), which offers assistance with editing and other technological aspects to many of the rainforest tribes. In Roddick's rather breathless account of the Altamira demonstration against the destruction of the rainforest, an event that is presented as spiritually transformative for the Euro-American environmentalists/tourists, there is no acknowledgment of a long history of indigenous activism and resistance that might bring about such an occasion. Similarly, bringing beads to the Indians to be fashioned into "one-of-a-kind" bracelets as a way to augment the Brazil-nut-oil industry resonates with tales from earlier European colonial encounters with "native" people; "trinkets" bartered for valuable resources have a long history that is refashioned here into a credo of noninterference with a way of life that is valuable only inasmuch as it remains utterly "different."

In discussing the Body Shop in *Beyond the Pale,* Vron Ware points out the classic "missionary discourse" and the correspondingly condescending tone in Roddick's interviews and advertisements, including an "uninhibited use of 'we,' meaning 'First World,' and 'they,' meaning 'Third World' (that is, underdeveloped)."[39] I would push this observation further because the distinction does not just simply exoticize the people Roddick meets in her travels or erase historically specific references to cultural and economic imperialism. As well, the Body Shop discourse establishes a complete dichotomy between developed and underdeveloped, between First and Third World, such that any complex distinctions and differentiations within those categories are conveniently suppressed. We are left in a vaguely postcolonial zone of vanishing natives who require managed altruism from a concerned source of capital development. There are no complex metropolitan sites in the Body Shop's representation of periphery, nor are there differentiated middle classes and elites in these locations who themselves have any complicated stakes in development *or* underdevelopment. There are only "natives" and the "West," mediated by the benevolent capitalism of the Body Shop. This is a representational practice that homogenizes through the construction of binary oppositions, depending on and recycling the stereotypes and bigotries of an earlier era, constructing a global feminism through the mystification of the operation of transnational capital.

PROFITS WITH PRINCIPLES: DON'T LEAVE HOME WITHOUT THEM

In the old days, the great British retailers may well have been driven by the profit motive
but they were also great philanthropists, functioning pillars of society and builders of the
community. Their monuments were museums and cultural foundations. Now what is the
retailing industry building? Shopping malls!
    —Anita Roddick, *Body and Soul*

It is precisely the proclaimed dissolution of public and private on the botanized asphalt of
shoppingtown today that makes possible, not a flaneuse, *since that term becomes anachro-*
nistic, but a practice of modernity by women for which it is important not to begin by
identifying heroines and victims . . . but a profound ambivalence about shifting roles.
    —Meaghan Morris, "Things to Do with Shopping Centres," in
    The Cultural Studies Reader

Trade Not Aid accounts for approximately 1 percent of the Body Shop's business. While
most of the company resources are not committed in this direction, a large proportion of
the corporate publicity is devoted to the representation of this policy. What is particularly
chilling to me is the Body Shop's *representation* of a corporate *replacement* of the nation-
state. It appears to be the Body Shop that funds and manages development projects, just
as it appears to be the Body Shop that addresses health care, financing, and environmental
concerns in its global reach. Because the liberal state has failed to address adequately
micropolitics and macroeconomics, luring its citizens with dreams of progress and inclusion even as it structures inequalities into governmental principles, it leaves itself open
to such "private" wish fulfillment. Who would not want some big, benevolent force to
come and take care of everything? (And who cares if the benevolence is based on a specific
profit margin?) Like the big fix-it shop that its name puns on, the Body Shop promises
quick, cosmetic solutions, feel-good capitalism, and warm, fuzzy geopolitics.

    As part of Roddick's dream to "cut out the middlemen" her representational strategy
is to excise all mediating agents. Regardless of country or location, there is little evidence
of governments, banks, local elites, or any other mediating factors or agents (except as
bumbling obstacles). There is only the Body Shop and the subaltern, indigenous subject
in need. Although in her memoir Roddick mentions numerous "helpers" and facilitators,
including translators and handlers, the catalog copy refines the discourse into a purer
form. Here, it is simply "Anita" who makes the treks, bargains and barters with natives,
and returns with stories and goods. While the company identifies target populations and
sites for increasing production and access to exportable products, it markets a nostalgic
narrative of "discovery" and entrepreneurial feminism. Thus, despite its global reach and
transnational representational strategy, the Body Shop also recuperates the center and
margin paradigm: as the American Express card ad reminds us, Don't Leave Home without It. Those of us who view this ad have "homes" in a "center" where we order goods
from a "margin."

    While the Body Shop ads are in many ways completely incoherent, their logic is that
proposed by a world-system model. They posit a world that requires salvation from
homogenizing globalization but that ensures further exploitation through the unequal

power relations of managed "modernization." The contradictory discourse of trans/national geographics represents a world that is composed of center and periphery, yet the periphery is always on the point of vanishing. That is, there is no part of the globe that is seemingly unreachable—Anita Roddick has been literally *everywhere*. In researching difference to provide products for her business, she reinvents the periphery; on the one hand, she embraces modernization in order to alleviate underdevelopment, while on the other, she constructs a world of differences that can never be homogenized for fear of depleting the imaginary resource of the exotic. Thus, to return to the American Express ad copy for a moment, the main narrative suggests a "story" of rational, managed exoticism in the periphery, where the extraction of "natural" ingredients for metropolitan cosmetics promises prosperity to a devastated local economy. Yet the last few lines of ad copy destabilize that parable of modernization: "The travel I do is dangerous"; "I am in bizarre places, remote places." Here comes American Express to the rescue, for apparently these dangerous, bizarre, and remote places are still linked to transnational capital—they "take" American Express!

Both the written text and images in these ads glamorize and seek to legitimate unequal transnational economic relations in ways that suture modern and postmodern. That is, these meticulously produced inducements to consume operate by suggesting the modern and postmodern simultaneously through recourse to the modern discourses of travel, adventure, "international understanding," and development mediated by extremely contemporary technologies. Mass consumption, then, becomes a mode of travel that uses nostalgia for the modern past as a panacea for an uncertain present. Consumption is also a mode of production; it produces dominant images of a world of difference without boundaries, and it creates sites or places where these ideas become practice. Mass consumption, as Robert David Sack puts it, is among "the most important means by which we become powerful geographical agents in our day-to-day lives."[40]

Yet trans/national geographic agency is not evenly distributed or unproblematically assumed. Back in the putative center, metropolitans have the luxury of manipulating the images of links and disjunctures, fantasizing *contact* with difference while maintaining a comfortable distance. Rather than use consumption as a way to learn about the operation of trade, to historicize the way the circulation of goods and money actually creates the world, to forge affiliations and alliances out of analyses of divisions of labor or patriarchal fundamentalisms, for example, metropolitans opt for romanticized representations of diversity. The shopping mall is the most obvious manifestation of this trend. A bigger and more postmodern variant on the collecting mania displayed in the bourgeois department store, the mall (like a mail-order catalog) forms a site of consumption where everything appears to come to the consumer, effortlessly and in excess. To quote Sack again, by severing our connections to the world, such "places of consumption encourage us to think of ourselves not as links in a chain but, rather, as the center of the world."[41]

Binaries of center and periphery, global and local, and other oppositional representations of the world seem to produce fantasies of boundarylessness that only reinscribe essentialized difference. The myth of a "world without boundaries" leaves our material differences intact and even exacerbates the asymmetries of power that stratify our lived experiences. In a world where nation-state power is eroded yet intact, where transnational economic systems are formed through differentiation and flexible accumulation, those monolithic formations can no longer account comprehensively for the construction of subjectivities and divisions of labor. To put it bluntly, few of us can live without a passport or an identity card of some sort, and fewer of us can manage without employment. Our access to these signs and practices is deeply uneven and hardly carnivalesque. In this context of proliferating fragmentation, power is never eliminated but differently organized and maintained. Thus, even as these deep reconfigurations of power and identity in postmodernity produce new asymmetries, historical opportunities for change, for shifts in imaginings and practices, also become possible.

We need to know how to account for agency, resistance, and subjectivity in the face of totalizing fixities or hegemonic structures without constructing narratives of oppositional binaries. We need deconstructive practices such as transnational feminist cultural studies to investigate the construction of global/local binaries in contemporary articulations of Euro-American culture, particularly in popular and visual culture, and especially in relation to feminist issues. As feminists we must ask how the binary concept of center and periphery operates in our theories. Are we inscribing monumental identities or are we producing critical practices that will aid our efforts to analyze our diverse activities and participation in contemporary transnational cultures of postmodernity?

In addressing the representational strategies of the Body Shop, I do not mean to suggest that it is a particularly reprehensible business (although it may be more duplicitous than some other corporations in protesting so vigorously against what it performs so well). I am interested in reading its representations against the grain simply to demonstrate that advertisements mask "business" or the workings of commerce in favor of the production of imaginary communities and subjects. It would be difficult to identify contemporary subjects who are *not* interpellated in the world-making activity of consumption. Collaborative studies of corporate practices, sites of consumption, and subject formation would contribute to a fuller and more accurate account of the phenomenon I have begun to examine here in a partial and preliminary fashion. Inevitably, as Meaghan Morris points out, the older models of travel will yield to other analyses of displacement.[42] If both the explorer and the *flaneuse* drop out of our deconstruction of the subject of mall culture, then what articulations remain? Rather than echo American Express's Enlightenment question ("Do you know me?"), we might well ask: What work must we still do to come to know each other without engendering violence? In deconstructing the historically specific representations of a world without boundaries, we come to recognize its powerful allure for Euro-American metropolitan feminism, an allure that can only be resisted and critiqued, and never, in these exact terms, bought.

NOTES

I'd like to thank Inderpal Grewal and Eric Smoodin for invaluable intellectual, emotional, and technical support during the preparation of this essay through several drafts. My thanks to Valerie Hartouni, Elspeth Probyn, and the Women's Studies Program at the University of California, San Diego, as well as Lisa Cartwright, Brian Goldfarb, Tim Walters, and the graduate students in the program in Modern Languages and Cultures at the University of Rochester for the opportunity to present versions of this essay. I am also grateful to the organizers of the New Economic Criticisms conference at Case Western Reserve University and Kamala Visweswaran and Carla Freeman, the conveners of a panel at the 1994 American Anthropological Association meetings, for giving me such useful forums for discussing this topic. Ella Shohat is always an inspiration and a friend. And I thank Stacy Kono for imaginative research assistance and for being such a good sleuth.

1. See Paul Fussell, *Abroad: British Literary Traveling between the Wars* (Oxford: Oxford University Press, 1980). See also my critique of Fussell's modernist aesthetics and Eurocentrism in *Questions of Travel: Postmodern Discourses of Displacement* (Durham, N.C.: Duke University Press, forthcoming).

2. Isak Dinesen, *Out of Africa* (London: Putnam, 1948); Beryl Markham, *West with the Night* (Boston: Houghton Mifflin, 1942). In their discussion of the Safari ads, Ella Shohat and Robert Stam argue that the "national identity of the White female 'character' is relatively privileged over the sexual identity of dark male figures." See *Unthinking Eurocentrism: Multiculturalism and the Media* (New York: Routledge, 1994), 166–67.

3. For an extended discussion of the historical construction of the harem in British culture, see Inderpal Grewal, *Home and Harem: Nation, Gender, Empire, and the Cultures of Travel* (Durham, N.C.: Duke University Press, 1996); see also Ella Shohat's groundbreaking discussion of Hollywood cinema's harem discourse, in "Gender and Culture of Empire: Toward a Feminist Ethnography of the Cinema," *Quarterly Review of Film and Video* 13 (1991): 45–84. I have discussed the feminist critique of Euro-American harem discourse in more detail in "'Getting to Know You': Travel, Gender, and the Politics of Postcolonial Representation in *Anna and the King of Siam* and *The King and I*," in *Postmodern Occasions: Cultural Difference, Gender, and the Politics of Representation,* ed. Michael Sprinker, E. Ann Kaplan, and Roman de la Campa (New York: Verso, forthcoming).

4. Renato Rosaldo, in coining the term *imperialist nostalgia,* makes ample reference to Hollywood films from the '80s that make "racial domination appear innocent and pure." Such acts constitute a particular kind of nostalgia, "often found under imperialism, where people mourn the passing of what they themselves have transformed." See Renato Rosaldo, "Imperialist Nostalgia," in *Culture and Truth: The Remaking of Social Analysis* (Boston: Beacon Press, 1989), 68–87.

5. Without constituting a complete list, some of the valuable work that has appeared within the past ten years includes Cynthia Enloe, *Bananas, Beaches, and Bases: Making Feminist Sense of International Politics* (Berkeley: University of California Press, 1990); Helen Callaway, *Gender, Culture, and Empire: European Women in Colonial Nigeria* (Urbana: University of Illinois Press, 1987); Margaret Strobel, *European Women and the Second British Empire* (Bloomington: Indiana University Press, 1991); Mary Louise Pratt, *Imperial Eyes: Travel Writing and Transculturation* (New York: Routledge, 1992); Nupur Chaudhuri and Margaret Strobel, *Western Women and Imperialism: Complicity and Resistance* (Bloomington: Indiana University Press, 1992); Jenny Sharpe, *Allegories of Empire: The Figure of the Woman in the Colonial Text* (Minneapolis: University of Minnesota Press, 1993); Laura Donaldson, *Decolonizing Feminisms: Race, Gender, and Empire-Building* (Chapel Hill: University of North Carolina Press, 1992); Vron Ware, *Beyond the Pale: White Women, Racism and History* (London: Verso, 1992); Sara Mills, *Discourses of Difference: An Analysis of Women's Travel Writing and Colonialism* (New York: Routledge, 1991); and Inderpal Grewal, *Home and Harem.* These studies, and others, are a vast improvement on previous work such as Pat Barr's pro-imperialist text, first published in 1976, *The Memsahibs: In Praise of the Women of Victorian India* (London: Century, 1989).

6. A small explosion of travel writing by so-called feminists has contributed to the reemphasis of this genre in local bookstores, leading to the reissue of such writers as Isak Dinesen, Sarah Jeanette Duncan, and Isabelle Eberhardt. See also the Beacon/Virago Press "Travelers" series of reprinted texts written by Euro-American women travelers for further evidence of a canon in formation. See also Dea Birkett's *Spinsters Abroad: Victorian Lady Explorers* (London: Basil Blackwell, 1989), as well as several texts on Mary Kingsley: Katherine Frank, *A Voyager Out: The Life of Mary Kingsley* (New York: Ballantine,

1986) and Alison Blunt, *Travel, Gender, and Imperialism: Mary Kingsley and West Africa* (New York: Guilford, 1994). Contemporary writers have played off the renewed interest in Euro-American women explorers and adventurers such as Mary Kingsley, Isabella Bird, and Flora Tristam. See, for example, Caroline Alexander, *One Dry Season: In the Footsteps of Mary Kingsley* (New York: Vintage, 1991). Travel writing by U.S. women of color and non-Western women is increasingly visible: see Vertane Smart-Grosvenor, *Vibration Cooking; or, the Travel Notes of a Geechee Girl* (New York: Ballantine, 1992); Nawal el Saadawi, *My Travels around the World* (London: Minerva, 1992). For a troubling emulation of nineteenth-century travel memoir genres, see Alice Walker and Pratibha Parmar, *Warrior Marks: Female Genital Mutilation and the Sexual Blinding of Women* (New York: Harcourt Brace, 1993). For an antidote to romanticizations of travel, see Jamaica Kincaid, *A Small Place* (New York: Farrar, Straus, Giroux, 1988). As these citations demonstrate, the field of women's travel writing is healthy, if under critiqued.

7. See Caren Kaplan, "Deterritorializations: The Rewriting of Home and Exile in Western Feminist Discourse," *Cultural Critique* 6 (Spring 1987): 187–98; and "'Getting to Know You.'" See also Chandra Talpade Mohanty, "Under Western Eyes: Feminist Scholarship and Colonial Discourses," in *Third World Women and the Politics of Feminism,* ed. Chandra Talpade Mohanty, Ann Russo, and Lourdes Torres (Bloomington: Indiana University Press, 1991), 51–80.

8. See Inderpal Grewal and Caren Kaplan, eds., *Scattered Hegemonies: Postmodernity and Transnational Feminist Practices* (Minneapolis: University of Minnesota Press, 1994).

9. I cannot attempt a comprehensive citation of this phenomenon here, but I would refer interested readers to the following discussions of the "local": Adrienne Rich, "Notes toward a Politics of Location," in *Blood, Bread, and Poetry: Selected Prose, 1979–1985* (New York: Norton, 1986), 210–32; Elspeth Probyn, "Travels in the Postmodern: Making Sense of the Local," in *Feminism/Postmodernism,* ed. Linda J. Nicholson (New York: Routledge, 1990), 176–89; Donna Haraway, "Situated Knowledges: The Science Question in Feminism and the Privilege of Partial Perspective," in *Simians, Cyborgs, and Women: The Reinvention of Nature* (New York: Routledge, 1991), 183–202; James Clifford, "Notes on Theory and Travel," *Inscriptions* 5 (1989): 177–88; Homi K. Bhabha, *The Location of Culture* (London: Routledge, 1994); Ruth Frankenberg and Lata Mani, "Crosscurrents, Crosstalk: Race, 'Postcoloniality' and the Politics of Location," *Cultural Studies* 7:2 (May 1993): 292–310; Chandra Talpade Mohanty, "Feminist Encounters: Locating the Politics of Experience," *Copyright* 1 (Fall 1987): 30–44; Katie King, "Lesbianism in Multi-National Reception: Global Gay Formations and Local Homosexualities," *Camera Obscura* 28 (1992): 79–99; Kobena Mercer, "Welcome to the Jungle: Identity and Diversity in Postmodern Politics," in *Welcome to the Jungle: New Positions in Black Cultural Studies* (New York: Routledge, 1994), 259–86; and my "The Politics of Location as Transnational Feminist Practice," in *Scattered Hegemonies,* 137–52.

10. See Cynthia Enloe, *Bananas, Beaches, and Bases;* and Hazel Carby, "White Women Listen! Black Feminism and the Boundaries of Sisterhood," in *The Empire Strikes Back* (London: Hutchinson, 1982), 212–35.

11. Rey Chow, *Writing Diaspora: Tactics of Intervention in Contemporary Cultural Studies* (Bloomington: Indiana University Press, 1993), 42.

12. On this point I have benefited greatly from reading and discussing Inderpal Grewal's work-in-progress, "Traveling Barbie: Female Bodies and Transnational Movements."

13. I am interested in the construction of female subjects in this essay, but my focus does not foreclose a discussion of this very process in the formation of male subjects.

14. Chow, *Writing Diaspora,* 30.

15. Here I must reference Gayatri Spivak's deeply illuminating, somewhat problematic, and always useful essay "The Political Economy of Women as Seen by a Literary Critic," in *Coming to Terms: Feminism, Theory, Politics,* ed. Elizabeth Weed (New York: Routledge, 1989), 218–29.

16. bell hooks, "Eating the Other: Desire and Resistance," in *Black Looks: Race and Representation* (Boston: South End Press, 1992), 31.

17. See Paul Smith, "Visting the Banana Republic," in *Universal Abandon? The Politics of Post-modernism,* ed. Andrew Ross (Minneapolis: University of Minnesota Press, 1988), 128–48. See also bell hooks's discussion of the Tweeds catalog ("Course of the Nile" issue) in "Eating the Other," 28–30.

18. Jonathan Rutherford, "A Place Called Home: Identity and the Cultural Politics of Difference," in *Identity: Community, Culture, Difference,* ed. Jonathan Rutherford (London: Lawrence and Wishart, 1990), 11.

19. Judith Williamson, "Woman Is an Island," in *Studies in Entertainment,* ed. Tania Modleski (Bloomington: Indiana University Press, 1986), 100–101.

20. In her memoir, *Body and Soul* (New York: Crown, 1991), Roddick attacks the cosmetics industry for spending "obscene sums" on advertising and packaging and points out that such costs are passed on to the consumer: "We have never spent a cent on advertising. At the beginning we couldn't afford it, and by the time we could afford it we had got to the point where I would be too embarrassed to do it" (12, 20).

21. The corporate annual report for 1994 notes that "someone buys from the The Body Shop some-where in the world every 0.5 seconds." The annual report for 1993 writes on its table of contents page: "On 29 February 1992, The Body Shop was trading in 41 countries and 19 languages. Numbers of stores worldwide: 727 (210 UK and 517 international). . . . Frequency with which shops open: 1 every 2.5 days."

22. Some versions of Euro-American feminist critique of mass culture and advertising have taken such a line. See, for example, Rosalind Coward, *Female Desires: How They Are Sought, Bought, and Packaged* (New York: Grove, 1985); Tania Modleski, *Loving with a Vengeance* (New York: Methuen, 1982); Erving Goffman, *Gender Advertisements* (New York: Harper and Row, 1976); and John Berger, *Ways of Seeing* (London: Penguin, 1972).

23. Smith, "Visiting the Banana Republic," 144.

24. Shekhar Deshpande and Andy Kurtz, "Trade Tales," *Mediations* 18:1 (Spring 1994): 34.

25. John Kuijper, "The Entrepreneur, Exotic Collecting, and Consumer Culture: A Critical Reading of Body Shop Practices and a Challenge to Change the Model Retailer," unpublished manuscript, December 1993.

26. Roddick, *Body and Soul,* 257–58. For more on the company's profits, see "Body Shop Reports Rise in Pretax Profit of 20% for First Half," *Wall Street Journal,* October 15, 1993, B8.

27. "Puff pieces" on the Body Shop appeared regularly in the *New York Times* throughout the late '80s and early '90s. See, for example, Linda Wells, "Venturers," *New York Times Magazine,* February 4, 1990, 58 ("Another dreamer, an Englishwoman named Anita Roddick, is shaking up the cosmetics business in profound ways"); Deborah Stead, "Secrets of a Cosmic Cosmetician," *New York Times,* September 23, 1990, 25 ("Ms. Roddick regularly treks to remote regions of Nepal and Brazil in search of natural oils, muds and methods"); and "Cosmetics Maker Adopts Renewable-Energy Plan," *New York Times,* May 29, 1992, D3 ("The British cosmetics maker Body Shop International P.L.C., which prides itself on not using laboratory animals and is an active campaigner on environmental issues, will now use windmills for its power needs"). In a column subtitled "Away from Home with Anita Roddick," Trish Hall profiles the company founder, rehashing the origin stories, reiterating the U.S. expansion plan, and noting a recent award from the NAACP, an invitation to teach at Stanford, and a guest stint along with Anita Hill and Gloria Steinem at the twentieth anniversary celebration of 9 to 5, the National Association of Working Women. See Trish Hall, "Striving to Be Cosmetically Correct," *New York Times,* May 27, 1993, C1, C8. More free advertising occurred in 1993 in an article on the Body Shop's project to raise awareness about AIDS. See Clifford J. Levy, "Body Shop Starting a Campaign on AIDS," *New York Times,* September 28, 1993, D4.

28. See John Entine, "Shattered Image: Is the Body Shop Too Good to Be True?" *Business Ethics* (September 1994). Press releases and newspaper articles referred to Entine as "Emmy Award-winning producer John Entine, a veteran of ABC's '20/20' and 'PrimeTime Live.'" Apparently not discouraged by

the Body Shop's thirty-two-page rebuttal, on August 31, Entine declared, "This story deserved to be told—I have told it." See Michael Swain, "I Stand by My Story on Anita, Gordon, and the Body Shop," *Evening Standard,* August 31, 1994, 16. The company appeared to take a heavy blow when the Franklin Research and Development firm, the largest independent financing firm to specialize in "socially responsible investing" sold its fifty thousand shares of the Body Shop International in response to leaks about the content of Entine's article, causing corporate stocks to plummet. On August 25, it was reported that Body Shop stock fell 9.5 percent from 242 pence, or $3.63 a share, to close at 219 pence. See Dirk Beveridge, "Uproar Threatens Body Shop Stock," *San Francsico Chronicle,* August 25, 1994, D1; and Michael Clark, "Body Shop Slides Further on Growing Concern over US Report," *London Times,* August 31, 1994 (business sect.). After an exchange of insults and impugning of integrity on all sides in the press, the furor appeared to subside slightly, leading to new headlines such as "Shares Rally for Body Shop" (*New York Times,* September 3, 1994, sect. 1: 36). In 1994, the Body Shop won a libel suit and was awarded significant damages against the producers of a British television documentary that made similar allegations to Entine's. Obviously, the corporation is entering a new era of litigation and public relations strategies.

29. An article in 1991 detailed stiff competition from Estée Lauder and the Limited while an article in 1992 mentions even smaller but persistent competitors such as H_2O Plus. In 1993, a feature article mentions "fears of market saturation." See Eben Shapiro, "The Sincerest Form of Rivalry," *New York Times,* October 19, 1991, L35, 46; Valerie Reitman, "Success of Body Shop Natural Cosmetics Attracts Imitators to the Scent of Profits," *Wall Street Journal,* September 4, 1992, B1–2; Judith Valente, "Body Shop Has a Few Aches and Pains," *Wall Street Journal,* August 6, 1993, B1, B3.

30. Noting that the United States has "traditionally been the graveyard of British retailers," Roddick details the care with which this new market was approached, stressing that the Body Shop had more than two hundred stores in thirty-three countries around the world before the first Body Shop opened in the United States in the summer of 1988. Roddick, *Body and Soul,* 131.

31. See Barbara Toman, "Body Shop May Need Ads to Sell Pineapple Facial Wash in U.S.," *Wall Street Journal,* March 15, 1989, B6.

32. Roddick, *Body and Soul,* 137.

33. I am quoting the text that appears in an ad in the August 1993 *Vanity Fair.*

34. Roddick, *Body and Soul,* 25.

35. Ibid., 165.

36. Ibid., 171.

37. See, for example, the discussion of video projects by the Kayapo and other indigenous peoples in Shohat and Stam, *Unthinking Eurocentrism,* 32–37; Terence Turner, "Visual Media, Cultural Politics and Anthropological Practice," *The Independent* (January/February 1991): 34–40; and Faye Ginsburg, "Indigenous Media: Faustian Contract or Global Village?" *Cultural Anthropology* 6:1 (1991).

38. Roddick, *Body and Soul,* 209.

39. Vron Ware, *Beyond the Pale,* 244.

40. Robert David Sack, *Place, Modernity, and the Consumer's World: A Relational Framework for Geographical Analysis* (Baltimore: Johns Hopkins University Press, 1992), 3.

41. Ibid.

42. Meaghan Morris, "Things to Do with Shopping Centres," in *The Cultural Studies Reader,* ed. Simon During (London: Routledge, 1993). Also published in *Grafts: Feminist Cultural Criticism,* ed. Susan Sheridan (London: Verso, 1988), 193–225.

DAUGHTERS OF SUNSHINE

Diasporic Impulses and Gendered Identities

Irit Rogoff

THE PRODUCTION OF "BELONGING"

The Modern Myth of the Jew as pariah, outsider and wanderer has, ironically enough, been translated into the post modern myth of the Jew as "other," an other that collapses into the equation: writing = Jew = Book. Such an exclusive address ultimately obscures the necessity of mapping out a space in which the Jew was native, not a stranger but an absolute inhabitant of time and place.
    —Amiel Alcalay, *After Jews and Arabs*

Amiel Alcalay's "Jew as Pariah" transformed into the "Jew as Book" is writ masculine, a metaphor extracted from material culture and conceived of in terms of the universalizing and homogenizing stereotypes of abstracted scholarship, out of time and out of place.[1] The discussion I wish to pursue, that of European Israeli feminine identity and its visual representations, is situated at the intersection of the two states described by Alcalay, those of belonging and of displacement, and of their inevitable and mutual interdependence. It is an intersection in which the desire for an "emplaced" belonging, enacted by European Jews in Palestine and refracted through the edicts of Zionism, produced an internally contradictory range of vehement, performative, and highly gendered identities. These produced identities would subsequently serve an ideological purpose: they would enable the laying of claims to land and the writing of histories for those claims. Within visual culture many of these visually produced identities are written as feminine and distinctly European. Their tasks, however, defy the conventional codes of traditional feminine activity: women laundering and breaking stones for road paving, women posturing as soldiers and modeling swimwear, women making contemporary art from the gendered scraps of forbidden nostalgias. The images of European women are equally conscripted into the fervor to produce and represent that elusive concept of belonging, mapped onto modern European bodies. At the same time they also act out a certain diasporic dissonance, a diasporic desire for a much hankered-after, yet unachievable state of belonging that is written in their bodies and gestures, in the veiling and performing of their sexuality, in their physically embodied challenge to the indigenous bodies around them. The extreme contrast between the representation of active, productive, machine-like European feminine bodies and the representation of passive, silent, immobile "oriental" feminine bodies within the visual culture of Zionism attests to this production of "belonging."

These very Western images supposedly exist within the framework of a nationalist rhetoric in which they are nothing more than the feminine counterpart to the radical socialist project of Zionism. By this I mean that they are the assumed representations of actual social, material, and cultural conditions and actions in which these women's bodies participated as part of the collective heroics of early Zionist activity in Palestine. It remains to be seen whether the conjunction of feminist theory, postcolonial analysis, and the study of visual culture can serve to puncture the surface of such totalizing nationalist rhetorics and nationalist imagery in order to reveal their fundamental contradictions. While feminist theory insists on the importance of situated knowledge, the study of visual culture insists that images are the sites of identity constitution rather than a reflection of the cultural and material conditions of their making. Furthermore, the emergent arena of visual culture analysis recognizes the importance of the bearer of the gaze and the range of subjectivities through which specifically thematized gazes and their cultural imaginaries reconstitute meanings. Thus the combined insights of both of these theoretical models of cultural analysis might work to reconfigure the purposes to which these wishfully charged images of women in Zionism were put, isolating their protagonists from any organic and naturalized relation to the land, so as to be able to lay a claim to that very land.

That so much of Zionist Israeli culture should have paid so little attention to the cultures of Arab Jews, whose histories of regional belonging have been so ancient and so complex, that these have not provided a model for the newly rewritten relation between a people and a place attests to the resolutely European nature of this model of a diasporic homecoming of the imagination. An analysis that genders every component of this process from the ideological inscriptions of images to the gestural codes of performative bodies might go some modest way toward dismantling the homogenizing aspects inherent in any modernist, totalizing, European ideology such as Zionism.

As a native Israeli I was taught to understand Judaism through the state of Israel, a moment of national coalescing that somehow also served as a rupture, or perhaps an assumed healing, within the paradigm of Judaism as pariahdom throughout the ages. Now I have begun to wonder about an inverse model, about the possibilities of reading Israel through the divergent histories of numerous Jewish communities outside of the state—perhaps as the possibility of reading the state as a national discourse that mobilizes the desire to belong through a new definition, an outsider's definition of what and how it means to belong. In adolescence, every story I heard, every picture I saw, every song I sang served that capacity of constructing a culture of belonging in which we were both actors and audience, simultaneously producing that belonging and culturally surveying it, being seduced by it. In a history so overdetermined by one overriding anxiety and one overriding concern, it is obvious that a totalizing set of ideological imperatives would sweep aside any consideration of what we today might term "difference" or differentiated experiences. In fact, much of the purpose of producing a culture of belonging was to eradicate the concept of difference, which had served to create the racial separation that marked European Jews as those outside the culture in their host countries—as those who do not "belong." How would such a notion of difference, of feminine or sexual difference in particular, affect the scenarios of belonging that were being woven in the culture I was raised in? It seems increasingly clear to me that one cannot have a culture of belonging without maintaining a consciousness of "not belonging," against which it exists in a permanent state of defiance and self-definition. On the one hand there was the historical model of the unbelonging of Jews in the so-called diaspora, and on the other the construction of a whole new category of unbelonging under the aegis of Zionism, such as that of Arab Jews and Palestinians. If this grounding binarism is indeed characteristic of the culture I am trying to engage with, then it is imbued with a necessary nostalgia and desire for the "old world" that are essential to its project but cannot be consciously acknowledged, for they are the very heart of what the new state has set itself to replace. So many of the avenues one would ordinarily pursue within a less forbidden and a less overdetermined terrain have been closed to me through moralizing historical discourses; a direct critique of Zionism by way of the terms it has set up and the paradigms it has determined are impossible, as they would only serve to sustain a true-false, right-wrong dichotomy. This is the reason I have ventured to examine the contradictory and conflicted desires of Zionist ideology through the representations of women within it.

Unacknowledged and unspoken ideological contradictions have always informed the ways in which cultures set up and represent femininity as a meeting point between rational and irrational discourses. Perhaps if I could gain insight into how the culture of belonging shaped the represented identities of women within it, I might also gain some perception of its own internal contradictions. Therefore, what I am trying to do in this piece about European, privileged Israeli feminine identity and its relation to the diaspora it left behind is not to define it in any way but to put together some of these elements of disruption, dislocation, and narration and to see how they work one upon the other.

While it is both ideologically imperative and politically urgent to address the complexities of other, marginalized, non-European feminine identities within modern Israeli culture, such as those of Arab Jewish women or Palestinian women, this does not absolve us of the responsibility of examining the actual identity formation of privileged positions. It is these Eurocentric cultural subject positions that have continued to dominate the popular imagination with regard to definitions of national identity and to determine all forms of Otherness as inferior to themselves. Since the European Israeli identity does not question its own values or regard itself as anything but normative and universal, as defining the cultural identity of the state and of its ties to the world (that is, to Europe and North America rather than to the so-called Third World), there has been little opportunity to acknowledge its own profound internal contradictions or to problematize its extremely uneasy relation to the European cultures on which it builds and draws its own overall hybrid identity. By using categories of gender and Eurocentricity to read across fortified and barricaded narratives of nation we may be able to illuminate some of the inherent contradictions that have worked to mold dominant Israeli culture in relation to the European cultures that had rejected its own founding fathers.

The critical models that have helped me think through some of the issues raised in this essay have emanated primarily from critical analyses of colonialism and minority discourse. These have posited complex and elaborate analyses of both the cultural systems constructed by old world colonialism as well as of conditions of cultural and racial marginality and hybridity within the contemporary postcolonial world. At the heart of all these discussions are trajectories of cultural power relations between colonizers and colonized or between dominant hegemonic culture and emergent minority identities. The subject position I am attempting to deconstruct in this discussion, however, cannot be fully or exclusively accommodated within this theoretical framework. While European, middle-class Israeli identity is undoubtedly a colonizing presence within the regional political map as well as within the internal ethnic map of the state, the feminine subject positions within it are simultaneously colonized and marginalized both in relation to dominant ideology and the ensuant internal contradictions of its own gender-specific identity. The attempt to understand and locate such split subject positions—historically oppressed, inhabiting a performative ideological stance and functioning regionally as a local colonial power—has resulted in this particular instance in a somewhat fragmented and inconsistent form of theoretical bricolage. I have, in recent years, encountered far too many analyses in which the female component of colonial or colonizing powers was assumed to be cognate with and acting out parallel imperatives as its male counterparts, albeit through a different set of social institutions, such as the domestic rather than the public sphere. Thus the ensuing fragmented account is offered in the feminist hope that it may ultimately be helpful in articulating an emergent set of contradictions that have been so firmly glossed underneath the rhetoric of Western, progressive ideology.

How, then, can one attempt to understand the inherent tensions within this Israeli feminine identity as well as to disavow the authenticity and coherence that it has tended to claim for itself? Part of my intention in so doing is to suggest possibilities for a greater plurality of coexistent, fragmented voices and identities within the geographical region of Israel/Palestine—identities that do not necessarily have to claim for themselves a fully representative coherence or authenticity and therefore do not have to masquerade as the sole legitimate representation of an indigenous population. If the conflicts and struggles between Israelis and Palestinians are to be understood as more than territorial—as a struggle over the possession of an authentic and locally rooted identity—then a major part of our attempt to critically address and understand these struggles must be invested in the claims that we make for our own identity. For as Theodor Adorno writes, "It is part of morality not to be at home in one's home," and it is in the name of (re)possessing this mythical home/land that much of the vehemently insistent nature of constructed Israeli identities has been mobilized.[2]

It is equally important, to my mind, to address these issues within the arenas of culture, of a

> struggle [that] is an essential counterpart to political and economic struggle. Since cultural hegemony continues to play an invaluable role in the production of subjects who are compliant toward the economic and political domination of internal as well as external colonialism, and since it legitimates the acceptance of one mode of life and the exclusion—or extermination—of others, the function of cultural criticism and struggle is to contest continually the binary oppositions on which such legitimation is founded.[3]

For it is within the arena of radical culture, unlike that of party political rhetoric, that fragmentation of voices can occur, that modes of representation can be seen to engage in legitimate contestation with one another, and that formal and stylistic disjunctures and experiments can be attempted to capture, to some extent, the "newly arrived at conscious-ness" of our incoherent selves. For, in the words of Arif Dirlik,

> an authentically radical conception of culture is not only a way of seeing the world but also a way of making and changing it. . . . Culture is not a thing, to paraphrase E. P. Thompson, but a relationship. It is not merely an autonomous principle that is expressive of the totality con-stituted by these relationships, a totality that once it has been constituted, appears as a seam-less web of which culture is the architectonic principle, exterior to the socio-political and logically prior to them. . . . Culture is an activity in which the social relations that are possible but absent, because they have been displaced or rendered impossible (or utopian) by existing social relations, are as fundamental as the relations whose existence it affirms.[4]

In attempting to introduce a dimension of sexual difference into the "possible but absent" social relations of Israeli identity, we may simultaneously be able to extend the axis and historical dynamics of internal fragmentation as well as work toward a reradicalization of culture.

NARRATIVES

A couple of years ago a friend and I were sitting astride the fortified outer walls of the an-cient crusader city of Acer on the northern Mediterranean coast of modern Israel. We were, as is our wont, ignoring the multicultural profusion around us—the Israelis and the Palestinians, the earnest pink-nosed English tourists with their Baedekers; the elegant, laconic French ones lolling about drinking local wine—for we were immune to such panoramas of difference. We had both been born into the newly founded State of Israel, into a babble of immigrant cultures and tongues soon to become that most excruciating of cultural experiences, the Melting Pot. Instead, as we dangled our feet toward the warm Mediterranean, we spoke of that most fascinating of all subjects, ourselves. "Our Tragedy," proclaimed my friend, "is that we believe we are the real Europeans, that those people out there in France, Germany, Spain are simply fraudulent parvenus who have usurped our rightful cultural place." "Look at you," he continued, pointing an ironic crooked finger, "ninth-generation in Palestine, first-generation of an independent Jewish state, the fulfill-ment of so many generations' dreams and hopes, and you spend your entire adult life im-mersed in the two cultures that have most oppressed your people in this century." He was referring to the fact that I did all my studies and lived for many years in Britain and that I work, when I can persuade myself to be geographically and historically specific, on mod-ern German culture. Look, indeed, but do not speak, for ours is the shared experience of a childhood in the shadow of the recent European Holocaust of which no one could speak, an omnipresent legitimating narrative for every form of aggression and discrimination perpetuated by the state and the culture, which could not, would not be acknowledged in language.

During this same time, I was reading a novel by Israeli author David Grossmann.

The novel, *See Under: Love,* defies any attempt at formal categorization or description. Suffice it to say that it is a series of narrative voices, Israeli and European, past and present, that attempt to construct a language of the Holocaust: lived, experienced, received, misunderstood, mythologized, and abused. At the novel's center is a nine-year-old boy named Mommik growing up in Israel in the 1950s, the only child of two haunted survivors and living in the midst of other survivors, whose utter disorientation is reflected in the confused babble of old and new tongues in which they communicate with the world, as if fearfully uncertain of who will be tuning in or of what they can speak about clearly and of what must remain coded and veiled. A secret society of mutes at the heart of the declamatory and abrasively proud new nation.

The following is a scene from the section of the novel about Mommik's childhood:

> Bella sits in one of the empty tables of her grocery/café all day long reading *Women's Own* and *Evening News,* smoking one cigarette after another. Bella isn't afraid of anything, and she always says exactly what she thinks, which is why when the city inspectors came to throw Max and Moritz out of the storeroom, she gave them such a piece of her mind that they had a [bad] conscience for the rest of their lives, and she wasn't even afraid of Ben-Gurion and called him "The little Dictator from Plonsk," but she didn't always talk that way, because don't forget that, like all the grown-ups that Mommik knew, Bella came from *Over There,* a place you weren't supposed to talk about too much, only think about in your heart and sigh with a long, drawn-out krechtz, the way they always do, but Bella is different somehow, and Mommik heard some really important things from her about it, and even though she wasn't supposed to reveal any secrets, she did drop hints about her parents' home *Over There,* and it was from her that Mommik first heard about the Nazi Beast. The truth is that in the beginning Mommik thought Bella meant some imaginary monster or a huge dinosaur that once lived in the world, which everyone was afraid of now. But he didn't dare ask anyone who or what. And then when the new grandfather showed up and Mommik's mama and papa screamed and suffered in the night worse than ever, and things were getting impossible, Mommik decided to ask Bella again, and Bella snapped back that there were some things a nine-year-old boy doesn't have to know yet, and she undid his collar button with a frown, saying it choked her just to see him buttoned up like that, but Mommik decided to persist this time and asked her straight out what kind of animal is the Nazi Beast, and Bella took a long puff of her cigarette and stubbed it out and sighed and looked at him and screwed her mouth up and didn't want to say, but she let it slip that the Nazi Beast could come out of any kind of animal if it got the right care and nourishment, and then she quickly took another cigarette, and her fingers shook a little and Mommik saw he wasn't going to get anymore out of her.[5]

The conjunction of these two narratives generated for me a series of speculations concerning diaspora and diasporic culture; traditionally, in our Israeli context the diaspora referred to the various scattered communities of Jews who had been exiled by the Roman conquerors of the land of Israel in the first century A.D. and had scattered throughout the world. In attempting to reconstruct that land in the twentieth century, we, the second generation in effect, seem to have reversed that relationship and have become in turn a diaspora of the host cultures into which our ancestors had been exiled and from which they had been banished. Ours, then, was a complex culture founded in nostalgias for imaginary, mythical locations in which we could function as oppositional marginals to the dominant order, as a constant disruptive Other against which the center could define itself. A new cultural construct had begun to emerge among us that viewed itself as the "diaspora's diaspora." This collapse of a clear historical order of center-diaspora relations led, in my mind at least, to the need to reevaluate the relations between history and geography, between collective cultural narratives of *Over Here* and the signification of that which is *Over There*. Mommik, the self-styled spy and investigator, eavesdrops whenever he can:

> Mommik is so excited he forgets to shut his mouth! Because they are talking freely about *Over There*! It's almost dangerous the way they let themselves talk about it. But he has to make the most of this opportunity and remember everything, everything, and then run home and write it down in his notebook and draw pictures because some things are better to draw. So when they talk about certain places *Over There*, for instance, he can sketch them in this secret atlas he is preparing.

ANALYSES

I am attempting to construct an argument concerning geography and identity that revolves around questions of displacement viewed by a former member of the Israeli intelligentsia, who has herself undergone several displacements backward to the cultures that were previously considered to be diasporas. The argument I am trying to present here concerns a contemporary siting that I would call the "diaspora's diaspora" and negates the very basic historical assumptions that an old people could conceivably have a genuine "new beginning." It seems to me that there are several dynamics between home and exile in existence within the problematic interaction of collective cultural and gendered identities as set up within the modern Jewish state.[6] The dominant narrative of "return home" is problematic not only for the legitimation it provides for territorial claims but also for the seamless naturalization of the concept of home, which it puts forth as a cultural metanarrative.

Instead, I wanted to use the rather interesting conjunction of Judaism, femininity, and modernity as an opportunity to speculate on the contemporary revisions and the internal contradictions of these supposedly progressive, egalitarian, and ungendered intersections. As in all so-called radical societies, and in the case of Israel, too, there was an imperative master narrative of struggle under which all other categories of potential difference and conflict were subsumed and trivialized. In the case of the modern Jewish state the dominant ideology of socialist Zionism assumed to speak for two categories of oppression, that of the Jews as an oppressed minority as well as that concerning their transformation from marginal, reviled serfs into a revolutionary working class linked to an international struggle. In effect, this was a transition from margins to center, countering traditional European anti-Semitism with its exclusions and persecutions of Jews with a participatory political project that aligned the Jews with other oppressed elements in society within the context of an international movement that transcended national or regional belonging and authenticity.

That these were to be transposed into the eastern Mediterranean, into a land already inhabited by a people with an equal set of claims to it, into a cultural location that could not be more different from the underground radical socialist movements of Central and Eastern Europe at the turn of the century, did not seem to overly worry the movement's ideologues. The supposedly seamless progressive identity of this society is constituted out of a discourse that is white, Eurocentric, bourgeois, and masculine and assumes itself to be the norm and the measure of what it is to be Israeli, while masking a huge array of differences in internal and external injustices and discriminations against oriental Jews, local Arabs, Palestinians, not to mention those against women. Given the prominence of Israeli and related affairs within the international media, there is no need to go into a detailed critical analysis of this supposed identity, for its internal incoherence is in fact constantly being exposed through a variety of much reported policies and the fierce debates that these generate both nationally and internationally.

For all this criticism, I am nevertheless a product of all these uneasy corollaries and find it necessary to try and unravel them in some potentially interesting and questioning mode. This, then, is a position of cultural hybridity that produces the need to problematize the seamless rhetoric of constructed national identity through the transnational critical tools evolved within my own generation's movements of resistance to hegemonic culture and the categories through which it establishes itself as normative and indexical. Thus an examination of specific feminine identities within the modern Jewish state can actually provide some useful insights into the overall patterns of internal conflict and contradiction, to which any form of Israeli identity would by necessity be subject. To begin with, feminine identity is positioned as filial, "the daughters of Zion" being a local variant of traditional Jewish femininity, which holds a secondary position within the traditional religious culture as well as being linked to the actual land in some filial and organic manner. But the subservient and secondary nature of this feminine subject position is further exacerbated by the passive shouldering of the burden of history.

In a poem titled "No License to Die," Esther Fuchs, a young feminist poet and daughter of Holocaust survivors, tells of her aborted attempt at suicide:

> Their faces as I was led away
> on the stretcher
>
> No *Gestapo*, no *Kapo* is upon
> you are after all newly invented
> A Bride of Sunshine
>
> How dare you?
>
> The forgiveness I beg—
> They were in crematoria smoke
> I have no license to die.[7]

Esther Fuchs's poem speaks of the despair of attempting to actually possess an identity of one's own in a society in which collective trauma has served to simultaneously infantalize and bind one to duty, to make one responsible for the existence of a supposedly better world in which such a genocide could never occur. Within this trajectory the concerns of

Figure 1. "Pioneer Women at Work." Photograph by Ada Maimon. From *Women Build a Land* (New York: Herzl Press, 1962). Reprinted with permission of Herzl Press.

women born long after the war had ended and the state of Israel had been founded could not be viewed as anything but self-indulgent desires aimed at a form of bourgeois, individual gratification. In my youth the culture abounded in sentences such as, "You do not know the meaning of horror, of hard work, of suffering, of sacrifice, of loss, of victimization," and so on. We were meant to be "newly born," but at the same time we were supposed to provide a daily, conscious, and, not least, grateful reminder of the negation of the old world. Women, whose experiences, needs, and desires had been completely subsumed under the rhetorical mantle of so much supposedly radical innovation and progress, seemed poised between two extreme models of femininity and identity, a radical European socialist one that served as an oppositional stance to the world they had come from and a passive, timeless, "oriental" one that served as a mythologizing perception of the world they had immigrated to.

Being much preoccupied with visual culture and the ways in which images construct meanings and mediate power relations, I would like to examine the following photographs as the officially circulating representations of fictive, idealized femininity functioning as binary opposites between which no actual identity could be formulated. The images derive from classroom textbooks and popular histories that circulate widely in modern Israel. The earliest images (figs. 1 and 2) show pioneer women who had immigrated from Eastern Europe at the turn of the century, performing both private and public chores, laundering the clothes and breaking up stones for the paving of roads and building of houses. In each case there is a staged quality to the photographic narrative. In the image of the laundering there is an Arab man idly languishing against a post in the

Figure 2. "Pioneer Women at Work." Photograph by Ada Maimon. From *Women Build a Land* (New York: Herzl Press, 1962). Reprinted with permission of Herzl Press.

background as if to declare that the women are doing this menial labor for reasons of ideological conviction and refusing to have it done by the indigenous population of the land, which could conceivably be hired to do so. In the stone-breaking image the two women are focused on their work while the numerous men stand about posing for the camera, unemployed. The fictions have to do with an attempt to dissociate the protagonists, the early pioneers, from the normative, exploitative codes of European colonialism in the eastern Mediterranean and with the myth of gender equality among the early communal existence of the first waves of ideologically motivated *aliyah*. Contemporary accounts, however, alert us to the mythologized nature of this equality; Fania, a woman pioneer of the second wave of immigrants and the heroine of a novel set in the Rosh Pina pioneer settlement in the 1880s, *Gey Oni* (valley of strength), complains, "Of all the things that were said, the one that constantly scorched her memory were remarks casually made by the doctor, 'There are nine Biluyim in Gedera and one woman,' . . . as if she were not a person! Nine persons and one something else."[8]

The dreamy, idealistic pioneer girls (see figs. 3 and 4) were within twenty years to become the thick-set, severe, bespectacled matriarchs of the Labor movement, political hacks like Golda Meir who did little for the cause of women and conformed in every way to the dominant, masculinist mode of party power politics.[9] As the building of the fledgling community progressed, we find images of women building houses, ploughing the land, working in the light industry and in service industries such as telephone and electricity (figs. 5–7). They are focused and attentive to their tasks; their bodies are veiled be-

Figure 3. "Young Women, Immigrant from Eastern Europe." Photograph by
Ada Maimon. From *Women Build a Land* (New York: Herzl Press, 1962).
Reprinted with permission of Herzl Press.

Figure 4. "Labor Movement Political Meeting 1932." Source: Emil Feuerstein, *Women Who Made History*, Israel Ministry of Defense Publications, Tel Aviv, 1989.

Figure 5. Source: Emil Feuerstein, *Women Who Made History*, Israel Ministry of Defense Publications, Tel Aviv, 1989. Photograph was untitled, without date.

Figure 6. Source: Emil Feuerstein, *Women Who Made History,* Israel Ministry of Defense
Publications, Tel Aviv, 1989. Photograph was untitled, without date.

Figure 7. Source: Emil Feuerstein, *Women Who Made History,* Israel Ministry of Defense
Publications, Tel Aviv, 1989. Photograph was untitled, without date.

neath layers of functional clothing; their sexual identity is negated; they are subjugating
themselves to their duties. Through their disciplined bodies, they have become work tools
within a socialist culture that valorized labor as the highest achievement and the greatest
agent of equality. It is important to understand how these bodies are used to make claims
to the land and to render those claims naturalized and organic. These representations of
women linked to the land posit a new relationship, one in which the land is not owned or
possessed as within the feudal or colonial systems that immediately preceded it but is
served and nurtured and made fertile. Thus both the land and its occupation are feminized through internally linked dynamics of subordination, service, and fertility. Their
direct counterparts are the "oriental" women (figs. 8 and 9): passive, quiet, and self-
absorbed, clothed in cumbersome traditional clothes that bespeak the exact opposite of
the pioneer women's public physical work, touting small babies or sitting in traditional
oriental poses, they inhabit an arena of ahistorical timelessness, an exotic Other against
which the pioneer women's activities seem even more extraordinary and their revision
of traditional femininity even more radical.[10] Not least, the fictive positioning of these
women as passive and subdued served as a legitimizing narrative for the imposition of
a set of foreign cultural values over the existing ones in the name of twentieth-century
progress.

In the period leading up to the so-called War of Independence and the establishment of the state in 1948, we see a shift in the photographic construction of femininity
circulating within the culture. On the one hand there is an obvious escalation in the real
level of participation by women in underground and military activities against the
British mandatory government and in preparation for what seemed to be an inevitable

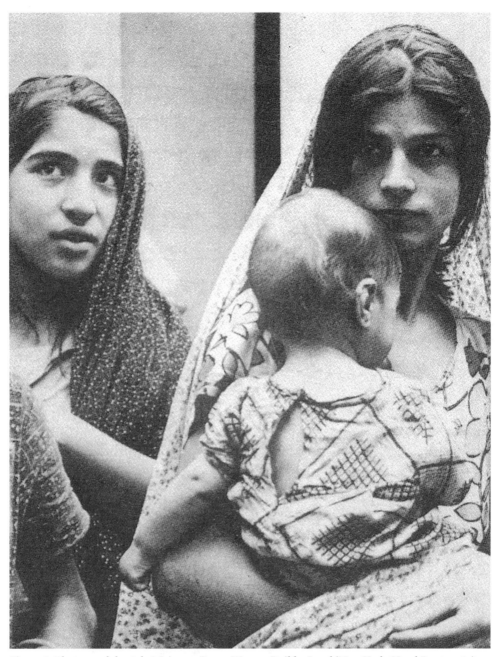

Figure 8. Photograph by Ada Maimon. From *Women Build a Land* (New York: Herzl Press, 1962). Reprinted with permission of Herzl Press.

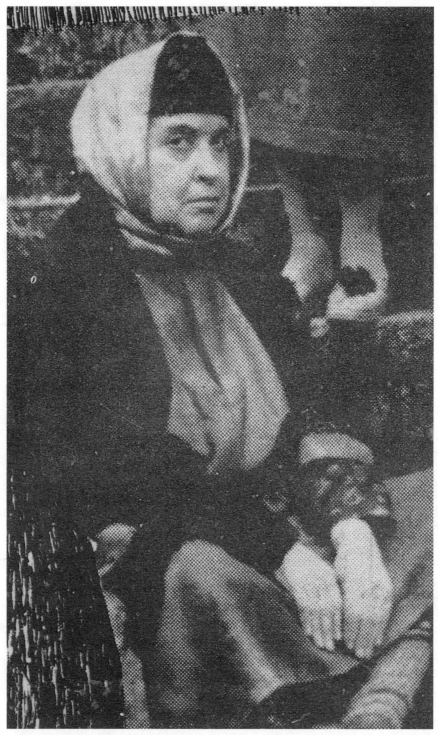

Figure 9. Photograph by Ada Maimon. From *Women Build a Land* (New York: Herzl Press, 1962). Reprinted with permission of Herzl Press.

conflict with the indigenous Palestinians and neighboring Arab states, a participation dictated by demographic scarcity, since the Jewish population of Palestine numbered no more than six hundred thousand at that point. The images, though, indicate another set of shifts, in perception of a femininity mobilized for a cause, dictated by circumstances rather than by the severe strictures of ideological purity (figs. 10–12). If we examine the images of the women—arming the mountain of hand grenades, crouched in tortuous and implausible positions; of the woman being led away by the British soldiers with her arms on her head; or of the woman soldier with her arms on her hips in a confrontational pose, apparently belied by a sweet and charming smile—a distinct pattern begins to emerge. The degree of physical confrontation and the far greater emphasis on gendering these bodies as female, on situating them as on display, begin the process of humanizing belligerence through an insistence on a new and self-consciously aggressive femininity. The difference in signification has as much to do with the shift from choice to necessity as it has to do with the cultural conventions of specific historical moments. More important, it concerns the moments at which the links with the two previously mentioned defining poles, the European and the oriental, get radically redefined in favor of a newly born construct, the "Israeli woman," who can be allowed neither the choices of the European woman nor the passivity of the oriental one. The surface aggression masks a level of filial subservience, this time to the state and the dominant Zionist ideology.

Forty years on the cycle of unceasing aggression, destruction, injustice, and loss of life, and it seems to continue without cease. The state of Israel founded on a rhetoric of socialist equality has been continuously shaken by accusations of racial discrimination against Sephardic Jews and by gnawing voices insisting on recognition for the Palestinians. The situation of women, who had started out as supposedly equal partners in the radical social experiment of Zionism, has remained sadly unevolved. There are few women in public life. Feminism is a marginal and ridiculed movement. The traditional family dominates every aspect of life and dictates the circumstances and priorities of women's existence and possibilities. And most important, we can perceive an exceptionally acute crisis of identity—the identity that had been forged between the two extreme poles of European and oriental has now receded back into those poles (figs. 13 and 14). The model in the Gottex conforms to every known cliché of the oriental beauty: dark-haired and dark-skinned, her hair an unruly cloud of curls, her costume vaguely reminiscent of the harem, she is supposedly situated firmly in the specific geographical region. The inherent contradiction between adopting a set of so-called oriental aesthetic values and then negating them through the display of the nearly naked body and the provocative posture is one that perfectly represents the internal conflicts of Israeli feminine identity. The model on the cover of *Naamat*—a vaguely feminist mass-circulation women's magazine in Israel linked to what was the Labor Party daily paper *Davar*—is adorned with a mask of glittering, sophisticated makeup that adheres to a European aesthetic of the remote and distant feminine. Attempting to adapt to a region with which it is engaged in active daily warfare, dreaming nostalgically of lost European worlds, cloaking itself in a mantle of emancipatory rhetoric, and living out a traditional and contradictory life, femininity in Israel is experiencing a crisis not just of identity but also one of context.

Figure 10. Source: Emil Feuerstein, *Women Who Made History*, Israel Ministry of Defense Publications, Tel Aviv, 1989. Photograph was untitled, without date.

Figure 11. Source: Emil Feuerstein, *Women Who Made History,* Israel Ministry of Defense Publications, Tel Aviv, 1989. Photograph was untitled, without date.

GENDERING DIASPORIC NOSTALGIA

These different representations have been circulating within the culture throughout this century as an increasingly coherent and solid mythical narrative. In recent years the internal contradictions of these gendered identities have become the focal point of a few, but far too few, interrogations within visual and textual culture. The cool, analytical work of Sigal Primor, a young Israeli visual artist who has only recently begun to exhibit her work internationally, is to my mind one of the most interesting speculations on this split identity.[11] The imaginary setting of the work is a fiction of urbane,

Figure 12. Source: Emil Feuerstein, *Women Who Made History,* Israel Ministry of Defense Publications, Tel Aviv, 1989. Photograph was untitled, without date.

Figure 13. Gottex advertisement. *Gottex International*, D.Sh.G. Ads, Tel Aviv, July 1989.

Figure 14. *Naamat* cover photo. *Naamat,* Tel Aviv, June 1989.

European culture centered on the world of opera houses and concert halls. With this she acknowledges the extraordinary symbolic and ideological centrality that classical music has in Israeli cultural life, which is flooded with orchestras, visiting musicians, and purportedly one of the largest classical-music-concert-going publics in the world. Aside from the obvious historical reasons that make music the most international, transient, and easily transportable of high cultural practices, it is also the one that supposedly transcends national cultural identities and thus can be appropriated as "our" cultural heritage, one that is exclusive to the European population of Israel and denotes their privilege without being obviously discriminatory. In Primor's work we see the entire gamut of romantic narratives associated with the world of high musical culture: violin cases lined with velvet are echoed by reduced-scale evening gowns of glistening taffeta and velvet in glowing jeweled colors, all alluding to an acculturation of women's bodies and a recognition of the seduction and sexual allure of high culture (figs. 15 and 16). The extreme artificiality and the emphasis on identity as a form of staged theatrical production are investigated through the endlessly intricate play with concert-hall balconies, parapets, and walkways, which immediately bring to mind the opera hall paintings of Pierre-Auguste Renoir and Mary Cassatt. Primor's work articulates a perception of identity as a feminized cultural spectacle; it is a complex cultural gaze in which subtle intersections of a longed-for mythologized heritage and a remote and privileged femininity intertwine and define one another as in those Central European novels of the 1930s such as those by Vicki Baum, in which spectacles of high culture (opera houses, cafés, grand hotels) supposedly masked internal differences and struggles. There is an acknowledgment of the simultaneity of insidership and outsidership, of the conjunctions of heady and rapturous cultural experience, and of the staging of desire through that experience.

In a work titled *The Bride and the Echo* (fig. 17) we see a photo of a generic European opera house, empty and cavernous as it draws us into its vast spaces through the promise of opulence, romance, and fulfilled desire that it holds forth to our cultural imaginations. It is surrounded by plywood cutouts of female images holding out some printed sheafs of paper, perhaps musical manuscripts, perhaps romantic scenarios. Superimposed over the entire image we find the slick, cold, metallic image of Marcel Duchamp's bride from the Large Glass narrative of the *Bride Stripped Bare by Her Bachelors, Even*. This image by Duchamp stands in as the referent for all that is "modern," European, technologically constituted, and progressive. In one single artistic reference, the entire contextual, geographically located world of the Near East and the Levant can be dismissed and denied. The invocation of Duchamp has little to do with his actual work but, rather, with its reception and its position as groundbreaking and paradigm-shifting modernist work in which a machine aesthetic for the human body acquired a sexuality that went beyond the utilitarian mechanized working bodies dominating the earlier historical avant-garde. In Duchamp's mechanized speculation on sexuality in the crisis of modernism, the bride in the upper part of the work is being anchored down by the bachelors in the form of chocolate grinders, titled *The Bachelor Grinds His Own Chocolate*. The two gendered panes of the Large Glass remain separate:

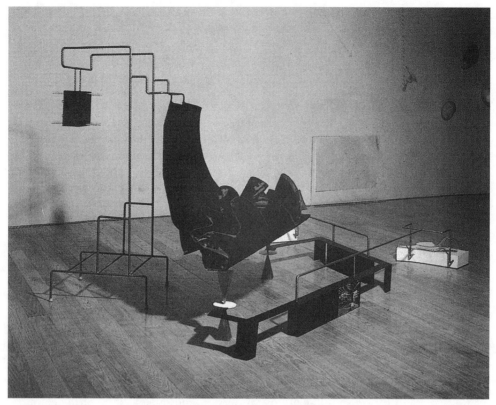

Figure 15. Sigal Primor, "Senorita" (1989). Courtesy of the artist.

> If the "Large Glass," and thus the "love operation" of the two machines had been completed, the Bachelor Machine, "all grease and lubricity" would have received "love gasoline secreted by the Bride's sexual glands" in its "malic" cylinders for ignition by "the electrical sparks of the undressing" and mixing with the secretions of the ever-turning Grinder, would have produced the ultimate union. In its "incomplete" state the Large Glass constitutes rather, an assertion of the impossibility of union—of the sexual alienation of man and woman in a situation which Lebel describes as "onanism for two."[12]

In Sigal Primor's works the bride has detached herself from the glass and from the oppressive binarism of the image of sexual alienation. Her mechanistic image of femininity, its metallic sinuousness representative of a rationalized female sexuality in the service of some modernist ideal or Other, hovers longingly in front of the photo of the opera house, eager to penetrate the luscious mysteries of cultural promise it holds out to her. It is a poignant image of cultural nostalgia, of the ideals of modernism looking back to the seductive fictions of the old world and its belief in culture's ability to transcend reality.

The Bride's Other is no longer the entire gamut of grinders and "malic" tools but the fictions of the past it wishes to escape into as if it holds some promise of a union, cultural rather than sexual, from which being trapped in Duchamp's mechanized Glass has barred her. The work viewed as a whole perceives culture as performative, as a gendered spectacle

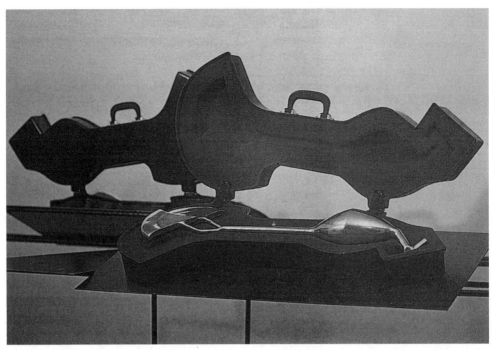

Figure 16. Sigal Primor, "Senorita" (1989). Courtesy of the artist.

of the desire for culture in which femininity is both staged and displayed, viewer and viewed. It seems particularly appropriate that all of these dynamics and desires are framed within the legitimating narrative of modernism, for like the relation between Zionism and international socialism, it, too, frames discourses within an illusionary international-ism and the shared goals and ideals of an ideology of "progress."

I am particularly interested in Primor's work because it seems to me to thematize and reflect on the condition of ambivalence and contradictory longings that the European-oriented cultural life of the state of Israel manifests. This is a Second World ambivalence toward cultures of origin rather than a Third World relation to these, as can be seen through a comparison with the condition described by Palestinian-born writer Anton Shammas, whose first novel was written in Hebrew, his second language:

> In my Humble case, as a Palestinian who was ungracefully deterritorialised by the Hebrew language (which Dante had described in the Fourteenth century as the language of Grace)— what I am trying to do is deterritorialise the Hebrew language, or, more bluntly to un-Jew the Hebrew language and make it the language of personal narrative discourse. In a certain sense, that is what most of the writers of the Third world are doing these days: undoing the culture of the majority from within. The deterritorialisation of the colonizers' language is the only way to claim their own territory, and it is the only territory left to them to claim as an independent state—the only one they can afford to call a homeland.[13]

The clear purpose of such a project is denied within European-oriented Israeli culture, at least overtly, since the relationship with its oppression is more complex. After all, it was

Figure 17. Sigal Primor, *The Bride and the Echo* (1989). Courtesy of the artist.

the Jewish intelligentsia in many of these originary cultures who contributed to its cultural formation or who took part in internal processes of its deterritorialization. Perhaps it is a nostalgia for such a position that we are experiencing, a hankering after diaspora that allows us an internal oppositional role. Perhaps those of us who occupy positions of clearly articulated ambivalence and who work to thematize and research those past European cultures from which our ancestors were expelled (and to which we at some level gravitate and try to make our own) have become "the diaspora's diaspora." Nowhere are these contradictions and ambivalent states more clearly visible than in the condition of femininity within the Israeli state as I have tried to map out in my brief and inadequate survey through encounters with a set of visual representations.

The value of Sigal Primor's work for my argument is in its insistence on critically examining the myths of cultural heritage and its uncompromising approach in pointing out the subtle and insidiously positioned superiority of the European heritage within collective cultural fantasies and identity formations. In her astute recognition that culture and cultural rituals are profoundly gendered and provide a refuge space away from the sorrow and the constant unease that accompanies daily life in the state of Israel, she is also exposing the rhetorical fictions of women's identities. The external trappings of the "new beginning" have collapsed back into the extreme poles of feminine identity, each in its own way a fantasy projection of an impossibly romantic ideal that claims a new identity but seems unable to actually provide a set of new, or even revised, values for that identity. Instead, it lives out its contradictory destiny and acute ambivalences through endless stagings of cultural desire and through the production of internally conflicted femininities, which attempt, with great difficulty and at great cost, to bring about some form of denied reconciliation.

NOTES

1. Of the many works, both scholarly and literary, that I have read in pursuit of these interests, two in particular stand out as having shaped my critical thinking on the constructed relations between European Jews and their sense of place. Amiel Alcacaly's *After Jews and Arabs: Remaking Levantine Culture* (Minneapolis: University of Minnesota Press, 1993) showed me clearly that while there had indeed been a relationship between Jews and place, it was not the claimed one of European Zionism but the lived one of the Arab Jews of the Levant and the religious Jews who settled there in the years prior to Zionist domination. Similarly, Ella Shohat's book *Israeli Cinema: East/West and the Politics of Representation* (Austin: University of Texas Press, 1987) first began to explore a model of thinking Israeli culture in terms of First and Third World tensions and through the analytical models of the critical analysis of colonialism. While their work may not be quoted here extensively, since my preoccupation is primarily to interrogate dominant ideology through an attention to gender and sexuality, it nevertheless serves to continuously inform and embolden my arguments.

2. Theodor Adorno, *Minima Moralia* (London: NLB, 1974), 39.

3. Abdul Jan Mohamed and David Lloyd, "Towards a Theory of Minority Discourse," introduction to *Cultural Critique* 6 (1987).

4. Arif Dirlik, "Culturalism as Hegemonic Ideology and Liberating Practice," *Cultural Critique* 6 (1987): 7.

5. All translations from Hebrew into English are my own: David Grossmann, *See Under: Love* (Jerusalem: Sifriyat Hapoalim, 1986).

6. For a radically new reading of the relation between Zionism, Judaism, and territoriality as articulated through the ideology of a return to a "homeland," see Boaz Evron, *A National Reckoning* (Tel Aviv: Dvir Publishing, 1988).

7. Esther Fuchs, *No License to Die* (Tel Aviv: Ecked Publishing House, 1983).

8. Shulamit Lapid, *Gey Oni* (Tel Aviv: Keter, 1984), quoted in Mira Ariel, "Creatures of Another Planet," *Politika* 27 (July 1989): 44–47.

9. Daphna Izraeli, "The Golda Meir Effect," *Politika* 27 (July 1989): 48.

10. Emil Feuerstein, *Women Who Made History* (Tel Aviv: Israel Ministry of Defense Publications, 1989).

11. Primor's work was featured in the exhibition *Feminine Presences* at the Tel Aviv Museum of Art in the summer of 1989.

12. William Rubin (incorporating quotes from Duchamp), *Dada and Surrealist Art* (New York: Museum of Modern Art, 1968), 40.

13. Anton Shammas's essay in *Critical Fictions: The Politics of Imaginative Writing*, ed. Philomena Mariani (Seattle: Bay Press, 1991), 77.

ARCHAEOLOGICAL DEVOTION

Jennifer A. González

Objects only make sense in the midst of practices of use and apparatuses of production and circulation. Artifacts are drenched with stories and dreams, and vice versa.
—Donna Haraway, interview with the author, August 1995

To leave the rush of Forty-Second Street traffic for the cool reflections of glass in the Philip Morris branch of the Whitney Museum of American Art is already to move between worlds that are worlds apart. In 1993 it was possible to encounter there another world—intimate, feminine—filled with objects collected and displayed with meticulous care, a museum, a boudoir, a shrine. *Venus Envy Chapter One (or the First Holy Communion Moments before the End)* by artist Amalia Mesa-Bains functioned like a microcosm within a microcosm, creating an unlikely space for the presentation of a Chicana cultural history in the context of corporate capital. In 1992, the year before Mesa-Bains's exhibition, the Williams College Museum of Art hosted *Sites of Recollection,* a group exhibition that included works by artists Renée Stout and Jenni Lukac. Each produced her own installation,[1] and each, like Mesa-Bains, constructed a sophisticated display of collected artifacts to represent private memories, public histories, and the formation of subjectivities using the *combined* spatial registers of religious sanctuary, domestic space, and museum display.

This slippage and overlap between spatial and institutional domains that are traditionally kept separate constitute one way in which the works participate critically in what James Clifford has called the "art-culture system."[2] The discourses of connoisseurship, ethnography, commodification, and authenticity used to differentiate "fine art" from "cultural artifact" are shown to occupy, in Clifford's Greimasian model, opposing and complementary positions. The artists recognize, as does Clifford, that material culture signs frequently travel between these domains, despite attempts to fix their positions. So-called tribal objects can appear in museums of modern art, fine art can be recontextualized as historical artifact, kitsch can become fine art, and so on. The works by Mesa-Bains, Stout, and Lukac present the possibility that not only objects but the context of their presentation (the museum, the church, the home) may accommodate more than one set of spatial practices. It becomes difficult to say to what degree their work is to be read as fine art or public ritual, as a private collection of objects or as complex cultural narrative, even whether the works should be read as "visual" or "material" culture.

Despite this categorical resistance, the works do share a common form of representation that references a private, domestic collection or display of objects. Serving as a site of psychic projection and introjection, such collections include what might be called autobiographical traces, such as photographs, travel souvenirs, heirlooms, religious icons, or gifts. These coveted objects can be seen to form a syntagmatic array of material signs using a spatial topography to represent a given subject's position within a network of social relations, what I have elsewhere called an "autotopography."[3] In the creation of an autotopography material objects are employed as a physical map of memory, history, and belief. The artifact in the autotopography becomes a grapheme, a prosthetic device, an element of writing, or a residual sign of the intangible aspects of desire, identification, and social relations. Here the writing takes the form of a juxtaposition of elements that are meant to be read as a spatial, rhetorical argument, inviting the viewer to interpret the metaphoric and metonymic relations between objects and images.

How does one read such a mode of "writing" or display? What are the particular topographies mapped by the artists' installations? What relation between subjects and their objects do the artists articulate? How does the work extend beyond autobiography to more general concerns with gender, ethnicity, and subjecthood? By reading the work of Mesa-Bains, Stout, and Lukac together, it is possible to better understand their contribution to a larger effort in the visual arts, of complicating simplistic representations of cultural identity by expanding the forms of its representation.

A RHETORIC OF OBJECTS

Speech and writing are linear. The reader knows where to begin, and follows the words through one by one in an ordered sequence. Faced with a room of objects, on the other hand, there is no set order or pattern to the way in which reading takes place.
   —Ian Hodder, *The Meaning of Things*

In the cinema the sequence of images, the sequence of the reading, is determined for us; whereas in the gallery we determine the sequence and the duration ourselves.
   —Victor Burgin and Homi Bhabha, "Visualizing Theory"

How does one "read" a collection of objects or a display of material culture? Is there, as Ian Hodder suggests, no set pattern to the activity of reading a room of objects? To what degree, in fact, is the sequence and duration of a gallery visit indeterminate? In a 1993 essay titled "Rhetoric of the Object," I attempt to address these questions and to argue for a way of reading collections of objects and artists' installations using the tropes of rhetoric.[4] Some of the arguments of this previous essay are repeated here and owe a certain debt to other scholars who have approached these questions in a similar manner before and since.

In his 1964 essay "Rhetoric of the Image," Roland Barthes analyzes the "emphatic" form of advertising images that combine both linguistic and photographic signs. His analysis concludes that not only words, which form a (repressive) textual anchor, but also the visible and identifiable objects in this image, along with their mode of presentation, possess the rhetorical means to convince and seduce the viewer.[5] Can the same be said of objects that have not been mediated by photography? Barthes does not explicitly explore this question, but he does observe that

> there is in fact a very great obstacle to the studying of the meaning of objects . . . the obstacle of the obvious: if we are to study the meaning of objects, we must give ourselves a sort of shock of detachment, in order to objectivize the object, to structure its signification: to do this there is a means which every semanticist of the object can use; it is to resort to an order of representations in which the object is presented in a simultaneously spectacular, rhetorical, and intentional fashion, which is advertising, the cinema, or even the theater.[6]

A "shock of detachment" may not be the intended goal of the art installations considered here, but the theater of their exhibition certainly situates the artifacts they employ in a "spectacular, rhetorical, and intentional fashion." A *rhetoric of objects* can thus be defined as the use of material culture within a context of presentation or display (such as commercial market, museum, private collection, or art installation) for the sake of producing a visual and material argument at a particular historical moment and within a legible semantic "code."

In the case of museums, for example, a rhetorical display may argue for the authenticity of a given artifact (in which case the object may be surrounded by documentary materials attesting to its origin—*aetiologia*); or it may concern the historical relations between objects (in which case a relation of contiguity may be created by proximate, linear placement—*chronographia*); or the cultural value of the object may require that it be given a place of honor (placed on a pedestal, under careful lighting conditions and security systems—*eulogia*), and so on. In *The Clothing of Cleo* Stephen Bann explores the rhetorical function of objects in the Musée de Cluny in Paris in terms of a shift from metonymy (which characterizes the chronological and comprehensive collection of Alexandre Lenoir, following a "classic" *episteme* of the "specimen") to that of synecdoche (which characterizes the idiosyncratic and "authentic" collection of Alexandre Du Sommard, following a "romantic" *episteme* of the "relic").[7] Here Bann recognizes that techniques of display reveal taxonomic organizations of history that lay claim to various kinds of realism: "It is this assertion of the experiential reality of history which the rhetoric of the museum both produces and annihilates. 'History' is made real through the fiction of the transparency of the historical syntagm."[8] In a more recent essay titled "Shrines, Curiosities and the Rhetoric of Display," Bann links the conventions of display in medieval churches to cabinets of curiosity of the sixteenth century. By drawing parallels between forms of symmetry, devotion, and performative narration, Bann suggests that cabinets of curiosity were concerned with a drive to recuperate the strategies of display that had been lost during an iconoclastic era. The very mode of curiosity, Bann suggests, was that of mourning—a mourning accompanying the loss of sacred relics as well as a general shift to a new, scientific paradigm:

Curiosity, therefore, is a term that indicates a historically and culturally specific attitude to the collection and display of objects, and would have had no meaning before 1550. . . . Attachment to objects—we might reasonably say, the cult of objects—was an inseparable feature of curiosity, and so was a particular style of display."[9]

Collection and display must still be read and understood through a lens of rhetorical tropes.[10] As Peter Wollen has observed, "Each historic period has its own rhetorical mode of display, because each has different truths to conceal."[11]

While it is generally taken for granted that art, like advertising, is "emphatic," it is rarely the case that art installations using material culture are understood as arguments rather than merely unorthodox collections or decorative displays. In the case of the installations produced by Mesa-Bains, Stout, and Lukac, the rhetorical success of the work relies to a large degree on audience familiarity with commonly encountered "theaters" of objects. Each artist borrows formal techniques from sites in which a material rhetoric already follows a sophisticated code—museums, shrines, commercial displays, and domestic collections.

These familiar forms are then used as the ground for a higher-level argument (the object as *signified* becomes the object as *signifier*). The artists construct their own realism, unlike that of Lenoir or Du Sommard, and more akin to a "surrealism" insofar as social relations are represented as careful arrangements of material evidence.

Like a concrete unconscious, the works of Mesa-Bains, Stout, and Lukac are made to be deciphered and explored, not taken in at a glance. Unlike other forms of artistic assemblage that follow a formal poetry of sometimes random placement, the legibility of these installations depends on the semiotic richness that comes from carefully choreographed juxtapositions of objects. As a result the work demands a close reading that is attentive to a spatial topology conceived as a rhetoric of objects.

SITE READINGS

Venus Envy Chapter One (or the First Holy Communion Moments before the End) (1993) is the first in a series of installation works by Chicana artist and activist Amalia Mesa-Bains that takes as its focus the iconic figures and institutional sites of identification shaping contemporary Chicana subjectivities. Both biographical and autobiographical, the work combines visual and spatial schemata found in religious shrines, ethnographic museums, and domestic interiors, using tactics of collection and display common to each of these settings to determine both the formal structure and discreet details of the installation (fig. 1). This overlay of spaces, public and private, sacred and profane, is clearly meant to demonstrate their mutual influence and interdependence in the formation of subjectivity and in the process of identification, particularly for women of Mexican descent living in the United States.[12]

The title of the work offers the first clues to the material rhetoric that follows. In the Catholic Church, first holy communion, as the artist perceives it, "occupies in the feminine landscape a fork in the road where the soul and the body are forced to separate."[13] This momentary ceremony, where confession is used to crystallize the consciousness of sin, marks for Mesa-Bains a young girl's first "loss of innocence." It also serves as a

Figure 1. Amalia Mesa-Bains, *Venus Envy Chapter One (or the First Holy Communion Moments before the End)* (1993), installation. Photograph by George Hirose; copyright 1993 George Hirose, reprinted by permission of the photographer.

metaphor for other forms of lost innocence, as *Venus Envy Chapter One* reveals how one might negotiate the terrain of a Catholic and Mexican American identity in the United States of the late twentieth century. The subtle conflicts between sexual desire and religious devotion are materially counterpoised with the political battles that face an economically disadvantaged community trying to maintain the rituals of its ethnic heritage. The installation simultaneously re-creates an autotopography of Mesa-Bains's own life, using intimate possessions and family snapshots to plot a personal narrative.

Filling a small square gallery *Venus Envy*'s evocation of narcissism is immediately apparent in the rows of mirrors that line the walls. Yet reflected there are not only the faces of gallery visitors, but also ghosts from the past: photographs of the artist as a young girl, of her ancestors, and of admired female icons haunt the interior of the glass where the reflective surface has been rubbed away. The audience is invited to consider the process by which they see, reflected in themselves, those others (parents, grandparents, ego ideals) from a real or imagined past—a past mediated in large part by photography. Time, the artist seems to suggest, is not a linear progression of birth and death, beginning and ending, but is little more than a conceptual obstacle to the recognition that the past always reappears in the present. Not a magical realism but another kind of realism pervades such an observation—that the mediation of images produces vision, and that it is only through this mediation that one sees oneself in the present.

The same heterochronic portraiture takes place in display cases placed in the center of the gallery space. Large and low to the ground, each case contains a different kind of

Figure 2. Amalia Mesa-Bains, *Venus Envy Chapter One (or the First Holy Communion Moments before the End)* (1993), detail. Photograph by George Hirose; copyright 1993 George Hirose, reprinted by permission of the photographer.

memorabilia. Referring to this part of the exhibition as the Museum of Memory, Mesa-Bains has organized a collection of artifacts that represent female rites of passage. A white dress from a young girl's first holy communion is laid out next to a confirmation gown and wedding dress.[14] Tucked into the folds and distributed across the surface of the smooth, creamy satin and delicate lace of these garments are antique dolls, crushed red rose petals (looking like drops of blood), dried fruit, tiny Mexican ceramic jars, and a postcard of Titian's *Venus of Urbino*. In another case is a doll in a nun's habit, wearing a wreath of flowers that symbolizes her religious initiation. These objects function not only as "evidence" of historical events per se but also as *metaphors for the psychic effects* of these events: the loss of corporeal freedom, the initiation into a hierarchy of purity and beauty, the conflicts created by a bicultural identity, and so on.

In another display case one can find snapshots of young Mexican American girls, again in the full regalia of Catholic ritual interspersed with other photographs of powerful adult females who project an entirely different sense of femininity: next to a traditional miniature image of the *Virgin de Guadalupe,* for example, is an image of the Virgin as a karate black belt (*La Virgen de Guadalupe Defendiendo los Derechos de los Xicanos* by Ester Hernandez); next to a snapshot of a young girl dressed in gloves and veil, hands demurely posed in prayer, is a photograph of muralist Judy Baca and one of her large-scale paintings of an indigenous land worker with hand outstretched to show the meager wages she earns (fig. 2). While creating a rhetoric of antithesis, such juxtapositions also serve as a developmental narrative for contemporary Chicanas: the cultural institutions (economic, religious, familial) that shape the identity of the female subject are filled with inherent contradictions. To be delicate and to be strong, to be pious and to be filled with desires, even to be a woman and to be an artist—all of these are conflicts mapped out in a neat array of oppositional signs.

In another corner of the gallery this structure of opposition is repeated in the spatial conflation of both piety and conceit, and of both Catholic and Aztec iconography. Draped along one wall, yards of white silk form the curtained setting for a stand of votive candles and a dainty vanity that combine to form what the artist calls a Boudoir Chapel (fig. 3). A small chair, set before a dressing table, is encumbered by a giant rosary that hangs to the ground like a beaded cape. Reflected in the glass of the oval mirror, however, is *Coatlicue,* the Aztec deity whose serpent head and death mask return the viewer's gaze. One symbol of the ancient culture around which the Chicano movement has established a myth of origins, Coatlicue here functions as the site of reflection on the artist's claims to a particular ethnic heritage, and to the indigenous traditions lost with the imposition of colonial Catholicism. For writer and scholar Gloria Anzaldúa, Coatlicue is also a figure or metaphor for contradictions in self-knowledge:

> There is another quality to the mirror that is the act of seeing. Of seeing and being seen. Subject and object, I and she. The eye pins down the object of its gaze, scrutinizes it, judges it. A glance can freeze us in place; it can "possess" us. It can erect a barrier against the world. But in a glance also lies awareness, knowledge. These seemingly contradictory aspects—the act of being seen, held immobilized by a glance, and "seeing through" an experience—are symbolized by the underground aspect of *Coatlicue, Cihuacoatl,* and *Tlazolteotl* which cluster in what I call the *Coatlicue* state.[15]

The "Coatlicue state" is one way to articulate the confluence of contradictory positions that must be taken up for a subject who is the object and the origin of scrutiny—both internal and external. Mesa-Bains's Boudoir Chapel locates this gaze in an imaginary relation between the subject and that sign or set of signs that interrupts its simple reflection. As an icon of death and regeneration, Coatlicue puts a new spin on the *vanitas* tradition, serving as a visual pun on the part of the artist, who links prayer with narcissism, vanity with mortality.

In some respects Mesa-Bains's collected artifacts resemble the vitrine displays and the "personal mythologies" exhibited by Christian Boltanski in the early 1970s. In both instances the collection reveals a system of memory in which disparate objects appear carefully ordered or gathered according to an autobiographical taxonomy. But the organizing logic of Mesa-Bains's installation also moves beyond a private language of display to what might be thought of as an iconographic revision. The virgin, the nun, and the bride are the ground on which and against which new images of womanhood are projected. Beyond this limited set of choices the artist offers a series of alternatives that are not so much a rejection of these iconic roles as a rearticulation of their social function. The title *Venus Envy* is clearly meant to be a play on the Freudian concept of penis envy in girls (a desire to have access to the power and privilege accorded to males and masculinity under patriarchy) and, simultaneously, an acknowledgment of a feminine sexual desire linked to fantasies of love and beauty. Identification is not limited here to the icons of the

Figure 3. Amalia Mesa-Bains, *Venus Envy Chapter One (or the First Holy Communion Moments before the End)* (1993), detail. Courtesy Steinbaum Krauss Gallery, New York. Photograph by George Hirose; copyright 1993 George Hirose, reprinted by permission of the photographer.

Mexican American community but is mediated, for example, by an identification with European standards of beauty (Titian's Venus). Gender is ultimately represented as a complex set of behaviors that are produced through an ambivalent relation to cultural hierarchies and prescribed "feminine" roles.

The installation as a whole points to the social and cultural institutions that shape a Chicana identity and simultaneously deconstructs the rules on which these institutions are grounded. In contrast to the purity of the childlike figure of the encased nun, for example, the artist includes wall text from the Beguines of the fourteenth century, demonstrating that the cloistered nuns, far from maintaining a truly celibate life, transferred their repressed sexual desire onto the Eucharist and proclaimed their own bodies as the marriage bed of Christ. In short, the artist layers the internal contradictions of the social institutions of religion against the subject's identification with them. Not only might a woman be impelled to identify with roles proscribed by different institutional paradigms, but those very paradigms may also contain their own internal contradictions.

Taken as a whole, the art installation also creates a new discursive formation for the interpretation of material culture. It organizes the context and legibility of everyday relics and icons, marking the domains of signification through which these objects are reread as part of a system of acculturation. In *Venus Envy Chapter One* the visual tropes of archive and museum display, shrine and sanctuary, are used to create a material cultural narrative. The artist also presents a topography of the psychic activity of identification that takes place for girls and women as they navigate their way through a maze of powerful cultural icons to a new interpretation of female roles. The work redefines the legibility of certain artifacts by removing them from an isolated discourse (of the Catholic Church, for example) and placing them in the context of other material discourses—discourses of activism, desire, domesticity, or history.

The use of material culture to visualize and locate ethnic and gender identification can also be found in the work of Renée Stout. In her installation *My Altar/My Grandmother's Altar* (1992) Stout re-creates a domestic living-room space as a terrain of debate across two generations. In the center of the room is a large patterned carpet, two well-worn over-stuffed armchairs, a small end table, and a lamp. Side by side, but situated in such a way that the table and lamp construct a barrier between them, the two armchairs face opposite walls of the room against which are staged two displays resembling private home altars. The installation thus invites the audience to feel "at home," while simultaneously suggesting a confrontation or conversation between opposing perspectives.

The altar that appears to belong to the grandmother consists of a large, color television set placed on the floor, atop which sits a dense array of framed photographs (fig. 4). Each appears to be a portrait of extended family members; infants, children, adults, family groups, and even a church choir are there. The photographs are carefully positioned to reflect the family ties that join them. Even unframed photographs crowd the top edges of the television set, neatly placed in rows. Keeping company with these images are artificial flowers, shells, and devotional figurines. The entire ensemble, in a balanced symmetry, rests on a white lace runner. Relying on her audience's familiarity with this kind of middle-class domestic space, Stout uses a conventional collection of photographs to serve

Figure 4. Renée Stout, *My Altar/My Grandmother's Altar* (1992), detail of installation. Photograph by Nicholas Whitman; reprinted by permission of the photographer.

as a family portrait. Relations of affiliation are thus easily extended to the other iconic figures of the piece. On the wall above the television altar are placed, in a hierarchical, descending order, a wooden crucifix, two chromolithograph figures of Christ and the Virgin Mary, a large, centrally placed photograph of two young boys appearing to date from the 1950s, and smaller reproductions of Christian religious icons. To make the extended family complete, the television runs a video loop of the pop religious figure Pat Robertson, whose smile and one-eight-hundred telephone number flash continually on the screen to remind his faithful viewers to send their donations to his *700 Club* fund. Such signs of devotion to family and church are echoed in photographs and keepsakes found on the small table in the center of the room and in the threadbare bible that rests on the seat of the grandmother's chair. Here a microcosmic view of the systems of faith and social networks that define an implied inhabitant of the scene are found in supplementary material evidence. Such evidence reveals that the figure of the grandmother exists at the nexus of several institutional frameworks: the Christian church, the extended family, and the evangelical media community.

The artist's altar—implied by the possessive use of the word *my* in Stout's title—is situated in and around a wooden curio cabinet that references both archaeological and museological display (fig. 5). A foot or so taller than the television set that faces it from

Figure 5. Renée Stout, *My Altar/My Grandmother's Altar* (1992), detail of installation. Photograph by Nicholas Whitman; reprinted by permission of the photographer.

across the room, the cabinet contains a diverse array of religious and cultural artifacts including a reproduction of a Hopi kachina doll; a reproduction of an African *n'kisi* figure; maracas; earth from several different countries in Africa, Europe, and Central America in labeled glass jars; bones; postcards and toys; feathers and dried corn. Open glass doors allow a closer inspection of the materials placed on the shelves inside. Two drawers at the base of the cabinet are also open, revealing collections of photographs and books about world religions. Like the grandmother's altar, the artist's altar is topped with photographs of what appear to be family, friends, and ancestors. An image of a black Christian saint hangs on the wall above, flanked on either side by brightly sequined icons of the vodun religion. Also atop the cabinet are four votive candles, an Aztec calendar, an incense holder, and a carved wooden figurine that appears to be of African origin.

Included in the artist's altar are signs that have been and continue to be elided by the mainstream religious culture to which her grandmother has assimilated—a compendium of countersigns that recuperates or invents tangible traces of the artist's complex ancestry composed of African, Mexican, Irish, and Native American cultures. Yet Stout is clearly not concerned with the authenticity of the objects but, rather, the intergenerational conflict staged *between* the two sign systems in the installation—the dialogue or debate that ensues when one kind of identity is positioned against another within the same family, the same gender. In reflecting on this piece, Stout has commented: "Between my altar and my grandmother's altar there is a clash in the middle of the room: between televangelism—where you are only allowed to think in one paradigm—and the other evidence of world religions. The center is a debate between the two positions."[16] But it is not only religious paradigms that are at stake here; it is also the act of marking a shift in systems of identification while demonstrating a parallel or shared practice. Scholar Lisa Lowe has observed a similar intergenerational tension in contemporary Asian American literary texts, commenting that, on the one hand, "the disruption of tradition" is often seen as a loss causing shame for the younger generations of immigrant families, while on the other hand, "traditional practices of family continuity may be oppressively confining," particularly in terms of gender roles for women.[17]

The articulation of a complex and heterogeneous identity demands that the subject in question be able to negotiate between inherited systems of signs and those they have "collected" themselves. Stout's critique of her grandmother's assimilation is simultaneously a rejection of its limited range and an effort to recuperate those cultural signs and ethnic affiliations that the grandmother herself relinquished years before. While the two displays stand in opposition, they also form a mirrored reflection. Grandmother and granddaughter are both shown to negotiate the ideological systems into which they have been interpellated, or the communities with which they identify, through the collection and arrangement of material culture signs. Functioning biographically as well historically, objects and artifacts in both parts of the installation are used primarily as metaphors for metonymic evidence—as *autotopographical* representations of intricate social networks. The implied dialogue is therefore not only between grandmother and granddaughter, but between the individual subject and the material signs with which she identifies. Renée Stout's work can be read as an archaeology of two separate discursive formations or social paradigms that come into conflict. To the degree that it implies a process

Figure 6. Jenni Lukac, *Votive Shrine* (1992), installation. Photograph by Nicholas Whitman; reprinted by permission of the photographer.

of intergenerational heredity, the installation can also be read as the transformation of one discourse into another, of one identity into another through the collection and display of objects. The artist is able to argue for a notion of identity that is not originary or pure but, rather, culled from a public discourse and maintained in private.

In a similar effort to link private lives with public history Jenni Lukac maps known and unknown, infamous and anonymous persons onto the landscape of a domestic shrine using news photographs, personal snapshots, postcards, cups and saucers, toys, keepsakes, and other material artifacts. Following the architectural floor plan of the nave and transept of a church, her installation *Votive Shrine* (1992) is also furnished as a domestic space (fig. 6). Small end tables, lamps, dressers, and chairs are placed throughout in a symmetrical pattern. The exhibition space is wallpapered in a somber brown and densely covered with framed portraits, wreaths, and elaborate *retablos* (home altars).

    Votive Shrine is primarily a memorial to martyrs. It is an exploration of the historical figures who have been sacrificed to wars, to disasters, to racism, to unlikely violence, to fame, but also to the everyday events of life, to the drudgery of time. The artist has commented that "the methodology of the placement of objects is greatly influenced by the theory of the memory palace, in which the positioning of objects and images stimulates the memory into reconstructing complex relationships, both physical and abstract."[18] The memory palace—an imaginary architecture originally intended, in antiquity, for the remembrance of rhetoric—is here made visible and concrete.[19] Lukac is interested, however, not in a remembrance of rhetoric but in a rhetoric of remembrance that is structured by the tropes of accumulation and comparison.

As in the work of Mesa-Bains and Stout, photography is central to Lukac's assemblage. She explains: "The photographic image serves as a mediator between ourselves and the past; our personal histories and the great rush of global events; between the living and dead."[20] A flat wooden box in the shape of a small house hangs at the back of the installation, graphed with a grim array of photographs depicting those who have suffered from systems of domination: concentration camp victims, Vietnamese children running from soldiers, political prisoners before and after death (fig. 7). The grid of images presents a rhetoric of equivalence: it argues for the equal status of human life across cultural and historical differences. Its lack of chronology, specificity, or documentary detail works against the tendency to historicize or rank forms of oppression. Yet it also avoids the naive idealism of any "family of man" revival.

There is little in the way of a textual anchor to stem the flow of connotations that may arise from the visual juxtapositions provided. Equivalences created by proximity do not, therefore, erase differences but, rather, point to shared elements within those differences. In a Boy's Shrine in one of the side chapels, for example, next to a photograph of young Chicano gang members, in a niche decorated with plastic guns and soldiers, cowboys and Indians, Lukac presents a newspaper photograph of Yusuf Hawkins—a young African American teenager who was killed by racists—and the two white teenagers tried for his death (fig. 8). As Lukac comments, "I saw a photograph of the three boys together, Yusuf and the two boys who killed him. I didn't want to look at the two boys, didn't want to see them. But I realized that three lives had been destroyed, and it was due to the whole social construct and the rituals of manhood and of ethnic polarity that still exist."[21] The presence of the plastic toys not only suggests the tragedy of the untimely deaths of young men but also points to the way in which masculinity is figured from a young age through the games and commodities available to boys.

Other syntagmatic arrays of images read like a history book, for those who are familiar with the references. A photograph of survivors of a German concentration camp for Jews is placed next to a photograph of Japanese military pilots taken during World War II; Anne Frank is pictured next to twins in matching coffins; a commemorative plate of the John F. Kennedy family sits next to a newspaper clipping of President Lyndon B. Johnson's swearing-in ceremony. Like the intimate spaces of Renée Stout and Amalia Mesa-Bains's installations, this space is populated with small dressing tables and chairs on which sit bouquets of artificial flowers, framed images, shells and coins, and albums open to pages filled with faces from the past. Indeed, the space of Lukac's installation is so filled with photographic portraits (literally hundreds) that it has the feel of an archive or the home of an obsessive collector. The public quality of the images themselves (some are canonical images by photographers like Richard Avedon or Dorothea Lange) suggests that this installation is less autobiographical than those of the other two artists. Nevertheless, the intimate quality of the space remains, and the artist herself claims that *Votive Shrine* is

Figure 7. Jenni Lukac, *Votive Shrine* (1992), detail of martyr shrine. Photograph by Nicholas Whitman; reprinted by permission of the photographer.

Figure 8. Jenni Lukac, *Votive Shrine* (1992), detail of boy's shrine. Photograph by Nicholas Whitman; reprinted by permission of the photographer.

"primarily about memory, both personal and cultural, and the mechanisms through which memory is encoded, transmitted, maintained and (re)contextualized."[22]

It is this last point—the notion that memory can be recontextualized—that I find most intriguing about Lukac's work. *Votive Shrine* is clearly not framing a question of identity or mapping the production of subjectivity in the same manner as the installations previously discussed. Nevertheless, it creates a rhetoric of comparison that invites the viewer to identify with the overlapping histories of those depicted within. The relationship between audience and image is personalized by the intimacy of the installation. Viewers are expected to identify with the faces in the photographs, trace a subjective path through the historical microcosm represented, and thus admit to a role as witness, past or present, to the events depicted; to accept the signs presented as part of a preconscious public memory. Histories can be retold, but can memories be reconstructed? By placing images that would not normally be seen side by side together in the space of this display, the artist appeals to the viewer's participation in his or her own reconstruction of memory.

Although the work makes reference to many forms of historical conflict, Jewish and African diaspora communities in the United States are a primary focus. The long history of animosity between these communities, illustrated by a rhetorical reconciliation in the installation, is clearly a motivating force behind Lukac's work, as well as one of its least re-solved elements. What is the history of these relations? How can they be understood in the present? What is lost in the equation of their representation? The work does not answer the questions it raises about the specific historical and social relations represented with visual and material artifacts. Instead, *Votive Shrine* reveals the repetitive cycles of power relations that create the conditions for martyrdom. Drawing parallels between forms of violence and suffering, the artist expands a critique of oppression beyond ethnic and national identities but also encounters there a resistance to the simple equations she would like to stage. Nevertheless, to present this critique in the context of domestic space and in the form of mundane objects productively collapses the artificial opposition that separates "great" historical events from the private lives of individual subjects.

DOMESTICITY, GENDER, ETHNICITY

Scholar Norman Bryson, writing about the history of European still-life painting, has observed that "the division between the exalted and the mundane is not simply a matter for neutral or philosophical debate, of world views between which an individual might freely choose"; rather, he argues, "the opposition does not exist in a vacuum: *it is overdetermined by another polarity, that of gender.*"[23] Bryson's analysis of still life suggests that the genre has been traditionally undervalued and therefore underanalyzed by art historians precisely because of its association with the domestic sphere, with the mundane, the decorative detail, and so with the feminine. The representational strategies of the installation works discussed here share this semiotic lexicon with the tradition of still life, extending its metaphoric and metonymic vocabulary from two to three dimensions. Of course, the artists also draw on a lexicon of cultural practices from their own communities, whether in the form of religious practice or forms of domestic display. The installation re-creates a space in which the subject is enshrined by the objects that represent the subject's absence. In both still-life painting and in these installations, material culture is used to point elsewhere, beyond the thing-in-itself to the social rank, cultural role, or invisible community that a real or imaginary subject inhabits. In addition, the artists here explicitly *exalt the mundane* in an effort to redraw the boundaries that have prevented consideration of the domestic sphere as a site for the renegotiation of power relations. The decision to produce installation art rather than works in traditional media suggests an interest on the part of these artists to create an environment within which the viewer will recall other, familiar sites. The artists perhaps recognize that the most important forms of ideological hailing may take place not "in the street," but in the home.

Amalia Mesa-Bains has explained her own work in terms of everyday practices that are common within her Chicana community: the production of *retablos* (home altars) and *capillas* (yard shrines) becomes "the focus for the refinement of domestic skills such as embroidery, flower making and hand-painting."[24] To clarify the culturally specific role of gendered spaces in her work, the artist has coined the term *domesticana* to denote what she calls a Chicana *rasquache*.[25] A form of "making do" with materials that are at hand, particularly in domestic spaces, *domesticana* is seen by Mesa-Bains as a creative process that affirms culturally specific values in combination with an emancipation from traditional feminine roles using "techniques of subversion through play with traditional imagery and cultural material."[26] As Mesa-Bains comments, "Because [the art] is rooted in popular practices, [Chicanas] are often misunderstood as still being naive folk artists or somehow ethnocentric provincials because we exhibit these popular practices and phenomena."[27] In fact, *domesticana* rejects the distinction between folk and fine art, enlisting flamboyant ornamentation for the sake of aesthetic subversions, such as those that appear in *Venus Envy*. *Domesticana* thus becomes the method by which the private spaces of the home—particularly spaces traditionally associated with women—are brought into the public spaces of exhibition, not merely to reflect but to actively construct new sites of identification for members of the audience who are invited to discover fragments of their own histories and memories in the signs presented. More important, Mesa-Bains's theorization of *domesticana* allows for the articulation of an *aesthetic of feminist critique* that simultaneously maintains a *commitment to cultural traditions*—a precarious but crucial position for the artist to occupy.

To the degree that certain forms of material culture have played a central role in the "objectification" of cultures—primarily non-Western cultures through the acquisition of their properties for the purposes of display—Stout's "domestication" of these same kinds of objects returns them to the realm of the subject and to a relation in which the artifacts are used in a process of identification rather than to signal cultural difference. In other words, the artist effectively resituates objects from one location in the art-culture system (that of ethnographic curiosity) to another (that of personal iconography) to another (that of fine art). Ethnicity here figures as an artifact of the subject: it is an inheritance that cannot be ignored, but it is also an edifice voluntarily constructed. The installation also draws on a domestic lexicon of signs to reflect on the changing gender roles that accompany the search for traditional values across generations. The work addresses a conceptual and material shift from the passive acceptance of narrow definitions of ethnic identity and gender roles (represented by the social hierarchies evident in the grandmother's altar) to one of active searching, critique, and discovery (as made manifest in the eclecticism of the artist's altar) through the staging of a dialogue. Stout's model of domesticity is one in which subjectivity is constructed through debate, through a cohabitation that may include confrontation but that also implies compromise.

Lukac's decision to organize *Votive Shrine* into gendered categories, she claims, is based on the fact that photography has historically figured men and women differently.[28] Thus photography, which is the dominant sign system of the work, is also its organizing principle. It seems that Lukac risks, in this decision, repeating the very grouping or stereotyping she has sought to avoid in other parts of the installation. But her decision appears to be motivated by the desire to produce visual associations that are only possible through such categorical collocation. Along with the boy's shrine discussed above are a men's, women's, and girl's shrine. The men's shrine, a somber but stately chest of drawers, into which the viewer can peer through a nineteenth-century stereoscope, contains recent and antique photographs of male politicians, male religious leaders, fathers holding children, and male sports heroes. Gillette razor-blade wrappers, golf balls, and other such paraphernalia fill the open bottom drawers. The women's shrine is less concealed and more ornate, decorated as a kind of mantelpiece or triptych with images of queens and political leaders, ordinary mothers and children, movie stars and saints along with flowers and statuettes. The girl's shrine houses miniature pink porcelain dolls and dance slippers. Lukac's choice of display points to the ways in which domestic architecture and even furniture design divide space into gendered territories. That men often keep personal mementos in drawers and that women often arrange them on shelves may have as much to do with the way domestic spaces are gendered as with conventions concerning privacy and display.[29] Lukac, despite her conventional mapping of gender identity, is observant in her representations of interior spaces as the sites where these conventions are played out.

What the artists observe about domestic space is that it is a site in which practices produce subjects. In *The Practice of Everyday Life* scholar Michel de Certeau, writing about the activity of "making do," suggests that to understand practices of use (in the context of consumption) it is useful to distinguish between "strategies" and "tactics." A strategy is defined as

> the calculation (or manipulation) of power relationships that becomes possible as soon as a subject with will and power (a business, an army, a city, a scientific institution) can be isolated. It postulates a place that can be delimited as its own and serve as the base from which relations with an exteriority composed of targets or threats . . . can be managed.[30]

Conversely, a tactic is a calculated action determined by the absence of power and "the absence of a proper locus" (37). Moreover, a tactical action depends on opportunities; it must "seize on the wing the possibilities that offer themselves at any given moment. It must vigilantly make use of the cracks that particular conjunctions open in the surveillance of the proprietary powers" (37). I would argue that the temporary artist's installation may already be a kind of tactical maneuver in the context of the institutional strategies of the art market. But more important, the kind of practices that these three artists represent, the domestic mapping of identities, the decorative aesthetic of making do, the rejection of "proprietary powers" all appear to be tactical responses to dominant strategies that may be racist or patriarchal.

DIASPORA, NARRATIVE, DISPLAY

Each of the installations is also the result of collecting, a gathering of disparate elements into an agglomeration of signs, legible to the degree that they follow familiar fixed syntagms (tables and chairs, candles and saints, photographs and keepsakes). The work suggests that the subject(s) represented in these spaces can be understood as a complex "accretion" of qualities that may be as much contradictory as complementary,[31] that this accretion can be indicated by synecdochic and metonymic signs, and that a display or collection of pseudoindexical signs can function to create an alternative iconography for this subjectivity. Critic Daniel Barbiero has suggested, in writing of Lukac's *Votive Shrine,* that "these relics and structures in their totality make up something we can term an historico-cumulus, i.e., a sedimented collection of worked material and categories of meaning."[32] The temporal structure of the work is neither neatly synchronic nor diachronic but, following Michel Foucault, what might be called heterochronic—combining signs that should be read *against* the temporality of other signs present, just as the subject's life is constructed out of constant interruptions, moments of the past appearing in the present (as symptoms), or geographical displacements creating disjunctions of space and an overlapping of visual signs, language, gestures, or artifacts. This articulation of the subject is similar to that put forth by Stuart Hall in his now well-known essay "Cultural Identity and Diaspora," in which he comments that the diaspora experience

> is defined not by essence or purity, but by the recognition of a necessary heterogeneity and diversity; by a conception of "identity" which lives with and through, not despite difference; by *hybridity*. Diaspora identities are those which are constantly producing and reproducing themselves anew, through transformation and difference."[33]

How is it possible to represent, to visually or materially display, this condition? The installations of Mesa-Bains, Stout, and Lukac offer one kind of solution.

Renée Stout, for example, reminds the viewer that neither religious affiliation nor cultural identity are "natural" categories. Rather, they are constructed through and maintained by material sign systems. The various images and artifacts that are collected in the installation become emphatic statements about such affiliations through placement and accumulation. In the grandmother's altar, each lovingly framed photograph is not merely a portrait of an individual but also one element of the larger family hierarchy to which it belongs. In the artist's altar, each individual element is not merely an "ethnographic" curiosity but a fragment that stands for cultural traditions, vast geographical locations, and the several different religious practices that are of interest to the artist. As critic Philip Brookman has suggested, "This room offers a kind of sanctuary for reflection and private thoughts about memory, family, and the assimilation of African American ethnicity and ethos by Christianity and television media."[34] It also offers alternatives to that assimilation, and it raises questions about the too-easy assignment of ethnic and racial identity to any individual.

"The installations serve as devices of intimate storytelling through an aesthetic of accumulation; accumulation of experience, reference, memory and transfiguration. Historical works . . . act as well for my personal narrative of life events," Amalia Mesa-Bains explains.[35] Accumulation and narrative may, in fact, share a similar rhetorical structure.[36] Scholar Mieke Bal has written an insightful account of collecting as a narrative practice in her essay "Telling Objects." Although Bal reads the practice of collecting as a far more systematic endeavor than the kind of activity in which the artists here engage, her reflections on the parallels between the narrative of the life of the subject and the narrative structure of the collection offer the important observation that "objects are inserted into the narrative perspective when their status is turned from objective to semiotic, from thing to sign, from collapse to separation of thing and meaning, or from presence to absence."[37] Bal argues that "a complex and hybrid kind of fetishism—indebted to childhood gendering as well as to submission to political history, to memory as well as to lived experience in the present—underlies collecting in the Western world" (112). Mesa-Bains's installations reconstruct the events of childhood gendering through the collection of trace elements— elements that are both signs of disavowal, repression, displacement as well as signs of an active affirmation of memory and history. A narrative forms the underlying structure of the installation to the degree that each material sign functions to denote a moment in a heterochronic development not only of the artist's life but in the lives of other Chicanas.

The kind of accumulative history told by Mesa-Bains, Stout, and Lukac is not strictly modern in its architecture. Their works might have more in common with those that

Gilane Tawadros examines in her essay "Beyond the Boundary," in which she argues that the artists Lubiana Himid, Sutapa Biswas, and Sonia Boyce engage with a conception of history that is predicated on an awareness of the historical limits of the modern, Western *episteme,* which privileges notions of continuity, development, and origins over and above notions of discontinuity, dispersion, and difference. This artistic historicism is to be read against a "nostalgic postmodernism" in which the appropriation of signs from the past serves to obscure "genuine historicity."[38] An aesthetic of multiplicity and eclectic assemblage in the work of these artists is therefore to be read neither as a pastiche of unrelated signs nor as the "authentic fragments" of a lost and rediscovered "original" or "pure" identity. Rather, Tawadros explains,

> The process of gathering and reusing, far from affirming the fragmentation of the black subject in terms of postmodernity, attests to the centrality and dynamism of the diasporan experience, of diverse cultural influences and discontinuous histories in opposition to the false unities of Western thought which reach their apogee in the "supreme fictions" of modernism. (124)

By rejecting a modernism that is blind to this diasporan experience (a rejection that may in fact owe a certain debt to the critical enunciations of postmodern theories of representation), the artists do not simultaneously announce the end of a coherent (not unitary), dynamic subject. Instead, the artworks display the manner in which strong subject positions are always *constructed across* conflicting conceptual and cultural paradigms. They might more accurately fall into what Sharon Haar and Christopher Reed call "resistant" postmodernism.[39]

By making the discontiguous contiguous, by linking spaces and signs that would never coexist (in the case of Mesa-Bains, the boudoir and the chapel, the museum and the bedroom; or for Stout the grandmother's altar and her own altar; or for Lukac the images of men or women from vastly different ethnic, economic, or historical domains), the artists are able to make a comparative analysis, to argue the problematic but necessary conflation of these domains. To chart the conflicts that exist between them, they make an imaginary space that can contain them. The installation, in other words, is the only site where these other worlds can be housed together. The literalness of the familiar signs employed is necessary for their recombination to effect a visual or spatial disjunction. The works are not intended to produce a simple reversal of signs; they act instead to redistribute the connotations of artifacts that are already heavy with iconographic associations.

Stuart Hall's essay "New Ethnicities" addresses a shift in black British cinema of the 1980s from a struggle over "the relations of representation to a politics of representation itself," from an effort to *simply be represented* to an effort *not to be represented simply.* He points out that while blacks in Britain had often been the object of representation they had rarely been the subjects *producing* those representations and that, in the 1980s, this situation began to change in the domain of filmmaking.[40] Michelle Cliff's essay "Object into Subject: Some Thoughts on the Work of Black Women Artists" makes a similar but more generalized case about the fine arts.[41] What both writers emphasize is the importance of the subject's ability to map a position within a complex social structure not merely in terms of difference, or in terms of oppositional Otherness, but as internally complex, layered, and diverse. This necessitates a nonracist context in which complexity is not collapsed into simplicity and an imaginary realism is not misread as an argument for authenticity.

If the installation art of Amalia Mesa-Bains, Renée Stout, and Jenni Lukac is representative of the formation of subjects, of the accretion of signs that shape and structure an identity and its context, what kind of relation is posited here between subjects and their objects? How can an archaeology of the site and an archaeology of the subject be read as somehow parallel?

It has been suggested that human subjects are *produced through* systems of representation that are understood as material, cultural practices: the mass media, visual arts, language, ideology. It has also been argued that the agency of individual subjects is lost in the general tendency to locate power in the larger social systems of which the subject is considered a mere effect. The temptation to replace one teleological chain of cause and effect (the discourse produces the subject) with another (the subject produces the discourse) should be avoided. For it is certainly the case that subjects are both the producers of discourse and produced by discourse. What is less obvious is the degree to which, in any specific instance, the relationships between discourses are structured. What Amalia Mesa-Bains, Renée Stout, and Jenni Lukac offer is one material and visual analysis of these relations.

For there is no reason to separate material artifacts from "visual" or "linguistic" artifacts in terms of their role in the formation of the social or psychic identity of individual subjects. Written and spoken languages may be the most commonly recognized sites of this formation for the reason that they are among the most conventional, rule-governed systems of cultural practice. However, the subject is also produced *through* the systems of objects that it encounters, that require or produce certain behaviors (what Louis Althusser might call material modalities), that mark or transform the subject through proximity or display, ownership or symbolic association.[42]

If, as Jacques Lacan suggests, the subject's first relation to an image is one of identification, then this image comes to be one way in which the subject is constituted, in which identity is shaped.[43] This image of the subject provides a certain "identity at a distance"— not within the body but in relation to it. This identity at a distance is a particularly useful description of the subject's attachment to objects. It complicates the division that is normally seen to exist between the body and the image or external representation of it. If early formation of the subject relies on the distinctions drawn between itself and objects in the world, such formation also produces identification with those objects. The semiotic legibility of material culture is likely to be established first as a system of things that to a child are accessible or inaccessible, desirable or undesirable, and that create the material environment that is its system of signification and through which its subjectivity is partially established.[44] In such a case the subject is less likely to identify *with* or *as* the objects in question as *through* them. Insofar as the subject can be constituted *through* a collection or display of objects, the form and properties of these objects are as likely to produce residual signifiers in the unconscious as other sign systems, such as language. The legibility of certain material-objects-as-signs will thus be "overdetermined,"[45] not only by the material artifacts encountered in childhood but also by the repetition of such artifacts in conjunction with other sign systems (such as language) in subsequent situations.[46]

If artifacts produce subjects at the level of the individual psyche, it is also the case that this production, while not following the strict rules of language, nevertheless has recognizable conventions both on the level of use and the level of signification. Disciplines such as anthropology and archaeology, as well as the historical materialism developed since Karl Marx, have long understood that material artifacts *represent* subjectivity or indeed *stand in for* relations between subjects (through gift-giving, wartime plunder, commodity fetishism, and so on).[47] The movement of the subject through such conventions (as consumer, as producer, as collector, as fetishist) produces that subject *as a subject,* according to the ideology governing such conventions, especially in the context of a hegemonic capitalism. In such a climate human subjects are clearly legible as the products of the objects they and others produce.

Teresa de Lauretis in her article "Semiotics and Experience" summarizes this process nicely: *"The individual's habit as a semiotic production is both the result and the condition of the social production of meaning."*[48] Extending the boundaries of Umberto Eco's theories, de Lauretis recounts the material role of the sign in the production of subjectivity, and in particular gendered subjectivity:

> In the first place, semiosis specifies the mutual overdetermination of meaning, perception and experience, a complex nexus of reciprocally constitutive effects between the subject and social reality, which, in the subject, entail a continual modification of consciousness; that consciousness in turn being the condition of social change. In the second place, the notion of semiosis is *theoretically* dependent on the intimate relationship of subjectivity and practices; and the place of sexuality in that relationship, feminism has shown, is what defines sexual difference *for women,* and gives femaleness its meaning as the experience of a female subject. (184)

De Lauretis is able to posit "a subject touched by the practice of signs, a subject physically implicated or bodily engaged in the production of meaning, representation and self representation" (182–83). This offers an understanding of semiosis as a process that can produce change through subjects, subjects who are necessarily already engaged in a "social practice" through which, among other things, gender is articulated. Despite the critiques leveled against the tendency to apply theories of gender to theories of race, I would nevertheless argue that de Lauretis's observations can be expanded to include questions of ethnicity, insofar as both ethnicity and race are also produced through the intimate relations of subjectivity and practice.[49]

Ethnicity and gender can become part of this material articulation of the subject when recognizable syntagms of artifacts are coded to produce familiar associations following surprisingly strict conventions such as that of the woman's boudoir or the ethnographic museum. In the artists' installations, these material syntagms are reorganized to present alternative or critical perspectives. In Mesa-Bains's installation, white dresses and rebellious virgins mark significant rites of passage and shifts in subject position for the young Chicana. Lukac exhibits a public memorial as a montage of photographs in a familiar domestic setting defamiliarized by its representation as a shrine. An African *n'kisi* figure in the company of family snapshots, bones, and Native American artifacts attest to the hybrid ethnic identity of the imaginary inhabitant of Stout's installation, while simultaneously disrupting those museum taxonomies that place such objects in mutually exclusive categories. Of course, other kinds of subjectivity are also produced through the collection, arrangement, use, and display of objects: determinations of class, profession, and cultural heritage often rest on the ownership or use of particular objects-as-signs.[50]

The art installations signify a dual interior, that of the artificial staging of domestic space that is installed in the museum or gallery, and that of the implied subject for whom the objects comprise imaginary parts, or constitutive supplements, a turning-inside-out of the incrustation of subjectivity formed by an accretion of objects. In addition, the audience is interpellated into a relation of identification with the implied inhabitant of the scene, positioned within a point of view or model of *looking* woven into the space of the installation. The act of contemplation is itself staged and orchestrated so that the audience is invited to imagine the kind of subject who is doing the looking, and the kind of subject positions expected of the audience. The architecture of the space, the placement of furniture, mirrors, and display cases imply several different kinds of seeing and being seen. In *Venus Envy* the mirrors, both on the wall and at the vanity, reflect a heterogeneous identity and suggest that mirrors are overdetermined sites of subject formation, whereas the vitrines in the center of the room distance the viewer from the personal effects of the artist by restaging a museological display that heightens the historical quality of the artifacts. In Stout's *My Altar/My Grandmother's Altar,* armchairs form the evidence of directed contemplation, a kind of studied focus that is dominated by the television in one instance and by a display of artifacts in the other. Lukac's *Votive Shrine* sets up an equivalence between domestic spaces of remembrance and public memorials. Looking at photographs becomes an act of witnessing historical events through another's private archive of souvenirs, which may in fact resemble one's own. In each case, a collection of what is certainly subject *matter* is presented as an archaeological portrait.

ARCHAEOLOGICAL DEVOTION

The work of Amalia Mesa-Bains, Jenni Lukac, and Renée Stout foregrounds an iconic mode of address while simultaneously staging a critique of those social institutions that depend on their own limited iconography: the museum, the church, the home. Reproducing formal elements found in each of these domains (the symmetry of the altar, the intimacy of the boudoir, the accumulation of the museum) is therefore both a rhetorical and tactical move on the part of these artists, who employ substitution as a primary form of subversion. Common visual tropes invite a reverent reading from viewers familiar with religious modes of display, but the content of display has changed and the icons themselves are new. Devotion here takes the form of a simultaneous celebration and critique of the religious institutions to which the installations make reference. Revealing conflicting worldviews, the installations also create a "home" for alternative signs and metaphors with which an individual or community may identify. This kind of subversion might be characterized, following Teresa de Lauretis, as a movement between the (represented) discursive space of the positions made available by hegemonic discourses and the space-off, the elsewhere, of those discourses; those other spaces both discursive and social that exist, since feminist practices have (re)constructed them, in the margins (or "between the lines" or "against the grain") of hegemonic discourses and in the interstices of institutions, in counter practices and new forms of community.[51]

In exposing otherwise repressed histories through what might be called a *discourse* of material culture, the works discussed here are participating in an archaeological enterprise that shares methodological concerns with those outlined by Michel Foucault in *The Archaeology of Knowledge.*[52] For Foucault, a material practice enters into a discursive state when it functions as the site of contention, contradiction, and transformation of other discourses. In order to map or to study such discursive formations, Foucault turns to the metaphor of archaeology. In contrast to a linear, progressive narrative that characterizes other analytic approaches to historical discourse, his archaeology can be understood as a methodology that outlines the conditions within which a particular discourse arises.[53] In this sense, for Foucault the archaeological method supplies that which is *not* coherent, *not* general, *not* part of a totalizing theory.[54] Rather, it finds that which has heretofore escaped systematic analysis within a particular discursive domain. The task is thus to redefine the parameter of a discursive domain through the recuperation of changes, contradictions, and transformations of the objects that form this discourse. It is for these reasons that I use Foucault's theorization of archaeology as a metaphor for the material practice of the artists in question:

> The horizon of archaeology, therefore, is not *a* science, *a* rationality, *a* mentality, *a* culture; it is a tangle of interpositivities whose limits and points of intersection cannot be fixed in a single operation. Archaeology is a comparative analysis that is not intended to reduce the diversity of discourses, and to outline the unity that must totalize them, but is intended to divide up their diversity into different figures. Archaeological comparison does not have a unifying, but a diversifying, effect.[55]

If the artists in question are participating in an archaeology, then it is one intended to create a material topography of those signs that constrain and allow for local subject formation and specific historical narratives. For Foucault the "archaeological" horizon does not require a historical description that relies on the notion of development, indeed it eschews this model of progression altogether. Similarly, the works discussed here present an image of history and memory that is made up of multiple and overlapping synchronic elements rather than a single diachronic development.

The primary difference between Foucault's archaeological practice and that of the artists in question is that while Foucault seeks to reveal how an order of *things* is reconfigured into an order of *discourses,* the artists discussed here seek to reveal how an existing order of things can be revised through a reordering of things. In other words, by producing installations, the artists confront archive with archive, taxonomic collection with taxonomic collection, material rhetoric with material rhetoric. All wish to reveal the gaps in discourse, primarily historical discourse, concerning certain subjects and objects. All work to include historical traces and signs that are not what would commonly be thought of as aspects of a traditional epistemology. For Foucault this practice is an archaeology of knowledge that forms a new analysis of the history of ideas. For the artists in question, this practice is an archaeology that participates in an ongoing *material debate*. Each installation piece produces a unique vision of history, ethnicity, and gender through a carefully orchestrated arrangement and display of gathered material signs. In response to hegemonic representations of gender and ethnicity, these installations provide an alternative material history, an agonistic rhetoric of objects. As an imaginary architecture, the installations rearticulate the social, economic, and cultural relations into which the artists and others have been woven as subjects.

NOTES

1. The term *installation art* has been used increasingly since the 1960s to denote temporary, site-specific artworks designed to surround or interact with the spectator and/or extant architecture in a given exhibition space. Formal and conceptual precedents are most often traced to dadaist and surrealist exhibitions of the early twentieth century or to the "environments" and "happenings" of the late 1950s and early 1960s that sought to disrupt the traditional semiotic and somatic boundaries assumed to exist between the audience, the work of art, the site of exhibition, and the world beyond.

2. James Clifford, *The Predicament of Culture* (Cambridge: Harvard University Press, 1988), 224.

3. See Jennifer González, "Autotopographies," in *Prosthetic Territories*, ed. Gabriel Brahm Jr. and Mark Driscoll (Boulder, Colo.: Westview Press, 1995), 133–50.

4. See Jennifer González, "Rhetoric of the Object: Material Memory and the Artwork of Amalia Mesa-Bains," *Visual Anthropology Review* 9, no. 1 (Spring 1993): 82–91.

5. Roland Barthes, *Image/Music/Text*, trans. Stephen Heath (New York: Noonday Press, 1977), 35.

6. Roland Barthes, *The Semiotic Challenge* (New York: Hill and Wang, 1988), 186. This comment is strikingly similar to that made by Christian Metz in the same year, who writes of film that "the relationships *in praesentia* are so rich that they render the strict organization of *in-abstentia* relationships superfluous and difficult. A film is difficult to explain because it is easy to understand. The image impresses itself on us, blocking everything that is not itself." Christian Metz, *Film Language*, trans. Michael Taylor (New York: Oxford University Press, 1974), 69.

7. Stephen Bann, *The Clothing of Cleo* (Cambridge: Cambridge University Press, 1984), 82–88.

8. Ibid., 88.

9. Stephen Bann, "Shrines, Curiosities and the Rhetoric of Display," in *Visual Display: Culture beyond Appearances*, ed. Lynne Cooke and Peter Wollen (Seattle: Bay Press, 1995), 23–24.

10. Another scholar who seems to be addressing the usefulness of rhetoric for the analysis of material culture is Katherine C. Grier. She delivered a paper at the October 1993 Winterthur Conference "Material Culture: The Shape of the Field" titled "Material Culture as Rhetoric: 'Animal Artifacts' as a Case Study." In the published abstract the author suggests that "if we pursue this concept of material culture as rhetoric systematically, it will 1) help to advance our analysis of one central problem in our field, how material culture communicates, as well as what it communicates and 2) help to link material culture studies more firmly to analysis of other forms of communication."

11. Peter Wollen, "Introduction," in *Visual Display*, 10.

12. My use of the term *identification* derives from the psychoanalytic definition of the concept. According to Laplanche and Pontalis, "identification" is the "psychological process whereby the subject assimilates an aspect, property or attribute of the other and is transformed, wholly or partially, after the model the other provides. It is by means of a series of identifications that the personality is constituted

and specified." I would simply add that this "other" need not be another person, but can be a system of signs, a social institution, an iconic figure, or a phantasmatic projection. J. Laplanche and J.-S. Pontalis, *The Language of Psychoanalysis,* trans. Donald Nicholson-Smith (New York: W. W. Norton, 1973), 205.

13. Gallery text from Whitney Museum of American Art at Philip Morris, New York, January 1993.

14. The display is reminiscent of French artist Annette Messager's *Histoire des Robes* (1990–1991). Messager's encased dresses suggest their own unique narratives but do not figure as part elements in a larger installation as do Mesa-Bains's.

15. Gloria Anzaldúa, *Borderlands/La Frontera* (San Francisco: Spinsters/Aunt Lute, 1987), 42.

16. From an interview with the author, 1993.

17. Lisa Lowe, "Heterogeneity, Hybridity, Multiplicity: Marking Asian American Differences," *Diaspora* 1, no. 1 (1991): 24–44.

18. Artist's written response to questions from the author, June 1993.

19. See Frances Yates, *The Art of Memory* (Chicago: University of Chicago Press, 1966).

20. Jenni Lukac, *Image/Object/Memory* (Richmond: Virginia Center for the Craft Arts, 1992), 4.

21. Jenni Lukac, interview with Julia Mandle, in *Sites of Recollection: Four Altars and a Rap Opera* (Williamstown, Mass.: Williams College Museum of Art, 1992), 60.

22. Jenni Lukac, letter to the author, June 1, 1994.

23. Norman Bryson, *Looking at the Overlooked: Four Essays on Still Life Painting,* (London: Reaktion Books, 1990), 157 (emphasis in original).

24. Amalia Mesa-Bains "Domesticana," in *Division of Labor: "Women's Work" in Contemporary Art* (New York: Bronx Museum of the Arts, 1995), 73.

25. Scholar Tomás Ybarra-Frausto defines the term *rasquache*: "In the realm of taste, to be rasquache is to be unfettered and unrestrained, to favor the elaborate over the simple, the flamboyant over the severe. Bright colors *(chillantes)* are preferred to somber, high intensity to low, the shimmering and sparkling over the muted and subdued. The rasquache inclination piles pattern on pattern, filling all available space with bold display. Ornamentation and elaboration prevail and are joined with a delight in texture and sensuous surfaces." Tomás Ybarra-Frausto, "Chicano Movement/Chicano Art," in *Exhibiting Cultures: The Poetics and Politics of Museum Display,* ed. Steven D. Lavine and Ivan Karp (Washington, D.C.: Smithsonian Institution Press, 1991), 134.

26. Amalia Mesa-Bains, "Curatorial Statement," in *Ceremony of Spirit: Nature and Memory in Contemporary Latino Art,* (San Francisco: Mexican Museum, 1993), 12.

27. Interview with the author, spring 1992.

28. Interview with the artist, July 1993.

29. See González, "Autotopographies." See also Mihaly Csikszentmihalyi and Eugene Rochberg-Halton, *The Meaning of Things: Domestic Symbols and the Self* (Cambridge: Cambridge University Press, 1981).

30. Michel de Certeau, *The Practice of Everyday Life* (Los Angeles: University of California Press, 1984), 36.

31. Victor Burgin, in a lecture delivered in Santa Cruz, California, November 12, 1990, described the development of the subject's psyche as an "accretion," using the metaphor of a coral reef. My own observations derive in part from this lecture. My meaning of accretion is also comparable, though not equivalent, to Alois Riegl's notion of "age-value." He writes of architecture (and I would apply the same observations to material culture): "Age-value manifests itself less violently, though more tellingly, in the corrosion of surfaces, in their patina, in the wear and tear of buildings and objects and so forth. . . . We are as disturbed at the sight of decay in newly made artifacts (premature aging) as we are at the traces of fresh intervention into old artifacts (conspicuous restorations). . . . Thus modern man sees a bit of himself in a monument, and he will react to every intervention as he would to one on himself." Alois Riegl,

"The Modern Cult of Monuments: Its Character and Its Origin," trans. Kurt W. Forster and Diane Ghirardo, *Oppositions* 25 (Fall 1982): 31–32.

32. Daniel Barbiero, "Jenni Lukac: Votive Shrine," *Art Papers* (January/February 1991): 64.

33. Stuart Hall, "Cultural Identity and Diaspora," in *Identity: Community, Culture, Difference*, ed. Jonathan Rutherford (London: Lawrence and Wishart, 1990), 235.

34. Philip Brookman, "The Politics of Hope: Sites and Sounds of Memory," in *Sites of Recollection*.

35. Amalia Mesa-Bains, unpublished manuscript, 1991.

36. See also James Clifford, "Collecting Ourselves," in *The Predicament of Culture*.

37. Mieke Bal, "Telling Objects: A Narrative Perspective on Collecting," in *The Cultures of Collecting*, ed. John Elsner and Roger Cardinal (Cambridge: Harvard University Press, 1994), 111.

38. Gilane Tawadros, "Beyond the Boundary: The Work of Three Black Women Artists in Britain," *Third Text* 8, no. 9 (Autumn/Winter 1989): 130.

39. "In its activist orientation, 'resistant' postmodernism is very much the heir to an earlier feminist engagement with the home, though its focus has expanded beyond the articulation of gender difference to include perspectives differentiated by race, ethnicity, sexuality and other forms of identity." Sharon Haar and Christopher Reed, "Coming Home: A Postscript on Postmodernism," in *Not at Home: The Suppression of Domesticity in Modern Art and Architecture*, ed. Christopher Reed (New York: Thames and Hudson, 1996), 261.

40. Stuart Hall. "New Ethnicities," in *Black Film/British Cinema*, ed. Kobena Mercer (London: Institute of Contemporary Arts, 1988).

41. Michelle Cliff, "Object into Subject: Some Thoughts on the Work of Black Women Artists," in *Making Face, Making Soul/Haciendo Caras*, ed. Gloria Anzaldúa (San Francisco: Spinsters/Aunt Lute, 1990).

42. See Jean Baudrillard, *Le Système des objets* (Paris: Denoël/Gonthier, 1968). See also Louis Althusser, "Ideology and Ideological State Apparatuses (Notes toward an Investigation)," in *Lenin and Philosophy, and Other Essays* (London: New Left Books, 1971). I am in agreement here with Clementine Deliss, who writes that "to look at the semantic fields of object-identification or visual communication in general is to suggest that interpretation might be conveyed through another dimension of signification. This approach does not deny the potential authority of language, as such; it merely attempts to introduce a new flexibility into the study of representation." Clementine Deliss, "Exhibit A: Blueprint for a Visual Methodology," *Third Text* 18 (Spring 1992): 33.

43. The movement of the Lacanian mirror-stage "manufactures for the subject, caught up in the lure of spatial identification, the succession of phantasies that extends from a fragmented body-image to a form of its totality." Jacques Lacan, *Ecrits,* trans. Alan Sheridan (New York: W. W. Norton, 1977), 4. This casting out into the world and drawing back is always the result of a connection with or passage through another object. This looping motion is a useful way of thinking through how meaning is anchored to an object, similar to the "quilting" that Slavoj Žižek discusses in *The Sublime Object of Ideology*. The object becomes the *point de capiton* within the chain of possible material signifiers; it becomes that which is the site of the passage of the Real to the Symbolic: "The *point de capiton* is the point through with the subject is 'sewn' to the signifier, and at the same time the point which interpellates individual into subject by addressing it with the call of a certain master-signifier ('Communism,' 'God,' 'Freedom,' 'America')—in a word, it is the point of the subjectivation of the signifier's chain." Slavoj Žižek, *The Sublime Object of Ideology* (London: Verso, 1989), 101.

44. I am not here trying to reiterate the arguments of object relations theory, which addresses a different notion of the object or part-object: the aim of the drive, which can be good or bad, such as in *The Psychoanalysis of Children* by Melanie Klein or *Playing and Reality* by D. W. Winnicott. Nevertheless, there are some useful parallels in certain instances, such as Winnicott's discussion of the "transitional

object," which is that material device that allows an infant to begin its psychic separation from the mother. Creating an attachment to a physical thing (a blanket, toy, etc.), the infant comes into a relation with the "original not-me possession." D. W. Winnicott, *Playing and Reality* (London: Tavistock Publications, 1971), 2. This possession becomes, for the infant, both an extension of itself (a prosthesis of sorts) and a kind of soothing presence external to itself. It is thus both internal and external to the infant's conception of self.

45. Laplanche and Pontalis define *overdetermination* as "The fact that formations of the unconscious can be attributed to a plurality of determining factors." Laplanche and Pontalis, *The Language of Psychoanalysis,* 292. From this original sense, the term has also been applied to domains other than the unconscious: political events, cultural signs that can be seen to arise from a combination of "determining factors."

46. Of course, the fetish is the most obvious example of such overdetermined signs. For an excellent discussion of fetishism and the possible functions of the fetish in the constitution of cultural identity, see Emily Apter and William Pietz, eds., *Fetishism as Cultural Discourse* (Ithaca, N.Y.: Cornell University Press, 1993).

47. See Baudrillard, *Le Système des objets.*

48. Teresa de Lauretis, "Semiotics and Experience," in *Alice Doesn't: Feminism, Semiotics, Cinema* (Bloomington: Indiana University Press, 1984), 179 (emphasis in original).

49. See Stuart Hall, "Cultural Identity and Diaspora."

50. See Pierre Bourdieu, *Distinction: A Social Critique of the Judgment of Taste* (Cambridge: Harvard University Press, 1984).

51. Teresa de Lauretis, *Technologies of Gender* (Bloomington: Indiana University Press, 1987), 26.

52. After writing this essay, I discovered an article titled "Exhibit/Inhibit: Archaeology, Value, History in the Work of Fred Wilson" by Irene J. Winter in the catalog *New Histories* (Boston: ICA, 1996) that makes a similar comparison between installation art, material culture, and Foucauldian archaeology. I am happy to see others thinking along the same lines.

53. An archaeology "does not imply the search for a beginning; it does not relate analysis to geological excavation. It designates the general theme of a description that questions the already-said at the level of its existence: of the enunciative function that operates within it, of the discursive formation, and the general archive system to which it belongs. Archaeology describes discourses as practices specified in the element of the archive." Michel Foucault, *The Archaeology of Knowledge* (New York: Pantheon Books, 1972), 131.

54. "Enunciative homogeneities (and heterogeneities) intersect with linguistic continuities (and changes), with logical identities (and differences), without any of them proceeding at the same pace or necessarily affecting one another." Ibid., 146.

55. Ibid., 159–60.

TRACING FIGURES OF PRESENCE, NAMING CIPHERS OF ABSENCE

Feminism, Imperialism, and Postmodernity in the Work of Sutapa Biswas

Griselda Pollock

It is one of the privileges of teaching fine art degree courses that I work in the presence of artistic practice. The challenging relations between art making and theoretical or historical reflection on and research in art history, when not kept in strictly segregated time zones, allow for a dialogue that can creatively alter each side. This article is a product of one such moment of exchange in which the relations between teacher and student, artist and art historian, structured and then recast two women's engagement with their practice, its politics, and the question of art.

I begin my writing on Sutapa Biswas with some memories. These are not mere nostalgia for those simpler days when we had just about gotten used to the idea that modernism was in for some serious critical revision and before postmodernism had begun to empty all our gestures of their intensity and hope. If I as a teacher at a formative moment of a young artist's education had any impact on Sutapa Biswas, she as an articulate young artist of Indian birth, taking on the possibilities and blind spots of a particular art department proud of its socialism and feminism but hardly self-conscious about its racism, has had a profound impact on me and my work. The opportunity to write about Sutapa Biswas's work is not only the outcome of an intellectual relationship forged in moments of becoming and difference; it is a product of a moment in the history of feminism, postcolonial discourse, and the artistic gesture. This moment has changed how I think and write, indeed has made these practices visible, susceptible to a creative and often critical self-consciousness, which abjures the possibility of remastering the shattered hegemonies challenged in the name of those they excluded. Instead, there is a double movement in which we have to find the positions allotted to us, the positions adopted by us, and the movements that can be made to create other relations of difference not premised on the phallocentric One/other models. Feminism of the class- and race-limited kind alerted us to the tropes of masculine imperialism before yet another more powerful internal complaint shattered the false unity of Feminism, recasting it as a perpetual process of self-provocation and dialogic covenant between the specific, singular, situated particularity of each of us who nonetheless uses this place, space, and discourse, rudely named "feminist," to grapple with the structures of power and position, desire and language, possibility and determination, in a world that by being called postcolonial or postmodern only makes us more alert to the perpetuated force of modernity and coloniality.

BEGINNING WHERE SOMETHING STARTED

Sutapa Biswas completed her undergraduate degree at the Department of Fine Art at the University of Leeds, England (1981–85). For some readers, this statement will immediately signify something quite significant. For others, it may indicate no more than educational background. The Department of Fine Art was one of the few in a British university to have the practice of fine art within its regimes of academic study.[1] After the appointment in 1975, and brief tenure of the Chair of Fine Art by social historian of art T. J. Clark, the faculty attempted to create a distinctive program for the study of fine art with art history by creating a course evenly divided between history/theory and practice/theory. By acknowledging the modernist legacy that had created a breach between practice and theory, the department undertook a historically and critically informed realignment that would as much challenge the shibboleths of modernist studio practice as it would demand the production of a new discourse in art history attuned to the problematics of artistic production.

The join between two sides of the course was created by the common interests shared by artists and art historians in the context of a politicized and increasingly theorized critique of modernism. Terry Atkinson, Fred Orton, John Tagg, Tim Clark, and I forged links through seminars, "crits" (studio-based discussion of students' work in progress), and lectures that bridged hitherto separated domains whose boundaries had been systematically policed as the condition of making ambitious modernist art.

Art history, itself being reshaped according to an emerging program for social and feminist histories of art, worked to provide a critical genealogy of the formation (1850s–60s) and disintegration (1950s–60s) of modernism. Artists in the studios explored these complex legacies and manufactured a critical practice that, while it was chronologically postmodernist, was not theoretically entirely symptomatic of those fashions now chaotically packaged as postmodernism. The critical difference between the two can simply be defined by the words *history* and *politics*. From several points of view, history—predominantly theorized through the tradition of historical materialism—ensured that theoretical revision was grounded in an understanding of interests, power, domination, exploitation. Such a conception of history stresses that there are important and concrete issues at stake in the challenges mounted to modernism's suspension of the social in favor of a formally isolated aesthetic domain. This engaged sense of the historical became a means to articulate a politically diversifying project, a naming of interests and an investment in concrete change rather than a fashionable substitution of ideas.

Feminism played a vital part in both the historical and political discourses that were developing at Leeds. As a historical perspective, feminism aimed to revise the canonical histories of art in order to acknowledge the presence and persistence of women artists over the ages. The realization, through such reclaimed histories, that femininity and creativity were not, as ideologically presented, incompatible, forced revision of the very practices of art history and criticism in order to understand the specificity and meaning of women's inscriptions on the texts of culture. Feminism necessitated a critique of modernist art and art history as much as of the critical revisions to it that were becoming the hallmark of the Leeds Department of Fine Art.

There can be no doubt that this academic environment—or, rather, this informal and still emergent conversational community, productively located in an art department that was considered marginal and provincial despite its prestigious past professors (Quentin Bell, Lawrence Gowing, Arnold Noach, Arnold Hauser)—influenced the development of Sutapa Biswas away from an immensely skillful and professionally accomplished figurative painting she had been producing as a student. Sutapa Biswas was encouraged toward an ambitious and critical intervention in contemporary art by means of multimedia presentations in the field of dominant representations, both local to Leeds and on a world scale.

Sutapa Biswas's presence in the course, however, was itself a factor in the evolution of the Leeds project. It was she who defined the absences in these seemingly radical discourses deriving from Marxism and feminism. It was she who named the imperialism that still structured analyses speaking in undifferentiated terms of class and gender, never acknowledging the issues of race and colonialism. It was her critique that forced us all to acknowledge the Eurocentric limits of the discourses within which we, the staff, practiced. Her challenge was mounted face to face, not at the level of abstract taunts. She directly engaged in dialogue with people sharing an intellectual and artistic space. We were thus assumed, by her political generosity, to be able and willing to enlarge the critical discourse we were developing to accommodate the subjects of class, gender, and race in their intricate and painful configurations between us and within us.

She demanded change. Response was made, and the course then altered. No longer repressing the question of imperialism and its racist practices, the space of the studio and the lecture theater had to articulate the pressure of the social and psychic relations that imperialism as a still powerful structure installed in us all. Instead of binary oppositions, Sutapa Biswas's practice as student and as producer of artworks systematically eroded the pairing of accusation and guilt to release the critical problem from defensive denial or mere liberal tolerance.

This is visible in the work she produced as a conclusion to her degree, *Housewives with Steak-Knives* (1984–85) (fig. 1). This vast tableau uses several pieces of paper mapped together with masking tape: "I sought to find a language that deliberately brought together components that were both of a Western and Eastern aesthetic and ideology. For me, the phenomena did not present such distinct borders, but in fact there were similarities and parallels in both camps."[2] This extended and hybrid space was constructed to house the collision of images, systems, meanings. At a formal level, the piece knowingly sets white against black, by imaging the Hindu goddess Kali, which means black, on white paper. Within Hindu thought, however, Kali represents the destroyer of evil, and the signification of this mission through blackness directly assaults the Eurocentric color symbolism that has been used in the imposition of the whitened, Christianized Europe's self-legitimating morality. The scale of the Kali figure and her adornment with both knives and flowers, with one of several hands raised in the Hindu gesture of peace, make this representation of she who pursues and punishes evil dominate the space of the picture and

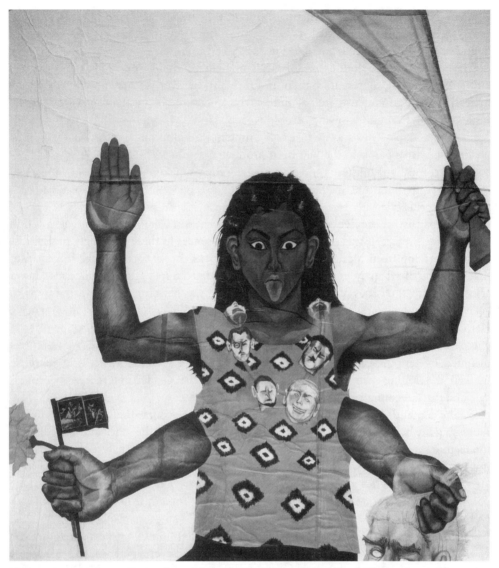

Figure 1. Sutapa Biswas, *Housewives with Steak-Knives* (1984–85). Oils, acrylics, and pastel on paper mounted onto canvas. 244 x 274 cm. Collection of Bradford Art Galleries and Museums, Cartwright Hall. Courtesy of Sutapa Biswas.

the space of the viewer. A centralized and frontal figure of a female goddess is not merely a signifier of power, which is, therefore, threatening. It is also a signifier of power and, therefore, comforting, because it is an allegorical figure of empowered femininity—the mother, who is too often misrecognized in Western patriarchal psychology as only the phallic mother.[3] Her power precedes the slightest intimation that the phallus might signify. The evocation of the maternal as a force of *both* order and power, of *both* anger and peace, reminds us of a measure of meaning other than that which European phallocentricism erects with its perpetual divisiveness. The binary opposition and hierarchical ordering of male and female, characteristic of the Western imaginary, are dislocated by this grand image of activity and moral purpose in the feminine. She sports a necklace of decapitated but still identifiable men's heads, which form a recognizably contemporary cast of political miscreants. These masculine trophies representing capitalism as well as communism, imperialism, and colonialism symbolize the evil that must be purged, in contradistinction to the Hellenic-Christian West's projection of evil onto women through the allegorical figures of Eve and Pandora, for whose apparent crimes all women must be punished. Hindu mythology provided Sutapa Biswas with a vocabulary with which to localize and reduce Western mythologies that, in permitted ignorance of other cultural systems, mistake their local stories and sexual mythologies for narratives of universal truth.

Hanging in one hand of Sutapa Biswas's Kali is a photocopy of another image of an active woman punishing male evil and threat, Artemisia Gentileschi's *Judith and Holofernes* (1625, Detroit Institute of Arts). This apocryphal story itself has a colonial dimension since a Jewish narrative was appropriated by Christian culture and reworked to convey completely refigured metaphoric meanings that erase the historical and ideological resonance of the story in its own national context. It thus becomes difficult to define what the considerable popularity of this imagery of a woman decapitating a man meant at the time a seventeenth-century woman painter, Gentileschi, began a series of repeated engagements with it. As part of Sutapa Biswas's image, the photocopy of a Gentileschi image further functions as a metonymic sign for contemporary Western feminist art history: for the photocopy is from *Old Mistresses,* a text used in the lecture series Theories and Institutions at the University of Leeds that Sutapa Biswas attended and critiqued.[4] Within feminist art history, still intoxicated in the early 1980s with recovering a "hidden heritage,"[5] Artemisia Gentileschi and her Judith paintings were celebrated as *exceptional* because by creating a murderous political heroine, the painted image seemed to disrupt and to counter prevailing assumptions about the inevitable passivity of women. Set in diminished proportions against Hindu culture's major deity, Kali, the counter but still Western femininity, signified by Judith as heroine/Gentileschi as artist, was relativized by Sutapa Biswas's picture. The powerful image of an active, divine, and politically insurgent femininity from Hindu culture functioned equally to displace racist stereotypes that currently represent Asian women as passive. The engagement with a culture's mythic sign in relation to lived sociohistorical femininities also addressed the complexity and contradiction within modern Indian culture itself as well as between cultures brought by history into both confrontation and potentially creative exchange.

TROPES AND THEORIES: CENTERS AND CIRCLES

Writing on "Imperialism and Sexual Difference," Gayatri Chakravorty Spivak has argued that feminism functions to expose the truth claims of the discourse of the privileged male of the white race, that is, to challenge their monopolistic claims on truth, defined according to their own interests. Feminism, however, has often failed by the same token to acknowledge its own complicity in imperialist discourse. Spivak argues for the necessary development from mere *oppositional* feminism, directed against patriarchal power, toward what she names a *critical* feminism that constantly examines its own complex imbrication in institutions and ideologies. Spivak exemplifies her point by noting, from within litera-ture studies, the different degrees of individuality ascribed to Western and non-Western women. Thus feminist literary criticism (and art history does much the same with its artist-heroines) struggles to create and legitimate for its women writers the very individu-ality that is the hallmark of Western bourgeois identity. Jane Austen, Charlotte Brontë, and Virginia Woolf are named in their complex subjectivities and ambivalent negotia-tions of identity and social place and become, as the effect of this attention, major icons of feminist discourse. By contrast, Western feminist scholars continue to produce studies on the undifferentiated collectivity of "Third World women." African, Asian, or Arab women are not endowed with a comparable privilege of either subjective particularity and com-plexity or of the capacity for resistance and negotiation of their sociopolitical situations. Thus if spoken of at all, African, Asian, or Arab women constitute a featureless collectivity, Third World women, the very icons of oppression.[6]

Sutapa Biswas's use of Kali as housewife deploys an image from Hindu culture precisely to overwhelm that objectification of Asian women, and its implied inequality in relation to modernity measured precisely by degrees of individuation. Equally, by set-ting this image in both a relation and a contrast to a figure from a Western mythology (Judith/Gentileschi), Sutapa Biswas retains the allegorical potential of the female deity to be a sign of a dense cultural and political freight that bespeaks the complexity of any cul-tural engagement with issues of power and sexual difference. She does not, however, flip back only to Westernize the Asian woman by creating for her a compromised, that is, im-perial and bourgeois, individuality, even though the features may be based on her own, giving the figure animation and immediacy. Finally, by naming such a figure, redolent with its place in high cultural discourses, a "housewife," Sutapa Biswas refutes a false ex-oticism. The woman is, after all, ordinary, working with her knives in the daily processes of domestic duty and familial transmission of language, culture, and its embodied stories. The artist thereby pays a certain debt to her own mother, to the place of domestic work, confusing and refuting the binaries that diminish the particular meanings of women un-named by History, though influential through personal and familial networks in particu-lar individuals' histories.

This major piece of "history painting" was produced in tandem with a remarkable performance, recorded and exhibited as a video, titled *Kali.* At the time, I had felt privi-leged and trusted to be invited to witness, so I thought, a performance Sutapa Biswas was preparing in order to explore her double vision.[7] Her feminism was larger, broader, and more finely calibrated to the questions of difference and power than that within which I had been allowed ignorantly to remain. When I arrived to watch the performance, I was kept inexplicably waiting in the corridor while preparations continued inside the room. At last I was ushered in to find myself not a spectator at the margins but part of the spec-tacle. The center, British imperialism, was to be put on discomforted display, and made to figure as part of the created ritual contesting its postcolonial hegemony. Obliged to sit in the center of a circle, hooded, though I could just see through the slits at eye level, I was made to function as an icon of imperialism around which Sutapa Biswas's enactments of resistance would be performed. Physically central by my actual positioning in the real space of the room, I was positioned as "I," the figured Subject of imperial colonialism. Yet that position was exposed and made vulnerable by being deprived of the privilege of being a protected observer, or a surveilling eye of power. The tropes of imperial power involve the excessive and objectifying visibility of the Other who consolidates the colonizer's subjectivity in its place of empowerment through the screen of the gaze. In the physical enactment and positionings created by the performance, these historical relations of power and visibility were reversed. The figure of imperial power was indeed secreted behind its hood; but its vision was impoverished, signifying the utterly partial and disfiguring nature of a disassociated understanding/ignorance of the culture and people it observed. Yet being placed in the ring, as actor in the drama, the assumed invisibility of the imperial as merely panoptical gaze from above or elsewhere was crudely exposed to everyone else's view. (The performance was also being filmed by a group of Indian students from both the department and other local art schools, so there were plenty of other viewers to witness this.) As bearer of this bared look, "I"/I could not distance myself from the mythological representation of a historically conditioned struggle that was concretized in Sutapa Biswas's experience as an Indian student in a British university art department. The performance's play between the larger histories that tied India and Britain and the local experience she was having at Leeds thwarted the processes by which colonialism seems to happen "elsewhere," over there, and not at home, and by which colonized peoples are displaced backward in time as if they belonged to a past, or a timeless zone, statically captured by religions and cultures that are ethnographically recorded as being stuck in time immemorial, Before History. The physical proximity of real persons in a room that performance rewrote as the space of history, power, and resistance became the signifying device for piercing the temporal ellipsis of colonialist discourse.

Because I was participant yet target, forced to hear and struggle to see meanings that silenced me, and to which I must react, an emotional register was activated to lend its intensities to the structural relations of colonization, which was the topic of the performance. I was made witness to the representational making of another configuration of subjectivities around the now-eroded binaries of colonizer/colonized. The performance exploded the oppositions black/white, Indian/English to demand recognition based on the experiencing of what might otherwise only be known abstractly, theoretically—namely, the radical interdependency of subjectivities and conditional nature of meaning within oppressive, oppressed, or resistant languages. Imperialism functions in its colonial as well as classed and gendered forms as the privilege of neutrality. The imperial subject is made to feel itself the norm, without color, sex, difference. Difference and its injuries are projected out, to be carried and signified by that which is othered in terms of class, race, gender, ability, and so forth. Purely positive endorsement of the Other's Otherness—any form of essentialist and uncritical celebration of ethnicity, class culture, femaleness—may offer momentary solidarity and necessary affirmation. Nonetheless, it confirms the mythic structure of the opposition, leaving it in place while, more often than not, merely and ineffectually reversing the evaluation of its terms. People who are the products of imperialism cannot sustain this binary opposition and its use of distance, for we carry the imbrication of world cultures within us. Whiteness, Europeanness, maleness, and so forth depend for their meanings on that which they Other, even while they use the Othered to exonerate and disguise themselves. In the global movements of peoples and the circulation of goods and cultures characteristic of colonial and international capitalism, there are no more discrete cultures and radically fixed differences. Some see the present situation as a kind of postmodern hybridity that is to be embraced. Others stress the ambivalence that underlies our inevitable complexity as postcolonial subjects. Sutapa Biswas's work operates in these mutually contaminated spaces through which she can explore this historically specific subjectivity that cannot be one and cannot be assumed, fixed, possessed, or simply affirming. The very use of performance as a media, utilizing the complex relations between actual persons in real space as an alphabet for a postcolonial script, enacted the pain, violence, and necessary hope that pulse across the hitherto masked interconnections of "the colonial subject."[8]

SPACES AND PLACES

Since that performance, Sutapa Biswas has traveled literally and metaphorically to other spaces, and her work now retains the imprint of this concern with space and the positioning of the viewer in relation to an experience of the work that is not contained by sight. Standard spectatorship allows the viewer a distance from the object. It renders what is seen an object, objectifying in turn the subject who has produced the work. Sutapa Biswas seeks ways to undermine this metaphorically imperialist spectatorship. Initially, this interest revealed itself in the way she used the spaces of the two-dimensional surfaces of drawings and pastels. Scale is important. To be confronted with very large pictures alters the spectator's own sense of importance in relation to the figured presences of the images. But Sutapa Biswas also uses the blank, unworked spaces of the paper. These read in several ways.

On the one hand, they imply a sophisticated engagement with the problematics of modernism, which specified the particularity of painting as the flatness of the support in opposition to the illusion of three dimensionality achieved by the use of perspective devices. Sutapa Biswas's figures elaborate that flatness while stressing it. Pastel is used to indicate the rounded forms of well-muscled arms, yet its own materiality insistently draws attention to its placing on and creation of the surface. Areas of dense color, which always threaten to advance or recede, are held in check by her use of a pattern shaped both like an eye and a mouth, which, for instance, appears on the garments of Kali and the figures in *As she stood, listened, and watched, her feelings were, this woman is not for burning* (Parts I and II, 1985, 1986) (figs. 2 and 3). Such devices, which so affirmatively define the surface of the paper on which she works, yield yet another semantic dimension. In refusing the eye the fascinations of the female body that are so adamantly not offered in Sutapa Biswas's densely worked pastel surfaces, modernist fidelity to flatness is made unexpectedly to serve feminist concerns. The saturation of the skin of color stands in, as signifier of modernist respect for medium and flat surface, for the body that masculine fantasy nonetheless desires to see. Her dramatic and uncompromising use of the female body by these reappropriated modernist moves, moreover, also bypassed the quarantine into which feminist artists and filmmakers had in the 1970s placed the representation of the female body.

On the other hand, the empty parts of her surfaces also engage with modernist concerns, critically rather than sycophantically. Sutapa Biswas refers to the impact of Robert

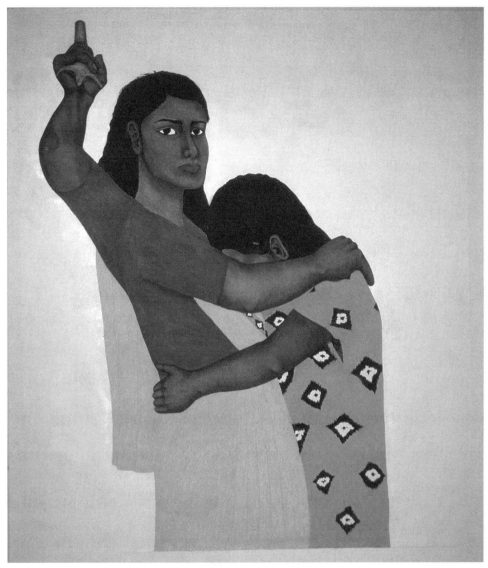

Figure 2. Sutapa Biswas, *As she stood, listened, and watched, her feelings were, this woman is not for burning, Part I* (1986). Pastel and acrylics on paper. 178 x 201 cm. Collection of Bradford Art Galleries and Museums, Cartwright Hall. Courtesy of Sutapa Biswas.

Rauschenberg's series *White Paintings*, encountered perhaps in Fred Orton's lecture course on American culture and society in the 1950s. Entirely blank canvases, ironically the epitome of modernism's purity, nonetheless, were full of incident, caused by their interaction with an environment and the spectators whose own presence is inevitably registered, however remotely, on the never entirely pristine surface. Sutapa Biswas used this insight in her own work quite differently at first. Large areas of unworked surface create not a blank space of nothing, but a counterpoint to what is so energetically worked in the

Figure 3. Sutapa Biswas, *As she stood, listened, and watched, her feelings were, this woman is not for burning, Part II* (1986). Pastel and acrylics on paper. 178 x 201 cm. Collection of Bradford Art Galleries and Museums, Cartwright Hall. Courtesy of Sutapa Biswas.

areas she has drawn. Using modernist notions of flatness and surface, she can make the figured and the as-yet-unmarked, the full, and the seemingly empty work in tension— a creative incongruity that makes the viewer recognize that what seems empty may still signify, and may still be active in contributing to the impact and meaning of the whole. This notion of other space, space off, brought into play, continues to be explored in a variety of practices that ultimately led Sutapa Biswas back toward the spaces of interaction so specific to performance, without abandoning the spaces of representation or, indeed, represented space.

Speaking of her own work, Sutapa Biswas has described the impact of a journey to India in 1987, the first in twenty-one years, a journey that involved going back both to the times and spaces of a remembered childhood and to the times and spaces of a historical India, one of the cultural compass points from which she had been working to negotiate her specific position as an Indian/British artist within contemporary British culture. She visited the cave temples of Ajanta and Ellora, the temples of Orissa and Khajuraha. She recorded the significance of the encounters with these architectural realizations of her interest in the interactions of individuals with physical space. What she found in these sites was a space that leads away from the fetishizing spectatorship typical of Western art to the multilayered semiotic experience characteristic of ritual or ceremonial architecture. With its varied uses of sculpture and painted imageries within a spatial totality, these great ensembles act on the participant through the sculptural figuration of the body that invites a corporeal empathy to create the channel of experience of the space and its mythological inscriptions.

These discoveries did not serve only formal purposes. The relation of Sutapa Biswas herself to these places was not merely antiquarian or scholarly. She came to them not only through space, from England back to India, but through time, from professional art practice in adulthood to childhood, memory, and family. What the discoveries in India offered, and why these places meant so much, were determined within a specific subject's configuration of a widespread contemporary condition of displacement, with its freight of loss, memory, and desire. Indeed, this condition may be one of the major decisive formations of the postmodern subjectivity that those writers and artists who do not merely straddle two cultures but embody the pain and pleasures of a historically shaped multiplicity are now finding forms to signify.

That this is a post- or anti-Orientalist program cannot be doubted. It is significant that Sutapa Biswas's art historical studies at Leeds involved a critique of what Edward Said called "orientalism" in Western painting, particularly of the nineteenth century.[9] *Orientalism* refers to the array of political, scholarly, and aesthetic discourses that turned a Western gaze on the Islamic world and constructed an "Orient," an "East" as the cipher of difference by which a European selfhood and identity were constructed as both superior and dominant. Orientalism is the form of domination constructed by a variety of strategies and devices. Orientalism is a projection of both fear of the Other and fascination with difference whose interactions create its characteristic myths of oriental backwardness, laziness, sensuality, cruelty, luxury, and indifference. Orientalism, furthermore, creates a temporal ellipsis, which projects that which is named as the Orient as belonging to a permanent past so that the European colonial invasion is represented merely as the inevitable rescue of dying cultures that will be brought into the present by becoming subjected to Europe, thus made synonymous with modernity. Domination thus reads as historically determined progress.

Orientalism is, in the words of Gayatri Chakravorty Spivak, a process of "worlding." The actual interventions of the European colonizers as soldiers, traders, scholars, artists, and governors involved a process of moving from ignorance about the societies and cultures that were illegible to them, treating India as a kind of uninscribed earth, toward the imposition of their own maps of "knowledge," the projection of their own schemes of meaning through which the colonized were then invited to recognize themselves. This metaphor of cartography, which marks the blank inert earth with the colonizers' meaning, thus making it a world that can be navigated and used, yielding meanings for its subjects, Spivak calls the "epistemic violence of the imperialist project."[10] It once again involves notions of space, for imperialist worlding is a political semiotics of space. Such cartography has to be engaged with and rewritten, and the field of experience must be reworlded by the artist who wishes to explore the ambivalence and multivalence of that history. Yet the return must also avoid the mythologizing of East, Orient, and Otherness, which by virtue of evacuating history remains in the imaginary spaces of Orientalism and imperialism.

Sutapa Biswas has written of her project as attempting to *demythologize* Otherness. This term, *demythologize,* takes us back to the critical work of Roland Barthes, whose study "Myth Today" was written at the height of France's Orientalist crisis, the Algerian struggles for liberation from France's colonial domination in the later 1950s. For his example of myth as the prevailing semiotic form of bourgeois representation, Barthes analyzed a provocative image from the magazine *Paris Match.* The cover showed an African soldier in French military uniform saluting the French tricolor. Barthes names myth a depoliticized form of speech. Myth works by appropriating one level of meaning or fully constituted signs, such as results from our decoding the color photograph as the picture of an African man in a French uniform saluting a French flag, then emptying these of their historical specificity—the agonizing struggle of the Algerian people for liberation—so that they can be filled up with a more dispersed, yet globalizing meaning, the natural acceptance of French imperiality. Barthes uses a number of terms to describe this complex process of ideological colonization of signs. Myth appropriates the first level of meaning, denotation, making it then the accomplice of the mythic sense. Myth deforms, distances, distorts. But it never completely obliterates:

> What French imperiality obscures is also a primary language, a factual discourse which was telling me about the salute of the African in uniform. But this distortion is not an obliteration: the . . . African remains here, the concept needs them; they are half amputated, they are deprived of memory, not of existence; they are at once stubborn, silently rooted there, and garrulous, a speech wholly at the service of the concept. The concept, literally, deforms, but does not abolish the meaning; a word can perfectly render this contradiction: it alienates it.[11]

Alienate has several meanings. It is about rendering something alien, making it other and foreign. It also means separating what belongs to someone from them, in the sense of alienating affections, or property, or in Marxist terms, the rights to the product of a person's own labor. In psychological parlance, it refers to the subjective experience of not feeling at one with oneself, or feeling cut off from those with whom we should or would like to feel close. *Alienate* is a promiscuous and labile word. Nonetheless, it captures the condition of the imperialized subject: made Other, thus cut off from her/his own center and made to feel separate from what should be close, affirmative, comfortable. It also contains the sense of being deprived of the products of one's own culture and labor, which is represented back as no longer available for use in the present. To demythologize is thus to undermine and resist that alienation, that being made to feel alien in one's own land, time, family, and person.[12] The myth produced by imperialism/Orientalism is that there are other lands, somewhere else and in another time. It obscures the fact that these are geopolitical spaces of interaction. To contest that myth is to refuse being constructed as "belonging elsewhere." In the 1980s there was a critical project to articulate this demythologized, de-alienated space, and it was undertaken by Indian artists born in India but growing up in Britain, and by those intellectuals who actively see themselves living across the geopolitical realities of a postcolonial world, through the accidents of birth and professional work or through growing up in the West as part of an Asian culture, refusing in their persons to confirm the mythic absoluteness of the division. The articulation of demythology can be achieved precisely in the spaces of representation, in "fabled territories," as the title of a touring exhibition of Asian photography in Britain, named it.[13]

Photography is a specifically cogent form of representation within which to work through this problematic. Sutapa Biswas has used it in her *Infestations of the Aorta—Shrine to a Distant Relative* (1989) and other works (fig. 4). Photographic space simultaneously contains fact and fantasy. It can make things seem concrete because we are led to believe in the existence of what we are shown photographically. Yet photography has always been a fantastic medium, a medium of fantasy, for it stills time, freezing the moment into a perpetual past that can uncannily still be held and looked at in the present. It can record, yet it also is the means of representing entirely fabricated scenarios that access memory and nourish desire. Barthes defines myth as depriving the image of memory while appropriating its existence. Sutapa Biswas's work demythologizes in precisely activating memory at the site of the now-ambivalent image. In a literal, autobiographical sense, she makes use of the memories that she reactivated on her trip India to revisit the places associated with her childhood (see *Blue Skies and Sunday Lunch*, 1989). But her installations also aim to create the space of memory, which is also historical and cultural. The personal can become a mythic signifier because it can be used to absent the historical context in which we are produced as subjects. The Othered, colonized subject is alienated from history and memory, made into a static fetish of its exoticism. To insist on subjectivity, through play of memory and desire, is to return time, history, and society as the context of our experience, our mediated relation to the structural determinations that made us subjects of time, place, and desire.

How can that be managed in an art practice? Sutapa Biswas orchestrates the space of her exhibitions so that she is the author of an entire installation. This was most marked in the piece/event/installation *Sacred Space* (1990). She used a room in the Slade School of Art, London University, a building that neighbors the Orientalist foundation, the London University School of Oriental and African Studies, established in 1909. Her presence in

Figure 4. Sutapa Biswas, *Infestations of the Aorta—Shrine to a Distant Relative* (1989), detail. Courtesy of Sutapa Biswas.

this room, hinged to its surroundings, forced into view the architecture of Orientalism. Edward Said quotes arch-orientalist politician Lord Cromer, advocating in the British Parliament the foundation of this school: "The Creation of a school [of Oriental studies later to become the London University School of Oriental and African Studies] like this in London is *part of the furniture of Empire.*"[14]

Sutapa Biswas carefully restored the room so that its pristine whiteness marked the division between its created and aesthetically charged space and that of the decaying building itself. Using lights installed outside the windows, the room became one vast white painting constantly reworked by the play of natural and artificial light in ways that Sutapa Biswas affirms were suggested by the paintings of rooms by American painter Edward Hopper. Mounted on the walls behind nonreflective glass were three large framed images, pastel, line drawing, and acrylic. Again these images were placed on large white surfaces whose edges were hard to discern against the surrounding whiteness of the walls. The subtle erosion of the boundaries between picture and space almost suggested that the images were directly drawn on the walls, and the viewer was incited then to move in for closer inspection. At that distance, the hanging of the piece and its size emphasized an architectural space, in which the viewer cannot imagine him/herself merely the mastering eye but is forced to know him/herself as a body in space.

On another wall were mounted, at a top eye level of six feet, a series of black-and-white photographic images. Printed on litho film and mounted as transparencies pressed between glass, they were further textured by the wall behind. Yet they were framed, holding the flow of space so that the viewer, coming close to read the images, constantly being eroded by light reflecting on them from outside, and the texts, had to work to see and read. Participant, engaged, worked on, the viewer becomes visitor to the installation, which put Sutapa Biswas's world, that which she as artist has "worlded" and thus inscribed with her meanings, into a special kind of encounter with that visitor. Like my own experience as decentered witness/participant object in her earlier performance, *Sacred Space* offered an invitation, drawing the viewer closer and making her work to read the signs within the mapped space of the installation. Paradoxically, it also challenged the viewer because the work so insistently embodied the subjectivity of the artist who made this space "sacred":

> Of memory, we change
> From one conversation to the next
> Always in search of
> The edge of the surface
> And of textures
> There is pleasure
> and sometimes none
> So thinking back to our space
> Marked only by fallen clay
> There is both absence and presence
>
> Of violated territories—
> You, whose spirit is dull

Brought me here
To the great mountain
Whereupon, I died in the thinness of its air
From violated territories
Its boundaries,
With fierce eyes
I watch
This sacred space.

—Sutapa Biswas (1990)

The images in the sequence of photographs are those of a bare foot stepping in foot-steps imprinted in the sand. For some this will conjure up both Sigmund Freud's reflections on Jensen's *Gradiva* and Victor Burgin's photowork of the same title, reflecting on Freud's essay, using the fetish of the beautiful and lost girl's unsandaled foot glimpsed at Pompeii.[15] Such formal parallels serve to give this work its sense of belonging, here and now, to a world that includes Freud and a critical semiotic art practice itself invoking psychoanalysis precisely to insist on questions of subjectivity in the production and consumption of art. Not nostalgia for some lost homeland but the complexities of desire are the animating terms of Sutapa Biswas's use of memory, image, and space. Psychoanalysis argues that in our formation as human subjects we become human only as we are marked by loss and lack. This condition results in the specific configuration of our subjectivity as split between conscious and unconscious. Each side of the division has its own characteristic modes of producing and connecting meaning. Between both, however, there is a regular, if displaced, traffic, by means of which the psychic journey we undertook to become a subject is perpetually recorded and reworked. Subjectivity is, therefore, not to be understood only as a developmental, organic achievement of simply living over time and growing up. Within the psychoanalytical model, the human subject is viewed as an archaeological site created out of a layering of experience through time and shifting and reframing of meanings because of both the accumulation and the division into conscious and unconscious that fracture our self-understanding and repress much of what nonetheless determines our ways of being. Every stage in this journey into subjectivity is sedimented within us. Its forms of survival or persistence, however, are affected by its configuration with all other stages and their related traumas, fantasies, and knowledges. The multilayered spaces of the subject can be evoked and addressed in the multiplaned spaces of an artistic installation, where image, surface, space, figure, body, and sign are put into orchestrated tension and play, overlapping, reconfiguring, and allowing meanings to be donated to sense in the gaps between.

The body in space—viewer in gallery and figured image on drawn page or canvas—functions as a literal sign for real subjects in a concrete history that is the territory on which we must engage in dialogue about the epistemic violence of imperialism and the violated territories that are its subjects. The acknowledgment of such a freight is neither comfortable nor painless for any of those caught in its historic webs. But there is no other space, utopic or nostalgic, that will heal the rifts, in our persons, as human subjects, in our social beings, as products of real histories. There is no essential mother India to salve the wounds of displacement and separation, but, in Sutapa Biswas's work, we experience a confrontation with loss and grief for an actual grandmother who was the beloved figure of territorially and culturally distanced childhood. There is no universal space called art or being human that can relieve the pain of learning about whiteness and Western power by attending to the articulation of the specificity of someone's experience, which is not Other but particular, distinct from, yet shaped by whiteness and its West, while also sustained by other memories, themselves historically contaminated but also resistant.

HISTORICAL SUBJECTS: SUBJECTS IN HISTORY

In Sutapa Biswas's complex aesthetic fashioning of the spaces of contiguity for India and Britain, these two poles of postcolonial formation are made contemporaries—thus signally a de-Orientalizing and demythicizing strategy—and while the particular interaction of the two is particular to Sutapa Biswas precisely because she makes their imbrication the condition of her practice, its historical hybridity and cultural opportunity become part of the viewer's world, too. The body in space functions thus as an allegory for the problems and disjunctions of communication: connection and disconnection, hearing and distortion, projection and confrontation. Made present by participating in Sutapa Biswas's work is the subject of history.

But even as I write this I realize that it once again inscribes a Western worlding. There is no subject, but we must always speak of subjects; there is no history, but always histories. I have stressed the issues of imperialism in subjectivities and histories so far because it is the condition of Sutapa Biswas's work. In our conversations at Leeds, it was its legacy of racism that rendered my feminism both local and imperial. Feminism is not displaced by the politics of race. For just as there has always been black women's creativity, there has also always been black feminism. Yet to qualify women's creativity and feminism with a signifier of color is to become enmeshed in the ideological constructions of racism. Sutapa Biswas's feminism challenged the ideological limits of what Valerie Amos and Pratibha Parmar call "imperial feminism."[16] Amos and Parmar quote bell hooks's argument about the racism inside the women's movement evidenced by the way that feminist scholarship is written as if black women were not a part of the collectivity, women.[17] Thus a feminism that perpetuates its own ethnocentricity actively sustains racism. Amos and Parmar critically examine some of the key theoretical concepts of white feminist literature. They examine their pertinence for black feminist theory. Difference, family, sexuality all are qualified by being considered in relation to the specificity of the experiences of Asian women and women of African descent. There is an important link here with *Housewives with Steak-Knives*. It is also a powerful text about femininity, setting in conflict and tension Western ideologies of Western and Asian femininity (stereotypes of passivity) with the interruption of both by the fact of Sutapa Biswas's active creativity and her use of an image of female power, Kali. Writing of Sutapa Biswas's work in the context of the politics of modernism and postmodernism, Gilane Tawadros calls this painting the "clearest enunciation of black women's creativity as a form of creative resistance":

Here, Hindu mythology is invoked to serve a political content which is quintessentially modern. The image of the goddess, Kali . . . has been appropriated by Biswas as a means of dissolving the absolute distinction and binary oppositions which characterised European thought. In opposition to these false and essentialist categories, the precepts of Hindu culture reflect the ascendance of ambivalence. Thus, the Western notion of "femininity" as essentially fragile and passive is contested by the ambivalent status of Kali who is at once goddess of both peace and war. In adapting the Hindu iconography of Kali, Biswas asserts the ambivalence of femininity, both pacifist (as opposed to passive) and aggressive, both "feminine" in a traditional sense and strong. She also affirms the existence, in terms of the Hindu system of knowledge, of a "zone of indiscernability," to borrow Gilles Deleuze's phrase, between myth and reality. Thus, Biswas implies, there is an element of the real in the mythologisation of "femininity," and equally an element of myth in the reality of black womanhood.[18]

Tawadros also suggests that by using icons and myths (from Indian and Western art and culture) Sutapa Biswas suggests a fusion between past and present, a way in which history is activated for the present, while also acknowledging other temporalities embodied in myth and religious thought. Finally, Tawadros points out the corruption of the key Western distinction between public and private, which is a gendering of social as well as psychic space, associating the feminine with the domestic and the private in opposition to the supposedly masculine domains of politics, power, and action. In this work, and later drawings from the same period, the housewife and her domestic tools, knife here, potato peeler in *The Only Good Indian* (1985), become tools of aggressive defiance because domestic spaces are perceived as equally penetrated by the politics of gender power and race power, both equally the site of resistance. Indeed, the family space is a critical space for Asian women in the struggle with white and black patriarchs, with the imperial state and its racist immigration and employment policies. The complexity of the mutually inflected struggles requires the production of artworks that are not ambivalent in a typically postmodern avoidance of accountability, politics, or ethics. They are cogently ambivalent in order to invent through the cultural inscriptions of a British Asian woman artist multiple registers of meaning that are activated in the spatial encounter between subjects, with bodies and histories.

Not so much beyond the boundary, this project works as a perpetual crossing, eroding, and unfixing of the frontiers where we must engage in dialogue, self-recognition, acknowledgment of difference within the realization of complexity and ambivalence. Through the use of many media, formats, and installations in space, Sutapa Biswas orchestrates a highly *affective* aesthetic staging for a nonhierarchical worlding—where desire, fascination, pleasure, and pain are inscribed and evoked. Footprints in the sand are fragile and transitory, yet their pressure leaves the trace of an Other's journey or pathway that we—any spectator—are invited to follow. Sutapa Biswas's materials increasingly invoke the notion of the trace, the fragile imprint in the historical and cultural archive of people's bodies, memories, and experiences. If we can all invest these traces with the full though not undivided subjectivity that they signify, we can begin to resist the alienation created by mythology (in Barthes's sense, the making foreign, the depriving of what is of or belongs to oneself), and in particular the West's destructive use of foreignness and its fear of ambivalence.[19] The binary oppositions of Western culture—white/black, self/Other, here/there, man/woman, to name but a few—are very local yet destructively hegemonic. Positioning her work as a historical practice, dialectical, full of interaction and mutual determination, while fashioning its poetics at the level of the intimate, tactile, personally charged, Sutapa Biswas produces a powerful, empowering, and critically feminist text that enlarges the world by overlaying and thus mutually redefining these oppositions, of which yet one more is that of center/periphery. Tawadros again:

> The constellation of voices and the plurality of meanings which are postulated by post modernity serve to obscure its continuities with cultural modernism, and suggests, perhaps, that this may not be a fissure or a "new dawn" in European consciousness but merely a transformation of the grand narratives of the West. In this context the "populist modernism" of black cultural practice, I would argue, signals a critical reappropriation of modernity which stems from an assertion of history and historical processes. Black women's creativity in particular expresses the ambivalence of identity and and redundancy of exclusive and unambiguous absolutes. It dissolves fixed boundaries between past and present, public and private, personal and political. (150)

The cultural practice of Sutapa Biswas, she argues, is the space of the diaspora, which is not predicated, according to Tawadros, on the primacy of difference and dispersion; rather, "the cultural expression of the margins and the periphery represents an aesthetic and political project which is predicated on resistance and change" (150).

POSTSCRIPT 1998

This essay was originally written on commission and in advance of the exhibition of Sutapa Biswas's *Synapse,* which first took place in Vancouver in 1992 (figs. 5 and 6). It was penned in ignorance of what that work would be. Yet some of the conclusions drawn from the analysis of her whole project to date sympathetically anticipated the new realization of these continuing concerns in the installation *Synapse.* The artist has written:

> Synapse is a metaphor for many things, but most recurringly, echoes that point of exchange between two or more components. That between the viewer, and the work of art, the artist and the critic. A relationship in which through the work, each individual is able to situate themself. The focus has been a concern for boundaries—a psycho-geographic journey between people, places, language, culture. As an artist, it is the journey to which I am constantly drawn.[20]

In medical terms, *synapse* refers to connections that permit transmission of coded information from one nerve cell to another. Degrees of expansion of shrinkage condition the number and quality of impulses transmitted through this branching network of possible connections. It thus becomes for her "symbolic of an undefined territory or space. Memory itself is of a shifting nature, vivid in places, with blind spots."[21] What conditions the degree of transmission, at this extended level, may be called Desire, which itself is the force that springs across the gaps and ties us into both a world of objects and an imaginary field of fantasy.

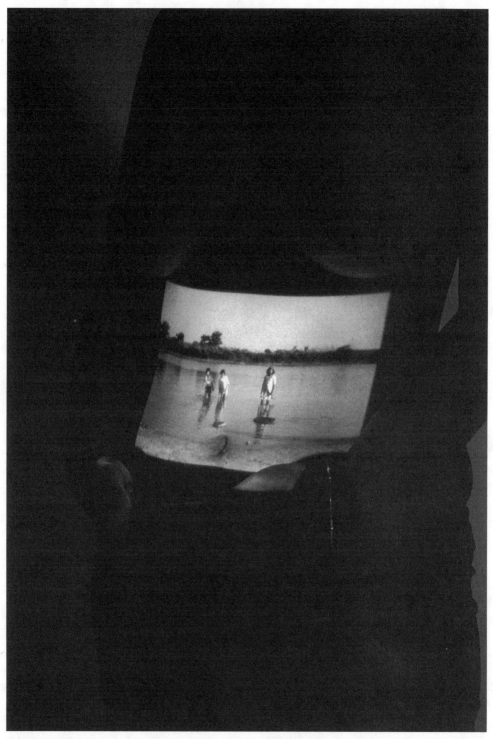

Figure 5. Sutapa Biswas, *Synapse I* (1992). Black-and-white photograph. 112.2 x 132.5 cm. Ms. detail. Collection of Oldham Art Gallery. Courtesy of Sutapa Biswas.

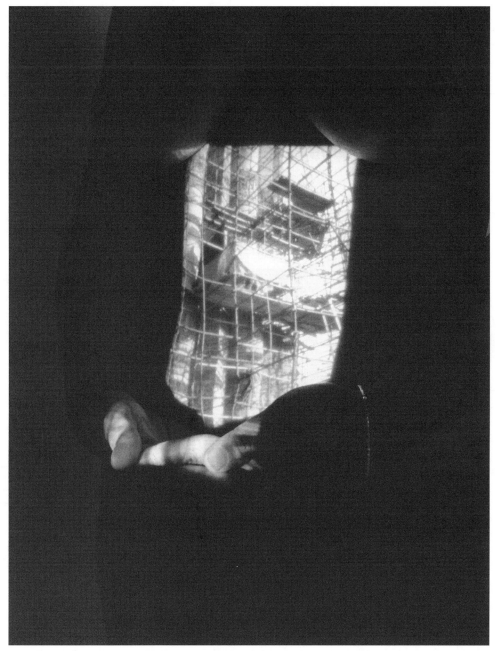

Figure 6. Sutapa Biswas, *Synapse I* (1992). Black-and-white photograph. 112.2 x 132.5 cm. Ms. detail. Collection of Oldham Art Gallery. Courtesy of Sutapa Biswas.

The project *Synapse* was largely photographic, although it included light-box pieces and a particular installation of boxes with memorabilia and other uncanny objects. Dominating the exhibition were nine very large photographs (52″ x 44″), which had been made by projecting slides, taken on the artist's 1987 trip to India, onto her own unclothed body. In this project, the process of making the work returned the artist to the arena of performance where the body of the artist works within the art, which is thus indexed to a lived, existential social body that is also the productive body at work. Unwitnessed but recorded, these images signify the artist's curious, wondering, desiring, intellectually motivated, and aesthetically responsive gaze on, for instance, the Khajuraha temples. At the same time, the artist is literally trapped in the beam of light from the projector and captured by the photographic gaze, which is not where she is. Reminiscent of Jacques Lacan's later theory of the subject as "photo-graphed," that is to say, found by the gaze, instituted by desire at the point of being in the field of the desire of the Other, *Synapse* opens poetically on this complex field of subjectivity as a dream landscape in which "I" am seen, "I" am a picture.[22] Thus the body in social space that made the work by performing it undoes itself to allow the body to signify as the support for a field of fantasy signified by projected images, themselves the captured memories of the artist negotiating her own relations as an artist to cultural legacies from both Hindu and Islamic components of the subcontinent's ancient and modern histories. In one sequence of these photographs, the velvety darkness is pierced by an image—a photograph of a piece of sculpture, a building wrapped in scaffolding, a holiday snapshot of children at the seaside—that seems to float unanchored. When we look more closely, the curve of a woman's breast or the interlaced fingers of two hands resting on a female abdomen, almost cradling the image, make us realize the intimacy of memory trace and body.

Just as the artist devised a means to create a forceful representation of an embodied femininity in *Housewives with Steak-Knives,* here she has also risked the issue in order to keep the tension between poststructuralist insistence on the psychic and discursive levels of our constitution as subjects and the materialist attention to socially constituted persons in concrete histories. The use of a medical term as metaphor for memory and desire itself encodes this rebellious refusal to be policed into a "correct" position on what must remain an undecidable and impossible distinction. Even at the heart of psychoanalysis, in the early work of Freud and now again in the important work of Julia Kristeva and the later work of Lacan, the question of the body, or, rather, of the corporeal as both image and uncharted site of drives, asserts itself as an always necessary dimension of thinking about subjectivity and desire. Sutapa Biswas's *Synapse* aesthetically connects more intimately than her previous work with this debate and offers a form within which the viewer can encounter not the argued terms and theories of that debate, but the substantive and affective material it tries to hook into analysis. The artwork, the product of a performance within the artist's studio, becomes a performance experienced by the viewer because of the precarious intimacy these photographs evoke for us between the inside and the outside, the body and the imaginary, the past and the present. One of the key crossovers is the recurrence of the image of a goddess figure set between two columns. In one photograph, she is carried on the body of the artist, crossed fingers echoing the formal patterning of the seated goddess's crossed legs. In another, the slide of the same sculpture is projected large, on a curving surface and the body of the artist appears to lie on the sculpture, swathed in dark shadow, with only the soles of her feet and the tips of her fingers illuminated. All the time the lighting and the composition oblige the viewer to examine her own curiosity, perception, attention. Nothing is obvious and explicit, while the scale and quality of the photographic prints provide the iconic frame for a series of reflections on the permeability of borderlines, the transmission of meaning, and their site: the subject in history, an embodied subject, and an inscribed history. The interchange between the artist's body and the historical monument stage another kind of "sacred space," offer another kind of postcolonial mapping, question the representations of femininity, trouble the boundaries between present and past. These are the questions that Sutapa Biswas has been pursuing across several continents, in varied media, and always with revealing effects.

NOTES

1. This has changed with the reorganization of higher education in Britain, which is no longer divided between "old" universities and "new" polytechnics. These latter institutions had absorbed the independent art schools and provided the majority of sites for the undergraduate programs leading to a B.A. in fine art. Until the early 1990s, when this binary system was abolished and all polytechnics became universities, there were only seven traditional universities that offered degrees in fine art, varying according to the origins of these departments in their balance between studio practice and academic study. At the University of Leeds, B.A. students in the fine art course were required to have high academic grades for entry and devoted half their time to art history/theory and half their time to studio practice in a program that aimed to integrate them into a self-critical artistic practice.

2. Sutapa Biswas and Moira Roth, "Sutapa Biswas: A Narrative Chronology," in *Synapse* (London: Photographers' Gallery, 1991), 23.

3. The phallic mother refers to an infantile, masculine fantasy that retrospectively endows the mother with the attribute of omnipotence; in fact, she is endowed with what the child attributes to himself.

4. Rozsika Parker and Griselda Pollock, *Old Mistresses: Women, Art and Ideology* (London: Pandora Books, 1981); rev. ed., 1995.

5. Eleanor Tufts, *Our Hidden Heritage: Five Centuries of Women Artists* (New York: Paddington Press, 1974).

6. Gayatri Chakravorty Spivak, "Imperialism and Sexual Difference," *Oxford Literary Review* 8 (1986): 225–40. See also the critique of this tendency in sociological writing by Chandra Mohanty, "Under Western Eyes: Feminist Scholarship and Colonial Discourses," *Feminist Review* 30 (1988): 61–88.

7. The phrase derives from the work of the American feminist historian Joan Kelly, "The Doubled Vision of Feminist Theory," originally published in 1979 and reprinted in Joan Kelly, *Women, History and Theory* (Chicago: University of Chicago, 1984). Kelly identifies *double vision* as that which embraces both the private and public spheres of Western bourgeois society. I am using it here for Sutapa Biswas's project, which creates two centers in conflict and dialogue, each having to acknowledge that the other is always already a part of the other, because they are both lived by the subjects—women subjects, colonial subjects (this phrase implies both colonizer and colonized and, in doing so, acknowledges the colonized as also a subject of the process, and not merely the passive object of Europe's Othering).

8. This analysis leans on the work of Homi Bhabha, "The Other Question: The Stereotype and Colonial Discourse," *Screen* 24, no. 6 (1983): 18–36. Bhabha's critique of Edward Said's *Orientalism* (London: Routledge & Kegan Paul, 1978) involves redefining the "colonial subject" as the ambivalent figure

where colonizing and colonized are structurally inseparable. Said's analysis revealed how the European self was produced by its Othering of the oriental, subjected in a Foucauldian manner, to the discourse of its own Othering. Bhabha uses a psychoanalytical model of the economy of the subject shaped in desire in conjunction with Foucauldian governmentality to paint a more complex picture of the psychic investments and effects of the colonial encounter in which both colonizer and colonized are constituted relatively. Thus the colonial subject signifies the ambivalent space of that complex constitution of subjectivity in the colonial/postcolonial field.

9. Edward Said, *Orientalism.*

10. Gayatri Chakravorty Spivak, "The Rani of Sirmur: An Essay in Reading the Archives," *History and Theory* 8 (1985): 251. Spivak derives her concept of worlding from the philosopher Martin Heidegger, who used it to define the origins of the work of art as resulting from the gap between earth and world, a gap filled by the texture and substance of the artwork.

11. Roland Barthes, "Myth Today," in *Mythologies,* trans. Annette Lavers (London: Paladin, 1973), 122–23, originally published in 1957.

12. This idea is powerfully explored in Frantz Fanon, *Black Skin, White Masks* (London: Pluto Press, 1986), originally published in 1952.

13. Sunil Gupta, *Fabled Territories: New Asian Photography in Britain* (Leeds: City Art Gallery, 1989).

14. Said, *Orientalism,* 213.

15. S. Freud, "Delusions and Dreams in Jensen's *Gradiva*" (1907), in S. Freud, *On Art and Literature* Pelican Freud Library, vol. 14 (Harmondsworth: Penguin Books, 1985).

16. Valerie Amos and Pratibha Parma, "Challenging Imperial Feminism," *Feminist Review* 17 (1984): 3–20.

17. bell hooks, *Ain't I a Woman? Black Women and Feminism* (London: Pluto Press, 1982).

18. Gilane Tawadros, "Beyond the Boundary: The Work of Three Black Women Artists in Britain," *Third Text* 8/9 (1989): 145.

19. Both themes have been treated by two important Western thinkers, Zygmunt Bauman, *Modernity and Ambivalence* (Cambridge: Polity Press, 1991), and Julia Kristeva, *Strangers to Ourselves,* trans. Leon Roudiez (Brighton: Harvester Wheatsheaf Press, 1991).

20. Sutapa Biswas, *Synapse* (Leeds: City Art Gallery, 1992), 27.

21. Ibid., 13. Cited by Moira Roth, "Reading between the Lines: The Imprinted Spaces of Sutapa Biswas," in *Synapse.*

22. J. Lacan, "The Gaze as *objet a,*" *Four Fundamental Concepts of Psychoanalysis* (1973) (London: Penguin Books, 1979).

YOU MAKE ME FEEL (MIGHTY REAL)

Sandra Bernhard's Whiteface

Ann Pellegrini

A particularly favourable occasion for tendentious jokes is presented when the intended rebellious criticism is directed against the subject himself or, to put it more cautiously, against someone in whom the subject has a share—a collective person, that is (the subject's own nation, for instance). The occurrence of self-criticism as a determinant may explain how it is that a number of the most apt jokes have grown up on the soil of Jewish popular life. . . . Incidentally, I do not know whether there are many other instances of a people making fun to such a degree of its own character.
  —Sigmund Freud, *Jokes and Their Relation to the Unconscious*

Without You *I'm Nothing,* the cinematic conversion of Sandra Bernhard's "smash hit one-woman show" (as she so frequently reminds us), represents a fascinating and offbeat interpretation of the Jewish female body as "performative accomplishment."[1] The film restages Bernhardt's successful 1989 off-Broadway show of the same name in predominantly black supper clubs in Los Angeles. Despite the fact that in the stage show within the film Bernhard repeats much of the "original" material, the film is not a literal record of the stage show. However, the film does employ some of the conventions of concert film and documentary, intercutting Bernhard's onstage performances with interviews with real people—except all the "real people" are performed by actors.

The operative conceit of the film is that Bernhard has gotten too big for her own good. The smashing success of her New York play has spoiled her; she is "way out of hand." Bernhard needs to return to her roots, to her *black* roots, as it turns out, in order to rediscover and recenter herself. So she goes "home," back to where it all began, back to Los Angeles and the Parisian Room. In moving from East Coast to West Coast, the play has also shifted audiences: from white to black and, perhaps, from Jew to Gentile. The reactions of the black audience to Bernhard's onstage antics vary from bewilderment, to boredom, to hostility.

Without You *I'm Nothing* functions as a parodic send-up of the conditions of spectatorship and spectatorial (dis)identification by signaling them so brazenly. By explicitly representing what Laura Mulvey has termed the "unpleasure" of the audience within the film (1989, 21) as it watches Bernhard's performances, the film, by accident or intent, interrogates the terms of spectatorial pleasure and identification. The film may also interrogate and challenge the terms through which Mulvey advanced her interpretation of the male gaze, visual pleasure, and narrative cinema. Mulvey locates the unpleasure of the male spectator in the threat of castration woman-as-lack represents (21). But the "unpleasure" of Bernhard's audience should not be understood as operating through the framework of sexual difference alone. To the extent that Bernhard may be seen to pose a threat to her audience's pleasure, that threat must be conceptualized as the anxious site/sighting of sexual *and* racial difference. Moreover, *Without* You *I'm Nothing* is not finally readable through a male gaze.

Without You *I'm Nothing* simultaneously teases and frustrates identifications.[2] The film forecloses an identification between its represented and "real" audience. Paradoxically, this foreclosure—what I am calling identifications found, then lost—reflexively calls attention to the misrecognitions that condition pleasure and subjectivity. It is the cinematic spectators—the audience "outside" the film—catching the audience within the film in the act of watching Bernhard who have the opportunity for recognition, self-recognition, as it turns out. True to its name, then, *Without* You *I'm Nothing* plays on the dialectic of within and without, self and other, present and absent. In its movement within and without, the film seems to evacuate any possibility of deciding, once and for all, on which side "realness" lies: hetero/homo, white/black, male/female, Christian/Jew, culture/camp.

Who is the *You* without whom Bernhard would be nothing? The film stages a number of (are they inclusive?) possibilities. First, and most visibly, *You* is a collective person; it refers to the predominantly black audience, whom the film depicts disinterestedly watching Bernhard perform at the Parisian Room. At the film's close, Bernhard, draped in an American flag, apologizes to her audience for lying to them. The critics were right, she admits: she is "a petty, bilious girl." She wishes she could refund the price of admission to each and every one of them because "without me—without *you,* I'm nothing." If Bernhard's near miss is "just" a joke, the joke is on Bernhard as it reveals her narcissistic self-involvement. "Without *me,* you're nothing," she nearly says. Yet the indifference verging on boredom of the depicted black audience has made clear that Bernhard means nothing to them. As Bernhard bumps and grinds her way through Prince's "Little Red Corvette," stripping away the Stars and Stripes to reveal patriotic pasties and g-string, the audience gets up and—one by one—takes leave of Bernhard. Only one woman, a black woman whose spectral presence haunts and even frames the length of the film, remains. (I will return, by way of concluding this essay, to this black woman's "framing" function.) This lone black woman, then, is also an overdetermined site and citational point of reference for Bernhard's directed address, *You.*

Bernhard wraps her verbal slip from *me* to *you* in the star-spangled spectacle and fantasy of a more perfect union—whether (only) with the black woman, within the national body politic, or between Bernhard and her collective audience is an open question.[3] In so doing, she gestures toward the wished-for containment and commodification of diffuse American cultural capitals—of which blackness is the film's most *visibly* represented term. These are processes of appropriation *Without* You *I'm Nothing* will both deliriously represent and ambivalently subvert.

In their contribution to the anthology *Fear of a Queer Planet,* Lauren Berlant and Elizabeth Freeman have interpreted Bernhard's American striptease thus: "Bernhard flags her body to mark a fantasy of erotic identification with someone present, in the intimate room: it is a national fantasy, displayed as a spectacle of desire, and a fantasy, apparently external to the official national frame, of communion with a black-woman-as-audience whose appearance personifies 'authenticity'" (1993, 194). Although I agree with much of their analysis, I want to unsettle the presumption of Bernhard's "whiteness"—an identification that seems, after a fashion, to ground their critique.

Bernhard's hyperbolic attempts to be black, as she impersonates Nina Simone, Diana Ross, Cardilla DeMarlo (in a wickedly lesbotic reinterpretation of "Me and Mrs. Jones"), Prince, and Sylvester, constitute an ambivalent acknowledgment of the conditions under which so-called minority cultures become visible to "mainstream"—which is to say, "white" and "straight"—America. A leading condition for the subaltern's visibility is re-authorization, via a commodifying exchange, by hegemonic culture. Expropriating the cultural products and even the "identities" of subaltern communities, majority culture transforms the historical particularities of racial, ethnic, or sexual identity/ies into the universal ground of "America" (hooks 1992, 31).

The issue here is not to adjudicate "origins" and "ownership," but to ask on whose terms and to what effects subcultural capital gets exchanged and differentially evaluated.[4] The multiple fortunes of hybridization are, of course, implicated in a postmodern (read: "late-capitalist") public-sphere-turned-shopping-mall. Nor is blackness the only term charged to and in consumer economy. For, if recent mass market (and even high theory) trends are to be taken seriously, queerness too has a certain exchange value. Madonna herself may be only the most celebrated instance of the "straight queer," the heterosexual who self-consciously takes on the signifiers of high-fashion queerness. The aestheticization of queerness, its reduction to a look and a manner of dress one can take on or put off at will, picks up the popular cant of homosexuality as a "lifestyle" choice and thereby contains the threatening difference of queerness. In this respect, then, the "straight" answer to Bernhard-as-Sylvester's question—*Do you wanna funk with me?*—is yes.[5]

On one level, then, Bernhard repeats a history of white appropriation of "blackness." Not only does she perform songs popularized by and even identified with black divas, but a woman playing Bernhard's manager claims that "Ross, Nina Simone, Whoopi Goldberg—they've all stolen from her."[6] Moreover, Bernhard seeks to produce her body as black. The first song she performs in *Without* You *I'm Nothing* is Nina Simone's "Four Women." Costumed in Africa, in a dashiki, Bernhard sings: "My skin is black, my arms are long, my hair is woolly, my back is strong. . . . What do they call me? They call me Aunt Sarah. . . . My skin is tan, my hair is fine (whichever way I fix it), my hips invite you, Daddy, my mouth, like wine. . . . What do they call me? They call me sweet thing."

As the second woman, "sweet thing," Bernhard invites both comparison and contradiction between her "black" body and the "authentically" black bodies of her band. In a visual citation of earlier close-ups of her male band members' lips, the camera closes in on Bernhard's mouth at the very moment she sings "my mouth, like wine." Has she displaced the sexual difference of her "feminine" lips upward and into an apparent "racial" similarity? Bernhard herself notes the racialized terms of her synecdochic identification with her (upper) lips: "They used to call me nigger-lips in high school" (in "Funny Face" 1992, 44).[7]

Bernhard is all mouth as she ventriloquizes blackness. Yet her ventriloquism should not, I suggest, be understood as an attempt to speak *for* blacks. Rather, she represents herself as trying—and flamboyantly failing—to speak *to* blacks *from* the place of blackness. Bernhard's inability to translate and communicate herself denaturalizes Black-Jewish solidarity, an alliance that has never been inevitable or finally achieved.

How might the contested history and meanings of Black-Jewish solidarity be thought through blackface? Michael Rogin has argued that one Jewish response to nativist sentiments in early-twentieth-century America was to see Jewishness in relation to other "monstrously alien" minority identities (1992, 438). Likening their own experience of anti-Jewish violence to lynchings and other forms of antiblack violence, Jews not only made common cause with African Americans in the struggle for civil rights but came in some instances to identify *as* black. Interethnic solidarity was most dramatically represented in the Jewish attraction to blackface entertainment. Jewish vaudeville performers like George Burns, Eddie Cantor, George Jessel, and Al Jolsen absorbed and revised blackface minstrelsy (Rogin 1992, 430).

Rogin suggests that Jewish blackface in the Jazz Age may also be viewed as a mechanism of assimilation. Blackface simultaneously posited a relation to black America and promised that blackness could be left behind, transcended in the process of becoming American. Blackness as masquerade had exchange value; it was a switch point through which Jewish identity could be made to appear someplace else. Rogin argues that Jewishness passes through blackness into whiteness only by "wiping out all difference *except* black and white" (447; emphasis added). Jewishness, in Rogin's reading, does not transcend or unravel the fundamental binary opposition between black and white but assimilates itself to the latter term.

Bernhard's blackface performances bear a different relation to the opposition black/white and to the history of black/Jewish relations in the United States. Parodically reiterating white appropriations of blackness, she destabilizes the binary operations of exclusion and denial whereby whiteness presumes to speak for blackness. Bernhard's blackface thus enacts a kind of whiteface; she imitates and parodies whites impersonating blacks. Seeking to deconstruct and reflexively critique white appropriations of blackness, Bernhard must perform that appropriation. As bell hooks observes, Bernhard "walks a critical tightrope" between criticizing "white appropriation of black culture" and repeat performance (1992, 38). Ultimately, the shifting positions occupied by the black audience in *Without You I'm Nothing* indicate the ambivalent fortunes of (re)appropriation and subversion. Simultaneously the screen against which Bernhard projects herself as transgressive spectacle and the silent register of her inability to translate herself across racial boundaries, the black audience within the film remains the voiceless measure of Bernhard's grand success (or still more grand failure). In this regard, *Without You I'm Nothing* seems to present its critique of white appropriation from the standpoint of whiteness—a whiteness masquerading, unsuccessfully as it turns out, as blackness.

However, what prevents Bernhard's impersonation from being a "simple" act of appropriation is its open failure to forge an identification between her black audience of address and herself. The audience withholds its belief, refusing to authorize Bernhard's vision of herself. Moreover, Bernhard sets herself up as an object of ridicule for that audience, conspicuously dramatizing the distance between her audience's and her own self-understandings. Bernhard's performance is self-ironizing. The audience does not "get" Bernhard; Bernhard does not "get" her audience. But the very misrecognition is to some degree what compels the performance.

Bernhard's failure may also disrupt the pleasure the cinematic audience takes in watching *Without You I'm Nothing.* Bernhard's theatricalization of herself as black is the occasion of extreme displeasure for the black audience within the film.[8] The visible displeasure of the textual audience renders explicit the identificatory fictions that produce and sustain whatever pleasure the cinematic audience takes. In this way, the film potentially challenges the illusions of self-identity that not only determine the pleasure of narrative film but also condition subjectivity. By showcasing the misidentifications between Bernhard and her audience, the film thus permits the cinematic spectators to gain some distance on themselves.

Nonetheless, the self-critique the film enables may also return to business as usual, reconstituting the self/other dichotomy. For the spectatorial pleasure of the white spectators, who comprise the vast majority of Bernhard's following, is founded in part on the represented discomfort or unpleasure of the black audience within the film. Yet so obnoxious is much of Bernhard's performance, so arcane many of her jokes, that the film ultimately frustrates any lasting identification between even its (phantasmatically) white audience and Bernhard, thereby leaving no place to "fix" identity within or through the film. Moreover, the startling and discomforting discrepancy between the laughter of the white or "whitened" spectators, on the one side, and the incredulity of the black audience (whether within or without the film), on the other, may literally represent the appropriations and resistances that condition all identifications.[9]

Throughout the film, it is Bernhard who is the preeminent site of mis-, dis-, and dissed identification. Twice, the emcee at the supper club where she is performing introduces her as "Sarah Bernhardt." Such a misidentification punningly installs Bernhard within a theatrical tradition, whose lineage begins with the Divine Sarah, arguably the first truly international star.[10] The name Sarah Bernhardt has also come to be identified with histrionics and over-the-top self-theatricalization. As a latter-day Sarah Bernhardt, Sandra Bernhard can point to the Jewishness, considerable talent for self-invention, and "notorious" sexual life of her predecessor with an assumed family resemblance.

If the emcee twice confuses Bernhard with her much more celebrated soundalike, neither can Bernhard herself seem to get her own identity straight. She refers to "me and my Jewish piano player," saying "we people get along so well." Bernhard's sardonic "we people get along so well" sends up claims of interethnic solidarity, for the visible gulf between Bernhard and her black audience, who do not respond to the joke, dramatizes exactly the reverse. "We people" also ironically undercuts claims to *intra*ethnic solidarity among Jews. Despite the resistance of her black audience within the film, who are not in on the joke, Bernhard persists in identifying herself as black, even to the point of intercutting scenes of her onstage performances with the figure of a young black woman, never named by the film, but identified in the closing credits as "Roxanne" (Cynthia Bailey). Roxanne, most famously, the name of another object of ventriloquized desire, Cyrano's.

It is not always clear whether the black woman appears as counterpoint to or confirmation of Bernhard's blackness. Is she Bernhard's mirror image or her mirror opposite? Bernhard's explicit response to this question is that "Roxanne" represents a reality check on her film persona's presumption to blackness:

> We [director John Boskovitch and Bernhard] just thought it was really funny to have this deluded white performer, who thought she was a black diva, perform for a black audience. It was like letting her know that she not only was *not* a black diva, but she had no idea what it was like to suffer, you know in that skin. And of course, at the end, the black woman—the *beautiful* black woman—has the final word, which is "Fuck you, bitch. You may *think* you're black, but I'm the one who's paid the dues." (in "Sandra's Blackness" 1992, 116; emphasis in original)

But who are "we" and why the emphasis on the black woman's beauty, as if—in the end—(only) the black female's *body* really matters? As Berlant and Freeman suggest, the symbolic function Bernhard assigns to the black woman "perpetuates the historic burden black women in cinema have borne to represent embodiment, desire, and the dignity of suffering on behalf of white women" (1993, 218). The black woman signifies but will not, does not, or cannot speak for herself. But is this the only way to see the black woman's symbolic role in the film, or, to put the question another way, is this the only way to understand Bernhard's relationship to her?

In *Black Looks,* bell hooks asks whether the black woman is "the fantasy Other Bernhard desires to become . . . or the fantasy Other Bernhard desires?" (1992, 38). Answering the former, hooks claims that the black woman functions as a critical "yardstick Bernhard uses to measure herself" (38). But are identification and desire only thinkable as mutually exclusive possibilities? What if identification is one of the ruses through and by which transgressive desires are rerouted?[11]

Identification and desire link Bernhard and the black woman throughout the film. Often, what mediates this transfer between identification and desire, Bernhard and the black woman, is a series of overlapping cultural references. The first time we see Bernhard, for example, she is sitting in front of a makeup mirror, concentrating all her attention on a strand of hair she is fussily trimming. Here *Without You I'm Nothing* and Bernhard wink at their audience as they conjure the image of Nico cutting her hair in Andy Warhol's *Chelsea Girls.* As Bernhard comes into closer view, the background music shifts from high European culture, signaled by Bach's first *Partita,* to the uniquely "American" sounds of jazz. Piling citation on citation, this scene will later be cited by the black woman. The black woman stands before a bathroom mirror, listening to Ice Cube, and carefully cuts a strand of hair. At other moments also the black woman appears either to retrace Bernhard's movements or give form to Bernhard's onstage monologues. During Bernhard's riff on Sonny and Cher's "The Beat Goes On," for example, the camera cuts from Bernhard's knowingly solemn intonation "And history has turned the page, uh-huh" to the black woman, in a chemistry laboratory, turning the page of a large textbook. Later, in a scene that registers the unstable border between identification and desire, we see Bernhard, on the bottom, being fucked by her black boyfriend, Joe the hairdresser. Bernhard seems to have usurped the black woman's position in a heterosexual economy of exchange, which posits sexual difference and racial "sameness" as normative criteria.[12] However, what if it is the black man who has taken the black woman's place? Perhaps, as Elspeth Probyn suggests, Joe substitutes for Bernhard's "real" object of desire and identification, the black woman (1993, 156). After all, the scene of heterosexual coupling was from the first a case of mistaken identity. Bernhard's insistent identification of Joe as a hairdresser, that redolent signifier of the homosexual and the effeminate, already promiscuously implied his "unmanning." Moreover, her complaint that Joe spent so much time in the bathroom "getting his look together" that she thought she was with a woman—"and from the size of [his] dick, I might as well have been," Bernhard quips—recasts the hypervirile, hypersexual black "stud," long a stock figure in a white racist imaginary, as not much more than a woman. That such a move, toppling the black man from his position "on top," is not necessarily a liberation hardly needs comment.

However, it is not just Bernhard who crosses over into the black woman's territory by becoming, or seeking to become, black. In one scene, the black woman puts herself, or is put, in Bernhard's "place." The black woman is seen leaning against what appears to be a kosher butcher shop. As Jean Walton notes in her lucid reading of this film, Bernhard's black stand-in holds a copy of Harold Bloom's *The Kabbalah and Criticism* in her hand.[13] This scene signals the possibility (or wish) that Bernhard's identification with blackness and the black woman might go both ways. The book title, which passes fleetingly into and out of the viewer's gaze, may also represent a teasing challenge to the filmic audience to subject the film and Bernhard to critical scrutiny.

The film's final, critical words belong to the black woman. As Bernhard stands before the now-empty supper club, gazing plaintively into the space her audience used to occupy, the camera's gaze and Bernhard's become unified, focusing intently on her last best hope, the black woman, who has materialized as if from nowhere. The black woman wears a flowing evening dress, her hair piled high on her head. She seems to return Bernhard's gaze, but with contempt (is this halfway to desire?), going so far as to mark that contempt in lipstick, femininity's signature. "Fuck Sandra Bernhard," she scrawls.[14] As the camera lingers over the black woman's parting statement, it also foregrounds a full glass of Remy Martin, the liquor to which Bernhard—in the persona of a black lounge singer—has earlier pledged her fealty. In high-culture contrast to Bernhard's bump-and-grind version of Prince's "Little Red Corvette," the black woman fairly floats out of the scene to the reprise of Bach's first *Partita*. The black woman is consumed by whiteness, as both she and the screen literally fade into white (Probyn 1993, 151)

In her analysis of the film, hooks argues that "all the white women strip, flaunt their sexuality, and appear to be directing their attention to a black male gaze" (1992, 38). But who are *all* these white women? There are only three "white" women in the film: Bernhard; her cigar-smoking manager; and Shoshana, an obvious parody of Madonna. Bernhard's "butch" manager hardly seems the type to be flaunting her sexuality and performing for *any* male gaze—at least not in the straightforwardly heterosexualized manner hooks ushers into (our) view. By "all the white women," then, hooks must mean Shoshana and *multiple* Bernhards. Evidently, performance and cinematic spectacle only go so far.

Hooks allows that Bernhard may be fragmented into pieces but seems to rule out the possibility that any of these performing "pieces" might be other than white. Hooks also insists that all the white women perform for a black male gaze. Yet who or where is the agency of that gaze? Does hooks mean the audience within the film (which includes both men and women), the boyfriend Joe, or a hypothetical black male gaze toward which white women in general direct themselves? The black male gaze within the film—if that is what it is—is textual, and it is *not* unified with the extratextual gaze of *Without You I'm Nothing*'s cinematic audience.

Hooks introduces but quickly drops the possibility that Bernhard might be performing for a black female gaze (1992, 38). Black women are Bernhard's "yardstick," not her objects of desire. Hooks chooses to read the interracial trajectory of Bernhard's desire heterosexually. This is, in my view, a telling misreading. The closing scene of the film, where Bernhard strips for the sole remaining audience member, suggests that it is black womanhood Bernhard desires and black women whose gaze she seeks to meet. Recoding lesbian desire through racial difference, rather than through the terms of sexual difference, stages the nonidentity of "same-sex" love. The "same" is restaged as and in the difference "between" white and black. All the same, this does not answer to the concern that it is the black female body that bears the burden of signifying the "white" woman's difference—a point also made by Probyn (1993, 158), and Berlant and Freeman (1993, 218). It does, however, queerly complicate the relations between "racial difference" and "sexual difference," identification and desire.

Blackness is not the only performative term the film tries to make visible. Does the black woman's disappearance into a screen of white light at the film's close represent only the territorialization of blackness by whiteness or/and does it destabilize the claims of either side—"whiteness" or "blackness"—to represent or incorporate "realness"? I want to suggest that this destabilization occurs through the introduction of an excluded middle term, which resembles both sides, but is identical to neither: Jewishness. This is a point that hooks, Probyn, Walton, and Berlant and Freeman overlook. Although hooks and Probyn at least cite Bernhard's Jewishness, neither fully addresses what the historical associations between blackness and Jewishness might mean in the context of Bernhard's will to blackness.

For hooks, Bernhard's "Jewish heritage as well as her sexually ambiguous erotic practices are experiences that place her outside of the mainstream" (1992, 37). Jewishness and unnamed, but sexually ambiguous (*because* unnamed?) erotic practices together place Bernhard at the cultural margins. But what does Bernhard's Jewish heritage have to do with her queer erotic practices? Has hooks inadvertently defined that heritage in erotic terms? The representations of Jewish women, not unlike the representations of (other?) women of color, have themselves been overburdened *as well as* overidentified with sexually ambiguous erotic practices. Hooks insinuates but does not finally clarify connections between Bernhard's assumed blackness, on the one side, and her Jewishness and queerness, on the other. She locates Bernhard's "outside" in an "alternative white culture," whose "standpoint" and "impetus" the film traces to "black culture" (37). Yet in Bernhard's pulsating tributes to (and as) Sylvester, "You Make Me Feel (Mighty Real)" and "Do You Wanna Funk," as well as in her knowing reference to *Chelsea Girls* and her later rhapsodic eulogy for Andy Warhol, she makes it clear that *queer* cultures, black and white, are also among the resources and expropriated sites of American (sub)cultural capital.

Similarly, when Probyn refers to Bernhard as a "white Jewish woman" (1993, 156), it is not obvious to me what work *Jewish* is doing here. On this, the first and last occasion Probyn will cite Bernhard's Jewishness, she qualifies it as "white." However, isn't the relation of Jewishness and "race" one of the things *Without You I'm Nothing* contests? Berlant and Freeman, too, seem to lose sight of Bernhard's "racial" specificity. They (mis)identify the film's and Bernhard's "aesthetic distance" as working through the "straightness of the *generic* white woman-identified-woman" (1993, 218; emphasis added). But what does generic whiteness—or generic blackness, for that matter—even look like? And does it look like Bernhard?

At the very least, Bernhard does not identify herself as white. Asked in a 1992 interview whether she "[related] to the world as a white person," Bernhard responded, "I never relate myself as a white person because I'm not a gentile; I'm a Jew. I feel like, culturally, I've gleaned from other cultures, but I also have a very rich one myself" (in "Sandra's Blackness" 1992, 116). In a 1993 interview (the too perfectly captioned "Egos and Ids"), Bernhard signals also the comparative *in*significance of her sexualized and gendered differences—as a woman-loving woman—when measured against the historical meanings of the Jew's "racial" difference:

> I feel more concerned about being a Jew than I do about equating myself with being gay. I feel like there's more anti-Semitism than there is antihomosexual feelings. It's like if the Nazis come marching through, they'll come after me as a Jew before they do as a chic lesbian. (Bernhard 1993, 4)

When pressed on the same point in another interview, Bernhard speaks even more directly of the inescapability of her Jewishness:

> If I am going to defend any minority part of myself, it is going to be Judaism. It's something that has formed my personality much more than my sexuality has. . . . You are born Jewish. It is not something you can deny or run away from. You can pretend you're not. You can get your nose fixed and play all kinds of games, but . . . (in Sessums 1994, 126).

Bernhard's Jewishness is not a "chosen" identity—even if accepting it or rejecting it is her choice. In contrast, she says, "You develop your sexuality" (127).

Whether or not Bernhard is right that the Nazis, or their contemporary equivalents, would come for her first as a Jew and only second as a "chic lesbian" seems to me beside the point. What interests me here is the way that Bernhard conceptualizes her Jewishness, on the one side, and her sexual "identity," on the other. In representing herself as born Jewish, but become queer, she aligns Jewishness with nature and sexuality with nurture. Another way to express this division would be essentialism versus constructionism.

In posing herself *as* the question of race, Bernhard appears to align herself with blackness not so much over and against whiteness as conceived through it. Her passage from blackness to Jewishness takes place through a caricatured whiteness. This transmutation through whiteness is dramatized in one of the film's early sequences. First, a "black" Bernhard performs Simone's "Four Women." After she completes the song, the black emcee encourages an incredulous audience: "Sarah Bernhardt, ladies and gentlemen. The lady came here all the way from New York City, so let's give her our support." Following Bernhard to the stage is "our very own lucky, lucky, lucky star, the original Shoshanaaaaaa," the Jewish name Shoshana rhymingly replacing the Catholic Madonna. As Shoshana wriggles her way through a performance whose bad taste is exceeded only by its poor execution, the camera cuts away from Shoshana's dancing fool to the anonymous black woman walking in front of the Watts Tower, then cuts back to Shoshana. Finally, Bernhard, performing "Bernhard," returns to the stage, where she attempts unsuccessfully to lead the audience in a round of Israeli folk songs. She talks about the joys of growing up in "a liberal, intellectual Jewish household" but also confesses to a Gentile family romance: "I'd fantasize that I had an older brother named Chip and a little sister named Sally, and my name would either be Happy or Buffy or Babe." It is the white imitation-Madonna and the buxom "Babe" who appear the most obviously "false" of any impersonation in the film. "Whiteness," then, is recast as always already an imitation—variously of blackness, of itself, of nothing. (This last possibility—"nothing"—recalibrates the distance and the difference between the subject-positions brokered in the film's title.) Bernhard also identifies whiteness with Christianity, concluding her rapturous "testimonial" to the joys of Gentile family values with the wish, "May all your Christmases be white."

It may be, as Mary Ann Doane has suggested, that "to espouse a white racial identity at this particular historical moment is to align oneself with white supremacists" (1991, 246). Moreover, as Doane also argues, "both whiteness and blackness cover and conceal a host of ethnicities, of cultural backgrounds whose differences are leveled by the very concepts of white and black. Whiteness and blackness are historically *real* categories only in their lengthy and problematic collision with each other in the context of systems of colonialism and slavery" (246). This, on my viewing, is one of the things *Without You I'm Nothing* achieves, or comes close to achieving: namely, the disruption of the totalizing logic either/or, white/black. Ultimately, however, it also seems to me that the film and Bernhard can only disrupt monolithic whiteness by reconsolidating blackness.

Nonetheless, Bernhard's *whiteface* performances, through which she mimes and parodies whiteness as the historical agent of colonization and cultural appropriation, complexify the relations Rogin traces in *The Jazz Singer*. Bernhard's blackface is not principally a mechanism whereby Jewishness transcends blackness and becomes white; her insistent equation of whiteness with Christianity troubles such a movement. Arguably, Bernhard's impersonation of whites impersonating blacks allows her to leave behind not blackness, but white guilt. In parodying the bald-faced failures of whiteness to speak for, or even to, blackness, Bernhard may be exculpating herself from any wrongdoings committed in the name of whiteness. This is a paradigmatically liberal gesture of disavowal and/as transcendence. It may also represent the reappearance of a political fantasy, Black-Jewish solidarity.

But just as the gender performatives of *Paris Is Burning* are not only about gender, the race performatives of *Without You I'm Nothing* are not only about race.[15] I believe Bernhard works "race," which she represents as blackness, as a way to situate and resituate also her Jewishness, queerness, and womanliness. That Bernhard thematizes whiteness as "being," among its other attributions, a relation to Christianity acts to denaturalize the claims of "race." At the same time, it indicates how Jewishness is articulated through multiple terms of difference: religion, race, gender, nationality, sexuality, class, *and* political affinity.

Blackness, arguably the constitutive elsewhere of American national identity, becomes a way of visibly re-marking and exteriorizing Bernhard's differences. Articulating her "otherness" through blackness reinscribes and potentially upends the historical terms of American "racial" definition.[16] Perhaps blackness is the performative term most often seen, or recognized, in *Without* You *I'm Nothing* because it "appears" to be the one identity category on display in the film that Bernhard does not "really" embody, because Jewishness or queerness or womanliness are somehow facts about Bernhard. She just is those things, right? This is appearance as ontology.

In sum, Bernhard's open avowal of the co-implicating structure of identity categories illuminates what so often seems just a theoretical abstraction: gender and race performatives. Moreover, we are able more clearly to recognize and identify (with) those processes that constitute and are performed as subjectivity when Bernhard is acting up and acting them out, than when "we" are "ourselves" becoming subject(s) through them. Meanwhile, if I take pleasure from Bernhard's performances at (and as?) the crossroads of gender, race, and sexuality, that pleasure is itself conditioned by the glimmer of recognition— I mean, self-recognition—provided in this occasion of spectatorship. It is prompted also by the prick of my desire, as if I were the phantasmatic *You* for whom Bernhard performs and without whom her "I" would be nothing.

Put otherwise, the *I*—whether mine, hers, or yours—is the intersubjective site, or citation, of the differentiating marks of desire and identification. However, to the extent that Bernhard articulates the specificities of her body by speaking through another Other's terms, she is yet caught up in the endlessly repeating and repeated logic of identifications found, lost, and found again at someone else's address.

NOTES

1. The term *performative accomplishment* is Butler's (1990b, 271).

2. For another reading of Bernhard's "tease" and "refusal," see Berlant and Freeman 1993 (193–229).

3. Cf. ibid., 193–94, 217.

4. It is worth considering, with Homi Bhabha, the ways in which commodification and economic objectification fold into colonial power/knowledge: "It [colonial power] is an apparatus that turns on the recognition and disavowal of racial/cultural/historical differences. Its predominant strategic function is the creation of a space for a 'subject peoples' through the production of knowledges in terms of which surveillance is exercised and a complex form of pleasure/unpleasure is incited. It seeks authorization for its strategies by the production of knowledges of colonizer and colonized which are stereotypical but antithetically evaluated" (1994, 70).

5. See, in this regard, the spate of 1993 articles on straight passing as queer in the *Village Voice* (Powers), *GQ* (Kamp), and *Esquire* ("Viva Straight Camp!").

6. The stage name Whoopi Goldberg indicates that blackness may also name itself through Jewishness. It also names a group whom this discussion occludes: African American Jews.

7. Bernhard's "inflated" lips are a point of frequent and sometimes even anxious discussion (Green 1992, 42; cf. "Look at Me" 1992, 14; and "Hips, Lips, Tits, POWER!" 1992, 8). Her mouth is cited as her

most distinguishing feature. An extreme close-up of her mouth is even the full-page subject of a Herb Ritts photo in his 1992 photo album of the "stars," *Notorious.*

8. In a 1992 interview with *Vibe* magazine, in which the flattering representation of "Sandra's Blackness" is in sharp contrast to the companion piece dissing "whites who think they're black," Bernhard was asked how black audiences respond to her black characters: "The black audiences love me. It's kind of amazing. They really get it. They're very receptive to me, it's the highest honor, because if black people dig you, you must be doing something right" (116). The displeasure recorded by the camera is a staged displeasure, then. According to Bernhard "real" black audiences "really" do "dig" her act. It is an open question whether Bernhard has here accurately represented—or spoken for—her impossibly unified "black audiences."

9. I do not here want to oversimplify the reception of this film. I am not claiming that all white people or all Jewish people (many of whom are also "white") like, or must like, this film. Nor do I mean to suggest that all black spectators (who may also be Jewish) are put off by Bernhard's bodily impostures. In neither case would this be "true" to the anecdotal evidence offered me by Jewish and African American friends and colleagues whose reactions to *Without You I'm Nothing* do not so easily fall into racial and/or ethnocultural line. Rather, I am trying to offer a schematic of the spectatorial positions idealized and produced by the film. At minimum, it seems to me that the very divergent reactions this film has prompted make amply clear how the scene of (dis)identification is mediated through race, gender, sexuality, and class positions.

10. Jesse Green's 1992 *Mirabella* article on Bernhard is even knowingly titled "The Divine Sandra."

11. Diana Fuss explores how identification simultaneously opens up and defends against the possibility of lesbian desire in the context of contemporary fashion photography (1992).

12. Butler has urged that feminist theory attend to the places where compulsory heterosexuality does not just prohibit homosexuality, but also regulates and demands racial "purity" (1993, 18). In other words, how do miscegenation and homosexuality together mark the boundaries of a reproductive heterosexual economy? The incest taboo—which is to say, the prohibition on mother-son incest—represses a prior prohibition on homosexuality and incest between father and son or mother and daughter (Butler 1990a). But the prohibition on (heterosexual) incest, which generates the extrafamilial exchange of women, produces an exogamy within limits, *racialized* limits. In this sense, the prohibition on miscegenation potentially preserves and incorporates the fantasy of incest by keeping reproduction within the bloodline and, thus, within the "family" of (or as) "race."

13. See Walton 1994, 255. Walton's fine essay on *Without You I'm Nothing* was published after the penultimate version of this chapter was written. As much as I am in agreement with and have learned from her reading of the film, Walton too fails to register the difference that Jewish difference might make for Bernhard's "whiteness."

14. Berlant and Freeman make a similar point (1993, 217).

15. For an analysis of the links between race and gender performatives in *Paris is Burning,* see Butler (1993, 121–40). Compare hooks (1992, 145–56) and Phelan (1993, 93–111).

16. During the first decades of wide-scale (read: visible) Italian, Irish, and Jewish immigration to the United States these marginalized "white" ethnicities—Irishness, Italianness, and Jewishness—were assimilated to blackness. For those whom historian David Roediger has called the "not-yet white ethnic" (1994, 184), assimilation to the American ideal has historically meant assimilation to "whiteness." In his study of common features in the symbolization of blacks and Jews in the American white imaginary, Nathan Hurvitz cites, by way of just one example, the "street expression and graffito" that "a nigger is a Jew turned inside out" (1974, 307). If this "joke" reverses the direction of Bernhard's performances and draws blackness through Jewishness, it yet arrives at the same "punch line." Neither the nigger nor the Jew is a subject *of* whiteness but is, rather, subjectivated through its terms.

WORKS CITED

Berlant, Lauren, and Elizabeth Freeman. 1993. "Queer Nationality." In *Fear of a Queer Planet: Queer Politics and Social Theory.* Ed. Michael Warner. Minneapolis: University of Minnesota Press, 193–229.

Bernhard, Sandra. 1993. "Egos and Ids: Goodbye to All That Cool Stuff." Interview by Degen Pener. *New York Times,* 8 August, sec. 9: 4.

Bhabha, Homi. 1994. *The Location of Culture.* New York: Routledge.

Butler, Judith. 1990a. *Gender Trouble: Feminism and the Subversion of Identity.* New York: Routledge.

———. 1990b. "Performative Acts and Gender Constitution: An Essay in Phenomenology and Feminist Theory." In *Performing Feminisms: Feminist Critical Theory and Theatre.* Ed. Sue-Ellen Case. Baltimore: Johns Hopkins University Press, 270–82.

———. 1993. *Bodies That Matter: On the Discursive Limits of "Sex."* New York: Routledge.

Doane, Mary Ann. 1991. *Femmes Fatales: Feminism, Film Theory, Psychoanalysis.* New York: Routledge.

"Funny Face." 1992. *The Face* (September): 40–46.

Fuss, Diana. 1992. "Fashion and the Homospectatorial Look." *Critical Inquiry* 18: 713–37.

Green, Jesse. 1992. "The Divine Sandra." *Mirabella* (August): 38–40, 42, 44.

"Hips, Lips, Tits, POWER!" ("Sandra Bernhard—Read My Lips!"). 1992. *The List: Glasgow and Edinburgh Events Guide* 21–27 August: 8–9.

hooks, bell. 1992. *Black Looks: Race and Representation.* Boston: South End Press.

Hurvitz, Nathan. 1974. "Blacks and Jews in American Folklore." *Western Folklore* 33 (October): 301–25.

Kamp, David. 1993. "The Queening of America." *GQ* (July): 94–99.

"Look at Me, I'm Sandra B." 1992. *Elle* (June): 12–16 (British version).

Mulvey, Laura. 1989. "Visual Pleasure and Narrative Cinema." In *Visual and Other Pleasures.* Bloomington: Indiana University Press, 14–28.

Phelan, Peggy. 1993. *Unmarked: The Politics of Performance.* London: Routledge.

Powers, Ann. 1993. "Queer in the Streets, Straight in the Sheets." *Village Voice* (June 29): 24, 30–32.

Probyn, Elspeth. 1993. *Sexing the Self: Gendered Positions in Cultural Studies.* New York: Routledge.

Ritts, Herb. 1992. *Notorious.* Boston: Little, Brown.

Roediger, David R. 1994. *Towards the Abolition of Whiteness.* London: Verso.

Rogin, Michael. 1992. "Blackface, White Noise: The Jewish Jazz Singer Finds His Voice." *Critical Inquiry* 18: 417–53.

"Sandra's Blackness." 1992. *Vibe* 1: 116.

Sessums, Kevin. 1994. "Simply Sandra" ("Sandra in Wonderland: Bernhard Gets Bigger"). *Out* (September): 68–73, 124–27.

"Viva Straight Camp!" 1993. *Esquire* (June): 92–95.

Walton, Jean. 1994. "Sandra Bernhard: Lesbian Postmodern or Modern Postlesbian?" *The Lesbian Postmodern.* Ed. Laura Doan. New York: Columbia University Press, 244–61.

CONTRIBUTORS

LISA BLOOM is currently associate professor of women's studies and visual culture at Josai International University in the Chiba Prefecture, Japan. She is the author of *Gender on Ice: American Ideologies of Polar Expeditions* (Minnesota, 1993). Her recent book project is *Ghosts of Jewish Ethnicity: Rethinking 1970s Feminist Art Practices in the United States.*

CHERYL DUNYE is the director and creator of the first African American lesbian feature film, *The Watermelon Woman,* which was awarded the best gay feature in the Berlin Film Festival, the Los Angeles OutFest, and the Torino and Creteil film festivals. She has written articles for *Time Out, Felix,* and *Movement Research,* and currently teaches in the Department of Art at the University of California, Riverside, and the Department of Media Studies at Pitzer College. She is a 1998 Fellow of the Rockefeller Foundation.

JENNIFER A. GONZÁLEZ is assistant professor in the Program of Art History at the University of California, Santa Cruz. Her essays concerning installation art, material culture, and historical memory have appeared in *Visual Anthropology Review, Inscriptions,* and *Frieze.*

INDERPAL GREWAL chairs the women's studies department at San Francisco State University. She is coeditor (with Caren Kaplan) of *Scattered Hegemonies: Postmodernity and Transnational Feminist Practices* (Minnesota, 1994) and author of *Home and Harem: Nation, Gender, Empire, and the Cultures of Travel.* She writes on issues of gender as they relate to class, nationalism, imperialism, internationalism, diaspora, and postcoloniality.

CAREN KAPLAN is associate professor of women's studies at the University of California at Berkeley. She is the author of *Questions of Travel: Postmodern Discourses of Displacement* and coeditor (with Inderpal Grewal) of *Scattered Hegemonies: Postmodernity and Transnational Feminist Practices* (Minnesota, 1994).

ZOE LEONARD is a photographer, filmmaker, and video artist whose work has been exhibited nationally and internationally. She created photographs for *The Fae Richards Photo Archive* that were used in the film *The Watermelon Woman*, by Cheryl Dunye.

AIDA MANCILLAS is an artist and writer living in San Diego, California. She is co-owner of Stone Paper Scissors, a public art studio, and is currently chair of the North Park Urban Main Street design committee. Her latest public artwork is the development of an urban park. Her writing is included in the anthology *The Citizen Artist: Twenty Years of Art in the Public Arena.*

FRANCETTE PACTEAU is the author of *The Symptom of Beauty*, and she is now cowriting (with Victor Burgin) *A Psychoanalytic Semiotics of Visual Representation.* Her current research is on the concept of the interior in architecture and psychoanalysis.

ANN PELLEGRINI is assistant professor of English and American literature and language at Harvard University. She is the author of *Performance Anxieties: Staging Psychoanalysis, Staging Race* and coeditor of *Queer Theory and the Jewish Question* (forthcoming). She also coedits the book series *Sexual Cultures: New Directions from the Center for Lesbian and Gay Studies.*

GRISELDA POLLOCK is professor of social and critical histories of art and director of the Centre for Cultural Studies at the University of Leeds. She is a founding member of the Centre for Jewish Studies and directs graduate programs in feminism and the visual arts. Her publications cover major debates in feminism and the visual arts, social histories of art, and the relations between femininity and alterity within the framework of Jewish history, philosophy, and art. She is the coauthor of *Old Mistresses* and *Framing Feminism,* and the author of *Vision and Difference, Generations and Geographies in the Visual Arts: Feminist Readings,* and *Differencing the Canon: Feminist Desire and the Writing of Art's Histories.*

IRIT ROGOFF has written extensively on modern German and European art. She is the editor of *The Divided Heritage: Themes and Problems in German Modernism* and coeditor (with Daniel J. Sherman) of Museum Culture: Histories, Discourses, Spectacles. She has taught critical theory and visual culture at the University of California, Davis. Currently she is a professor at Goldsmith College, London University.

SHAWN MICHELLE SMITH is assistant professor of English and American studies at Washington State University. Her book on gender and race in nineteenth-century American visual culture is forthcoming. She is also a practicing artist and has recently exhibited her photographic work *Fragments from a Family Album* in Seattle and Kansas City.

RUTH WALLEN is a nationally exhibited artist and writer living in the San Diego–Tijuana region. Much of her work, in the form of installation, artist books, public art, and critical essays, focuses on examining the biological and cultural environment of the border region. She currently teaches at Southwestern College and the University of California, San Diego, and was recently a Fulbright lecturer at the Autonomous University of Baja California in Tijuana.

MARGUERITE R. WALLER chairs the women's studies department and teaches in the English department and the Film and Visual Culture program at the University of California, Riverside. Her current interests include new feminisms evolving in militarized situations (including the U.S.–Mexico border), constructions of space and time in non-Hollywood films, and the shooting and editing of her own videos. She has published extensively on Italian cinema and Renaissance European literature.